D1193998

CANADA: The Uneasy Neighbor

CANADA:
The Uneasy Neighbor

By GERALD CLARK

DAVID McKAY COMPANY, INC.

New York

CANADA: THE UNEASY NEIGHBOR

COPYRIGHT © 1965 BY GERALD CLARK

For my daughter Bette

Foreword

MANY PEOPLE—Canadians included—think of Canada as a benign country complacently enjoying a high standard of living without stress or strain. Yet Canada in truth is filled with conflict—so much so that a government-appointed commission was impelled in 1965 to express concern over "serious danger" to its continued existence as a nation. The specific and immediate fear was caused by hostility between English Canadians and French Canadians. But the tensions spread in many directions. Even within the French-Canadian group itself there is conflict: between those who seek a moderate adjustment to French Canada's status within the present union and those who demand speedy action—if necessary at the cost of bloodshed—to wrest independence from the English-speaking majority.

Conflict in one shape or another has existed from the minute the first soldiers and settlers arrived, even if it implied only a contest with Nature. The same people who live today in a narrow belt alongside the American border, where the climate is relatively hospitable, continue to dream of a destiny in the Arctic or Far North, where the struggle is relentless and unrewarding. Canada is so big, physically, that seven of the world's twenty-four time zones cross its territory. The geographic vastness promotes regionalism, and this in turn contributes to a constant and nagging friction between provincial governments and central authority. The appearance of secessionism is by no means confined to Quebec, though, curiously, English Canadians are held together by an overriding fear of domination by the United States. This is probably the greatest of all of Canada's conflicts: between her own interests—or imagined interests—and those of the United States.

More than one historian has commented that if there were no United States, Canada would have to invent it. The implication, of course, is that Canadians are united *solely* out of mistrust of the United States and American intentions. The point is debatable, but the fact is that the presence of the United States casts a shadow that makes many Canadians uneasy. This presence plays a part, either consciously or unconsciously, in Canada's major decisions of international scope, whether economic or political or military. If the United States, in turn, had at one time covetous thoughts about Canada, its policy now is to support a strong and unified neighbor. From a strategic aspect alone, Canadian cohesion is important to the security of the United States. What happens, for instance, if Quebec does separate and forms its own republic under an extremist government? Will the St. Lawrence Seaway, which begins in Quebec and penetrates the U. S. Midwest, become endangered? Will the whole of North America's integrated defense system be threatened?

I had been across Canada at least a dozen times in the past, but those were trips of short duration and for immediate newspaper purposes. Now, in six months of travel and research from one end to the other and from the U. S. border to the Far North, I saw Canada in another perspective. Now I was deliberately dissecting it and trying to determine what made it function. I had one advantage. Though I was born and educated in Canada, I had been away for much of my professional life; now I was coming back after a stretch of nearly a decade in the United States and Europe. And so I had the benefit of almost fresh eyes and ears, applying,

I hope, the kind of objectivity usually reserved for foreign countries. In a sense I was a stranger in my own country, for much of what I saw was new, and some of it I found alarming or disturbing. While material changes were everywhere dramatically plentiful, the regionalism was more acute than I had remembered it. So was the uncertainty about the future.

Fundamentally, there are two dominant themes: English Canada vis-à-vis French Canada, and Canada as a whole vis-à-vis the United States. It is within this framework that I have written this book, and fellow Canadians will do themselves a disservice if they try to ascertain whether one geographic area is given more attention than another. I am not interested in regional statistics as much as I am in the mood of the country and how this mood affects internal harmony and over-all relations with the outside world. The big question is whether Canada will survive or whether it will disintegrate into segments, some of which will seek liaison with the very nation, the United States, whose presence has always meant anxiety.

GERALD CLARK

Montreal
August, 1965

Contents

Foreword vii

CHAPTER 1. Time to Enter History 1

2. The Neighbor Upstairs 51

3. Dollars or Domination? 84

4. The Quebec Rebels 110

5. . . . and the Venetian Princes . . . 144

6. Ontario: Key to English Canada . . 181

7. Blow-Me-Down, Canadian Yankees . 207

8. "Wacky" Bennett and His Empire . 250

9. The Prosperous Prairies 273

10. The North's Frontier: Myth and Fact 316

11. Culture on Guard 359

12. Days of Affluence and Strain . . . 393

Index 421

CANADA: The Uneasy Neighbor

1.

Time to Enter History

WITHIN THE PERIOD of twenty-four hours not long ago a half dozen youths appeared in a court in Montreal to answer charges varying from conspiracy to capital murder in connection with a French-Canadian secession movement; and a cabinet minister rose in the House of Commons in Ottawa to announce measures designed to keep Canadian banks and other financial institutions from falling under American control. The two events were connected in spirit and drama, for Canada is undergoing the dual anxiety of remaining intact as a nation and simultaneously protecting its autonomy. The eventual outcome is of some consequence not only to 20 million Canadians but to the people of the United States, who, mostly with misguided nonchalance, assume that the sprawling country to the north provides a solid and steady and secure front of neighborliness.

The half dozen young men—four of them students—had been arrested after seizing automatic rifles and other weapons from a firearms company, two of whose employees were shot and killed. In court they made a rather forlorn and unprepossessing sight as one of their colleagues, turned witness for the prosecution, described a so-called camp hidden in the Laurentian hills.

"What was the purpose of this camp?" asked the judge, Emile Trottier.

"It was a military camp," said the witness, Marcel Tardif, almost in a whisper.

"But there was no war on."

"No, but we were training to fight the enemy."

"Would it be too indiscreet," said Judge Trottier, leaning forward slightly, "to ask who your enemy was?"

"The federalists," replied Tardif, his face extremely pale.

As it transpired, this hardly could be described as a Castro-type operation with the equivalent of a guerrilla army secreted in the Canadian Sierra Maestra. The small group of revolutionaries were impressive neither in training nor in acumen. They owned an arsenal of three rifles; military drill consisted of mounting guard around a camp fire for the week and a half they spent in the woods. Their strength would have been increased, of course, had the raid on the firearms company succeeded. But even so the consequences might have been brief and slight. Police, just about this time, were picking up the last batch of weapons another clandestine would-be *Armée de Libération* had taken several months previously in a theft from an armory and never used.

Of far greater significance than the firepower was the general dolour represented by the extremists: an uneasy mood even among many moderate French-speaking residents of the Province of Quebec, of general discontent with the state of union with the rest of Canada, of wanting substantial changes—but instinctively holding back from too drastic a move lest it break the country into fragments and rob French Canada of any individuality by throwing it into the melting pot of the United States.

On the part of English-speaking Canadians—"the federalists"—there was annoyance with French Canada and even some militant hostility toward its enigmatic aspirations, largely because of the timing. Canada was just emerging from a profound period of self-doubt when the French Canadians began to assert themselves in the early 1960's, thus shaking the flimsy and fresh inner confidence. But more importantly, English Canada was struggling for the meaning of identity, especially in relation to the powerful United States, and trying to decide what measures to take to protect independence. Economic nationalists looked with horror at the raw statistics: half of Canada's factories and mines were now owned by Americans; as long as Canadians continued to demand a high and rising standard of living they would go on selling their resources piece by piece every year—so that within another generation Canada would be completely an economic colony of the United States. The nationalists had their spokesman in Walter Gordon, the finance minister, who introduced to parliament a program limiting the percentage of stock nonresidents—that is, Americans—could hold in Canadian banks, insurance and trust companies.

"It has been evident for several years," said Gordon, a mild, pleasant Torontonian in his late fifties, "that there has been increasing concern about the problem of retaining Canadian ownership and control of Canadian enterprises."

The concern embraces equally the realms of culture and history. Few Canadians will object to the institution of frozen television meals copied from the United States, though they might deplore the taste; some will even boast that Canadian supermarkets are more elaborate and bewildering than the prototypes south of the border. But the flagrant Americanization reaches deep into the soul of Canadianism. There was a simple illustration when the Canadian Broadcasting Corporation, itself a public service designed to encourage a Canadian character, bought a packaged television series for children by Walt Disney. One of the episodes depicted heroes of 1776 in conflict with treacherous colonials who were opposed to the American Revolution. It was a fine show for a United States audience. But, since the villains happened to be the United Empire Loyalists who soon afterward founded much of English Canada, it hardly indicated a glowing educational approach for Canadian children. The fault, it will be noted, did not rest with the Americans, who produced the show or sold it purely as a commercial venture. It remained with the Canadians who bought and accepted it, a theme that is both bewildering and persistent in the story of present-day Canada.

"Canadians are generally indistinguishable from the Americans, and the surest way of telling the two apart is to make the observation to a Canadian." This shrewdly perceptive remark was written by Richard Starnes in one of his Scripps-Howard newspaper columns. Starnes also discerned that what appears to be anti-Americanism in Canada should more accurately be described as pro-Canadianism. But he might have added that if the label of anti-American must be applied, it fits Canadians naturally; all other anti-Americans around the world are tenderfeet by comparison. Canada had its start a couple of centuries ago, when the early settlers realized that for reasons of climate and geography the United States was destined always to be immensely richer and mightier—and the everlasting problem would be how to keep out of the vortex created by this huge and dynamic society.

Part of the modern dilemma—demonstrated whenever Walt Disney sells his television films—is that the big neighbor possesses a power for influence and absorption without even conscious awareness of it. And because the majority of Canadians value a separate nationality they are concerned with preventing any unwitting annexation from taking place. This they must do by resisting the pressures—political, economic, cultural—that are always at work, like mechanical pumps, drawing people and ideas through the same funnel. Occasionally a politician takes advantage of acute Canadian sensitivity by introducing the spectre of *deliberate* American intervention—the most hideous fear of all. John G. Diefenbaker, in a 1963 election campaign, after six years as Prime Minister, called into use the then controversial issue of whether defense missiles in Canada should be fitted with United States nuclear warheads. In speeches across the country he constantly exclaimed: "Policies made in Canada. . . ." Left dangling was the end of the sentence. If the syntax was faulty, the psychology was sound. Listeners simply filled in the rest . . . "and not in the Pentagon."

One can go through the Diefenbaker record and find practically nothing that in direct quotation could be considered anti-American. It is the half-sentence, the innuendo, the sneer that carries the meaning. But even here it is misleading to think of Diefenbaker or followers of his technique as "anti-American." The formula of anti- or pro-American is a dangerous oversimplification even when applied to such countries as Brazil or Venezuela. In Canada it is doubly imprecise or unsophisticated because Canadians consider themselves, as North Americans, almost—but not quite— members of the same family as the United States. Since policies made in Washington frequently have a direct bearing on them, they feel as uninhibited as Californians in expressing opinions, often unfavorable. At the same time, the Canadian abroad is resolutely the United States' best ambassador. Some of the liveliest skirmishes in the Second World War were conducted by Canadians against the British —in London and country pubs—when anti-Yankee diatribes disturbed the visitors' sense of justice. With familiar ease each Canadian almost invariably would open the rebuttal with the same words: "You don't understand Americans the way I do. . . ." A similar pattern goes on today when the Canadian tourist tells the Italian hotel keeper that not all Americans are extravagant or brash or belligerent.

Mixed with this role of interpreter is an inevitable sense of smugness. It goes back again into history when Canadians were intimidated by the people next door flexing their muscles. Americans hardly helped by speaking of Manifest Destiny that directed them to rule all the lands of North America, including Canada and Mexico. Canadians felt bullied in the War of 1812 and fearful of invasion again in the 1860's because Civil War armies might spill over the border. Despite the apprehension, however, there was the self-satisfaction that for a change the omnipotent nation was in difficulty. It possibly was a typographical error when a newspaper in Halifax, Nova Scotia, appeared in 1861 with a column of American news under the heading: "UNTIED STATES." But the next issue made the malice clear when the heading was corrected to "DISUNITED STATES."

The modern version of Canadian vainglory unveiled itself during the McCarthy era. If only a small number of American liberals seemed horrified by the witch-hunting in their midst and willing to do something about it, the entire Canadian people—French and English—were united for once in an outburst of indignation: against the "narrow-mindedness" of the United States, against the creeping signs of a "police state," against the "decay of democracy." Canadians hardly recognize among themselves today a related kind of intolerance when they suggest that federal police—the R.C.M.P.—should ferret out French-Canadian secessionists from federal posts, or take them off the air, or isolate them so they will not contaminate the youth. Precisely the same rationale is used as was heard under McCarthyism: "In the national interest." The fact that civil liberties have been protected speaks more for the delicacy of the French-English position than it does for genuine public sufferance.

Canadians deplore racial malevolence in the United States, and yet religious bigotry in Canada lingers to a degree hardly known in the United States. A Protestant mistrust of Catholicism—which had its most forceful expression under Ontario's Loyal Orange Society—continues to spring up and pollute internal relations. Ontario itself, particularly Toronto, has emerged from the domestic version of the Thirty Years' War, but much of the rest of Canada continues to engage in it slyly. In the tiny eastern province of Prince Edward Island a veteran editor, Burton Lewis, recalled for me his boyhood in rural Ontario, where his father, a Methodist pastor, was ostracized because he refused to join Orangemen in the persecution and condemnation of Roman Catholics. Lewis, in his sixties, said: "Prince Edward Island is at about the same stage in many social matters as my home town was when I was growing up." In western Canada I found the mentality of Orangeism common in Alberta and British Columbia, where the unease or ignorance about Quebec is often switched from political to religious grounds. "Those French" are equivalent to "papists," and therefore linked with an indefinable but diabolical Roman plot to spread Catholicism.

The hypocrisy that occasionally shows itself in the Canadian character overflows into American relations. To some people the new kind of nationalism—of a nature that accepts United States finances on one hand and deplores inroads on the other—is repugnant and immature. It is the kind of nationalism that Harry G. Johnson, an argumentative Canadian economist who taught at the University of Chicago, claims has diverted Canada into "a narrow and garbage-cluttered cul-de-sac," and has given rise to "two-faced anti-Americanism" that distinguishes it from any other type of anti-Americanism in the world. One can quarrel easily with the Johnson approach, and the usual rejoinder is simple: "What are we to make of it when we are told that our claims may be asserted only so long as they are not 'anti-American'?" In fact, the kind of anti-Americanism that does exist in Canada is not the same as the Brazilian or Venezuelan varieties because it is not virulent or based on a bitter resentment of American wealth. The Canadian standard of living may be about 25 per cent lower than the American, but nonetheless it is extremely high: along with Sweden's the second highest in the world. In practice the differentiation between it and the American scale means that a Canadian, instead of driving an Oldsmobile, drives a Chevrolet. Such economic jealousy that prevails is internal and has, as we shall soon note, regions of Canada scowling at one another in place of the United States.

The late and great editor B. K. Sandwell once said that Canadians like England but dislike Englishmen; they like Americans but dislike the United States. The validity of the observation continues today. In the first part, the affection is for British justice and institutions; the antipathy is toward the haughtiness of some Englishmen who act or talk as though Canada were still a colony. In the second part, any objection toward the United States is based on the chronic fear of being engorged, while individually Canadians have an affinity for Americans and share the same tastes and ambitions.

Canada's "anti-Americanism" is rather in keeping with a trait found in Americans themselves: the need to be liked, or if not liked at least understood and not ignored. Canadian distress over the United States may have its origin in history, but currently it is caused by American unwillingness to learn not only some of the facts but the motives and anxieties that lie behind Canadian behavior. United States ignorance shows itself in trite ways: tourists driving over the border with extra spare tires because they are not certain they are available in Canada; tourists reaching Toronto for a week end, hoping to have a quick side trip up the Alaska Highway (2,500 miles away).

Most of these anecdotes no longer offend Canadians. Nelson Eddy and Jeanette MacDonald left such a lasting imprint of the Frozen North and mushing dogsleds and serenading Mounties that Canadians shrug in resignation and do not even attempt to dispel the myths. What does irritate them is the opposite kind of ignorance that dismisses Canadians as unworthy of much time or attention because "they are just like us." American tourists so busy snapping photos of Mounties in their vivid scarlet tunics are perhaps unaware the color was copied in admiration of the same "redcoats" who were objects of American derision and hatred.

Walter O'Hearn, executive editor of *The Montreal Star,* now and then lectures editors of United States papers on their failure to cover Canadian news adequately. He reproaches even "that vast compendium," *The New York Times,* for giving prominence to long stories about Canadian fish and game laws while burying reports of significant elections. O'Hearn rejects the usual explanation by American editors ("since you're similar to us, you're safe and therefore dull") and offers instead a unique theory based on his several years as a correspondent in New York. In those days resident aliens had to report every few months to an immigration office on Columbus Avenue to have their work permits stamped. Some of the people lining up with O'Hearn hoped eventually to become naturalized United States citizens—but a number of them had no such intention. And so, with monotonous regularity, they made the long trip up to Columbus Avenue—retaining their own citizenship by choice. O'Hearn recalls the consternation and the aggrieved manner of immigration officers for whom United States citizenship was the highest privilege to which man could aspire. The other was a voluntary choice these officers could not understand: "It made us appear in their eyes daffy, deplorable, perhaps even subversive."

The O'Hearn exposition follows:

The millions of United States citizens who have traveled north are struck by the similarities of mood, architecture, and accent. Some Americans say they find this reassuring. Yet if they were to plumb their unconscious, would our neighbors find reassurance? I believe there is a deep, if unrealized resentment. They don't like to read about us every day. They don't want to be reminded daily that we exist. They are affronted by the presence next door of Americans who don't want to be United States citizens. By merely getting along, by managing to be like them without going all the way, we disturb something deep down, which may be their faith in themselves. We upset them as no Englishman, Thailander, Cuban or Russian could.

As unorthodox as is this analysis, it dovetails in a way with the more traditional view that if Canadians spoke Spanish they would be taken more seriously simply because they would sound different from Americans; or if Canada suddenly emerged with a Communist or Fascist government Americans would be forced to learn more about it in six weeks than they had troubled to learn in sixty years. However, the strange truth is that while the Canadian at one minute demands attention, at the next instant he hates himself for being petty enough to show this human frailty. Here, as in so many other areas, there is a contradiction that makes the Canadian character far more complex than it appears on the surface. When Canada is snubbed by the American press, or taken for granted, a prickly Canadian pride lets loose resentment. When it receives headlines, it questions the balance or tastefulness. In 1963, for instance, the United States press all at once discovered Canada because of a serious conflict between Ottawa and Washington over continental defenses. Even those Canadians who despised Diefenbaker challenged American publications for making him out to be a villain.

Diefenbaker's virtue, at least, was that he drew notice to the country and its difficulties. One Washington paper even published a map showing "the major trouble spots of the world." Canada finally was in the same company as Cuba, Panama, Viet Nam, China, and the Congo. The caption, unfortunately, destroyed the momentary giddiness: "Canada, unlike Cuba, is firmly in the Western camp."

There was, inescapably, exasperation over this oversimplified yet fundamentally sound fact of international life. This, of course, is the basis for whatever complacency does exist in the United States: in any showdown Canada is hardly likely to go over to the enemy side. But the fact tends to obscure the intricacies of Canadian problems.

Occasionally a workmanlike, serious job of interpreting Canada is done without a sensational news development to justify or confound it. One such series of articles was written a few years ago by Carl T. Rowan, former director of the United States Information Agency, and at the time a staff writer for the *Minneapolis Tribune*. Rowan had some relatively minor misconceptions to dispel—such as the notion that Canadians live in a perpetually frozen belt. About three of every four Canadians, he pointed out, live farther south than International Falls, Minnesota. He also relayed the cutting and characteristic pique of an Alberta farmer: "Just tell 'em where the fish are bitin' and which part of Canada the next cold front is coming from and the Americans will have all the information they can digest." This much he almost expected to hear and to learn. But on a broader and more thoughtful level the Canada Rowan did detect was not what he had anticipated:

> I discovered that the much-heralded "undefended border" between the United States and Canada now is being fortified on the Canadian side with a host of cultural and economic artillery. I found that while we have been wincing and watching the nationalism of distant lands we have failed to note that an equally fervid nationalism has fired up our next-door neighbors. . . . It would be silly and sensational to say there is danger of a "Cuba to the north" in either the near or distant future. Yet, it would be journalistic malfeasance not to pass along this comment by a noted former Canadian, Dr. Jacob Viner, professor of economics at Princeton University: "One must never underestimate the power of a nationalism chafing under real or imagined grievances."

Fundamentally most stresses and strains between Canada and the United States shrink to two causes: American ignorance, Canadian touchiness. Several years ago Canadians were deeply concerned—as they almost always are—about their balance of payments with the United States. In what became a famous golf game played between the Canadian Prime Minister and the United States President, Mr. Eisenhower said that while he knew Canada was the United States' best customer he was amazed to hear of Canada's huge trade deficit with the United States. Canadians felt justified in voicing shocked grief over a presidential lack of awareness of a problem central to economic well-being. The Canadian petulance, on the other hand, sometimes reaches ludicrous heights. During a Montreal by-election local newspapers published long accounts of the activities of a United States vice-consul interviewing a French-Canadian candidate on his views about neutrality and nuclear weapons. The press tone was one of shock, with the implication that this was American interference in Canadian politics. There was no acknowledgment of the standard practice of consulates and embassies all over the world to gather political information in the normal course of duties.

There are some Canadians—unfortunately a relatively small number—who are not perturbed merely because most Americans are uninformed about Canada. After all, the reasoning goes, the United States has an excessively heavy load to carry, much of it directly related to urgent matters of peace or war; Americans should be able to relax sometimes, somewhere, with someone—and not feel that up-to-the-minute homework is crucially important. If not with Canadians, with whom? One can even forgive Americans who do not understand all the nuances of Canadian independence. Canada does not pay taxes to Britain, as many Americans still believe; nor is its foreign policy controlled by London. But the confusion, if not entirely excusable, is at least understandable. In 1965 Canadians themselves were still talking of removing their constitution from British hands and placing it exclusively in their own.

If Americans are unacquainted with the names of the Canadian Prime Minister or the leader of the chief opposition party, or the fact that there are ten provinces, Canadians themselves are hardly immune from criticism. Who was Sir John A. Macdonald? The question was asked of high school students in Toronto, and it received such common replies as: "He tried to unite Canada and the United States," or, "He was the first governor of Toronto." The same students could identify George Washington and Abraham Lincoln, yet they failed to realize Macdonald was a mixture of both: Canada's first Prime Minister, and the molder of a union of scattered and quarreling colonies. On a Montreal radio quiz program a group of twelve-year-old children hardly did better when they were asked to cite the significance of the year 1867. The contestants were able to identify several personalities in television and sports—mostly Americans—but the date of Confederation defeated every one of them.

Partly the fault can be attributed to the teaching of history, but not entirely. Canadian nationalism until recent times was so low-keyed that it discouraged flag waving or other blunt manifestations of patriotism. To some extent this was because the two distinct peoples who made up the original Canada—French and English—each had its own cast of heroes, and often the idol for one was the scoundrel for the other. But there was yet another reason: a perverse shrinking away from "American" characteristics, from the extravagant symbols of nationhood of those "loud Yankees." Strident nationalism might be all right for the unsophisticated, but Canadians were dedicated missionaries, the do-gooders who could move suavely and quietly around the world with an international spirit. If the Americans made a fuss about the birthday of Washington or Lincoln, this was all the more reason Canadians could afford to be blasé and let Macdonald's slip by unnoticed. To this day the only observance of Macdonald's birthday is by a small band of faithful inheritors of his Conservative Party who each year place flowers beside his tombstone in Cataraqui Cemetery on the outskirts of Kingston, Ontario, a burial ground obscure to most Canadians.[1] And only in 1964 was the first tangible dedication made to Macdonald and the country's other founding fathers with the opening in Charlottetown, Prince Edward Island, of a Memorial Centre—a cultural complex consisting of a theater, art gallery, and museum— in their collective honor. Lamenting the languor, Frank MacKinnon, a college principal, and president of the government foundation that put up the Memorial Centre, pointed to the Washington Monument, the Jefferson Memorial, and the scores of other tributes paid by the United States over the years to its creators. "I've always felt," said MacKinnon, "the reason we are so unemotional about our beginning is that Confederation was a constitutional development, and not the result of a popular revolution. If we had only hated George III it might have been different."

There is also good reason to suspect that in the Canadian personality lurks an innate resentment that the United States, with all its chauvinism and razzle-dazzle, has captured a spirit of unity and purpose, the dearth of which now bedevils the Canadian nation.

Several features make Canada different from the United States, among them a loyalty to monarchy and membership in the Commonwealth, the fraternity of Britain's former colonies. But the most important without doubt is the existence of a French Canada, and with it the interplay between the two groups known as English Canadians and

[1] In 1965 federal, provincial and municipal political figures gathered in Kingston to attend a banquet and hear speeches about Macdonald. But the circumstance was exceptional: the 150th anniversary of his birth. The ceremony served mainly to remind editorial writers across the country of how Macdonald's memory has been shunned.

French Canadians.[2] The majority of men, women, and children of French lineage, almost five million, live in the Province of Quebec. They are the most cohesive, tenacious minority in North America. Another million or so are scattered in communities—some of them substantial—in other provinces. Together they are the oldest inhabitants of North America, next to the Indians and Eskimos. Their story can be traced back to 1605, when Samuel de Champlain, the greatest of the early French explorers and colonizers, set up the first permanent colony in Acadia, an area the English subsequently called Nova Scotia. Three years later he founded Quebec City as the center of France's activities in the New World. Like the original English settlers in Virginia, the French were ruled by a company of merchant adventurers; but there was one striking difference. They were ruled also by missionary priests—the Récollets and later the Jesuits—who, filled with the zeal of the Counter Reformation, worked boldly to preserve Roman Catholicism among the fur traders and to spread it among the heathen Indian trappers.

For a while New France was an illustrious place, supplying furs in abundance for the hats of the men of Paris and

[2] This is cumbersome nomenclature, and the phrase "English Canadians" in particular is inexact since it implies persons of English or Anglo-Saxon descent. In fact only about 40 per cent of Canadians trace their ancestors to the British Isles (for census purposes: English, Irish, Scottish, Welsh). Another 30 per cent, of European origin, are included in the broad term "English Canadians" since their main language is English rather than French. Thus the majority—seven out of ten—are lumped together to distinguish them from the minority whose mother tongue is French. Several other forms of identification have been attempted, including "Anglo-Canadians." French Canadians commonly say *"les Anglais."* But recently the Montreal newspaper *Le Devoir* revived the word *Anglophone* to teach its subscribers that just because someone speaks English he is not necessarily of Anglo-Saxon stock. If this is not sufficiently confusing, French Canadians refer to themselves as *les Canadiens,* but, as will be related in a further chapter, there is also a distinctive group known as *les Acadiens.* For the sake of the reader's sanity, I will keep mainly to the old-fashioned but manageable "English Canadians" and "French Canadians." Occasionally, as a reminder that not all "English Canadians" are English, I will use still another phrase: English-speaking Canadians.

timber for the French fleet. But by the latter part of the seventeenth century Louis XIV began to lose interest in his colony. He did not want to "depopulate France," as he put it, in order to reinforce the thin line of eight thousand settlers huddling in the regions of Quebec City, Trois Rivières, and Montreal. Nor did he like the idea of spending even a few thousand *livres* a year to administer what Voltaire later was to dismiss contemptuously as *"quelques arpents de neige"* (a few acres of snow).

New France was more or less forced onto its own resources. As explorers pushed farther inland to find better pelts they encountered hostility from their competitors, the English fur traders from Albany, each side using Indian allies to harass the other. By the middle of the eighteenth century the antagonism was sharply increased when war in Europe between France and Britain spread to North America. William Pitt, the British Prime Minister, shrewdly recognized France's apathy toward its overseas possession and aimed the main thrust there. Even when the French did stir themselves to ship out reinforcements, they were turned back by the British, who controlled the seas. The French commander in New France, the Marquis de Montcalm, could call on no more than 6,000 regulars and 10,000 militiamen to defend a vast territory. But at least the city of Quebec, on the formidable heights dominating the St. Lawrence River, appeared immune to any attack by land or water.

Then, in what was to become a classic and dramatic example of an amphibious operation, the British general James Wolfe sent his Highland troops on flatboats, borne silently by the tide in the darkness of a calm night, to the Anse au Foulon, a cove at the foot of the cliffs leading to the Plains of Abraham at the west of the capital. A small French patrol was overpowered, and by dawn five thousand British regulars had climbed the cliffs and were in position for battle. Montcalm, who had anticipated a showdown elsewhere, hastily moved four thousand militiamen and Indians to meet the enemy. In fifteen minutes on a September day in 1759 the fate of New France was settled.

The British conquest gave rise to a variety of reactions. For people in the Thirteen Colonies to the south it was the signal for much rejoicing; the old foe who for years had been ambushing them, and leading Indians in forays of scalping and slaughter, were finally out of the way; French forts that had been obstacles would now provide protection for the push of settlers into farther fields; Fort Duquesne would be renamed Fort Pitt (and later Pittsburgh); and the American colonists, freed from worry about the French, would begin to lose their sense of dependence on England. For the people in France there was hardly a moment spent in sorrow; the Seven Years' War was still being fought in Europe, closer to their own farms and homes than the savage and costly and undesirable land a thousand leagues away. For the people of New France, however, "The fatal hour had sounded and it was necessary to bow to the inevitable. ... No more help could be expected from France."

Those words, written by the French-Canadian historian Thomas Chapais in the twentieth century, reflect the sad but proud reaction to an event two centuries ago. Barely sixty thousand *Canadiens* were faced with the challenge of their preservation as a whole people in a world suddenly turned English; theirs was neither the instinct nor desire for assimilation. But the problems were immense. Most of the French administrators returned to the mother country as British governors replaced them. Left behind was a leaderless collection mainly of peasants and small merchants, some *seigneurs,* or members of the landed aristocracy—and a total of one hundred and sixty-four parish priests and monks. The clergy were the essential, pivotal group, for they ministered not only to religious and educational needs but took over much of the secular direction as well—to provide French continuity. The Roman Catholic Church was to remain the principal defender of the French-Canadian way of life from generation to generation, meeting defiance only in recent years.

At first the British thought of absorbing the vanquished by attracting masses of settlers from the Thirteen Colonies; but Ohio valleys and warmer lands were beckoning, and few showed up. However, merchants from the Thirteen Colonies, and from England and Scotland, quickly appeared and assumed control of Quebec's economic affairs. By the early 1770's the British had framed a new and relatively generous policy to win support at least from the two most influential classes: the clergy and the *seigneurs*. The seignorial system of landholding, canceled after the conquest, was restored; but, most important of all, the new British colony was given the right to be French in institutions— such as civil law—and to continue with a guarantee of freedom for the Catholic religion and education. In a Protestant empire, this was a considerable concession; and in return the Church preached allegiance to the British crown.

The English largesse was not entirely altruistic. The governor, Guy Carleton, accurately estimated the growing discontent in the colonies to the south (in a fashion, the conquest of Quebec created the United States, for not only did the colonists feel less need for England's protection, but England itself created antagonism by looking for new tax sources to pay the heavy debts accumulated during the war with France). Carleton reasoned that a loyal Quebec would be invaluable as a strategic base in case of trouble; moreover, the *Canadiens* might recruit a useful militia. As it turned out, he was partly right. When leaders of the rebellion in the American colonies exhorted French Canadians to "seize the opportunity presented by Providence itself" and join them, very little interest was aroused.

But if the *habitants,* or peasants, were not for the revolution neither were they sufficiently against it to flock to arms. Carleton called them "the most ungratefullest wretches." The simple fact was that the masses were lukewarm toward the British and especially irritated over having to start paying again seignorial dues and church tithes. But at the same time they could see no advantage in joining the Americans. After all, in Quebec the English were only a minority; but if Quebec were combined with the other colonies then the French would be the minority. On top of this was the recollection that until only a few years back the colonists who now offered friendship had been their deadly enemies. Some of these colonists, in turn, became enemies of the American Revolution. Between forty thousand and sixty thousand—United Empire Loyalists, supporters of the crown—left the new United States of America in two main branches. One moved by sea to Nova Scotia; the other traveled overland to found what became known as Upper Canada (later Ontario). They, rather than the original conquerors of New France, were the principal colonists of British North America. Ill at ease amidst French customs and law and language, only a relative few stopped in Quebec itself (Lower Canada). The settlers in Upper Canada, clearing forests in a world apart from the *habitants* of Lower Canada, lost no time in bringing in the freehold land system. They also supported laws designed to make their new province "the very image and transcript" of England. Thus, at an early stage were drawn the basic distinctions between English and French Canada.

Meanwhile, the *habitants,* a quiet people, grew steadily in numbers despite the end of any possible migration from France. By 1790 Quebec's population rose to 160,000, an increase of 166 per cent in one generation. Keeping pace with the biological achievement was the strong sense of nationalism. There was little sentiment for the country that had let them down; they regarded themselves as *Canadiens* —the true Canadians—and not as Frenchmen. The clergy took up the earnest task of preparing a new middle class in keeping with a Catholic outlook: a professional class rather than one of commerce or industry or science. The old seminaries were the starting points for the lawyers—*notaires* (solicitors) and *avocats* (barristers)—and later the doctors and journalists who joined the new *bourgeoisie*. Meanwhile the English of the governing and merchant classes found their soulmates in the *seigneurs,* an alliance of money and power that was to change only in the degree that eventually the landed-gentry partners were replacd by French-Canadian politicians.

Little more than a hundred years after Wolfe's landing, French Canadians were in the remarkable position of negotiating a new status. In 1840 Upper and Lower Canada had been joined into the Province of Canada, a union that satisfied neither the French nor English inhabitants. Now, in 1867, the British North America Act was passed by the British parliament to provide for the formation of the Dominion of Canada. The B.N.A. Act divided the region again into the Provinces of Ontario and Quebec, and simultaneously brought them into wider Confederation with the colonies of Nova Scotia and New Brunswick. As an article of Confederation, French was given a secure constitutional guarantee and designated one of the two official languages of the Dominion of Canada. In slightly less than the next hundred years the Confederation became ominously precarious, because French Canadians regarded themselves as aliens, as second-class citizens, a colonial people exploited by foreigners who happened to be their own English-speaking countrymen.

In the interval, the old social structure had gone through drastic upheaval, most of it only during the last generation and a half. What had been primarily an agricultural life and economy was changed; Quebec became a manufacturing province. French Canadians, who had formed the most traditional society on the continent—intimately identified with the land and the parish priest—moved to towns and cities to work in factories. More than seven out of ten, many of them suddenly, were exposed to urban pressures; inevitably there were some emotional adjustments, including a beginning of anticlericalism now that the local *curé* no longer exerted his influence. But any deeper stirrings were kept under control. The last *seigneur* was a sharp politician, Maurice Duplessis, who as premier and quasi-dictator of Quebec, starting in 1936, catered to French-Canadian nationalism by speaking of the province's "autonomy," but simultaneously treated his subjects as though they were still living in a feudal age. Only he was capable of knowing what was proper for them (children under the age of sixteen were not admitted to movies, but a girl could be legally married at the age of fourteen).

Duplessis appeased physical needs by such measures of patronage as building roads; he also built a corrupt political machine that extracted $20,000 in graft from a café or restaurant owner each time he needed to buy a liquor license worth $18. His seignorial arrangement with the industrialists —most of them English-speaking, as in the past—was simple. They supported his machine, and introduced more industry, in return for which he provided them with trouble-free labor that cost much less than in the neighboring and more advanced province of Ontario. Any major threats on the labor front, such as strikes, were handled by the provincial police who used notoriously crude strong-arm techniques.

Moreover, though ultranationalism, even secessionism, was always a latent force, Duplessis had it effectively channeled so as not to cause uneasiness among the province's English-speaking minority. His legislature rubber-stamped a so-called Padlock Law, which entitled police to clamp a bolt across the door of any house or building in which "Communist activities" took place. If the term was loosely defined or the power abused—as happened regularly —one could, in theory, appeal to the attorney general for legal action. Duplessis happened to hold also the title of attorney general. Once his provincial police closed down a printing shop because it turned out a double caricature of Hitler and Stalin, which folded over to make a likeness of Duplessis. When a bridge in Trois Rivières, his home constituency, collapsed he blamed "Communist saboteurs." Later it was discovered that the costly mishap was caused by defective steel that had passed provincial inspection; but there was no retraction.

Duplessis' blend of ruthlessness and paternalism was based on a shrewd evaluation of his own people. He judged, accurately, that his strength came from the noneducated in the smaller towns and the rural areas [3]—people who wanted a father figure to keep them safe from unsettling changes in the alien world outside and secure in familiar values and standards, even though some might be outdated. In any event he was by nature a mid-Victorian, an apostle of the *status quo*. Ill at ease with new ideas or concepts, which his conservatism rejected automatically, he kept power by feeding only a slight degree of advancement at a time— marked perhaps by the opening of a technical school. His rationale was much the same as that found today in backward Latin-American countries: that if you offer people too much knowledge too quickly, they will get out of hand.

The social sciences faculties at the two great French-language universities, Quebec City's Laval and the University of Montreal, were outstanding; but when professors analyzed the province's ailments and suggested remedies, Duplessis denounced them as leftists—and cut off grants. Some of the younger people, especially students and intellectuals breaking for the first time into social sciences and applied sciences, loathed him. There was little mourning among them when Duplessis died suddenly on September 7, 1959, at the age of sixty-nine. Lieutenants in his Union Nationale party carried on until the next election—June 1960—but, with "the chief" gone, the machine crumpled into defeat.

[3] Quebec has had compulsory schooling only since 1943, and during the Duplessis régime much of this was on paper.

The provincial Liberals came into office on the campaign slogan *"C'est l'temps qu' ça change!"* ("It's time for a change!")

Duplessis was one of the few men in Canada who assessed with prescience the extent of the smoldering fire within Quebec. On one occasion he told some of the younger members of his party, including Daniel Johnson, a future successor as Union Nationale leader: "When I'm gone you'll face the outburst." He was right—except that the man to face it was the new premier, a forty-eight-year-old lawyer named Jean Lesage, whose team of honest and energetic and idealistic administrators were dedicated to haul Quebec quickly into the twentieth century.

For a few months there was no visible recognition among French Canadians—especially the more youthful—that they were emerging from the Dark Ages. The memory of Duplessis and his despotic methods was too fresh and deeply imbedded. But then the release from frustration began to exhibit itself. Scrawlings in white paint on walls—*Québec Libre, Front de Libération Québecois*—were rather meaningless and unheeded at the start. These were followed by crude but passionate attacks on symbols of federal and "Anglo-Saxon" authority: dynamite bombs left in mail collection boxes in a Montreal suburb, Westmount, the residence of the wealthier English-speaking Quebecers. The incidents shocked the bulk of the usually peaceful French Canadians as much as they did English Canada. Such violence might be expected in Algeria or Cyprus, but, after all, this was Canada: a country of moderation, of stolid people!

The bombings, which ended with the capture of several young men, were written off as acts of a lunatic fringe element, sporadically organized, few in numbers—a correct evaluation as far as it went. Apart from the fact that disorder continued in other forms, the larger message began to appear: Quebec as a whole was dissatisfied and restless. Some of the discontent was aimed inwardly, against old religious mentality, against the social order, but much of it, for psychological reasons, took another direction: against the realm of the "conquerors." Practical areas for attack were not hard to find. Though Canada was supposed to be a bilingual country, at least for official purposes, most of the federal government's business was conducted in English. French Canadians, who made up 30 per cent of the population, held no more than 13 per cent of the senior federal civil service posts. Ottawa itself, the national capital, could count one third of its inhabitants as French-speaking, but the mass of them were in menial or subordinate jobs: running elevators and printing the forms for others to fill out.

It is because of this role—"the hewers of wood and drawers of water"—that the greatest resentment is felt. Fewer than seven out of every hundred corporation directors in Canada are French Canadians. The picture comes into more strenuous focus inside Quebec itself, where most of the major industrial, mining, and mercantile companies are owned and operated by *les Anglais.* The fact that much of this group, in turn, is controlled by Americans is of incidental interest to the average Quebecer. The consideration that Duplessis encouraged outside capital to enter the province, by promising to control his own people, is also irrelevant. The average French Canadian knows only that executive positions—at least up to now—have not been available to him. He has been expected to perform the function of a skilled or unskilled worker, with a standard of living 25 per cent lower than in Ontario. And if his own lack of modern education is a contributing factor, then—he argues defensively—perhaps he would be better off putting more of his province's revenue into a crash program closer to home, instead of contributing it to a central government in Ottawa. A word heard at intervals in the past in English-French relations—but never so volubly—has come into everyday conversation: *séparatisme.*

Every French Canadian is sentimentally a nationalist,

that is, conscious of the history and feat of sixty thousand people of 1759 who clung to language and customs to establish a "nation" within what is called Canada. Every French Canadian is also a potential secessionist or separatist, the degree depending on how far he feels he must go to protect his language, culture, and self-respect. In 1965 active separatists were in the minority. The questions troubling the moderates are whether English Canada is willing to understand that French Canada is undergoing two substantial and belated revolutions at once—social and industrial—and whether enough changes can be made in the existing structure and mood of Canada to satisfy the wants of French Canadians.

Almost three thousand miles from Quebec and its ferment, I sat with Bruce Hutchison in his home in Victoria, British Columbia. The tranquility of the West Coast setting, with roses still in bloom late in November, only served to accentuate the despondency of the thoughts he expressed. Hutchison—journalist, editor, and author—wrote one of the first general books on Canada to have international appeal: *The Unknown Country*. That was back in 1942, when there was no internal strain. Nor was there unease about the United States. "We had another crisis—the war—to make us take our minds off ourselves," he recalled. The pattern of Canadian history almost invariably has been that at a time of great stress or dissension a depression or war has come along to pull the country from its immediate and consuming problem. Now it is different. "We are at the point," Hutchison judged, "where all the strange, mysterious, dark forces of the Canadian nature are coming to the forefront, with the Quebec issue forcing us to decide whether we want to be a nation. If we're not big enough to see this through, we won't have a nation."

Not long afterwards, I sat in the study of J. A. Corry, one of Canada's most distinguished political scientists, and principal of Queen's University, in Kingston, Ontario. He made the observation that if Canadians are unimaginative and unadventurous there is a reason:

> The challenge has been just a bit too much for us, partly because of hard physical conditions and the fact that political leaders always must be sensitive to English-French relationships. This makes you cautious. I can see it even in university matters. When we—the English-language universities—meet to decide what we can do in common to urge on the government, we are terribly careful to consider: will this offend the French? So, Canadians don't go in for a wide, sweeping, daring show—unlike the Americans who can say and do things with more abandon.

In general he feels Canadians are groping because "the old labels have worn out." For instance, two labels that dominated Canadian thinking for generations were "dominion status" and "social reform," the attainment of which Canada eventually saw. Both were positive objectives. Now the slogan deals with the United States—"economic and cultural independence"—and this, Corry argues, denotes a negative perspective.

The uncertainty or hesitation conveyed by Hutchison and Corry, and by virtually every thoughtful Canadian today, is due largely to the blow to self-confidence suffered within the last few years. Until the Second World War Canada had been so busy looking over her shoulder at the United States or Britain, and then fighting the great depression of the 1930's, that any curiosity about her own identity was of secondary consideration. Canada emerged from the war, however, with a buoyancy and optimism unknown in the past. She had mounted a mammoth military effort, and now she was the third largest trading nation in the world. While much older and more populous countries—Germany, Japan, France—were recuperating from damage and dislocation,

Canada's vastly enlarged and intact factories were pushing out goods and materials for hungry foreign markets.

Domestically, expansion was almost unlimited. New oil fields competed for attention with new uranium or iron ore finds, and living standards rose sharply. Canadians threw away their old reputation for reserve and self-effacement. Instead, they swaggered around, almost like Texans, proclaiming their land the biggest, the best, the most glowing and promising in the whole world. Perhaps most heartening of all, the two main language groups had come through the war with far less strain or bitterness than during the First World War, when French Canadians opposed conscription for an overseas fight they considered the business of a remote British Empire and not of Canada. The prospect for healthy national unity was never better, and it was symbolized in 1948 by the choice of a French Canadian, Louis St. Laurent, as Prime Minister.

Apart from the material prosperity and internal harmony, there was considerable pride in the stature that Canada had achieved internationally in spite of its relatively small population. During the war Canada had struggled in vain for a voice in major Allied decisions. The closest it came to these moments of history was when Mackenzie King, the Prime Minister, acted as host to President Roosevelt and Prime Minister Churchill during their two conferences at Quebec City. But King never entered the conference chamber itself. Afterward, Canada purposefully moved to the forefront of the "middle powers" at San Francisco in laying down the structure of the United Nations—and restricting the authority of the major powers—so they could find suitable functions for themselves. Not much later a remarkable diplomat and personality, Lester B. Pearson, emerged as a global statesman. Pearson, Secretary of State for External Affairs, possessed just the right mixture of knowledge and compromise to work quietly behind the scenes to win acclaim for Canada far beyond its actual capabilities. The importance of "middle powers" was never greater. Pearson's effectiveness was shown in his personal triumph of resolving the Suez crisis in 1956, for which he was awarded the Nobel Peace Prize.

The scope of Canada's mission was exaggerated, both in the public and the official minds. It was perfectly true that many of the freshly emerging nations—small, and wary of old colonial empires—placed more faith in Canada's altruism than in the power struggles of Britain and the United States on one hand, and the Soviet bloc on the other. But before long the reality of international life became increasingly clear: in any veritable crisis only two countries, Russia and the United States, made the decisions over life and death. Even this implicit awareness, however, did not account completely for the psychological decline in Canadian prestige and influence. One indirect reason for it, at least in theory, was the maturing of the United States itself. In effect, John Foster Dulles, with his unyielding policy, was largely responsible for the number of times Pearson was called in to act as conciliator and mediator among the powers. John W. Holmes, now director general of the Canadian Institute of International Affairs, but Assistant Undersecretary of State in the Department of External Affairs during its period of renown, analyzes it another way: "When a nation has the bloom of youth and chastity in a naughty world and has not been out and about long enough to step on many toes, it can achieve diplomatic success which becomes progressively more difficult to get away with." In any event it may not be coincidence that Canada's role waned as the United States began to receive recognition for greater flexibility and patience.

If any single year had to be picked as the turning point in Canada's economic and diplomatic position and self-confidence, it would be 1957. Factories in Germany and Japan were back in their stride, and Canada no longer was the third trading nation. Business charts slipped, caught up in the general North American recession, and people started to question whether this was indeed the most lustrous nation on earth. Unemployment reached the worst levels since the 1930's. The year 1957 coincides, too, with the inauguration of the prime ministership of a small-town lawyer, John Diefenbaker, who had delusions of his own grandeur on top of Canada's flimsy grandeur. His failure internationally was his inability to understand that diplomacy requires finesse and skill different from the techniques of getting votes from prairie constituents. While, under Pearson's strategy, Canada had worked unobtrusively to gain results, the reverse prevailed under Diefenbaker, who made bellicose or bragging statements out of place with actuality.

The inadequacy and superficiality of Canadian foreign policy during the Diefenbaker era was illustrated by the appointment of Howard Green as foreign minister. Green, a friendly and decent man, had performed well as minister of public works. But his interest in, and knowledge of, foreign affairs was indicated in the fact that he had never visited Washington and his last contact with Europe was as a soldier in 1918. Soon after his appointment, Green flew to London. Within minutes of his landing at London Airport, a waggish Fleet Street reporter asked him how he found London after an absence of forty years. Green, incredibly, fell into the trap and said that, flying in, he had noticed many changes. To Europeans, who had learned great respect for Pearson and his methods, the next few years were to mark the sad loss of Canada as a forceful link between the Old and New Worlds.

The circumstances of the postwar period and the need of the world for many of Canada's products had contributed to the notion that the twentieth century belonged to Canada. Sound minds were now asking: Why should it? What had Canada done to earn such a claim? There was almost masochism in some of the harsh self-analysis that became customary in the late 1950's and continued into the 1960's.

There was extra fuel, too, in the letdown suffered after a glowing Diefenbaker promise of opening up "The North"—the Arctic and wastelands—into a new and enormous and bountiful source of energy and wealth. The public became aware that the North would remain much as it had always been: a cold and unprofitable challenge, and little else.

The searing soul-searching included the very substantial matter of rethinking the Canadian role, of Canadians deciding what they might accomplish in fact, rather than fancy. This appraisal was just getting underway when the Quebec crisis burst into the open, causing added confusion and irritation. And just about the same time, the new government, formed by Lester Pearson as Prime Minister in 1963, came under severe rebuke for a crude attempt to control the rate of United States investment in Canada. In the furor Canadians were made more conscious than ever of the dilemma of their position vis-à-vis the United States. Roy A. Matthews, an economist with the Canadian-American Committee, a private, nonpolitical, nonprofit organization that watches objectively the relations between the two countries, expressed it this way:

> As a practical matter, the Canadian ship of state has been obliged throughout its history to steer a difficult and sometimes uncertain course between the two shoals of absorption by the United States, on the one hand, and loss of economic advantage, on the other. The curious aspect of the present situation is the ostensible appearance of a new and baffling threat: that of being shipwrecked on both rocks at once.

Bruce Hutchison adds a point:

> I despair for us. We are crybabies. We turn against the Americans and accuse them of trying to dominate us, when we can't even solve our own problems. ... What few Canadians and fewer Americans understand is that Canada is no longer debating some minor aspect of policy but is struggling for survival as a nation.

The strange reality is that the two parts of the struggle —Canada's unease about the United States, French Canada's discomfort with English Canada—are parallel. Both are based on economics and culture, rather than pure politics, and both have traits that seem illogical and nebulous, and at least emotional. Nevertheless, these symptoms are very genuine to the peoples concerned. Just as the English Canadian sometimes is irked when his child comes away from watching a United States television show and pronouncing the word "loo-tenant" instead of "left-tenant," so a French Canadian bridles at the sound of "le baseball" and other Anglicizations that creep into his language. It is not, of course, the mere fact that impurities enter French-Canadian speech. It is the symbolism, the fear that French Canada, in relative terms a gradually diminishing minority, eventually will be digested entirely by English Canada.

The retention of the Canadian idiom as such is really of minor importance to the English-Canadian nationalist; he is worried about the inroads of Americanization all around him. In each instance, the trifle is just the indicator of the vast and complex problem of retaining an identity. What French Canada wants from the rest of the country is acceptance that Quebec is not simply another province, like Ontario or British Columbia, but that it is a way of life: in effect, a nation with a soul of its own that must be maintained and protected from mightier forces. The demand even of moderate Quebecers today is for a reframed political system that would give Quebec the right to control its own taxation and finances, and plan its own economic destiny— possibly along socialist lines—without conformity to central planning from Ottawa. In practice, a loose federation would exist with common trade and central control over such matters as defense and foreign policy.

The average English Canadian reacts with instinctive indignation and says: "Why should any minority dictate to the majority?" This is where the nub rests. French Canada, while numerically a minority, does not regard itself as one in spirit. Nor does it feel it is forcing English Canada into anything unreasonable. Since it looks upon itself as a nation within a federation, it wants to be left alone, and in return is prepared to leave English Canada alone to work out its own problems. The average English Canadian again has a ready rejoinder: "This makes no sense. It is not merely a question of five or six million French Canadians in relation to fifteen million Canadians who speak English. It's this whole continent they've got to think about. They're outnumbered by more than two hundred million people who speak English." Where the average English Canadian commits his error is in the still deeper fact that he argues with the hard logic of an "Anglo-Saxon," while what is involved is an ingredient that is not necessarily cerebral. The Spanish have an expressive word for it: *dignidad*. There is a common *latinité* in the French Canadian, who, striving to be comfortable with his dignity, may allow emotion to outpace logic. This is the part that has not been grasped by English Canada. It carries with it the greatest hazard, since it implies a clash between cold polemics and aroused emotions.

Essentially what English Canada resents is the rocking of the boat—especially after the traumatic experience of the 1950's when Canadians found themselves not as vigorous or as prominent in the world as they had once believed. But the tension in Canada today can be expressed another way: English Canada, after many years of searching and struggling for an identity, and now animated by the alarming growth of American influence, has finally begun to look on itself as a nation; in order to consolidate this feeling among peculiarly diverse provinces, it requires a strong central link or government. But French Canada also feels now the need to assert its nationhood: a nationhood dependent on strong provincial authority, and therefore a weakening of federal jurisdiction. This is where the fundamental discord begins, and it was demonstrated in two events in 1964:

the debate over the introduction of a distinctive Canadian flag, and the visit to Canada of Queen Elizabeth.

Though Canada had existed as a country for almost a century, it had never agreed on a flag of its own. During the first three quarters of its history it simply showed Britain's Union Jack. During the Second World War the Red Ensign of the British merchant marine, embellished with the Canadian coat of arms, and designated for the use of the troops overseas, became popular. It was at least more acceptable to French Canadians than the Union Jack, which they rejected as blatantly British. Quebecers also flew their own provincial emblem of the fleur-de-lys—not through any sentiment for old royalty of France, which had forsaken their ancestors, but because it was as *canadien* as anything else flying.

On and off over the years, Canadians spoke of getting a unique flag—one that would cling neither to the British nor French past. But it was not until May 1964 that anyone did anything tangible. Prime Minister Pearson, fulfilling an election promise, unfurled his idea of how a Canadian flag should look: with the central theme the maple leaf, Canada's natural emblem, and no sign either of the Union Jack or the fleur-de-lys. Pearson made this pronouncement before a national convention of the Canadian Legion—a veterans' group exceeded in conservatism only by the American Legion—and was angrily shouted down. One veteran jumped to his feet and cried: "You are selling Canada to the peasoupers!" (French Canadians.)

Despite the initial and disheartening test, Pearson a few days later presented his flag in detail to parliament: three red maple leaves on a single stem on a field of white, and flanked by vertical blue bars to represent the national motto, "From Sea to Sea." His flag resolution also contained an unexpected—though characteristically Canadian—compromise. Apart from the official maple leaf flag, the Union Jack would continue to be flown as a secondary sign of Canada's membership in the Commonwealth and allegiance to the crown. Public opinion polls indicated general approval. It was far from the end, however. Instead of entailing a clean and simple move to fill—as Pearson intended—a unifying need in the country, it turned into a parliamentary brawl thick with racial overtones. John Diefenbaker stood by the Red Ensign and declared: "A flag that does not contain the greatness of your heritage is no flag for a nation." The mayor of Ottawa, a bumptious woman named Charlotte Whitton, referred to the new design as "a white badge of surrender waving three dying maple leaves." This was the recurrent reaction of the opponents: "betrayal" for the benefit of French Canada. Members of Pearson's Liberal party who spoke strongly in favor of the flag found themselves jeered at by Conservatives, one of whom said of French Canadians, "It is they who are dividing the country, not us."

French Canadians in general approved the flag, but with an air of ennui. For all the good and sincere intentions, Pearson's gesture was late—several years late. The grievances of French Canada were beyond solution by a token. Arthur R. M. Lower, the eminent historian, observed sorrowfully that "the flag issue sums up our whole historical experience," because opposition to it was a cover for racial antagonism. "It is for the majority to show forbearance, tolerance, and chivalry towards the minority," wrote Lower. "Here is the hardest lesson Canada has to learn.... for our psychology is anything but tolerant and chivalrous. Racial antagonism comes from both sides of the fence."

The arguments against the flag reached farcical excesses. In the House of Commons some members said that the maple leaf motif looked like a beer or flour advertisement. Amateur heraldists said that vertical blue bars to represent the sea were unacceptable; the proper form should be wavy, horizontal lines. Finally, in disgust over a Conservative filibuster, Pearson accepted a formula placing the choice of a design in the hands of a fifteen-man committee representing all five federal parties.[4] The committee examined nearly two thousand designs; one even featured the Stars and Stripes to show a North American affiliation. Six weeks later it came up with its recommendation: the same theme, but now a single red maple leaf with red vertical bars instead of blue bars. Again Diefenbaker led his party in filibuster. Parliament dragged on, into its longest session in history— and one of the nastiest. Then Pearson invoked cloture, a procedural device for ending debate and securing an immediate vote used only eight times in the annals of Canada's parliament.

A nation stunned into boredom by the long wrangle— thirty-three days of debate, 252 speeches—sighed with relief when the House of Commons approved the new red-and-white maple leaf flag by a large majority. It was an anticlimax. In the House, members sang "O Canada" followed by "God Save the Queen," some of the vanquished standing with sullen stiffness. But no cannon sounded across the land, no fireworks went up in the kind of display to which any newly emerged nation would have treated itself on such a noble and historic occasion. In Montreal a few people stood at a street corner and applauded while a makeshift flag, the first in town, was hoisted into a brisk December wind. In Alberta members of the Progressive Conservative Association wore black arm bands to mourn the passing of the Red Ensign. *The Montreal Star,* anticipating the best, summed up: "The new flag may never be the flag of the old or the middle aged, but it will be the flag of the grandchildren of the one and the children of the other." A couple of months later, simple flag-raising ceremonies were held officially in Ottawa, provincial capitals, and at Canadian embassies abroad.

[4] In addition to the two major parties—Liberals and Conservatives—three smaller ones sit in Canada's parliament: the socialist New Democratic Party, the "funny money" Social Credit Party, and its French-Canadian splinter of Créditistes.

Those Canadians who previously had complained because the United States paid little heed to Canada could take dubious comfort from the fact that the flag issue attracted widespread comment. "We have graduated from the *National Geographic* to the *Atlantic Monthly*," said one erudite wit. The *Memphis Commercial Appeal* charitably pointed out that controversy still surrounds the Stars and Bars: "It was, after all, only recently that the Interior Department ruled that the flag of the Confederacy cannot be flown over Fort Sumter in Charleston Harbor, where the first shots of the Civil War were fired." *The New York Times* hoped that now that the flag debate was out of the way, Pearson could persuade parliament "to get on with legislation designed to meet some of Quebec's aspirations for a greater voice in its own affairs." Problems that exist between Quebec and the rest of the country, the *Times* wisely noted, "are more profound than mere differences of language, symbols or national anthems." Some papers recognized how strange, and petty, it was to find such an item as a flag dominant in the thermonuclear half of the twentieth century. In Paris, *Libération* said: "It is a fortunate nation that is able to quarrel over such an issue."

In the aftermath, one could speculate reasonably validly that English-Canadian hostility toward a flag that discarded the British insignia was due more to reasons of psychology than to any sentiment. For the Union Jack, or any derivative of it, stood for the conquest of Quebec and a comfortable collective security. The same unspoken attitude lay behind the reaction to Quebec's reception of Queen Elizabeth in October 1964. The Queen—Canada's monarch, as well as Britain's—had been invited three years in advance to attend ceremonies in Charlottetown and Quebec City commemorating the centennial of two conferences that led to Confederation. The planning was announced well before F.L.Q. (*Front de Libération Québecois*) terrorists had gone into action, and in fact only a couple of years after a 1959 visit to Quebec when Duplessis was still in control and when the Queen spoke appreciatively of "peace, generosity and union." But 1964 was not 1959. Two specific points made it different. First, separatists declared publicly that the Queen would not be welcome and that her life might be in danger; second, the terrible memory of the assassination of President Kennedy was barely ten months old. A fear that Quebec City might become another Dallas turned what should have been a rather routine visit into a tense and major drama.

The irony is that all previous royal tours had been enthusiastically received in Quebec. If anything, the Gallic flair resulted in more lusty welcomes than in staunchly "British" but durably restrained Ontario. No matter how frequent or bothersome the clashes between English and French Canada, French Canadians had never forgotten it was the British crown that had guaranteed the continuity of their language, religion, and customs. There is also no doubt that the symbolism of the crown was essential to English Canadians looking in another direction: it made Canada and its constitutional monarchy different from the United States and its republicanism. But now the separatists were using that same crown as the pivot in their fight for Quebec autonomy. Their protest was not so much against the Queen as it was against the anniversary of the union she was commemorating—a union they now considered to have no validity.

More than one thousand reporters and cameramen arrived from all parts of the world, many of them simply with the ghoulish assignment of standing by in the event of an assassination. A British television crew even dug out a supposed terrorist cell and filmed members removing from some hideaway brush near Quebec City a "cache" of weapons. It consisted of two or three rusty rifles. But the fear of exposing children to possible violence, plus apathy and antipathy and bad weather, kept people away. Only a few thousand of Quebec City's 200,000 residents turned out to greet the

Queen. Moreover, a few hundred youth booed when the Queen's car drove by, or shouted, "Elizabeth go home." Local police, massed in full strength, pushed back the chanters. Paris reporters observed that Quebec police behaved much as Paris police, roughly and impatiently flailing a clump of demonstrators. American reporters were reminded of Birmingham police using precisely the same tactics of striking out indiscriminately with nightsticks to keep a mob moving. One United States reporter, noting how police smashed into a group of maybe a dozen singing teenagers, said sardonically, "At least we let our Negroes sing." Meanwhile, the ghoulish aspects were not completely overlooked. Radio reporters kept repeating over and over again on the air, "Nothing has happened to her—yet."

The fact that nothing did happen, that the anxiety about attempts at assassination proved groundless, was largely overlooked in the post-mortem of the visit itself. Both English and French papers deplored that the crown appeared, at least momentarily, divisive rather than unifying. There was, at the same time, a sober and shocked realization by many French Canadians—normally hospitable and gracious —that they had been intimidated into staying in their homes while unruly agitators took over their streets. Moderate voices, silent up to now, began to demand of the *Rassemblement pour l'Indépendance Nationale* (R.I.N.) and other separatists that they confine their activities to elections and see how poorly they would do.

The reaction from English Canada was more worrisome. While many newspapers across Canada saw the Quebec visit as a valuable lesson in pointing up just how sick Confederation really was, and urged a better understanding of French Canada, this positive approach was far from overwhelming. At least as common was the bitter and hostile comment that the Queen had been insulted—the Queen in this sense representing English Canada. Columnists and editorialists, speaking of French Canadians, in effect repeated the sentiment of two centuries ago when Governor Carleton called them "the most ungratefullest wretches." Richard Sanburn, editor of the *Calgary Herald,* wrote: "I'm not being entirely facetious when I suggest a rerun of the Battle of the Plains of Abraham—with the subsequent script rewritten to make more sense."

The dilemma, reduced to its raw essence, is this: For the first time in its life Canada has a grievous and complicated problem to overcome on its own. In the past, debates between French and English Canada could be mediated by Britain. Canada did make a separate declaration of war against Germany in 1939, instead of accepting the British declaration as automatically binding, and it was an act of self-assertion, of growing toward manhood. But still the country continued to lean on Britain in other ways, psychologically. For instance, Canada's equivalent of a written constitution is the British North America Act, by which the country was established in 1867. Since the B.N.A. Act was passed by the British parliament, all amendments to it have come by the London route. Thus, almost a century after theoretical nationhood, Canada remained one of the few sovereign states in the world powerless—at least on paper —to alter its own constitution.

It was not, however, a typical case of a "mother country" trying to keep a last greedy grasp on an impatient offspring. It was the opposite. Westminster gladly would have voted itself out of formal Canadian involvement at a moment's notice—but Canada held back from making the appropriate request. One major reason was Quebec's lingering dread of being smothered without the British insurance to shield it from the English-speaking majority. In a period of thirty-five years the provinces met with the federal government at a half dozen conferences to try to work out a formula that would placate Quebec's fears and also satisfy other provinces that their entrenched habits would not be violated. Finally, late in 1964, such a formula was arrived at. It was complex in detail, and gave the provinces a power of veto in certain types of amendments, but at least made it possible to bring the constitution home to Canada. Still—almost as an old reflex—provincial and federal parliaments insisted on more debate, lasting into 1965, before the actual transfer could be made.

In another small but typical sample of holding onto vestigial attachments, Canada continues to rely on Britain for much of its consular work. Ottawa, of course, maintains embassies in all principal countries. But in about half the world, where there are no Canadian consulates, would-be immigrants are told to deposit applications with British consulates, which do the processing on Canada's behalf— at no charge. Ottawa simply takes the free service for granted. It has never occurred to officials in Canada's Department of Citizenship and Immigration to ask the British if they mind performing these chores; this is the way it has always been done, and the officials express astonishment that it might represent degrading or unconscious unwillingness to cut completely the umbilical cord. The British do not raise objection, regarding the consular handout as simply a fringe reward for Commonwealth membership.

But this is a relatively uncomplicated external matter. Britain has no part in Canada's internal predicaments, nor desires any part, prompting W. L. Morton, the historian, to remark:

> About the year 1960, the key year, French Canada instinctively realized that Britain was out of the picture—a vague, casual, elusive thing, but important. Today English Canada realizes it, too. The United States certainly wants no entanglement. And so for the first time in our history we have to solve our own problems, in our own way, and without anyone to turn to. This is part of our groping.

It is also one reason why some English Canadians, though they are neither numerous nor vocal, would like to see Canada declare itself a republic: to break the protectionist "mother" image Canada has of the crown, to drive home sharply that an urge for someone else to carry even part of the load is no longer valid or healthy.

It was phrased in another fashion by France's President de Gaulle when a visiting Canadian cabinet minister complained to him about some of Canada's difficulties. "It is about time," said de Gaulle tartly, "that Canada entered history."

The history conceivably could take a dramatic and bloody turn. English Canada's attitude toward Quebec sways; at times it shows patience and forbearance, at other times such animosity that, as in the cry of Editor Sanburn, it sounds like a call to arms. What is usually overlooked in the debate and discussion going on in Canada is that there is no clear-cut, legal way in which Quebec could secede even if a properly elected party such as the R.I.N. should come into office with an avowed separatist mandate. Political scientists sometimes refer to a "contract" between the provinces, but constitutional lawyers shun the word as being invalid. F. R. Scott, former dean of law at McGill University, and one of Canada's outstanding constitutional authorities, says that more of a case could be made for secession in the United States, because the original colonies that broke away from England were bound only by the laws they enacted among themselves. In Canada's case, the original colonies were united through an act of parliament in Britain, and only an equivalent act of parliament could change the Confederation.

But beyond the legalities, historians draw a parallel with the experience in the United States little more than a hundred years ago. In the 1850's many Northerners said they did not care if the South decided to break away. First they felt the South would collapse economically without the North and its mills and manufacturing industries; and then they did not think the South really meant it. But when the act of secession was a fact, the same Northerners said they must fight to save the Union. Something of this order is happening in Canada now, with English Canadians arguing that Quebecers would collapse economically without the rest of Canada. And so the impetuous expression is: "Let them go if they want to." In a showdown, however, the reaction might be precisely as it was in the United States, with English Canadians saying they must fight to save Confederation. W. L. Morton comments: "We may be in our 1850's. English Canadians will not stand idly by and allow French Canadians to break up the country. It is a mistake to think that Canadians cannot be bloodthirsty."

The analogy with the United States of a century ago ends there. Times and geography are not the same, and physically Quebec would be in no position to resist for long any federal force. Since the psychological tragedy would be incalculable, few people talk even of the remote possibility of a clash. The farthest they are willing to go is to speculate about a nonviolent end to Confederation and its probable effects on various sections of the country. The moderates, of course, discourage even this pessimism and say that a healthy accommodation is being arrived at between English and French Canada. Generally, as a rough index, the English Canadians with the greatest understanding are those closest to Quebec: the minority within the province itself, and next those in Ontario who come into reasonably frequent contact with French Canadians. By the same measure, people in British Columbia are the least informed and sympathetic toward Quebec's aspirations.

As to the practical effects of a separate Quebec, the area most vitally concerned would be the Atlantic Provinces, which would be isolated from the rest of Canada. This region in all likelihood would then be pushed into a position of seeking alliance or union with the United States. Conceivably, Canada from Ontario westward could keep together, but just as credibly it could fall apart, with a portion such as British Columbia establishing its own nationhood. Others might find it economically essential to request liaison with the United States. Aside from whether such a confrontation would suit the United States politically or economically, Washington has to ask itself the question of what happens to mutual continental defenses—and to the strategic St. Lawrence Seaway, its heartland in Quebec—if there is a secession. United States policy, based on a harmonious and unified Canada, would be in for radical reshaping, and Americans would be forced into a keen look at the people who inhabit the top half of the map.

Quebec, since it is in a state of social and industrial revolution—with political rebellion always a possibility—is by far the most exciting part of Canada today. It is inevitably more so than Ontario, which conducted its industrial revolution closer to the American timetable and now abides with a secure and high rate of material progress, and a kind of placid contentment that comes from absence of fiery challenge. This does not mean, however, that Quebec is the *only* part of Canada, though Quebecers, living in a constant condition of inward searching and dissecting, tend to think so. Each area has its own objectives: to secure prosperity, as in the case of the Prairies, where less than a generation ago drought and poverty were the commonplace; or, as in the case of Nova Scotia and New Brunswick, to find it for the first time since the days before Confederation. The fact that simple bread-and-butter issues come before the complex nuances of English-French relations is indicated by a survey in 1964 in which Canadians listed Quebec's separatist movement as only sixth in a list of problems facing Ottawa. Well ahead of it were such matters as unemployment, the rising cost of living, and relations with the United States.

One can divide the country broadly into a half dozen regions: the Atlantic Provinces, Quebec, Ontario, the Prairies, the North, the West Coast. The division is determined by differences in geography, economics, and customs. If one factor linking the various sections is a resolve not to become part of the United States, another, oddly, is distance: the common feeling of vast space, the stretch that must be overcome before neighbors can communicate. Russian philosophers long have written how a special factor in the Russian character and psychology is the steppe, the open and endless land that sweeps from one horizon to the other. Much the same might be said about the interminable expanse of Canada and the sensation of loneliness it creates. It is not merely that a relatively small number of people live in a land mass exceeded in size only by Russia itself. It is how this mass is shaped, with half of it lying within the inhospitable Arctic and sub-Arctic, and much of the rest an empty wilderness of lake and forest.

Most Canadians make their homes within two hundred miles of their country's southern border. Some geographers and historians have argued that an East-West trade route and an East-West political union were the natural results of geography—the direction, for instance, of the St. Lawrence River's flow—rather than an illogical attempt to defy it. In any case, the fact remains that this narrow inhabited strip lends itself to quick contrasts, the oldest and most glaring being the concentration of industry and capital in the "central" provinces of Ontario and Quebec—to the detriment of industrial development in other provinces. The resident of Vancouver, on the West Coast, may have little affinity with the Montrealer or Torontonian, but he can feel something of a kinship with the resident of Halifax on the East Coast. Both are pitted against the English-speaking Establishment of Toronto and Montreal. To the prairie farmer, too, "the East"—meaning Ontario and Quebec in one package—must be regarded with a suspicion and contempt born in the days of depression and dying only slowly. "The East" is synonymous with trust companies and banks and foreclosed mortgages.

The United States, of course, has similar regional rivalries and recriminations. The supporters of Barry Goldwater in the last presidential election offered a reminder of this when they railed against the "Eastern Establishment." But the United States derives fundamental unity from a land mass held together by one nationality. The two-nation concept of Canada—culturally, if not politically—means in effect a homogeneous French-speaking population in Quebec, with the English-speaking majority in the remainder of the country lumped into what is sometimes referred to as a "Canadian mosaic." The phrase "melting pot" is inapplicable, partly because it is resented as the working model of the United States, and partly because the ethnic groups have never been encouraged to abandon their original identities. "Mosaic," as the name implies, denotes bits and pieces mixed together, with the hues and shapes somehow remaining distinct.

Bruce Hutchison once called Canadian nationalism "a dim impalpable and dumb thing, beyond our power to express or even name." More recently a seminar at the University of Toronto came to the conclusion that a French Canadian knows who he is, but the closest definition of an English Canadian is the negative one: He is not a French Canadian and he is not an American. To make Canadian life just a bit more obtuse, there is the statistic that nearly one third of Canada's citizens are neither of French nor British ancestry. More specifically, more than 10 per cent of the population, known by the discriminatory label *New* Canadians," were born abroad and came to Canada only since the Second World War. They are beginning to talk of themselves as a "third force" in bringing some sense to the pattern laid down by the so-called "two founding races."

In the meantime, some persons believe the simple answer to Canada's lack of consistent nationality would be entry into the United States and therefore absorption in the melting pot. The question is asked regularly in surveys: "Do you want Canada to join the United States?" And just as regularly a majority say "no." In a 1964 study sponsored jointly by *Maclean's* magazine and the Canadian Broadcasting Corporation, 29 per cent of those questioned advocated union with the United States, one of the highest proportions yet on record. (A Gallup Poll shortly afterwards brought this proportion down to 20 per cent.) The examinations are consistent in showing that most of those who favor a merger are in the undereducated, low-income groups; they are expressing a belief that their standards would rise. Canadian nationalism is strongest in the middle classes.

Even from the earliest days in Canada there have been active and vociferous groups urging the dismemberment of the country. Separatism as a phenomenon is not a Quebec monopoly. It has existed in British Columbia, Nova Scotia, and virtually every other province on occasion, though not with the same following as in Quebec. Some people consistently have urged amalgamation with the United States. But the significant fact is that the prevailing pattern of the majority has been to keep Canada intact and prevent annexation by the United States or union with it. At the same time, few Canadians delude themselves about *Realpolitik;* if the United States thought it in its self-interest today, as distinct from the past, to see Canada splintered so the segments would clamor for statehood, there is little doubt that State Department practice would be to fan the flames. United States policy, in fact, calls for a strong Canada with a Commonwealth link. Any converse notion proves embarrassing. Officials at the United States Embassy in Ottawa relate how awkward it is for them when they receive requests from local school children, at work on class projects, for information on how union between Canada and the United States would be beneficial. The children are referred to the Ottawa public library for material. Almost as mechanically, the children are then told by librarians: "Why don't you try the American Embassy?"

The other question—why don't you want to join the United States?—hardly ever brings a definitive answer. Often the reply is facetious: "I couldn't stand all the hoopla of an American election." More steadily and thoughtfully, one of Canada's greatest public servants, George Davidson, Secretary of the Treasury Board, expresses it this way: "I want to be different from people in the United States, because it is good for us and good for them. But in being different it doesn't mean I think I am better." In Winnipeg, Mr. Justice Sam Freedman of the Court of Appeal, and Chancellor of the University of Manitoba, said: "I've had a long and public love affair with Canada. It represents something of unique value. It is dedicated to the idea of unity without uniformity."

These expressions are about as close to any sounds of nationalism as one is likely to find in Canada. But the objective of unity is still much to the forefront and the subject of incessant dialogue between federal and provincial leaders —and not only because of the claims presented by Quebec. One of the contradictions about Canada is that the English-speaking portions instinctively pull together, and think in terms of strong central government, when they look with apprehension at Quebec. But simultaneously there is a tug in the other direction for each to go its own way if it is advantageous. Three quarters of Canada's life has been marked by a contest between the center and the periphery. A television comedian, Dave Broadfoot, once described Canada as a collection of ten provinces with strong governments "loosely connected by fear."

It was not always this way. On the contrary, since Confederation was framed during and immediately after the Civil War, Sir John A. Macdonald and the other founding fathers had no hesitation in drawing a lesson from the United States. The main flaw in the American system, they believed, was the division of powers which gave the individual states strength and left the federal government weak.

If the new union of Canada was to be safeguarded from collapse, they further agreed, it would need firm centralization: a kind of unitary command, with the provinces acting as little more than administrative zones. Quebec and Ontario, however, objected to total loss of their influence, and this brought on a modest touch of federal compromise.

Still, the authority of the central government, as established in the B.N.A. Act, was so sweeping that Macdonald and the others had good reason to feel sure it could never be challenged on any question of "states' rights." The provinces were given control only in a few specific areas, local in application; these included direct taxation within the province, the construction of roads, and jurisdiction over education. But everything else—without being spelled out —was left in the federal sphere. Macdonald was convinced that a wonderfully flexible arrangement had unfolded. "We have given the central legislature all the great subjects of legislation," he said in exultation. "We have thus avoided the great source of weakness which has been the cause of the disruption of the United States." But just the opposite of what was intended took place over the years: the provinces gained greater powers while the central authority diminished; and, ironically, in the American system so studiously avoided, it was Washington that emerged with increased dominion.

The conflict between regional and national loyalties grew partly out of economics. Confederation was not providing the great boom that had been promised; in fact, recession, particularly in the Maritime Provinces, was the occurrence. By the 1880's provincial governments were brazenly defying laws passed by Ottawa, and since these involved constitutional rights, appeals went to the highest court: the Privy Council in London. In most instances the Privy Council bent the B.N.A. Act to support the provinces. But, by the early part of the century, economic improvements resulted in fewer challenges to central command. Canadian wheat was

in demand in Europe; hundreds of thousands of homesteaders moved into the Prairies, and the East-West railway
system helped stimulate a boom and make sense of Confederation. Ottawa spurred developments on a national
scale, and by the First World War the kind of central power
Macdonald had envisaged flowed into the federal capital.

After the war the country returned to regional wrangling,
and Mackenzie King inherited a precarious union, which he
held together partly by wheedling and sly dealing. The depression of the 1930's followed the tension of the 1920's, and
in this fresh crisis the central authority reasserted itself because it had to bail out the provinces. National relief payments to Manitoba and Saskatchewan alone amounted to
more than $700 million. Centralization again reached its
height during the emergency of war. Starting in 1939, the
provinces relinquished most of their tax-collecting privileges, and Canada in a sense again became Macdonald's true
unitary state. This reasonably efficient arrangement continued into the postwar period and the prosperous early
1950's, but was shaken up in the past few years when the
bigger provinces felt they should retain more of the tax
dollar for their own development rather than share it with
less bountiful neighbors. In Quebec's case the motive is
largely dictated by its pressing social and industrial upheaval, accented by French-Canadian nationalism. But
other provinces, notably British Columbia, are equally ada-
mant about advancing themselves.

The attacks on the central structure are remarkable not
only for the financial or other practical problems they present to Ottawa. They provide also a clue to "nationalism."
Paul W. Fox, a political scientist at the University of
Toronto, is struck by the peculiarity that almost everywhere
in Canada when he uses the term "government" people
think he is referring to provincial government. So ingrained,
he concludes, is the habit of thinking of regional autonomy
or self-reliance that Ottawa comes second to mind. Ontario

offers an exception, Fox notes, "but in any event Ottawa is regarded as an incorporated suburb of Toronto."

One feature that makes a federal system difficult in Canada is the size of some of the provinces. In confederate theory, all voices are equal, but Ontario, Quebec, and British Columbia overshadow the others in wealth and strength. Either Ontario or Quebec—each with about one third of the national population—has the power to threaten disruption for the entire country. In the United States neither New York State nor California can begin to touch this position of dominance. Even British Columbia, with a much smaller percentage of the population, was able, during international negotiations on the Columbia River power treaty, to hold out for what it wanted and get it—not only from Ottawa but from Washington. Among other regions, the so-called "have not" provinces—such as Nova Scotia and Newfoundland—favor strong central government, which can pump in finances and resources to help elevate them to national levels.

2.

The Neighbor Upstairs

PRESIDENT LYNDON B. JOHNSON, with obvious good intention, once remarked: "Canada is such a close neighbor and such a good neighbor that we always have plenty of problems there. They are kind of like the problems in the home town." This aroused comment from an alert Canadian political scientist, James Eayrs: "They are kind of not like that at all. They are the problems not of neighbors but of friendly foreign powers." It was a shrewd summation of a situation and an attitude shared by many Canadians. Canada's broad problems of war and peace may be similar to those of the United States; and home towns, physically, may look alike. But it is more realistic to argue that many of Canada's difficulties are caused by her determination to be different from—and independent of—the United States. The historians vary in shades of interpretation, but there is general agreement that Canada's evolution from British colonial status to independent nationhood was hesitant and ambiguous because Canadians themselves were driven by this compulsion *not* to be Americans. Nothing is more basic to a Canadian consciousness than the decision to retain a separate identity. In the process, Britain did not necessarily force its authority on a hapless colony. A good deal of the time Britain was clung to—like a confused parent unable to send an offspring into the world.

Canadians attained a substantial measure of self-government as far back as 1848, but a long period elapsed—until the present century—before they felt sufficiently secure from American military and political pressures to welcome complete release from British protection. In the meanwhile, the colonies of British North America got together to form what is now known as Canada largely because they desired unity *against* the United States. In actuality, the War of 1812 had already faded into insignificance, and if anything the United States was beginning to be a friendly attraction rather than a frightening menace. But this was just another nuance in the complications of Canadian life that loiter to this day. In that Confederation year some people suggested naming it the Kingdom of Canada. A mature Britain, sensitive to the republican sentiments of Americans who might resent a blatantly British monarchy next door, recommended the benign title of Dominion of Canada.[1] And so the lesson is both complicated and simple: Canada in its youth grew up fearful of the United States and simultaneously conscious, always, of any action that might offend the United States.

"Fearful" is too strong a word today, for there is no longer American talk of a Manifest Destiny to acquire the whole continent even at the price of a military invasion of Canada. Nor does the United States possess covetous political ambitions; the era of the Champ Clarks and Bertie McCormicks has ended. However, Canadian concern on the economic and cultural levels remains very real, as we shall see in later chapters. Since this concern is imbedded in history, the histo-

[1] The designation "dominion" has fallen into disuse in recent years. Through fortunate wording of the B.N.A. Act, the dropping of it did not entail special legislation, which almost certainly would have created controversy as in the case of the flag debate. The government's tendency to refer simply to "Canada," rather than "Dominion of Canada," began before the Second World War and was carried on in earnest in the last decade.

rians deserve a good deal of attention. One can question whether Canada has produced many notable novelists or literary figures, but as a group the historians happen to be outstanding. This may not be sheer coincidence. A member of the group itself, Frank H. Underhill, has observed that Canadians do not seem to be at ease with general ideas, with letting their minds play speculatively on a broad problem; they are happier when they can keep to well-ascertained facts.

But what are the facts about Canada? To start with, what is a Canadian, and how is he different from an American? Some of the historians set out the negative perspective that the Canadian basically is a defeated person: the French were defeated by the English, and the English—at least the bulk of the early settlers, the United Empire Loyalists—in turn were defeated by the American Revolution. This leads to the next point presented by Arthur R. M. Lower, one of the most controversial of the historians, that generally the Canadian who exists even today is not a go-getter or a dynamic success. Lower contends that the robust, the industrious, the ambitious, have migrated to the United States, leaving behind the withdrawn people, the sedate, and those with the least energy or ability.

This theme was developed in a series of books culminating in *Canadians in the Making,* a social history of Canada published in 1958. But it hardly adds up to a succinct or firm answer for a nation concerned with a growing Americanism and strident French-Canadian nationalism. More recently when I put the question to Lower: What do Canadians stand for, what do they represent?—it was at his home outside Kingston, Ontario, where he lives in retirement. "This is a poser," he confessed. "Separately I think I know a little of what English Canadians and French Canadians stand for, but the two together? I don't know." He thought for a while, and then referred to another of his favorite themes, the land—the literal importance of geography that

53

connects people and gives them an identification. And since —he said—neither religion nor social customs nor affection binds together the peoples of English and French Canada, perhaps a love for the land is the common denominator. Lower had just completed a trip around the world, and he observed of the Australians that they feel the power of their land because it is an island. "We have almost the equivalent of an island, because there is the great mass of the United States below us," he said. "In New Zealand I was amused to hear the suggestion that Australia was a 'threat,' that it might pop over and gobble up New Zealand."

Lower does not believe that it is Quebec that gives Canada a distinctive character: "I am inclined to think that if there had never been anything else but English Canada we would have been conscious of our existence just by reason of the American presence." And so here we were back on the same negative footing: A Canadian is someone who lives in his country because he does not want to be an American. Lower recalled the more appealing definition once offered by Arthur L. Phelps, an acute analyst of the Canadian scene: "A Canadian is one who is increasingly aware of being 'American' in the continental sense without being 'American' in the national sense." Lower, anyway, said he was unconcerned if the identification was vague. "I don't think these things are important," he commented. "It used to be said that the best way to tell a man's nationality is to ask it."

But since the definition of a Canadian is a nagging one, and people do strive for it, we shall go on, with the next stop in Winnipeg, where W. L. Morton is professor of history at the University of Manitoba. "A Canadian," said Morton, "is someone who knows he is going somewhere, but isn't sure where." Morton, however, was emphatic in the rest of his statement. After making the point that Canadian history is *not* a parody of American history, he noted that it is "rather an important chapter in a distinct and even a unique human endeavor: the civilization of the northern and Arctic lands."

(Sixteen hundred miles to the east, in Liverpool, Nova Scotia, Thomas H. Raddall, the historian-novelist, had made somewhat the same reference when he said he felt the differentiation between Canada and the United States was like that between various levels in a house: "The Americans fell into the great fortune of finding themselves roaming through the comfortable lower floors. The Canadian found himself in the attic, surrounded by a lot of bulky objects and always aware there was snow on the roof.")

Morton developed his theme about the civilizing of a raw and inhospitable land: From the start, it drew fewer people than the United States. This factor in itself introduced in pioneer days a concept of law and order—different from that of the United States—that survives into the present. Because there were fewer people, there was, by necessity, more yielding to authority. In the United States relatively large numbers of men moved into the West, driving out and slaying Indians, and taking the law into their own hands. In Canada a few hundred Mounted Police were sent to the Prairies ahead of settlers, making peace with the Indians, keeping law and order for Indians as well as for whites.

The sociologist steps into the historical field at this juncture and points out that the American from the beginning was an individualist who took the attitude that every man must be capable of looking after himself. Canadian frontiersmen, on the other hand, were organization men, held together not only by police and law but by big corporations and enterprises—the Hudson's Bay Company, the Canadian Pacific Railway—which, with state blessing, possessed authority to distribute land and favor. Results of the dissimilar heritages are noticeable today. For one thing, the quieter respect for law and order in Canada is due only partly to British traditions; it is due also to the disciplines learned in the earliest days in a harsh and lonely environment. For another, the American has retained an obsession for "rugged individualism" or personal initiative, while the

Canadian, never cognizant of these incentives in the same degree, takes it for granted that society as a whole will share in his protection and welfare. Even the United Empire Loyalists, destitute on their arrival from the Thirteen Colonies, learned the first lesson when the government handed them food, land, and tools. One of the striking contrasts between the United States and Canada today is the calm approach a Canadian makes to a subject anathema to an American: socialism. Though, by European standards, Canadians are only now catching up in measures of welfare, by United States terms they are virtually socialists with cradle-to-the-grave security.[2]

There are, of course, other obvious differences. Canada, for instance, retains the parliamentary system of Britain and spurns republicanism. But one of the greatest points of departure between Americans and Canadians took place early in history and has left a mark ever since: the fact that the United States received its independence through revolution while Canada reached its autonomy through a gradual, evolutionary process. This has bothered some historians, among them Frank Underhill, who says:

> I think it would have been better for us as Canadians if we had a little more of the revolutionary tradition in our Canadian make-up. One of the things that makes the Americans great is that they have a great tradition of a rebellion

[2] Regardless of income, all families receive children's allowances of $6 to $8 a month per child. Everyone, again without a means test, receives a pension of $75 a month on reaching the age of seventy. In a new, partly contributory, pension scheme being introduced, couples will get $225 a month, single persons $150, with lesser benefits to those who prefer retirement at 65. But the security is far broader than indicated by direct benefits. Hospitalization throughout the country is free, and medicare is in effect in varying degrees in several provinces, beginning with Saskatchewan where doctors work under a state program. In addition, Canadians consider it normal for the government to operate several key enterprises, including the biggest transportation system (Canadian National), the major airline (Air Canada), and the most important radio and television networks (Canadian Broadcasting Corporation).

that succeeded; it stiffens up your backbone. Our one attempt
at revolution was a dismal failure; in fact it was a fiasco.

That "revolution" took place in two parts in 1837 and 1838
in Lower Canada (Quebec) and Upper Canada (Ontario),
and was largely in protest against the domination of the
majority by small ruling cliques. But such was the limited
scale of active participation that when a few hundred men—
mostly poorly armed farmers—marched on Toronto and were
confronted by a sheriff and twenty-seven men, both sides
fired, turned, and fled. Two days later the uprising was over.
Yet it had a practical result. The British government,
startled into consciousness of discontent, sent Lord Durham
to Canada in an investigation that ended in a report that
freed Canadians from strong imperial control and established a durable relationship that animated the colonies to
remain in the British Empire.

What are the red letter dates in Canadian history? I asked
this of several historians. Though each had his favorite milestone, almost invariably it related more to concern over
threatened American domination than desire to end dependency on Britain. For Thomas Raddall the significant date is
1812: "After the American Revolution the big question for
us was whether we could live independently of the United
States. But it was not answered until 1812. The War of 1812
was our war of independence, because it made Canadians
aware of a reason to fight." Even though the Americans were
engaged by British regulars, alongside the redcoats were
Canadian militiamen, including those who spoke French.
The two races had their disputes, but the French remembered words preached to them by their own clergy after
Wolfe's victory: "The best way to remain French is to stay
British." And freshly in mind was the example of Louisiana
falling into the American melting pot.

All along the border, towns and villages were affected.
Even if Maritimers had little inclination to battle their New

England neighbors, there were some sharp and meaningful engagements elsewhere. Raddall calls Queenston Heights "our Bunker Hill," for in the first year of war the Americans who crossed the Niagara River into Upper Canada, in the misguided expectation that the local population would greet them as liberators, were forced to surrender. The war dragged on for eighteen months, and if neither side won it was in effect an impressive achievement for Canada simply to preserve its territory in a confrontation with the much more heavily populated United States. Anyone who dismisses this as insignificant or forgotten history needs only to drive today along the St. Lawrence Seaway to the reconstructed Upper Canada Village, a handsome tourist attraction. There a minor victory against the Americans, at Crysler's Farm, is commemorated in an elaborate park. This memorial would be understandable if it had survived intact from the early part of the last century. But in fact it was created only a few years ago by the Ontario government. The old Crysler farm was among other sites that had to be flooded in the construction of the Seaway. But before this was done, soil from the battlefield was reverently moved to higher ground in remembrance of the "Loyal British Regiments of America."

The Seaway itself, of course, is a tribute to the present spirit of trust and cooperation between Canada and the United States. But those who want to talk solely in glowing terms of "four thousand miles of undefended border" might note that it was only after the Boer War, in 1906, that the last detachment of British regulars was withdrawn from garrison duty in Canada. To an eminent historian, Donald Creighton, the Boer War was a turning point in Canadian affairs. Canada had made no attempt to escape from British leadership in diplomacy "because we were terrified of the United States and its political pressures." But then two developments took place. Canada sent a small expeditionary force (seven thousand men) to South Africa: "The first time troops ever went the other way—down the St. Lawrence instead of up it." And simultaneously Canada was involved in a dispute with the United States over the Alaska boundary. Canada wanted neutral arbitration, but President Theodore Roosevelt threatened the big stick unless his view of a settlement prevailed. Britain, enmeshed in South Africa, and also trying to work out a deal with the United States over the future of the Panama Canal, was in no mood or position to help Canada, physically or spiritually. "This," according to Creighton, "was our moment of truth. We had at last the reality of our destiny—that so far as North America was concerned, we'd set out to make a nation, and now we had to establish it not only vis-à-vis the United States but with the whole world, including Britain."

The next scene is selected by Gerald M. Craig, of the University of Toronto, who feels the most important single event in Canadian history was the First World War. Canada put into the field a corps command of its own, and even though it came under over-all British command there was a true sense of Canadian identification. The losses suffered were enormous, proportionately fivefold those of the United States. But they had the strange effect of pushing Canada into the world at large. Craig, a specialist in the history of Canadian-American relations, points out that the deepening pride and self-confidence of Canadians was heightened by the postwar retreat of the United States from world affairs. No longer was there overt political danger from the giant next door. Now, finally, a developing Canadian nationalism could concentrate on cutting or weakening the British bonds. This was essential psychologically, for, although Canada had boasted sovereignty since 1867, matters of foreign policy had remained in British control. The big drive in the era now was for Canadian emancipation from a mentality of "colonial" status.

For Ramsay Cook, another University of Toronto historian, the next significant step led to independence in foreign affairs. It was taken in 1923—at an Imperial Conference in

London—when Canada's Prime Minister, Mackenzie King, opposed a common foreign policy for the British Empire. As a practical result of that conference, Britain accepted the view that each dominion had the right to negotiate its own international treaties.[3] The ultimate stage was reached in 1931, when the Statute of Westminster repealed outmoded laws dating to colonial times, and legally established the autonomy that already existed in practice. The term British Empire also went into decline with the official definition of the Commonwealth of Nations as a free association of self-governing nations.

On September 3, 1939 Britain declared war on Germany. In 1914, when another war had broken out, Canada automatically was included. But now, at the outset of the Second World War, Canada waited a week, and Mackenzie King led parliament in its own formal declaration. There had never been any real doubt that the move would come: first because of English Canada's strong sentimental attachment for Britain, and also because of a genuine conviction that a victory for Hitler in Europe would be disastrous for the world, Canada included. But the date of Canada's official war proclamation, September 10, 1939, was a symbolic, even if belated, graduation certificate for the Class of 1931. King acted as he did to drive home to Britons and Canadians alike the reminder that any "colonial" complex no longer was valid, that Canada now possessed the freedom of choice to join the war or stay out. Canadians also needed—and received—command of their own army for the first time, and put into action their own naval and air force units.

King was prime minister of Canada for a total of twenty-one years. During his administration Canada not only attained full stature as a nation but improved its relations with

[3] The first international treaty Canada signed alone, in 1923, was with the United States, and it dealt with fishing rights in coastal waters. Previously, a British representative had always been present at such negotiations.

the United States and learned the full meaning of a policy of striving for countervailing weights. King spent much of his lifetime fighting off British influence, and, so far as he could, called in the United States for that purpose. He negotiated trade agreements with Washington, and held talks on common defense problems. In the process, Canada took on a useful function as a connecting link between Britain and the United States, but this was only incidental to King's major objective of balancing one against the other.

King was a mystic who believed in spiritualism, but otherwise there was little of the picturesque in his personal life. More than any other individual, perhaps, he represented how Canada came to be constructed in the first place—and how, fundamentally, it differed from the United States. Compromise and balance were the two key postures he adopted; he could not afford, as Canada has never been able to afford, an aggressively dynamic attitude either externally or internally. This benign or moderate image is not offensive to one of King's biographers, H. Blair Neatby. "Compromise," argues Neatby, "is a method of achieving a principle. It is not an evil, a selling out." In the case of Canada, with its English and French structures, the principle is unity. To be a national leader in Canada, Neatby argues further, "means you cannot be as dogmatic or even as colorful as when you lead one group, or a relatively homogeneous group, as in the United States. The mere fact that some compromise has to come in, makes it impossible to be dogmatic." And that is why, in effect, Canadians can afford to have authoritarian or jaunty or dramatic political figures on a provincial level only, such as in Newfoundland or British Columbia, where the populations are more or less homogeneous.

Mackenzie King handled disagreements between English and French Canada with skillful instinct. In his diaries he talks of being "suspicious" of "Catholics." In the fashion of his Presbyterian ancestors, he did not trust them. Nevertheless, he had an awareness that the Gallic way of thinking was not necessarily the same as that of the Anglo-Saxon. Neatby develops this theme to illustrate that just as King understood that Quebecers rebelled when they felt unjustly imposed upon, so he realized how Canadians as a whole resented it when taken for granted. That is why King insisted on legal autonomy and the Statute of Westminster—not because he wanted to withdraw from Empire or Commonwealth affairs but because he knew if London ever assumed again it could speak automatically for Canada, or commit it in any way, the indignation would be immediate and perhaps disastrous to the extent of rupturing Commonwealth membership. And it was important for Canada to retain that membership if it was to pursue a policy of balancing the external forces in its life.

The problem of "colonial" inferiority to Britain was resolved under King. The United States, meanwhile, had become flaccid or flabby in its isolationism, and was no threat to Canada, at least in the 1920's and 1930's. Moreover, from 1940 and 1941 onward the United States had taken on the role of a military associate and ally of Canada—the exact reversal of its earlier stance. But suddenly in 1945 it dawned on the Department of External Affairs that Britain had come out of the war weak and almost toothless, and the United States once more was the big and dynamic force to be watched. King's generation had concentrated so strenuously on the British question that this fact took some time to be widely accepted. But the vestigial "colonial" reflex flared up again, and remains to this day. By old habit it reacts sharply against anything American that resembles pressure or intervention or even gentle coercion.

When John F. Kennedy made his first trip outside the United States as President in 1961 it was, fittingly, to the "good neighbor" Canada. Kennedy addressed a joint session of the Canadian Senate and the House of Commons, and, in passing, suggested that Canada should join the Organization of American States. Up to that point, in the press and public debates on the subject, there had been considerable support for the notion of Canada taking a more active part in hemisphere matters. The mail received by the foreign minister of the time, Howard Green, ran heavily in favor of Canada joining the O.A.S. But the day after President Kennedy's mild utterance, the mail turned abruptly the other way: three to one against.

The incident itself is slight, but it accentuates two or three important features about Canada and its external relations. In the first place, of course, it was acute Canadian pride and sensitivity that caused an immediate and unfavorable response to the Kennedy submission. Canadians long have shown preference and affection for Democratic presidents, especially Roosevelt and Kennedy, but the automatic thought in the Canadian mind was: Who is *he* to tell *us* what to do? Unconscious memories brought up actions of the past in which the United States treated all the Americas as its domain. A United States citizen, reared in the modern and sincere belief that his country has never wanted to be any less than a friend to everyone, may find it difficult to understand Canadian hesitation or suspicion over a statement that appears harmless on the surface. However, a Mexican—still brooding over territories lost to the United States in the nineteenth century and over "aggression" by President Wilson at Vera Cruz in this century—will understand instinctively the Canadian wariness of the giant next door.

Another unintended feature of the Kennedy proposal was its quiet reflection of the whole range of Canadian-American relations. Officially, and so far as the public knows, the reason Canada has resisted membership in the Organization of American States is because of its traditional interests that go in other directions: toward Europe and the British Commonwealth. Aside from the United Nations itself, the two principal associations Canada cherishes are with the Commonwealth and the North Atlantic Treaty Organization. Canada, the argument goes, is simply not ready to change or expand its East-West orientation to take in yet another bearing that would embrace twenty countries to the south. But the real reason for the holdoff is more subtle and pertinent. Latin-American nations for many years have urged Canada to come into the O.A.S. to serve as a North American buffer between them and the United States—in other words, for Canada to occupy its characteristic role of middle man or interpreter. It is precisely because of a desire to avoid this function that Canada has been reluctant to enter into collective relationship with the other hemisphere states. No one in the prime minister's or foreign minister's office will state so publicly, but there are already enough problems in bilateral relations between Canada and the United States without opening the way for others.

For instance, Canada, like Britain, does not believe in economic sanctions or embargo as an instrument of policy. Canada, again like Britain, has continued to trade with Castro's Cuba and to maintain diplomatic relations, the cause of some irritation on the part of the United States State Department. But what would have been the repercussions in Washington if Canada, as a formal member of the O.A.S., had spurned the Organization's resolution in 1964 to break diplomatic and trade contacts with Cuba? At the very least it would have run the risk of accusation by Americans of being greedily uncooperative. And what attitude would Canada have been expected to take when Panama, earlier that year, got into a violent dispute with the United States over the Canal Zone? Latins themselves shrank from joining a commission of investigation, lest they find the United States responsible for the first provocative rifle shots. Could Canada—if the evidence so dictated—have been sufficiently honest to face the charge of disloyalty or betrayal of its best friend? An even more troublesome example was the armed United States intervention in the Dominican Republic in 1965. The Canadian public as a whole, in common with most Latin Americans, deplored and condemned Washington's unilateral action of sending in the Marines, though at an official level Ottawa kept a discreet silence. Thus, while the Canadian government proceeded to say it looked "sympathetically" on the idea of joining the O.A.S., in fact there remained grave doubts to be overcome in official Canadian thinking. In a survey conducted by the Department of External Affairs among its ambassadors in Latin America, half expressed their opposition to Canadian membership.

The irony, in a detail little realized today, is that Canada once did want to enlist but was rejected by the United States. In 1942 Mackenzie King expressed willingness to have Canada join what was then called the Pan American Union. Franklin Roosevelt and Cordell Hull, the United States Secretary of State, disapproved of the overture. Technically there was the excuse that only republics were eligible, and Canada, of course, was a monarchy. But other factors entered into their disinclination to see Canada in equal liaison with the Latin-American countries. The United States had just experienced the end of isolationism thrust on it by the war, and even such men as Roosevelt and Hull retained an ingrained fear of Britain entering hemisphere affairs through the back door. Though they realized that by now Canada's foreign policy no longer was dictated by London, there was a nagging suspicion that Canada was indoctrinated in "British" thinking and subject to British influence. This in itself, they believed, would lead to some sort of mutilation of the Monroe Doctrine that reserved the Americas for the Americans. The change in Washington's attitude toward Canadian participation came around 1949, by which time Canada itself had turned cool and used the excuse that no one had extended a formal invitation to join the club. The results of a specific bid, such as the Kennedy invitation, have already been noted.

The case history of Canada and the O.A.S. illustrates several points, starting with the fact that until the Second World War Canada never had much of a foreign policy of its own, since it concerned itself with keeping strong Empire or Commonwealth connections as an insurance policy against American domination. And then, as Canada began to evolve a policy, United States suspicions of the old British attachment and sentiment stood awkwardly in the way. Therefore, it leads to the conclusion that the relationship between the two countries has been, at best, a peculiar one marked by mutual failures at times to grasp the nature of that relationship. Today, of course, it narrows down to a simple truth: what Americans magnanimously like to label a "partnership" in North America is a partnership between two unequal partners.

For a while, until just a few years ago, Canadians took themselves seriously enough to believe their country actually was a power—not in a sense of kilotons but at least in terms of influence and prestige. The notion proved fallacious. For one thing, there was the realization that since the United States carried the major burden of Western defenses, the United States was going to act decisively, when it thought it necessary, without consulting "partners," as demonstrated during the Cuban missile crisis of 1962. The question about any relationship, then, is this: How much privilege have the powerful to prescribe policy and the weaker partners to go their own way? In Canada's case the dilemma includes not only political facts of life but economic and cultural issues that also result from inequality. In a college classroom, for instance, one of the first comments a freshman hears from his economics professor is: "When the United States sneezes, Canada catches pneumonia." [4] It is true, of course, that a recession or depression

[4] One measure of the difference in potency of the two countries: Merely the increase in the gross national product of the United States in a single year almost equals the total gross national product in Canada.

66

in the United States affects the whole world, but Canada's proximity makes its intimacy, even in the area of economics, unique. Each country is the other's best customer, yet even in this sense it is a partnership of unequal proportions. The United States takes nearly three fifths of Canada's total exports; Canada takes about one fifth of the United States' exports. But since the absolute value of American goods is so much greater, Canada chronically has an unfavorable balance of trade.

The rest of the significance is in the message that the United States has nearly reached self-sufficiency economically; exports represent only about 5 per cent of the gross national product. In Canada, by contrast, exports account for 20 per cent of the gross national product. For the United States a decline in exports is not disastrous, while in Canada it affects one in every five workers, one in every five dollars. Britain not long ago was Canada's most valued customer, but now about two thirds of Canada's international trade transactions are with the United States. By this measure alone, the cornerstone of Canada's foreign policy used to be reliance on Britain. Today the cornerstone is friendship with the United States: neighbor, ally, biggest buyer.

People in Ottawa's East Block, which houses the offices of the prime minister and the foreign minister, do not like to make such an open confession, a natural enough reticence in a country still trying to strike a balance between North American realities and older kinship with the Commonwealth. They prefer to put it this way: "We won't do anything without first considering its effect on the United States." Here a question of degree enters the process. For instance, Canada does not consider its Cuban policy *deeply* offensive to the United States—at least not as offensive, say, as recognition of Communist China would be. And so, even though Canada for many years has questioned the wisdom of Washington's attitude toward Peking, it has held off extending its own recognition, for the very simple reason that on balance any gains would not be worth the inevitable cost of embarrassing or antagonizing Washington. This deference to United States sensibilities, however, has not prevented Canada from picking up a share of the trade in nonstrategic goods. John W. Holmes, of the Canadian Institute of International Affairs, put it brightly when he told a San Francisco audience: "In the absence of any agreed allied policy to starve China into submission, it has seemed foolish to us not to relieve the Chinese of their dollars in return for our surplus wheat." [5] Holmes, a former officer in the Department of External Affairs, also pointed out that diplomatic or economic embargoes, to serve any purpose, should have some achievable political object: "not be merely expressions of righteous indignation."

Basically Canada's foreign policy, as any other nation's, is one of self-interest. In this instance it turns principally around keeping the United States unruffled, partly so that when important issues do arise Canada's voice will not be shut out. On a very broad international level, this means trying to have impact on any action likely to involve all the Western allies, though Canadian officials no longer pretend their influence is unusually high. In more immediate or domestic terms, it means, as one policy-maker expressed it to me, "not irritating the Americans with such incessant nagging that they won't listen to us when we have something vital to say about trade or balance of payments." On virtually every level of my inquiry, dealing with joint enterprises, diplomatic relations, defense, commerce, and other matters of Canadian interest, the record in recent years shows an astonishingly high degree of American willingness to listen and to comply with Canadian requests and complaints, sometimes even to the disadvantage of the United States' own interests.

[5] In recent years, Canadian exports to China have amounted to about $100 million annually, mostly in grain. Exports to Cuba come to around $16 million, almost entirely in food and livestock.

The Canadian public, for example, for a long time was under the impression that the United States State Department had stepped in to block the sale of one thousand cars by Ford of Canada to Communist China. This embargo, the story went in 1958, was invoked under United States law, which prevented American companies or their subsidiaries from trading with China. There was an immediate and public outcry in Canada that an American law was being applied in Canada. But this was false. What happened in fact was that a Vancouver import-export firm had asked Ford of Canada in a very general inquiry whether vehicles might be available for shipment to China. Ford of Canada took it up with the parent company, which in turn received clearance from the State Department. Later, President Eisenhower, on a visit to Ottawa, reiterated that Canada was not to lose business as a result of regulations applicable in the United States. The broad principle was that whenever a United States subsidiary was invited to sell to China, and there was no completely Canadian-owned company in a position to make the same product, the State Department could raise no objections.

The query from Vancouver turned out to be purely hypothetical; no order for cars ever was placed. But to the present day the "China car deal" is often cited, erroneously or mischievously, as an example of United States "interference" in Canadian affairs. In other instances where adverse decisions have aroused Canadian indignation they usually have been the fault of civil service bureaucracy rather than any official Washington malevolence. In 1961 special unloading equipment was needed for freighters carrying the first shipments of Canadian wheat to Chinese ports; the equipment was made only by a manufacturer in the United States. The Canadian press reported in fury that the United States firm was not allowed to sell to Canadian shippers dealing with China. The Department of External Affairs intervened, and the State Department investigated. It soon turned out that the restrictive order was issued by a relatively junior official in the United States Treasury Department acting under authority of the Foreign Assets Control Act. The State Department had the order rescinded, and the large Canadian wheat sale, which had hung in the balance, continued on its way. External Affairs people themselves cite this as an example of how Washington, if it wanted to be unpleasant, could invoke dozens of small, legal tactics to hinder Canadian activities.

Not long ago in a moment of pique, when a British manufacturer sold buses to Cuba, the United States government cut off its existing military aid to Britain: value in the sum total of $7,400. Canada has never accepted military aid, nor any other form of direct aid, from the United States. But no one is under any misunderstanding about the extent of Canada's indirect dependence on the United States. Dean V. W. Bladen, of the University of Toronto, who once made a study of the automotive industry on behalf of the Canadian government, gives full marks to the United States for being gentle with Canada. The English-born economist, speaking of the relative strength of the two economies, said: "We can't retaliate, really. But their power to hurt us, if they wish, is very great indeed."

The economic weapon possessed by the United States is forceful enough to make any good neighborly act by Canada a necessity, and even if it is never used it remains always an unspoken threat. Occasionally, it emerges in open view, as in 1964 when George W. Ball, the United States Undersecretary of State, warned the Canadian government not to adopt economic policies which "are discriminatory and inequitable" toward American industry. His reminder—"any change in the existing ground rules can have immediate and substantial repercussions"—was pointed and unnecessary. Canadian officials are well aware that the economic deterrent in United States possession is mightier than their own, and American officials know they know it. Ardent economic nationalists in Canada stress precisely this point: that even if the United States does not draw its sword, the potential hazard to Canada's political freedom grows with the increase in economic meshing. In actual practice, however, a cabinet minister told me quite frankly: "We can always win an argument with the Americans." How? "First we invoke the principles they subscribe to, such as morality. Then we say: 'You have so many investments here,' a slight hint that, Mr. Ball notwithstanding, maybe those investments could be curtailed." As a final observation—and with a smile—he commented: "We're sharpening our wits constantly with Americans, hence our good civil service."

A brilliant, former member of that civil service, Mitchell Sharp, who became Minister of Trade and Commerce, confessed that he takes "a simple approach" to Canadian-American relations. "We can never change the fact that we are situated next to a giant," he said. "All we can hope to achieve is that Canadians will be given a freedom of choice, so they will never be overwhelmed by American goods or culture." The practical experience reported by a variety of government officials indicates that the freedom does exist: American negotiators can be exasperating when they betray ignorance of specific Canadian problems, but they make up for this by avoiding table-thumping or other postures of belligerence. Often they appear to lean backward to accommodate Canadian needs and sensitivities. Certainly they respond to a Canadian cry of "crisis."

An example of this occurred in July, 1963, when President Kennedy announced the proposal to levy an "interest-equalization tax" of 15 per cent on the purchase by Americans of foreign bonds and stocks. The reasoning, though complex in detail, had the pure and broad purpose to discourage foreign borrowing and so reduce the serious deficit the United States was experiencing in its balance-of-payments position. The move was not designed with Canada specifically in mind; it was aimed generally at big borrowers in twenty-two countries. Canada happened to be one of them, but this is where the problem turned out to be the most acute because Canada was the most heavily involved. On the morning of July 18, the United States Treasury sent an emissary to Ottawa to inform Canada's finance minister, Walter Gordon, of the legislation proposed by Kennedy. The President's message was actually before Congress at the moment, and it was too late for Gordon to warn Washington of its likely effect on Canada. But the result showed itself dramatically within hours. Stock exchange sales indicated an almost hysterical flight of capital; traders were afraid that Canada would be unable to support its dollar without easy continuity of American capital.

Within twenty-four hours—that is, up to Friday the 19th —Canada lost $110 million in foreign exchange, and if the pace continued unchecked the nation was in grave danger of having its entire reserves wiped out within a week. Gordon and several leading officials, including Louis Rasminsky, governor of the Bank of Canada, flew to Washington the next day for an emergency meeting with Douglas Dillon, Secretary of the United States Treasury. The highly respected Rasminsky, with a world reputation as a member of the executive board of the International Monetary Fund since its inception in 1946, and an executive director of the International Bank for Reconstruction and Development since 1950, had no difficulty in backing the Gordon case. The simple facts were these: in the decade between 1952 and 1962 Canada bought from the United States $14 billion more in goods and services than it had been able to sell to the United States. In the same period United States investors put $8.5 billion into Canada. But this still left Canada $5.5 billion in the hole, a process that added to Canada's own balance-of-payments burden but actually was of considerable help to the Americans in alleviating theirs. Now—the argument continued—if the United States went ahead with its new bill, a slowing down of Canadian borrowing would cause an even greater balance-of-payments problem for Canada, forcing her to cut down on United States imports. Thus, in the cycle, the United States would lose more than it would gain. The logic of the case was quickly accepted by Dillon and his associates. By Monday morning —before the stock market opened—Ottawa was able to announce that Canada would not be classed with the other twenty-one nations, and, by discretion of the President, was to be exempt from the proposed regulations. The flight of capital ended.

Later, Gordon said the episode provided a sharp illustration of how senior Washington officialdom is not always aware of the brittleness of Canada's position next door, and how, even unwittingly, the United States can deliver a nearly lethal blow. Later, too, Treasury people confessed that in the haste to prepare the President's message to Congress they had not done their homework on Canada and simply needed to be reminded of the facts and figures, as Gordon and Rasminsky subsequently presented them. Though clearly it proved in the self-interest of the United States to keep a free flow of money across the border, there is also no doubt that Gordon obtained a quick and receptive hearing because it was a *Canadian* financial crisis; complaints from other countries would not have been heard as readily.

Relations between the two countries in recent years have not always been so agreeable. They declined gradually during the prime ministership of John G. Diefenbaker, from 1957 onward, and then early in 1963 came to a precarious stage over the issue of defense. Looking back over the record since the Second World War, a senior External Affairs officer said the only substantial fault he could find with American behavior toward Canada was a single, but devastating, State Department press release criticizing Canada's nuclear policy and touching off a political crisis that was resolved only in a general election. He conceded that United States officials might have felt provoked and irritated after a long series of setbacks in negotiations and broken promises about the stationing of nuclear warheads on Canadian soil. Nevertheless, in the eyes of professional diplomats the act by the State Department was the type that one power rarely invokes against another; it was a gross attempt to bring about the defeat of a government, intentionally and deliberately. Not all Canadians, as we shall soon note, agreed with this assessment. But the curious point, overlooked in most of the debate that attended and followed the 1963 affair, was that defense exemplifies more incisively than any other field how closely in fact Canada has integrated itself in practical matters with the United States, despite intense nationalism.

It can be argued easily that Canada has enjoyed the comfort of knowing it would be defended, regardless of the circumstances, ever since President Franklin D. Roosevelt made his celebrated pledge in 1938 that "the people of the United States will not stand idly by if domination of Canadian soil is threatened" by any foreign power. The significance was that war clouds were gathering in Europe and that Canada was much more likely to become directly involved than the United States, which still maintained a policy of isolationism. In any global war now, of course, the United States would be one of the principal protagonists; and Canada, if only because of her geographic position, still would be drawn in. For Canada, therefore, the situation remains basically the same as it was a quarter century ago, with powers mightier than herself determining the course of events. The chief difference is that the United States, rather than any nation farther away, is certain to provide the guideposts. Where Canadian military orientation once was purely East-West—that is, toward Britain— it is now largely North-South. The small Canadian navy is still run broadly on British lines, though more and more equipment is of American design. The army is geared for

NATO requirements, which brings it partway between British and American emphasis.

It is in the air force, the principal arm of modern defense, that the most dramatic changes have taken place. The Royal Canadian Air Force until recent times was almost completely of the same identity as the Royal Air Force: from uniforms to manuals to procedures. In the Second World War, the R.C.A.F. flew British aircraft, and for a period Canadian squadrons were part of larger British formations. Today just about the only remaining links with the R.A.F. are the similar style of uniforms and the system of ranking, and even these are in the process of change. Canadian airmen fly United States fighters, and follow United States manuals and procedures. They are part of the integrated command known as NORAD—North American Air Defense Command—the key to hemisphere safety from bomber or missile attack.

This combined operational command was established in 1958, a few years after completion of another cooperative military effort: the Distant Early Warning Line, the continent's northernmost radar screen. The principle of American bases on Canadian soil had already been established with Newfoundland's entry into Confederation, but under Prime Minister Diefenbaker arose the question of "sovereignty" of the DEW Line stations in the Arctic. They had been built by the United States at a cost of $400 million (and maintained by the United States at a total cost of $40 million a year), and had been manned chiefly by civilians—a mixed bag of Americans, Canadians, and Britons— since the required knowledge was in electronics rather than in tactics. But Diefenbaker thought it would be more fitting to put in a few Canadian air force personnel, and so the R.C.A.F. assigned a total of twenty men, five at each of the four principal stations, to assume titular command. In effect, said a Canadian Defense Department official, "It was to make sure the Canadian flag flew at the same height as the American flag." The same official recalled it was "embarrassing" to negotiate the new arrangement, but that his American counterparts understood the meaning of politics or nationalism and presented no obstacles.

However, within the next two or three years the Diefenbaker attitude grew from concern with relative triviality into something of far greater complexity. First he decided to scrap production of the supersonic interceptor CF-105 Arrow, designed to be Canada's main contribution to continent defense, on the grounds that the Soviet bomber threat had diminished. Then, to overcome the intense controversy that arose in Canada, he persuaded the United States to move two of its projected Bomarc antiaircraft missile sites from south of the United States-Canadian border to north of the border. The United States spent $77 million, Canada spent $14 million, and the two Bomarc squadrons, under R.C.A.F. command, were installed in North Bay, Ontario, for the defense of Toronto, and at La Macaza, Quebec, for the defense of Montreal. The only flaw was that they were unarmed and useless: that is, the Diefenbaker government, unwilling to depart from conventional armament, would not accept the nuclear warheads for which the missiles had been conceived. As one R.C.A.F. officer, with great bitterness, put it, "After conning the Americans into a deal to get us off the hook, we double-crossed them." It was an oversimplification, though in effect true. No formal agreement had existed, Diefenbaker said, for Canada to acquire nuclear warheads. But at the same time—though he did not acknowledge it—the Bomarcs were never intended for other than nuclear warheads. A similar argument arose against the arming of Canadian fighter planes, overseas under NATO command, with nuclear-tipped missiles.

The real problem was that Diefenbaker was attempting to sit astride two competitive horses at once. His Defense Department was working in close harmony with the Pentagon. But his Department of External Affairs, under Howard

Green, was trying to push for world disarmament, with the first step aimed at confining nuclear weapons to the countries already in possession of them, thus excluding Canada. Diefenbaker was unable to reconcile what was clearly a contradiction of interests or to establish anything resembling a coordinated policy. Meanwhile Americans felt, with some justification, that their own defenses had been weakened by Canada's vacillation.

The question of whether or not there had been a commitment on nuclear arming was sharply and authoritatively answered on January 3, 1963. General Lauris Norstad, who had just retired as supreme commander of NATO forces, visited Ottawa and told a press conference that he considered that Canada had undertaken to provide its fighter squadrons in Europe with tactical nuclear weapons, and in failing to do so was not meeting NATO requirements. Four weeks later the State Department issued a press release to reporters in Washington to refute the most recent statement by Diefenbaker. In a House of Commons speech Diefenbaker had claimed that at a meeting in Nassau, the previous month, President Kennedy and Britain's prime minister, Harold Macmillan, had "placed under doubt" the R.C.A.F.'s nuclear role. The State Department in effect called Diefenbaker a liar when it pointed out that the agreements made in Nassau were fully published and "they raise no question of the appropriateness of nuclear weapons for Canadian forces in fulfilling their NATO or NORAD obligations." This blunt language was met by equally hard words from Diefenbaker, who said that Canada would not be "pushed around" or turned into a "satellite" of the United States, expressions calculated to appeal to the inherent Canadian suspicion of the United States. Diefenbaker also ordered the recall of the Canadian ambassador to Washington, an unprecedented move in Canadian-American relations, and one just short of the actual severence of diplomatic contact between two nations.

Lester Pearson, leader of the Liberal party in opposition to the Conservative government, had little heart for nuclear armament himself. But he took the position that Canada had indeed made commitments and therefore had to live up to them. Diefenbaker's own defense minister, Douglas Harkness, also believed there had been betrayal of a firm understanding with the United States, and accordingly resigned. The drama reached its climax a few days later when the Diefenbaker government lost a vote of confidence in the House of Commons and was compelled to resign. The accusations of deliberate United States meddling to cause the downfall of a government were now at their loudest. They sounded at least as angry on the United States side of the border as on the Canadian. Walter Lippmann, in one of his columns, described the State Department statement as a "critical mistake." *The Washington Post* called it "impolitic and undiplomatic, but worst of all, foolish." *The New York Times* saw it as "deplorably heavy-handed." But the *Times* also saw it, accurately, not as a blow that by itself toppled a government. It was, rather, the catalyst in a political crisis that had been simmering for many months over issues created by Diefenbaker's chronic irresolution in domestic matters as well as in defense and international issues. Much of the Canadian press put the State Department action into this perspective, justifying it as necessary for the sake of NATO solidarity on defense strategy. It was regarded as a case of maintaining a principle rather than any deliberate intervention.

In the ensuing general election Pearson and his Liberals won enough votes to form a minority government. Part of their campaign was fought on the moral obligation of Canada fulfilling an agreement and thus restoring the nation's credit abroad. Later on, said Pearson, the matter of keeping nuclear warheads on Canadian soil could be renegotiated, but in the meanwhile Canada had to show it was a reliable ally. Relations between Canada and the United States had degenerated to their lowest point in modern times; within a few months, however, the old accord was appreciably restored. Even more remarkable was the public reaction to nuclear weaponry once it became a *fait accompli*.

What many people in the United States failed to understand about the Diefenbaker indecision—and the over-all debate in Canada—was the instinctive feeling of Canadians that since they were relatively small cogs in the modern war machine, it did not really matter in a practical way whether or not they picked up nuclear arms. Many intellectuals took up the argument that, apart from preventing the spread of such weapons, a valid case could be made for the division of functions within NATO between nuclear and nonnuclear powers. In this sense Canadian reluctance was the opposite of European eagerness to acquire nuclear weapons, and really was based on a trust of leaving them entirely in American hands. In the passion of debate of early 1963 this remarkable feature became greatly clouded by the Diefenbaker overtones of anti-Americanism. But a year later the passion had so died out that when the actual warheads for the Bomarc missile sites were brought into Canada and placed into readiness the news was hardly considered of front-page value; most papers carried a brief item inside.

Military men themselves required little adjustment, for even at the height of the Diefenbaker controversy Canadian and American airmen continued their close relationship. There had been reports that old friendships and professional trust had broken down to such a degree that Pentagon officers would hastily lock filing cabinets whenever Canadian opposite numbers walked in. Air Vice Marshal Max M. Hendrick, who was living in Washington during this period as Chairman of the Canadian Joint Staff, says this was not so. In maintaining intimate liaison with the Canadians, Pentagon officials, says Hendrick, showed "forbearance and wisdom." Basically, he feels, it was not even a question of Americans being patronizing. It was more an attitude built on a closing of ranks: military versus civilian thinking. United States Air Force planners had engaged in innumerable battles of their own with Congress and other civilian bodies, and they instinctively understood what the R.C.A.F. was going through.

Hendrick left Washington to become chief of Canada's Air Defense Command. Tall and lean, and a vigorous fifty-five years old, Hendrick, in common with other senior Canadian military men with whom I have spoken, notes proudly that the joint Canadian-American defense arrangement is unique in the history of the world. Not even in wartime has there been such an example of two nations working so closely, "all the more significant when you consider that one is powerful, and the other is not so powerful." Hendrick recalls the conflict between the R.A.F. and the R.C.A.F. during the war, when the British wanted Canadian bombers to function entirely under R.A.F. command. In NORAD, Canadians not only retain their own formations but assume command of Americans. NORAD's deputy commander is a Canadian, and a large percentage of the officers at Colorado Springs headquarters are drawn from the R.C.A.F. Under this arrangement, the vital decision to put United States–Canadian air defenses into action might well come from a Canadian. Even in day-to-day flying operations, R.C.A.F. officers command regions that overlap United States territory.

During the Diefenbaker era bombers of the United States Strategic Air Command had to receive prior permission to fly over Canadian territory with nuclear loads—a delaying process that was particularly irksome to Washington in the critical days of the Cuban missile crisis when aircraft all over the world were being deployed as a precaution in the event of war with the Soviet Union. The procedure, now that Canada has broken its own nuclear ice, has changed. Hendrick sums up the general respect of the Canadian professional for the attitude of the United States: "The truth, as any military man knows, is that the United States doesn't have to consult Canada. It could fly through our skies at will if it wanted to, but it doesn't. On top of this, our people are given credit for capabilities far out of line with our total contribution to continental defenses." [6]

It may be that the U.S.A.F., more than any other American agency, is particularly alert to Canadian pride and moods. Its record in dealings with Canada is exceptionally fine. In the first stage of construction of the DEW Line, in the mid-1950's, the United States Air Force used its own transport planes and supplies. But on the suggestion of the Canadian government it quickly switched to private Canadian carriers and supplies bought inside Canada. Though possibly no extra expenditure was involved, there was no real obligation for it to turn tens of millions of dollars' worth of business over to Canadian firms. In recounting this example, John Baldwin, Canada's Deputy Minister of Transport, said it was done purely with "the good grace of understanding." This understanding, I saw in Newfoundland, can go to extremes of self-sacrifice. Harmon air base provides the principal industry for the adjoining town of Stephenville. Thirteen hundred U.S.A.F. families live in rented trailers or houses in Stephenville, many of them subject to gouging more blatant than in the usual service town. But the official policy is to say little for the sake of "community relations." In this instance, much less is said because the base is in Canada rather than in the United States.

In Stephenville, incidentally, there was virtually no adverse reaction when Pearson announced that nuclear warheads might be stored at Harmon. The general attitude was one of stoicism: that since the town depended for its life on the base, the element of additional risk was inconsequential. The only tangible expression of opposition came at La Macaza, when a small group of ban-the-bombers from Montreal paraded through the Laurentian hills and sang the

[6] The R.C.A.F. has 14,000 men under NORAD; the U.S.A.F. has 200,000.

hymn "We Shall Overcome." Even the neutralist movement, which had a fairly devoted following particularly among intellectuals in the late 1950's and early 1960's, appears to have lost its force in recent years. One of the most popular cases for Canadian neutrality was made by James M. Minifie, Washington correspondent for the Canadian Broadcasting Corporation, in a widely discussed book, *Peacemaker or Powder Monkey.*

The neutralist theme is a familiar one: that there is little a country of Canada's size can do to alter the strategic struggle between East and West—that is, between the giants of Russia and the United States. On the contrary, by freeing itself of commitments in NORAD and NATO, and becoming unaligned, Canada might find an unprejudiced role as mediator and peacemaker. Minifie did not suggest pacifism for Canada; rather, he thought of armed neutrality. This approach has been condemned even by the socialist New Democratic Party, which has opposed nuclear weapons for Canada but said—as one member put it—"we can't contract out of North America." The contemporary view on neutrality was best expressed for me by Andrew Brewin, a New Democratic representative on the Parliamentary Committee on Defense:

> It may be feasible for countries like Sweden or Switzerland to think of armed neutrality, but the expense of trying to do the same in half a continent would be ludicrously high. Any talk of being on our own is sheer madness. We have to be part of continental defense with the United States. For anyone to go further even than Minifie, and say that we could do without all arms because the United States would defend us anyway . . . this would be utter hypocrisy.

Neutralism for Canada has been emphatically rejected. What the nation is striving for now, within the context of integrated defenses, is a function that can be realistic and useful beyond the hemisphere. The long-range objective is to develop a highly mobile, streamlined striking force that, for instance, can move into action at the request of the United Nations to hold back any potential explosion in a Congo or a Cyprus; this would tie in broadly with a foreign policy that leans heavily toward the United Nations. The first step in streamlining came in 1964 when Paul Hellyer, the Defense Minister, announced a radical overhaul of bureaucracy, eliminating many duplicate jobs by combining the administration of the navy, army, and air force. The operational elements of the three services remain distinct, but tight cohesion is the ultimate target. Defense people point out that there is no need to renegotiate at the moment on nuclear arms, because commitments to NATO and NORAD run only to 1966 and 1967, by which time the present equipment will be obsolete. In addition the world emphasis may have altered, with the two major blocs around the Soviet Union and the United States drawn more and more into a tolerable understanding.

For Canada the circle is almost complete, starting many generations ago with a fear of American military domination and developing into an appreciation of good relations. Even if they do not often say so aloud, Canadians sense that in the modern age of elaborate technology and enormous military costs the word "alliance" is misleading. Certainly, as we have observed, there can be no equality between "partners." The Western alliance is more aptly described by Max Lerner as a power cluster, with the United States as its epicenter. Canadians who may not be prepared to accept American jurisdiction in the field of economics or culture are tacitly acquiescent to the military facts of life, which dictate that in the final analysis the big strategic calculations can be made only in Washington. Instinctively, perhaps, Air Marshal Hendrick speaks for the nation when he says Canadians are fortunate to have an omnipotent neighbor who at least is willing to cater to Canadian sensitivities.

3.

Dollars or Domination?

We started our national existence as colonies of Britain just as you did. You secured your freedom and independence through revolution. With us the route was evolution and it took us longer. But we have achieved political freedom and independence. We have fought to defend it in two great wars; subsequently we have contributed to the collective defense of freedom. Now what we fear is that inadvertently we may lose our economic independence.

> —Walter L. Gordon, Canada's Minister
> of Finance, in an address to
> The Economic Club of New York, 1964

BURTON KEIRSTEAD, a soft-spoken man in his late fifties, is an economics professor at the University of Toronto. His background is as "Canadian" as one would wish, since he was born in New Brunswick of parents descended on both sides from United Empire Loyalists. The name Keirstead was introduced to North America in 1658 when a young medical student, accused in Holland of grave-snatching, was banished to New Amsterdam. The family property grew to include what became the site of the Astor Hotel in Times Square, but this was—unfortunately—forfeited when the Keirsteads opposed the American Revolution and joined the Loyalists in the trek northward. The professor's ancestors remained sensitive to any incursions—threatened or real—by the United States, and Burton Keirstead retains to this day an ardent insistence on Canada's uncompromised political freedom and integrity. Much of the anxiety shown by Walter Gordon about Canada's position in relation to the United States is based on the belief that the greater the economic dependence, the greater the potential loss of political independence.

What does the deeply patriotic and proud Keirstead believe? He refuses to accept the Gordon thesis or to become alarmed that his heritage is in danger. In common with the majority of academic economists, he says: "Three quarters of the nations of the world want foreign capital. That is, all countries outside the Communist bloc want it. Here is lucky Canada, so near the United States that it gets it easily, while others cry out." He goes on to express the opinion that much of the complaint against United States ownership of industry in Canada is caused by a degree of awkwardness of Americans who come up and think they are simply in another backwoods section of their own country; they fail to realize they are in a foreign country.

Keirstead cites an example of the pitfall: He was called in to mediate in a labor dispute involving the branch of a United States electronics firm in Quebec. Part of the difficulty, he found, was over a lack of communication between management and staff. The plant manager, an American, could not speak a word of French despite the fact that almost all the employees were French-speaking. Nor was the foreman, the obvious go-between, any more knowledgeable. Keirstead recalls asking the manager about the foreman: "Do I detect in him a Boston-Irish accent?" Right, said the manager, as he proudly pointed out that the Bostonian had been specially selected and sent to Quebec for the post because he was Roman Catholic and this would immediately give him a common bond with French Canadians. Few choices could have been deadlier; in Quebec the enmity between Catholics of Irish origin and French-Canadian origin is far greater than between Catholics and Protestants.[1]

The parent company should have known this, but did not and therefore committed a serious blunder despite its good intentions. Keirstead offers this general advice to Americans operating in Canada: "Realize you are in a country that is superficially the same as the United States but has a different history and different institutions—and a touchy pride. Let Canadian industry grow as it can, and consult our labor laws and labor procedures, which are not the same as in the United States. And have your company identify itself with the community."

The formula sounds simple. But no matter how the academic economists express themselves in rebuttal of Gordon, who felt sufficiently stirred to attempt to introduce highly controversial legislation designed to limit United States investments in Canada, the fact remains that some Canadians are worried that they are losing the battle that created Canada in the first place: the desire to prevent inundation by the United States. If the fear of *direct* political domination has been eased, it has only been replaced by fear in two other areas: culture and economics. And yet both are naturally related to the political, for total or even wide-

[1] Partly because French Canadians in the past have resented a people sharing their religion but not their language, partly because English-speaking Catholics felt crowded out by the more numerous French-Canadian Catholics and thought their backwardness reflected adversely on the Church as a whole. A French-speaking priest in a small Quebec town advised the manager of a paper mill on how to go about hiring a foreman. The first choice, he said, should be a French Canadian from Quebec City, because it was not so big that it had lost the common touch; if necessary, a French Canadian from Montreal would do. But if no French Canadian was available, an English Protestant from Ontario should be considered next. Because of the different faith, said the priest, the Ontarian would make no effort to be patronizing. He gave other suggestions—including a warning against bringing in a Frenchman from France—but ended by saying: "The very last on the list should be an Irish Catholic from Quebec."

spread domination in one or the other narrows the reason for Canada to remain separate from the United States. The question of whether Canada actually is in peril of economic control by the United States, and whether it should curtail foreign investment, remains open to argument and interpretations that vary in complexion. Some facts, nevertheless, are fairly well established, and they tell how the economic debate has become a part of Canadian life. If it has appeared particularly strong in the last few years, this only sharpens the generality that for more than a century Canada has worried about the dangers of absorption or exploitation by the United States.

From the start of its history, Canada was "exploited." Long before the United States came on the scene, France —and then England—had taken on the northern territory with the purpose of extracting natural wealth and shipping it back to the Old World. Furs were the first export commodity, and then followed fish and lumber. As degrees of self-government under the British grew in the nineteenth century, the colonists themselves set more of the economic policies; they decided to keep to the existing pattern of shipping raw materials to ready markets in the United States and Europe, and to import in return consumer goods. At the time of Confederation in 1867, the only manufacturing industries of any size were ship-building, boot-making, and the fabricating of farm tools and equipment. But by the 1880's the "National Policy" of Sir John A. Macdonald, the prime minister, was well under way to encourage development of secondary industries. Partly the policy was decided upon because the United States had put up tariffs, thus curtailing one of Canada's principal markets. But the ideological purpose was to reduce Canada's reliance on outside markets and sources of finished goods, and so protect the fledgling nation's independence. The apprehension about economic smothering by the United States existed then as now.

Some Canadians had urged mutual free trade—reciprocity —with the United States. The popular mood, however, was in favor of a tariff wall. "No great nation has ever arisen whose policy was free trade," said Macdonald. "There must be a mixture of industries to bring out the national mind and national strength." The reciprocity issue arose again in 1891 and in 1911, but each time the electorate, stirred by national slogans ("No truck nor trade with the Yankees"), turned decisively against it. In effect, Macdonald's National Policy, basing itself on tariff protection, remained the cornerstone of Canada's economic structure, even though the design itself was altered to allow preferential trade arrangements with Britain and the Commonwealth. Manufacturing industries did grow, so that today Canada ranks sixth among the industrial nations of the world. But because of a relatively small home market and high labor costs, the products of Canadian factories are still, for the most part, unable to compete with imported goods without some tariff protection.[2]

Today the United States has more money invested in Canada than in any other part of the world: $20 billions. This represents almost 30 per cent of all the investments made by Americans outside their own country. Moreover, nearly two thirds of the $20 billions is in the form of "direct investment": that is, ownership of subsidiary companies in Canada. How did this enormous development take place, especially with such an accelerated pace in recent years? At the turn of the century most of the external financing in Canada continued to come from Britain, and most of this was in the form of bond purchases—for railway expansion, for example. United Kingdom investment (more than $1

[2] In commenting on this point, economist Roy A. Matthews notes: "Allowance must be made for the movement towards international trade liberalization that has occurred in the past twenty years and in which Canada has been prominent. Today Canada is not, by any means, a high-tariff country."

billion) overshadowed United States investment ($168 million).

The first major shift occurred at the end of the First World War, when Britain's predominant position as the world's leading creditor and trader was seriously weakened. At the same time the position of the United States as an economic and financial power was greatly enhanced. There was an increased demand in the United States for raw materials that Canada could supply: minerals, pulp and paper. The result was that by the mid-1920's, a major period of capital inflow in Canada, the United States took first place from the United Kingdom in the league of foreign investors. Though Americans owned or controlled less than 20 per cent of Canadian manufacturing, there was already a hint of things to come: the takeover of old Canadian firms as well as the establishment of new branch plants. Colonel R. S. "Sam" McLaughlin, central figure in a homegrown success story in Ontario, produced a high-riding motor car in 1908, thus founding Canada's auto industry; but before long the profitable McLaughlin Car Company was sold to General Motors, which built its own plant at Oshawa, Ontario.

By the 1960's nearly half of Canada's manufacturing industry was in American hands. No other country in the world could arrive at the same conclusion—disquieting to some Canadians—about such a high proportion of its industry being under control of a single foreign power. Some economists stress that this was Canada's own doing, and therefore not part of any American "plot." The normal procedure would have been for United States companies simply to ship goods northward across the border. "But we forced them to come in here because we established a tariff wall to do business in our country," said Eric Kierans, Quebec's Revenue Minister. "They had to leap over it. They had to establish subsidiaries or branch plants. And once they did that, the inevitable happened. The subsidiary has a tremendous competitive advantage over any domestic corporation." [3] The tariff wall was not, of course, the sole reason for commercial invasion. In the 1930's, after preferential trade agreements were concluded among British Commonwealth countries, some United States companies set up shop in Canada to take advantage of Canada's privilege to sell under these low-tariff arrangements. The automobile industry, in particular, expanded, with General Motors and Ford becoming mechanical giants in Canada.

After the Second World War, the enlargement of Canada's manufacturing capacity, stimulated by the war itself, encouraged the entry of further American capital and secondary industries. Europeans, involved in their own internal reconstruction, could not consider significant participation in Canadian development, thus throwing the proportion of foreign ownership more and more in United States favor. Americans, for instance, now control 52 per cent of the mining and smelting in Canada, with only 7 per cent held by all other foreign interests combined. Americans control 95 per cent of the automotive industry, 90 per cent of the production of rubber products, at least 75 per cent of petroleum, and 65 per cent of electrical appliances. The trend is such that, at the present pace, something like four fifths of Canada's manufacturing industry will be under United States domination within twenty years. This trend, says Walter Gordon, must be stopped—for a variety of reasons. First there is the practical problem of balancing the books; then come the more amorphous political and national considerations. "It is a question," he says, "of how much you can absorb before it becomes indigestible."

The first point revolves around the interest and dividend

[3] The advantages accrue from the fact that large portions of administration expenses can be passed off to the holding company in the United States; also, in the costly process of establishing themselves in Canada, the parents—under United States tax laws—can claim losses against profits at home.

payments that flow out of Canada, aggravating the country's deficit in international payments. To stop part of this outflow and at the same time discourage foreign incursions in some areas, Gordon in 1963 proposed legislation that would have increased from 15 to 20 per cent the withholding tax on dividends that subsidiaries in Canada paid to foreign owners, and imposed a 30 per cent tax on takeovers of Canadian companies. Gordon's philosophy was almost an echo of Macdonald's: "No country can survive for long if its citizens are not proud of their national identity and are not prepared to pay some price for its preservation." The obvious price, in any flight or restriction of American dollars, would have been a drop in Canadian living standards, at least temporarily. There was an immediate outcry against the Gordon proposals—not only from United States investors but from Canadian businessmen and politicians, among them members of Gordon's own Liberal Party. The press almost unanimously joined in condemnation, calling Gordon destructive and fumbling. The proposed restriction on takeovers was dropped immediately; and by the time of his second budget speech, the following year, Gordon withdrew the proposed increase in withholding tax.

So devastatingly hostile was the reaction that the effect on the government in the interval was almost traumatic. Even though other members of the cabinet shared Gordon's concern about protecting Canadian interests, there undoubtedly would be a setback of several years before any government would pick up so bluntly the perplexing challenge of United States ownership of Canadian industries and resources. The question of outright takeover came sharply into the news in 1964 when Milwaukee's Jos. Schlitz Brewing Company bought control of the third largest brewery in Canada, John Labatt Limited. It was a textbook example of what Gordon had been attempting to prevent through tax on the sale of Canadian companies. But now neither Gordon nor any other senior Canadian official said or did anything about it.[4]

About the same period, a rather sad and subdued fifty-eight-year-old Walter Gordon declared: "Some people say our standards will decline if we lose United States investments. I am afraid they will decline if we let matters drift on." A few years earlier, in his book *Troubled Canada*, he had put it another way: "Canada as a separate and independent nation will be able to do more for its own citizens ... and more for the world at large than she could do as a dependency, even a semi-autonomous dependency of another country." For one thing, as he expressed it to me later, since half of Canadian manufactured goods come from factories controlled from the United States, it means that a large proportion of Canadian businessmen, when they talk of "our economy," are speaking as employees of companies with headquarters in Detroit or Chicago or New York, and are unlikely to speak completely objectively in Canada's own interests.

For another, the parent companies themselves are under obligation first to their own country's interests rather than Canada's—to see, for instance, that the operations of their Canadian subsidiaries do not contravene United States laws, especially the antitrust laws and the Trading with the Enemy Act. Though, as observed in the previous chapter, some of the allegations of United States "intervention" in Canadian trade with countries such as Communist China are exaggerated, the fine point is this: the United States State Department will not raise objection to an American subsidiary doing business with China *only* so long as a purely Canadian company is unable to fill the order. But this still leaves hanging overhead the principle of one country apply-

---

[4] *The Financial Post* listed 143 Canadian-owned firms that had been acquired by foreign investors, mostly American, between 1960 and 1964. The enterprises ranged from insurance and finance companies to stove manufacturers and department stores.

ing its own laws in extraterritorial fashion. For in the field of electronics—in which purely Canadian as well as American-owned firms are engaged—the subsidiary could not sell its Canadian-made equipment to China without placing the president of the United States parent company in danger of going to prison.

Some of Gordon's other main points are these: Under extensive "absentee ownership" the tendency is to fill promotions in subsidiary plants with appointments from the home office, to discourage research in Canada, since much of it is done by the parent company, to use United States advertising agencies to sell products in Canada, to inhibit the development and training of Canadian business managers. Others who think in sympathy with Gordon claim that subsidiaries are seldom allowed to go into competition with parent companies either in the United States or in foreign markets. Michael Barkway, editor and publisher of Canada's *Financial Times,* makes this case:

> Of course Americans have created some wealth here. But too often it has been the very minimum return for the exploitation of natural resources of ours, which are not inexhaustible. American tariff policy has always favored raw materials against finished or even semi-finished products. It's easier to sell rough lumber than finished woods; and this duty rises steeply if we try to sell furniture or TV cabinets or even window frames. We can sell newsprint but not fine papers. We can sell blocks of frozen fish but not fishsticks. And so on, pretty well across the board. Yet in spite of tariffs, we are beginning to sell more manufactured goods in the United States, and so we're running into another problem of American ownership. The Americans, after all, didn't build plants in Canada to compete with their parent companies in the States or in overseas markets. Yet we've got to export more manufactured goods; many Canadian plants can't achieve an economic volume from the Canadian market alone.

These, however, are relatively petty strictures in the view of the majority of Canada's economists, businessmen, and politicians. Even fellow government agencies dismiss the Gordon thesis as out of tune with modern needs and desires for expansion. The Economic Council of Canada was established by an act of parliament in 1963 to encourage development and promote a long-term high level of employment. In its first report, published in 1965 and signed by its chairman, John J. Deutsch, a noted economist, the Council warned that the labor force of Canada was starting to grow at such an unprecedented rate that the country would have to increase the number of jobs by 1.5 million by 1970; a 50 per cent boost in industrial output was urged as a prime target. "Deliberate policies calculated to create a more insulated and isolated economy will not, and cannot, point the way towards an alternative route to high economic performance in this country," said the report. Later, in less formal style, Deutsch said of United States investments and Gordon allegations: "Performance is what we're looking for, and we'll get it wherever we can get it."

The first major academic study of the effect of American holdings in Canada was conducted in 1957. Looking back, Irving Brecher, professor of economics at McGill University, and co-author of the study, said: "We found it difficult to escape the conclusion that economic advantage was enormously on Canada's side. In almost all instances, the Canadian economy could not have grown rapidly if not for United States investments, and in some cases nothing at all would have been accomplished." A more recent survey was sponsored by the Canadian-American Committee, the nonprofit organization concerned with problems arising from the growing interdependence between Canada and the United States. The survey dealt specifically with the policies and practices of American subsidiaries in Canada and concluded that while a good deal of Canadian criticism is valid, often it involves sweeping generalizations based on the misconduct of a few companies, and it "ignores the sincere and successful efforts of many U.S.-owned firms to be as good 'corporate citizens' in Canada as they are in the United States." [5]

The latest report on the subject was prepared in 1964 by A. E. Safarian, head of the department of economics and political science at the University of Saskatchewan. Safarian examined the behavior of three hundred companies that hold among them a total of 40 per cent of the direct foreign investments in Canada. Safarian used a computer and a great number of fresh statistics to supplement the findings of Walter Gordon, the Canadian-American Committee, and Irving Brecher. At the end, his general feeling was almost identical with that of Brecher. "In terms of economic gain," he said, "taking the contributions to the income of the community and deducting such costs as interest and dividends paid in the United States, the net result is overwhelmingly in Canada's favor." Constantly, in his analysis, he asked himself the question: Is a given case of alleged malpractice typical or isolated? Almost invariably he discovered it was a fringe case. In the example of exports by subsidiaries, about half the firms Safarian investigated did not sell outside Canada. However, in most instances the restrictions were associated with patent rights or trade marks that limited franchises to the domestic market. "When I've looked at Canadian-owned companies and their agreements with European companies over patents, the same restrictions apply," Safarian said. On the question of research and development, he acknowledges that conducting research inside the country would be more beneficial than buying it from abroad. But then he asks: Are the foreign-owned companies in fact doing less research and development than purely Canadian companies? He answers: "It's embarrassing to say this, but I'm not sure they are."

[5] *Policies and Practices of United States Subsidiaries in Canada,* by John Lindeman and Donald Armstrong. The Canadian-American Committee, Washington and Montreal, 1961.

Safarian is highly critical of Gordon, accusing him of careless interpretation of statistics when he speaks of a large degree of the industry in Canada falling dangerously under United States ownership. Manufacturing, argues Safarian, is not the only significant index in economics. Added to such classifications as mining and manufacturing, he asserts, should be utilities, such as railways and electric power. Americans owned 12 per cent of the shares of Canadian power companies in 1958; this has since declined to 4 per cent, largely because of public takeovers. Using this kind of measure, says Safarian, United States companies own or control 27 per cent of industrial Canada, including manufacturing, a figure that has remained constant for several years. "Does this represent a 'political threat'?" he wonders. "That expression is the last refuge of a man who is backed into a corner in an economic argument."

Other people's reactions to the Gordon philosophy are put even more tersely. Eugene Forsey, director of research for the Canadian Labour Congress, says: "I'm fed up with all this talk of American economic domination. It's eyewash." Robert Thompson, leader of the Social Credit party, says: "I don't believe in penalizing Americans for doing a job we've failed to do ourselves." The premier of Newfoundland, Joey Smallwood, who has recruited United States capital to extract his province's enormous deposits of iron ore, says:

> As an individual with emotions, and being intensely pro-British—as are nearly all Newfoundlanders—I resent the growing Americanization of Canada through movies, magazines, and television. I also react emotionally when I see American capital taking over our resources. But when I think with my head, and not emotionally, I know that Canada would be fifty years behind where she is without United States capital. Remember, the United States itself was virtually created by British capital. In every instance of British financing, a country has paid back its debts as it

has become more and more industrialized and less of a market. I feel the same about the present situation. One day we will repay the United States, and therefore there is no risk to our independence.

It is precisely on this point that the disciples of Gordon demonstrate their greatest anxiety. Britain's capital investments in the United States and Canada in the nineteenth century were largely in the form of bonds, which were redeemed as each country grew and prospered. United States investment in Canada is mainly in outright ownership of branch factories and mines, which cannot be bought back so readily. Peter C. Newman, a journalist of distinction who holds a master's degree in economics, rebuts the Safarian argument that the Canadian autonomy is in no danger since United States firms control only slightly more than a quarter of all industry. What counts, says Newman, is the *significant* area of control. Manufacturing is the key because it involves the consumer directly. Moreover, remarks Newman, if you look at companies with more than 5,000 employees the majority are American-owned, and they dominate the most dynamic sectors of the economy. In order to protect this stake and their pre-eminence, they must rely on a "politically safe" Canada. Some United States corporations—charges Newman—already have begun to make contributions to Canadian political parties, "thereby becoming involved in our political affairs for their own self-protection." For Newman, the Gordon fear is justified because it is predicated not merely on hard economics or material standards of living—the factors on which nearly all the academic economists base their opinions—but rather on the less tangible issue of Canadian political freedom.

Among young politicians, much the same attitude is fairly common, though it lacks coordinated expression. Pauline Jewett, a political scientist who was elected to parliament as a Liberal in 1963, came to Gordon's defense when he was condemned by older members of the party. She agreed that, from a purely economic point of view, the professors were probably right when they talked of "free flow" and "unrestricted" investments. She quoted United States economists who argued that what Franklin D. Roosevelt did during the New Deal was against traditions of free enterprise—and that perhaps today there would be even greater economic growth in the United States had the New Deal not intervened. "But," observed Miss Jewett firmly, "the New Deal, coming in a depression, was absolutely essential for social reasons, apart from any economic ones." This is her continuing disagreement with the economists: that sometimes considerations beyond straight economics must be weighed, and in Canada's case these add up to a national identity. "We have gone in for much more welfare than the United States," she notes. "What would happen to this trend if we were forced more and more into economic and ultimately political union with the States?" Miss Jewett rejects mere flag-waving as her incentive. She believes, rather, that Canada should be preserved as a "window" through which progressive experiments can be observed. "We serve," she says, "as a kind of loyal opposition to traditional conservatism in the United States. And that's good for American liberals, too. Gordon is right when he talks not so much about economic inroads as the implicit dangers to our way of doing things."

In a manner curiously pertinent to the current Canadian scene, apprehension is also expressed by Jacques Parizeau, noted Quebec economist, who warns that English Canada has yet to learn what French Canadians have felt for a long time: the "demoralization" of seeing outsiders control the economy. "French Canadians," he says, "have known for generations what it means to have all resources developed from the outside. This has created a psychological problem—the feeling that if an enterprise is interesting, the 'foreigners' will be in it. And if they're not in it, it can't be interesting. So you just sit back and wait until others do for you what you should be doing yourself." Speaking of "foreigners," in this instance, Parizeau includes Ontario companies as well as American. He figures "the limit of one hundred per cent outside ownership" has just about been reached in Quebec —in the sense that most head offices of factories are located outside the province. Translating this into broader terms, Parizeau estimates that English Canada is "three or four decades" behind French Canada in awareness of what foreign ownership means. Just as French Canadians complain that English-Canadian management relegates Quebec employees to subservient positions, so he predicts Canada as a whole will realize eventually what it is like to discover that "the highest post you can reach is that of district manager for southern Ontario." Then, he adds, "even the illusion of running our own country will disappear."

The key question, of course, is whether there is any virtue in a "Canadian identity" related to economics, or even, in fact, whether such a state is possible or desirable in this age of customs unions and common markets. Harry G. Johnson, a Canadian analyst and critic who has taught at major universities in Canada, the United States, and Britain, says that economic nationalism is lunacy and that Canadian economic policy so far has "consisted only of a series of bumbling efforts to turn back the clock." If some people suffer confusion or emotionalism in trying to equate political and economic freedom, Johnson undergoes no such conflict. A free enterpriser and free trader, he regards economic integration between Canada and the United States as eminently desirable; until that stage is reached he condemns as cowardly any efforts to discourage takeovers or to control the extent of United States investment in Canada. One of his points is that Canadians have a markedly higher propensity to invest in the United States than Americans have to invest in Canada—about one and a half times as much per capita. He also delights in talking of "Canadian exploitation" of the United States—the half-billion dollars or more of corporate taxes that Canada collects from American investments come "more or less directly at the expense of the United States Treasury." Such arguments raise loud outcries from nationalists who reply that 20 million Canadians buying individual shares of stock in the United States are hardly in the same category as 200 million Americans buying factories in Canada. Johnson's hypothesis is that economic efficiency should be the predominant factor, and that any interference with a free market for the sake of political or cultural considerations is deceitful. "More integration," he believes, "means a richer and more prosperous Canada; and nobody is as independent as a man who can afford to pick up his own cheque."

Johnson aroused considerable controversy when a collection of his speeches and papers appeared in book form, *The Canadian Quandary* (McGraw-Hill, 1963), and he struck the theme that "if the public is to be taxed for the privilege of having a national identity—which is what the protectionists are really arguing for—there are far more worthy monuments to national independence than a second-rate manufacturing sector that could be constructed with the money." This irritated a member of the economics department of the University of Toronto, Abraham Rotstein, who, condemning the "political innocence of the economic liberal," wrote:

> If Professor Johnson is right, it does raise the question of what other national dross can similarly be turned to gold. For example, what of our second-rate defence establishment and our second-rate foreign service? The Americans might run our defence establishment at half what it costs us at present—they might even do it free—and the English have a proven record of running our foreign service efficiently. Also the banks and the mass media could be made similarly efficient, while Canadians would pocket the proceeds and build monuments to their independence.[6]

[6] *The Canadian Forum,* June, 1964.

Since Johnson suggests that political union might well follow the development of closer economic ties, Rotstein dryly accuses him of proposing the novel idea that a state should pursue a policy geared to its own dissolution.

Other economists are wary of Johnson's emphasis on complete economic integration. Roy A. Matthews, Canadian director of research for the Canadian-American Committee, says he is quite prepared to take a look at the virtue of free trade between Canada and the United States, since the economies of the two countries are so closely interwoven anyway; his criticism is that Johnson thinks too much like a pure economist, "and this you cannot do if you want to take into account the individuality and personality of a country." Still others prefer an approach that would fit the traditional Canadian policy of offsetting the pressures from the United States by retaining British and European connections. The shift in orientation is dramatically evident in the statistics of Canada's foreign indebtedness. In 1914 Britain occupied the present position of the United States; British investment accounted for about three quarters of all foreign capital in Canada. Today it is scarcely 15 per cent—less, even in absolute terms, than fifty years ago. Thus Canada has been deprived of its historic counterpoise to the weight of the United States.

"If we went into a common market alone with the United States, it would increase our dependence on the United States," says Professor Clarence Barber of McGill University. Professor W. Y. Smith, of the University of New Brunswick, agrees. He wants a North Atlantic free trade area in which Canada would be one of several members instead of having to bargain alone with the most powerful nation in the world. "Then if we would have differences of opinion or approach with the United States," he points out, "the others would be there to redress the imbalance."

Many politicians and government leaders, while reluctant to push for the controversial kind of safeguards advocated by Walter Gordon, go along with the doctrine of Barber and Smith: the implicit attitude being that any exclusive economic arrangement with the United States would present an unwarranted danger to Canada's autonomy. Lester Pearson, both in and out of office as Prime Minister, has indicated his opposition to a bilateral economic union with the United States and has spoken vigorously in favor of a North Atlantic free trade area in which Canada would be dealing "on the broadest multilateral basis." In the chronic debate on Canadian-American relations, though, there are economists and businessmen who maintain that Canada cannot wait for the idealistic formation of Atlantic community free trade and that, anyway, the natural attraction is southward to the United States. There was wide applause in Canada when Prime Minister Pearson and President Johnson signed in 1965 an agreement to remove tariffs on automobiles and parts going into each other's country. Basically it was a scheme to encourage the big car manufacturers to make better use of their production capacity in Canada and thus open up more jobs for Canadians, though in effect it was a "free trade" compact. Canadian officials denied, however, that there was active planning to extend the principle to other industries.

The hesitancy is by no means one-sided. Americans themselves have shown little leaning toward free trade with Canada. Considerable opposition arose over the importing even of auto parts, and Congress held up ratification of the Johnson-Pearson agreement. The Canadian-American Committee, in presenting a new study of how a hypothetical free-trade plan might look, brought out an interesting point: free access to the Canadian market would add, in terms of population, about 10 per cent to United States industry's present domestic market; but for Canadian industry, free access to the United States market would add about 1,000 per cent to the size of its present domestic market. Though large adjustment of the Canadian economy would be involved in the easier flow of goods, the other part of the drama remains pertinent: What untold strength would be possessed by Washington lobbyists, seeking to protect favorite industries, in quoting the 10 per cent benefit for the United States as against the 1,000 per cent for Canada?

What does the Canadian public think about free trade or a common market with the United States? Two out of three Canadians, according to a *Maclean's* survey, favor economic union with the United States, despite the fact that almost the same proportion are opposed to political union. In other words, the average person does not believe that economic union—which classically is defined as not only a common market but complete coordination of all trade and economic policies—would lead to political domination by the stronger of the two participants. All the recent arguments about the virtue or evil of foreign ownership appear to have confused many people. But their bewilderment is understandable when even leaders in banking and industry are vulnerable to fluctuating points of view. Harry Johnson says loudly that the arch-villains who seek protection for Canadian industry —and do so for greedy rather than patriotic reasons—are the men of Toronto's financial district: "the small, smug mind and large, larcenous hands of Bay Street." But when a correspondent of *The Times* of London asked "some leading Toronto industrialists" about Canada's growing dependence on the United States, he received the general answer that complete integration with the United States is inevitable and that Canadians are not prepared to reduce standards of living just to halt the process. This stimulated the reminder that Henri Bourassa, a staunch French-Canadian nationalist, had predicted a half century ago that if a movement toward annexation by the United States ever started in Canada, it would be led by "the imperialists of Toronto."

The only group I met across Canada with any semblance of unanimity on the subject of Canadian-American economic collaboration were English-speaking university students. This generation confesses little fretfulness about the extent of the United States stake in Canada. In some instances, students suggested that the Canadian government should attempt to direct the flow of United States capital into industries that need development, rather than permit it to go into established industries; but even this approach is not pursued too strenuously as a realistic one. In Vancouver, a young Arts student, Gordon Galbraith, expressed a prevalent opinion: "The existence of an artificial line thirty miles from here should not hinder the flow of capital." In Toronto, a city synonymous not many years ago with arch-conservatism and the pro-English motherland, the consensus among students was that Canada should welcome closer relations with the United States in every area. David Grace, twenty-four years of age and working for a master's degree in history, said: "I'm all for closer economic ties with the United States, and in the long range I'm not opposed to organic union with the States. It's a positive ideal to work for."

And so, on the basis of the attitude of students and the generation they represent, one might reasonably forecast that as time goes on there will be less and less resistance toward the inflow of American wealth or concern about inherent political dangers. But among the present generation of Canadians, a minority—including men of substance and influence—still show considerable apprehension. Jacques Parizeau says: "When I started to think about the problem of foreign investment in Canada, I believed that marginal controls—a little legislation here, a little tax there—could do the trick. But in the last few years I've become more and more convinced that marginal controls are not enough, that something massive must be done." The basic limitation to Canadians developing industry themselves—as Parizeau sees it—is the lack of pools of equity capital. He also says the aim of the Canadian government should be twofold: to discourage takeovers of existing companies and to encourage the rise of new industries under Canadian auspices.

At the moment United States companies operate individually in their own self-interests and without desire or collusion among them to swallow up Canada. But, says Parizeau, "in the long run there is no doubt that there will be increasing interplay between corporations of any country and their government, since there will be considerable coincidence of interests. This tendency is apparent now in Europe, and it is bound to reach the United States." And so, almost inevitably, the argument keeps coming back to political considerations making United States capital dangerous for Canada. Parizeau wants to prepare safeguards now by establishing pools of capital on a federal level in much the same way that Quebec is doing provincially. (The province is designating contributions to a public pension plan to be piled into a general investment fund along the Swedish model: to lend money to industry or to start important projects on its own and so stimulate development.) Something of this order was, in fact, mentioned as a federal target in 1963, but it was quietly dropped, presumably because it smacked of socialism. In 1965 it was introduced again, but in diluted dosage, when Gordon announced that a Canada Development Corporation would be organized to create a billion-dollar pool of capital, partly to buy up existing crown corporations, partly to outbid foreign interests attempting takeovers of Canadian industries. The government intended to retain 10 per cent of the shares, offering the rest to individual shareholders.

Parizeau accuses English Canadians of being more inward-looking even than French Canadians, at least in the field of economics. He points out that a number of ideas for Quebec's advancement have been borrowed from the experiences of France, Belgium, and Sweden. Even the notion of using government funds for development, he notes, goes back to the time of Louis XVIII ("and there was no mention then of 'socialism' "). Apart from providing capital, another purpose would be served: to drive away would-be gormandizers of existing companies. Parizeau contends that any government that offers finances to industry has a right to "keep a finger in the pie, to retain some part of ownership —maybe 10 per cent." This, he says, will discourage takeovers, because no private investor likes the idea of a government representative on his board of directors.

In the meanwhile, much subdued, Gordon repeats in public statements his argument that if relatively mild steps are not taken now to protect Canadian interests, more drastic ones will be required later. Fifteen months after his disastrous "Canadianization" effort of 1963, Gordon again presented measures to control certain stock sales and thus impede takeovers. But these were considered quite reasonable and acceptable, because they were limited to financial institutions—banks, insurance and trust companies—the backbone of a nation's commercial structure. Nevertheless, economists such as Safarian continued to deplore any proposals which in principle invoke "unnecessary restrictions." Safarian takes the approach that if and when an abuse arises you deal with it specifically, "but otherwise you don't pass general legislation in advance when there's no need for it." Unsaid by many economists, but implicit, is the final point: Canada, if it feels threatened, can always emulate Mexico, which expropriated American oil companies in 1938, or even take the extreme measures of Castro in outright seizure of foreign property.

And so the battle goes on, with the American investor, caught in the middle, asking in consternation:

Just what do the Canadians want? They say they need our capital, that without it their standards would drop. They acknowledge freely that they have high standards because of American capital, and that their own businessmen haven't the capital or won't take risks if they do have it. And when we incur the risks and build new industries, and provide people with jobs, we're accused of trying to take over the country and run it.

The American investor has a virtually unanswerable grievance, for he is confronted by a diffuse kind of nationalism: rather illogical at times, emotional and intuitive, but nonetheless real—in its own way as difficult for Americans to penetrate as it is for English Canadians to understand what all the unease is about in Quebec.

There are some factors that even work against an American's chance for comprehension. For example, he does not see Canadian nationalism in the same perspective as it is viewed by a Canadian. The Canadian-American Committee found that when an American hears of Canadian nationalism he tends to think of it as something akin to the parochial "patriotism" of Texas or California. Moreover, "Few in Connecticut are worried because du Pont is incorporated in Delaware, or because a lot of local real estate is owned by New Yorkers.... Why should Canadians worry about such things?" The American in Canada receives no sign of open hostility—as he might in Venezuela—for the simple reason that there is no overt hostility. Anti-American student riots are nonexistent, "Yankee go home" signs are never put on display, and, despite the undercurrent of economic nationalism, the country does not pursue the kind of restrictive policies found in lands where chauvinism is so violent that the threat of expropriation is always present. Canadians speak the same language as Americans, they throw a party in a manner that is so reminiscent of home that it is not thought about as taking place in a foreign country, they build the kind of houses that are found in Iowa or Pennsylvania. The American businessman who is stationed in Latin America, and who conducts himself and his enterprise differently from at home because he is conscious of the mood of the people and government of the host country, relaxes in Canada. If this is flattering it is also unfortunate, for he should make a special effort to realize he is up against a special type of sensitivity.

Robert M. Fowler, co-chairman of the Canadian-American Committee, and president for the last twenty years of the Canadian Pulp and Paper Association, approaches the subject with great sympathy for both sides. He observes that when a Canadian firm transgresses in a manner considered harmful to the national interest it is merely a poor citizen; but when an American subsidiary commits the same misdemeanor it brings abuse on all American investors. "What this means," he says, "is that American subsidiaries in Canada need to reach a higher level of performance and pay closer attention to Canadian touchiness than a purely Canadian firm needs to do." He repeats the theme that Canada is *not* the United States, that Canadians are *not* Americans; that different laws and customs and attitudes prevail in Canada. And because of this it is not enough for a United States parent company to operate a subsidiary in Toronto as though it were a branch plant in Topeka.

One of the principal criticisms made by Canadians of American subsidiaries is that, just as they do not conduct enough research in Canada, so they fail often to sell their shares to Canadians or to include Canadian directors on their boards. Fowler joins in this chorus, but rather than draw on sentiment he reasons along practical business lines:

> Corporate decisions that neglect to include the differences in attitudes and laws between the two countries are obviously not as effective as those that do. Canadian directors and Canadian shareholders can reflect distinctive Canadian feelings and objectives. Research conducted in Canada can touch actual market requirements and preferences. It adds up not just to good manners but to sound business acumen.

With this much said to and about Americans, however, there are two general points for Canadians to remember: First, none of the studies so far indicates any sinister United

States plan to take over Canada through its business establishments; nor have Americans landed in the tradition of freebooters. Second, the motivation of American companies operating in Canada is the same as the motivation of Canadian companies themselves: to make a profit. It is this inducement that largely determines practice. If it is profitable to have a subsidiary in Canada ship its product into the United States or abroad, this is done; but if the parent company can see a higher return or a tax benefit through selling its own production, then this is the overriding criterion. In other words, United States capital participates in Canada's economy because it is worthwhile in dollars and cents and not because of either extreme of altruism or territorial ambition.

The high rate of investment may not go on much longer at the old pace, according to a forecast by the economics department of McGraw-Hill Publications. Though Canada continued in 1964 and 1965 to take the biggest single portion of the huge United States private investment abroad—between 28 and 29 per cent—the share in 1966 is likely to fall to 20 per cent, with Asia and Africa the chief beneficiaries. One wonders, if this prediction holds true, what kind of outcry will then assail American ears. The most pungent summation of the dilemma for Canadians was contained in two short sentences in a report sponsored by the Canadian-American Committee: "They do not want to be engulfed. But neither do they want to stem the tide."

4.

The Quebec Rebels...

PIERRE BOURGAULT is a personable and intelligent French Canadian, thirty-one years of age. He was born in the Eastern Townships, a region in Quebec closely identified with the early history of English Canada. The Townships were settled by farmers from Vermont and New York soon after the American Revolution, and remained an enclave of English language, customs, and thinking in a predominantly French-speaking province. When Pierre was nine years old, his father, a county registrar, was transferred from a place called East Angus to another place called Cookshire, which had a population of around nine hundred people, mainly English-speaking. Pierre remembers them *all* as English-speaking and in control of local property. He recalls how the family first was compelled to live in a hotel while his father looked vainly for a house to rent. No one would lease a dwelling to a French Canadian, and even the local Anglican minister—Pierre was told—preached openly against admitting more French-Canadian families to Cookshire, for this would mean the end of the English-speaking hegemony in the area. There were other humiliating experiences later in life, he says, though the imprint at the age of nine was the most lasting. Pierre went on to college, and then to work as a journalist. In 1961 he joined the *Rassemblement pour l'Indépendance Nationale,* a separatist group, and three years later became its president—dedicated full time to the overthrow of the present arrangement known as Canada and to the emergence of Quebec as a republic of its own. Bourgault and his followers have even calculated that Quebec would be the ninth biggest country in the world in area, and fifty-sixth in population.

I discussed the Bourgault case history with two men: the first a prominent English-speaking psychiatrist who dismissed the Cookshire incident as insignificant, in the sense that it did not by itself lay the foundation for animosity toward English Canada. Rather, said the psychiatrist, Bourgault and French Canadians generally have frustrations created among themselves, but they have shifted their resentment onto others, such as English Canadians. For instance, Bourgault at classical college would have been ridiculed by teachers and students alike because he was of the lower middle class rather than of the "French Establishment"—that is, the heirs of the old seignorial class. Made to feel inferior by his own people, but unable to take out his vexation on them, he automatically would have aimed his attack in another direction. Bourgault's rejoinder to the analysis is that he was never debased at college or anywhere else by fellow French Canadians. Curiously, on a recent return visit to his college Bourgault was shown by one of his old teachers an essay he had written in 1952 entitled "Canadian Unity." It sang the virtues of Confederation. It was only in later years, when he thought more carefully about the problems of English-French relations, that he came to the conclusion that separatism was the only answer.

The second person with whom I discussed Bourgault was one of French Canada's outstanding figures, Gérard Pelletier, former editor of *La Presse,* the largest newspaper in

Montreal. Pelletier, a moderate who is opposed to separatism, said the Bourgault example was as good as one could find to illustrate the reason for the groping and restlessness of present-day Quebec. "Every French Canadian," said Pelletier, "has a Cookshire experience somewhere in his background." Pelletier's own family record is also linked with the Eastern Townships. However, it might as aptly fit any part of a province whose majority of inhabitants—four out of five—are French Canadians, but whose industries, finances, and communications are commanded by English Canadians. Gérard Pelletier's father was employed by the Canadian National Railways as a station agent at the town of Victoriaville. Pelletier the elder, despite the Gallic name, had not learned to speak French until he was in his teens; brought up in Vermont, his first language was English. The job with the railway was fine, but the ambition of every rural agent was to get the station at Richmond, the hub of the district. Pelletier, eligible in seniority and ability, was passed over when the prize was handed to a man named Brown. This choice, Gérard Pelletier knew even as a boy, was made because Brown was an English-sounding name. The irony, however, as officials at the head office in Montreal discovered too late, was that Brown spoke hardly a word of English. He was representative of those Quebecers—rather numerous—who bear purely Scottish or English names (the result often of marriages contracted by Wolfe's soldiers) but who are thoroughly French-Canadian.

Not long ago Gérard Pelletier recalled for Donald Gordon, president of the Canadian National, the story of his father a generation back, to point out how deep and old and justified is the rankling of French Canadians who feel English-Canadian prejudices working against them. Gordon had just been hanged and burned in effigy by a furious group of students from the Université de Montréal; he had made a hapless remark that no French Canadian was a vice president of the publicly owned railway because he had never met one with the proper professional qualifications.

Pelletier, unlike Bourgault, does not carry any childhood bitterness to the extent of rejecting union with English Canada. On the contrary, his is a sane and thoughtful voice in the midst of intense nationalism. But he is now in his middle forties; and, when he was Bourgault's age, his rebellion was necessary in order to set the stage for Quebec's present revolution. It was against Duplessism. Pelletier was one of the very few men or women who stood up and fought actively against the machinations of the late Premier Maurice Duplessis, a demagogue determined to keep the province comfortably safe and backward and corrupt. Pelletier did so as one of the founders and editors of the progressive and intellectual review *Cité Libre,* as a trade unionist, and as a newspaper commentator. A colleague described him at the time as "a thin, intense young man who looks as if he never got enough sleep." He continues to burn himself out, writing and lecturing, because he is appalled by the chasm that has appeared between English and French Canada. Pelletier's objection to separatism, on simple practical grounds, is that Quebec's individuality could not survive in an overwhelmingly English-speaking continent, most of it an American crucible, without some form of guarantees for language and education such as presently exist in Canada. But he does not condemn Bourgault harshly, because the separatists, by their agitation, have brought national attention to the fact that there is widespread discontent with the limitations of the present Canadian structure.

Pelletier lived for a while in Belgium after the Second World War. He draws an analogy between the Belgium of 1946 and the Canada of today. Belgians were hungry and restive and in search of new answers to old social problems. The Communist Party was strong and active and constantly pushing; and because of this challenge and goading, the more responsible elements took action. In this sense he hopes the separatists, unwittingly, will prove of some value by making English Canada respond to the emotional and philosophical and technical needs of Quebec. In the same way, though a step farther off, Bourgault and his R.I.N. party while seeking control through a popular election and while dissociating themselves from the bombings and criminal acts of terrorists, do not decry the publicity aroused for the Quebec extremist cause.

Pelletier is a "federalist." [1] He considers that Quebec has an enormous amount to do to reshape its society without diverting its energy wastefully in a major wrangle with the rest of Canada. And while he holds that constitutional reform is necessary in order to set out a special status for Quebec, he feels this can be achieved within the framework of the existing Confederation. The essential difference between the federalist and the separatist is that the latter is convinced Quebec can attain real progress in the economic, social, and cultural fields only by leaping first into independent nationhood. Between these two ideologies is yet a third body of opinion in intellectual French Canada. No label is applicable to it, but its adherents are closer to the federalists than they are to the separatists, in the degree that they want to retain a Canada composed of an English-speaking part. They speak of "associate states." Roughly, Quebec would set its own economic and fiscal policies, and possibly its foreign and even military policies; the rest of Canada would do as it wished; the common bond would consist of such ingredients as currency and trade. This kind of covenant calls for a tearing up of the present constitution and the writing of a completely new one, and is hardly more acceptable to English Canada than outright separatism.

Relatively few students—contrary to the general impres-

[1] The precise term should be "cooperative federalist," based on a phrase that is used frequently by moderate Quebecers as well as by Canadians in other provinces: "cooperative federalism." There are various definitions of "cooperative federalism," but broadly it implies the seeking of solutions to federal-provincial problems within a federal structure.

sion in English Canada—are *active* separatists. At the University of Montreal, with an enrolment of twelve thousand, the R.I.N. could claim only fifty-seven members four years after its founding, though perhaps as many as 20 or 25 per cent of the students are sympathizers. The majority tend toward "associate statehood," and this is what distinguishes their generation from both Pelletier's and Bourgault's. For instance, to Claude Bachand, aged nineteen, Bourgault is neither inspiring as a leader nor is his platform realistic. Bachand has great respect for Pelletier, but he feels the editor-crusader belongs to a stage in history eons back. Bachand was scarely fourteen years old when Duplessis died, and though at home he heard of the evils of that era it now seems in the remote past—five centuries, not five years ago. Bachand's generation disowns any connection with former times and looks only to a fresh future for which it can take responsibility. This is why he says he cannot subscribe to Pelletier's claim that the British North America Act supplies Quebec with enough flexibility to do an effective job of housecleaning while awaiting constitutional changes. He demands a new constitution and new statehood. "It is like a child reaching the age of eighteen," he explains. "Suddenly he is a child no longer, and he insists on breaking away from a father's discipline. For us in Quebec the father has been Ottawa, and now we feel we can manage without his supervision."

One wonders about this plea. In effect the disciples of associate statehood want life two ways: they crave the stimulation of separatism but require the security of federalism. This suggests the need yet for an umbilical cord—similar, in a manner, to Canada's clinging to psychological vestiges of British security in the form of the crown or consular services. Claude Bachand, who is studying law, is well aware of the excitement of living today in Quebec. He wears his hair fashionably brushed forward, in addition to a wisp of a beard ringing his face—but he is no beatnik. He is, rather, a young Quebecer, and this in itself is a fraternity understood only by those eligible, in age and spirit, to be part of it. Algeria had its rebels, and so did a score of other countries within memory even of some of the young men. But Canada is not Algeria, no matter how hard the fanatics try to find a comparison. Bachand makes this point strenuously. The bombs of the F.L.Q. (*Front de Libération Québecois*), the first terrorist group to go into action, shocked Montreal's 2,200,000 French and English inhabitants alike. The targets were, according to grandiose communiqués, "colonial institutions" (such as federal post offices) and media of the "colonial language" (newspapers and radio stations using English). And so for eleven frightening weeks in the Spring of 1963 homemade explosive charges were dropped in mail boxes and around federal property. One innocent man was killed, and another was horribly maimed. When the police rounded up the group—a score or so—they turned out to be mostly in their late teens or early twenties. Some were college students, others were artists and bohemians, and almost all were from good, respectable families of at least middle-income level. Claude Bachand, in retrospect, looks on them as misguided, even if sincere, and symptomatic of the bewildered aimlessness of that particular period. Within eighteen months the pace was to become less frantic but no less weighty. Quebec's revolution would go on, steadily, whether or not dramatic interludes of violence drew world-wide attention.

And what kind of a revolution is it? It embraces three principal components: nationalism, socialism, secularism. That is, the objective is to create a French-Canadian state, at least semiautonomous, in which basic economic planning will be in the public sector, with the Roman Catholic Church stepping aside from education and politics and confining itself to religion. Quebec might well become the first truly socialist state in North America, and Claude wants to be thoroughly a part of it. He stresses his good fortune to be born into this epoch's exhilaration. "Here," he recognizes, "we have the security and freedom of North America, with the revolutionary atmosphere of Africa. Where else in the world can you be a revolutionary in such comfort?" His choice of physical settings for discussions on the revolution is wide. He could, if he desired, sit at a table at the Cochon Borgne (the One-Eyed Pig), a night club hangout for R.I.N. members. Here, in a walkup on St. Catherine Street East in Montreal, the atmosphere is appropriately noisy and smoky, the sketches on the walls are in the Paris style, and the addicts are youthful and enthusiastic. In keeping with numerous satirical clubs in the past in Montreal, a *chanteuse* stands on a tiny stage and throatily sings a sly lampoon of Canadian politics—but with a difference. In the old days the humor usually was warm and clever; now it is nasty and vulgar and filled with obscene gestures of what separatists will do with the new flag of *"les Anglais."*

The star of the show is a youth named Richard Bizier, who is of the same age as Claude Bachand. Bizier, a former elevator operator, lacks a singing voice, but he does have heroic appeal: he served six months in jail for planting a time bomb in a building of the Royal Canadian Air Force. Bizier, who did it for the F.L.Q., and openly boasts he would do it again if necessary, is baby-faced and unexciting, except to the audience who scream his name—Bi-zier, Bi-zier—with the frenzy once identified with Hitler Youth. Bizier chants the words to a battle hymn: "English, get out. If you don't, we'll make you." When it is over, the crowd in the room—the pretty girls in sweaters, the young men in corduroy blazers —stand and shout and hold aloft two fingers in a Churchillian but chilling salute. Then everyone sits back to sip beer and debate half-formed, heady ideas of the world of revolution and how lessons can be applied to Quebec. Some quote Marx—or more frequently misquote him. They are, however, reasonably well informed on the economic ramifications of the Algerian revolution. This appears to be their guidepost, and they speak admiringly of Ben Bella: of what he did, and when he did it.

"Some people," comments a twenty-year-old commercial artist, "think we are stupid and would repeat the silly things Castro did, especially to seize the property of Americans and antagonize them. How much better is the example of Algeria, where Ben Bella took over French property, but paid for it, and kept a relationship with France which today is very useful." Hovering in the background is the short, squat Reggie Chartrand, a former professional fighter who now spends part of his time leading street demonstrations and being carted off in Black Marias. Chartrand operates a boxing school—probably the only place in the world where one can find side by side copies of Karl Marx's *Das Kapital* and Nat Fleischer's *Ring Record Book*. Wearing a deep blue sweatshirt, with white lettering on the chest—"Québec Libre"—Chartrand is something of an idol around the Cochon Borgne, where he says: "I used to fight for the profit of Anglo-Saxon capitalist managers, now I fight for my people."

I asked Claude Bachand whether he had ever visited the Cochon Borgne. He had not, and in fact had only heard of it a few weeks previously—thanks to an N.B.C. television documentary on the Quebec situation, some of it filmed at the night club. Montreal has hundreds of cafés, and the Cochon Borgne is really known only to its R.I.N. devotees. Bachand's favorite rendezvous is Chez Vito, a pizzeria on Côte des Neiges, a few blocks from the University of Montreal. The walls are of wood veneer paneling, the pictures are cheery, and the atmosphere is subdued. Students gather for a cup of *capuccino* and to reject what they consider the half-baked notions of Marxism quoted by some of the extremists. There is, among many students, a sophisticated approach to socialism and a mixed economy, just as there is annoyance with too many comparisons with other revolutions. A separatist or terrorist who talks of the example set by the Mau Mau, "fighting for the independence of Kenya," is laughed at as unworldly or ill-informed. Quebec, regardless of the F.L.Q. claim, is not an "occupied colony" that needs liberation. Nor, as the R.I.N says, is its revolution another "Negro Revolt." A parallel can be drawn between French Canadians and American Negroes only in that both regard themselves as second-class citizens economically; but beyond that any collating is deceptive. Unlike Negroes in the United States, Quebecers have enjoyed the vote for as long as it has existed in Canada. In addition—and at their own insistence—they have complete control over their educational system, without federal interference.

Young Claude Bachand is inclined to agree with Gérard Pelletier, who has developed the thesis that the type of revolution going on in Quebec does not fall into familiar or traditional patterns. None of the usual conditions apply for a "nationalist" upsurge. There has been no strangling of civil liberties. On the contrary, political freedom is so highly advanced that the R.I.N. can speak out publicly and run for elective office with the avowed motive of toppling the prevailing system. Quebec, though not as highly industrialized as Ontario or the neighboring state of New York, stands up favorably alongside most parts of Europe. More than two thirds of its people lead an urban life. The per capita income may be $500 a year less than in Ontario; but, conversely, Quebecers, at $1,500 a year, earn an average of $500 more than Newfoundlanders and enjoy social security, comforts, and luxuries unheard of in "developing" areas of Africa or Asia and most of Europe. And so the nuances of the mood and desire of Quebec exclude glib comparisons with other eruptions and make it difficult for French Canadians to answer with logical precision the English Canadians who ask, either in frustration or irritation, "Just what *do* you want?"

Bachand, sitting at his favorite table in Vito's, says: "When I visit other parts of Canada I have no feeling of belonging. But I would die for my country." This is not a contradiction in terms. It is, rather, a pure and very representative expression of young Quebec. Bachand, whose English is flawless, has no difficulty in communicating with people in other provinces. He finds, however, there is little to communicate. French-Canadian and English-Canadian attitudes are so different that he says he might just as well be visiting the United States. When he speaks of his "country," therefore, he means French Canada. "Country" is another word for security and understanding set on a foundation of language and culture and philosophy. Bachand approved when student associations of French-language universities withdrew from the national body, the Canadian Students' Union, to form their own Union Générale des Etudiants du Québec. It was not, he insists, separatism. It was the foretaste of associate statehood. Previously when youthful French Canadians of the three principal universities—Laval, Sherbrooke, Montreal—met English Canadians of more than a score of universities at national conferences they had a minority voice only. This, comments Bachand, was perhaps natural— but degrading. Now when they meet at the top level they do so as two organizations "side by side." Bachand does not stress the term "equality," but it is implicit. The significance is deep, for the French-Canadian student today closely approximates in motivation and animation and influence the student of Latin America. He is usually a committed being, unlike the bulk of students in the United States or English Canada. Where one can expect as many as three quarters of English-language students to be apathetic or uninvolved in politics or campus activities, the opposite ratio is the pattern among French-Canadian youth. The majority are engrossed in the changing shape of their Quebec now, and are likely to remain so as adults.

Claude Bachand thought at one time he might like to enter the foreign service: that is, the federal Department of External Affairs. Now he is aiming for a career with the Quebec government, preferably in *its* foreign service. Bachand will take his bar exams, and retain law in the background as insurance in case a civil service career does not work out. But, in keeping with many of his generation, his heart is in doing a job for his own people. Among exponents of the "associate state" proposition are those who go to the limit of saying Quebec should be responsible for its own international diplomacy. Bachand is one of them. "We would be especially effective in acting as liaison between the former French colonies in Africa and the rest of the world," he says. "We have at least the same language in common." Bachand would also like to see a distinctive defense department. His argument is that basic commands in the Canadian army are given in English, even when units are French-speaking—and he feels this is the way it always will be in a country with majority rule.

Many of the supporters of the "associate state" idea say it is precisely in such fields as defense and external affairs that a superstructure, Ottawa, should maintain control. The disciples of this school include Claude Valois, who is a tall, clean-cut twenty-two-year-old political science student. Like Bachand, Valois hopes for a career in the service of Quebec, but unlike Bachand he sees it flowering in closer economic and political collaboration with English Canada. Partly this is because of his age. Twenty-two-year-old students in Quebec tend to be less radical than nineteen-year-olds! Largely, however, it is because of the difference in social and economic positions. Bachand is of the upper middle class; his father, a lawyer by profession, is in the field of public relations and also serves on the directorial boards of a bank, a food company, and an automobile agency. Valois, by contrast, lives in a rather shabby section of Montreal; his father works in a dry-cleaning establishment.

The Quebec revolution has some of its fieriest advocates from the professional middle class. Those of humbler circumstances are more conscious of security—federal pensions and allowances, among other items—and in their ranks hard-headed Gallic logic and caution take over. What would happen under separatism to all the social security measures provided now by Ottawa? What would happen if associate statehood were carried almost as far? Valois, as a specialist in political science, also knows that the ultimate dual-state concept would be valid theoretically only if the English-speaking provinces formed a homogeneous unit. He is aware that geography alone—especially with Quebec acting as a physical and spiritual barrier between the Atlantic Provinces and the rest of the country—encourages regionalism. However, beyond the fact that English Canada is only now in the process of developing an identity, there is the instinctive English-Canadian response of hostility to a nineteenth-century kind of Austria-Hungary relationship.

Obviously there is no simple, single reason for the Quebec revolution. Neither Pierre Bourgault's childhood experience nor the psychiatrist's analysis provides a total explanation. To find the interrelation of several factors, one starts with the conquest of New France by the British, and the establishment—in theory—of two cultures. Barely eighty years later came Lord Durham's celebrated description of "two nations warring in the bosom of a single state." Lord Durham, however, fully expected an end to the emotional conflict through the assimilation of French Canada by English Canada. When the absorption failed to materialize, the speech-makers provided a twist by declaring at every observance of Confederation that here was an example for the world to emulate: two races living together in harmony.

But how susbtantial was the fraternity, really? A modern indication of the unease that was never far from the surface showed itself in 1955 in the unlikely setting of a sports event. One of the folk heroes of French Canada, Maurice "Rocket" Richard, star of the Montreal *Canadiens* hockey team, and the greatest scorer up to then in the history of the game, was suspended for rough playing. The timing of the suspension was unfortunate, for it barred Richard from the crucial Stanley Cup championship playoffs. Even more unfortunate was the fact that the man who decided on the suspension, as president of the National Hockey League, was named Clarence Campbell. Richard fans—especially younger ones—went wild and stampeded through downtown Montreal, smashing shop windows and overturning cars. It was not a mere case of booing the umpire. Though it was hardly recognized at the time, it was a classic example of built-in frustration, racial and political and economic and every other variety, that suggested *"les Anglais"* again committing a terrible act against the people of Quebec.

In 1917 there had been other riots, when the federal government enacted military conscription. Though some French Canadians had volunteered for overseas service, relatively few accepted the English-Canadian argument that if England and France were defeated Canada would be attacked. Most French Canadians regarded European wars much in the same way as did the Americans. These were events happening in a part of the world from which they had been cut off for generations; their most honest course, they felt, was to strive for as much neutrality as possible. Sentiment for a mother country hardly came into it; France had deserted *les Canadiens,* England had conquered them. Now the dreaded device of conscription was being enforced. To English Canadians the draft was simply a means of ensuring that everybody did his equal share; to French Canadians it was, on the contrary, a case once more of the conquerors imposing their will on the minority. The country was precariously split in 1917, and motions were presented in the Quebec legislature to break Confederation. During the Second World War the conscription issue was less serious, partly because of a decline in French-Canadian isolationism and a corresponding rise in voluntary enlistment. Nevertheless, the recurrent fear that the majority were imposing their will on Quebec led to something of a crisis atmosphere.

The crisis of the 1960's is different from anything in the

past, and graver, for the good reason that it is taking place at an entirely new point in history. For one thing, even if logical comparisons with the Algerian uprising and other postwar revolutions are not valid, the mood created—"international nationalism," some people call it—reminds French Canadians of the meaning of their own struggle that has lasted two centuries. Basically, French Canada is concerned today, as it has always been, with preventing an "English will" from swallowing up its language and customs and personality. But new factors have a bearing. The political scientist points out how the Algerian revolt—and its technical use of plastic bombs—stimulated the F.L.Q., which, in turn, brought attention to the R.I.N. and separatism. The historian points out that while secessionism is not a novel phenomenon—at previous intervals it attracted some students and intellectuals—now, for the first time, it cuts across a wide section of the *bourgeoisie* and has drawn prominent politicians into its orbit and debate. On top of these specific definable features are shapeless components that have turned the separatist movement into a much broader arena of general discontent and probing: such amorphous things as the need for recognition and acceptance and dignity. The sociologists and psychologists point out that these are higher levels in human development desired after the more basic attainment of material security.

The political scientist and the historian again enter the investigation and talk of yet another powerful undercurrent: hostility toward the "Anglo-Saxon" because of his "arrogance." Or, put another way, there is reaction against traditional "Wasp" domination. The "Wasps," White Anglo-Saxon Protestants, have been so identified in recent years because of the increased awareness that their command in the world of politics and commerce is under challenge. In the United States the obvious defiance comes from the Negro; in Asia and Africa it comes from former colonial subjects of the British. "Anglo-Saxon arrogance is manifest everywhere," says Arthur R. M. Lower, the historian. "In South Africa the Afrikaners detect it in English South Africans, and this is the foundation for much enmity. The French Canadians, of course, find it all around them." Gérard Pelletier tells of a typically revealing sample. Pelletier, who lives in the mainly English-speaking suburb of Westmount, was called to his door one evening by an enumerator gathering information for census purposes. The caller, a woman, started to question Pelletier in English. He interrupted and said: "Don't you speak French?" She said no. Irritated, Pelletier demanded to know why the federal government would send a nonbilingual person on such a mission, to which the woman replied: "Oh come, Mr. Pelletier, everyone knows if you live in Westmount you speak English." [2]

Pelletier does not relate this type of incident with pleasure. He suffers double shame: first because he feels that despite all the gestures of English-speaking people in recent years—some, for instance, studying night courses in French —the insensitive enumerator represents a deeply imbedded attitude or "Anglo-Saxon" frame of mind; second because he allows himself the human frailty of exasperation. This is a remarkable inner conflict among French-Canadian intellectuals. I have spoken with dozens of them on the subject; almost all tell of experiences and reactions similar to Pelletier's. On one hand they believe they should be beyond submission to petulance; on the other they undergo uncontrollable indignation. Mme Solange Chaput Rolland, a prominent critic and broadcaster, is the wife of a textile-mill owner. They live in St. Jerome, a town twenty-five miles north of Montreal, and frequently entertain English-speaking business acquaintances. Language has never been a problem because the Rollands are fluently bilingual. But

[2] The crux of the problem is that English is the working language of Montreal. French Canadians, who want to advance, must have a knowledge of it. But fewer than 27 per cent of "Anglo-Saxon" Montrealers are bilingual.

one evening at dinner not long ago Rolland snapped at an English-speaking guest: "For heaven's sakes, talk French." Mme Rolland recounts the event only because of her own surprise; her husband, whom she had always considered a mild-mannered person, had shown an unexpected—and revealing—limit of patience.

Typical of French Canadians—and contrary to the misconception of much of English Canada—the Rollands do not expect people in Vancouver to speak French (though Mme Rolland once inadvertently used her own language to start a conversation with a Vancouver woman who broke in to ask: "Do you speak white?"). They know that from an economic point of view they must speak English to survive in the continent of North America, while no one else need speak French. But at the same time Mme Rolland confesses that today she walks out of any Montreal shop when she is not answered in French. "It is illogical," she says, "but it is the way I feel. And this is a point to remember— the difference between English 'logic' and French temperament. If only English Canadians would understand it is emotionalism, and not always reason, that underlies much of French Canada's behavior, then we would be a step forward."

The Rolland attitude, of course, is founded on more than irrationality. Fundamentally it originates in a search for confirmation that at least English-speaking Quebecers, a minority forming barely 20 per cent of the province's population, are willing to respect the principle of biculturalism and bilingualism. And even this is not merely to prove a point but to give some reassurance that French Canada's identity will last into the future and will not be pushed farther and farther into a corner, eventually to disappear. Quebecers want to ensure the continuity of language and culture where French-Canadian minorities still exist—in such provinces as Ontario, Manitoba, and Saskatchewan— and to do so through guarantees for the educational rights of those communities.[3] But first they sense that the willingness of *"les Anglais"* must show itself within their own province, if there is to be any real degree of understanding by English Canadians farther afield. Abbé Louis O'Neill (despite the name, a French-Canadian priest), who is professor of ethics at Laval University, says that he rarely undergoes moments of umbrage in Quebec City, where 95 per cent of the residents are French-speaking and the rest know the language. But he reacts furiously when he arrives at Montreal airport and pauses in a shop to make a request, in French, and receives a blank stare in return. Like the other intellectuals, he hates himself for the reaction, but adds softly, "I can't help it."

Abbé O'Neill, young and progressive, says he is not irritated when he visits Toronto. He relaxes more there than in Montreal, because he does not expect Toronto to be bilingual. When a Torontonian makes a courteous gesture by trying a few words in French he is all the more delighted. But he blames the past haughtiness of Montreal's English-speaking inhabitants—who comprise fewer than one third of the city's population—for much that has gone wrong. The historian is inclined to agree with this view, recalling that by the middle of the last century, when English-speaking people were in the majority in Montreal, the mercantile aristocracy was solidly English or Scottish. The sociologist carries the past into the present. Professor John Porter of Ottawa's Carleton University, who specializes in power

[3] Studies published in the Jesuit magazine *Rélations* show a steady decline in the use of French as a language by French-Canadian minorities outside Quebec. In British Columbia, where a generation ago more than 54 per cent of the French-Canadian community retained their mother tongue, today two thirds are assimilated to the extent that they do not understand any French. In Quebec sociologists and linguists are concerned because nine out of ten immigrants are becoming integrated in Montreal's English-speaking rather than the French-speaking community. But there is no imminent threat of total Anglicization. Apart from the fact that the proportion of people of French origin in Montreal is higher than a century ago, about 60 per cent speak no English at all.

structures, dispels the commonly held notion that Toronto epitomizes Canada's "Wasp" Establishment. Rather, he says, one has to look at Montreal, which contains a much more tightly knit group of the financial and industrial élite than Toronto; it consists primarily of men of Presbyterian or Anglican affiliations and educations in Lower Canada College and McGill University. Porter argues it is harder for a Jew to become a member of the Montreal Stock Exchange than of the Toronto Stock Exchange—and this he attributes to an indirect reason. The Montreal "corporate" Establishment has striven so rigidly to keep out French Canadians that it has protected itself automatically against all other groups, such as Jews, lest any exceptions be made.

Translated into practical figures, Porter's data has provided distressing reading for French Canadians. For instance, he has calculated that only 6.7 per cent of the directorates of major Canadian firms are composed of French Canadians. The usual rejoinder of English Montrealers is that French education—of classical college vintage—has not turned out managerial, executive types. Very often there is validity to the defense, but one of Porter's academic colleagues, Philippe Garigue, dean of social sciences at the University of Montreal, injects a further note of complication. He says that since French Canadians are mostly in menial jobs, a hostility develops along class lines. "What we are seeing in French Canada," he believes, "is not merely a minority struggle. It is also a class struggle. Stated in a very simple way, it is the 'haves' versus the 'have-nots.' "

In the Garigue sense the have-nots are not necessarily indigent. Colonel Yves Bourassa lives in a fine home in the Town of Mount Royal, a Montreal residential district of upper income levels. Distinguished in bearing, and now in his middle fifties, he worked for fifteen years as vice president and manager of French services of the Montreal branches of Canadian and United States advertising agencies. What is it like to be a French-Canadian executive in a big English-Canadian or American-owned company? "It is not easy," Bourassa replies. "One feels—and cannot help but feel—that there is a ceiling that you reach quite quickly, and then you keep bumping your head on it." He illustrates the effect of this by relating a personal experience. One day a senior agency man, in from the Toronto office, turned to Bourassa at the end of a management committee meeting and asked: "What's all this separatist talk about?" Bourassa answered: "There are seven or eight of us sitting here who can aspire to become president, and eventually maybe chairman of the board, except one—and that's me."

Bourassa recalls there was a long silence around the table, and then someone said, "Well you know, Yves, it's a matter of language." Bourassa, who speaks impeccable English with the neutral accent and idiom of a well-educated Chicagoan, surmised that what was meant was not language but extraction. He became an example of an internationally educated and oriented French Canadian who decides his future is not with an American or English-Canadian corporation, and who suddenly lets his heart show itself because of the pressures all around. Bourassa realizes that the pressures are much the same as those on English Canadians who are sensitive to United States domination—and says because of this he cannot understand why English Canadians have so little comprehension of the French-Canadian mood. In any case, he left the agency and took on a temporary promotional post with the powerful St. Jean Baptiste Society, which preaches extreme French-Canadian nationalism.

Bourassa had an outstanding military career as commanding officer of Les Fusiliers Mont-Royal, an infantry battalion, during the Second World War. When asked point blank whether, as an officer and obviously a patriot, he would turn against English Canada and break up Confederation if necessary to attain a goal for Quebec, he hesitates, thinks for a while, and then answers that he hopes it will never come to such a decision; but if it should, his place would have to be with "my own people." Part of the tragedy is that the group with which he has now clearly identified himself, the St. Jean Baptiste Society, is pushing for associate statehood of a variety just short of outright separatism—with Quebec's sovereignty to include "Quebec citizenship" for its residents. The Society also threatens economic boycott of stores and businesses where the English language is predominant.

The Bourassa case history was televised by the National Broadcasting Company to tell of the frustration sustained by French Canadians of executive caliber. One immediate reaction from English-Canadian advertising people was that Bourassa had gone as far in the field as his ability would take him, and that he was charging discrimination unfairly. This, of course, is a matter of opinion, but the main point is that Bourassa *felt* he had the ability and experience and knowledge to go higher but that he was limited to a position as head of "French services." The brooding, in other words, remained—whether or not English-language associates thought he should be satisfied. In the same vein, a French-Canadian doctor—prominent in bacteriology—tells how resentful he is when he meets with English-speaking doctors who keep the conversation to small talk: Does he know any good new restaurants? "They seldom deign," he says bitterly, "to discuss medical matters." There may have been some explanation many years ago for English-Canadian doctors looking with disdain on French-Canadian doctors; the medical training and hospital standards of the latter were of inferior quality. But this factor no longer applies, and the offended French-Canadian doctor says: "It is the continuing condescension or overbearance that grates on me."

Possibly the most dramatic and poignant and revealing story of the French-Canadian quandary is represented by Leo Plouffe, a lieutenant detective who is the Montreal police department's bomb disposal expert. Plouffe, a massive forty-one-year-old who trained with the F.B.I., worked at a frantic pace dismantling dynamite bombs during the F.L.Q.

scare. At one point he went sleepless sixty hours responding to emergency calls. Haggard from weeks of strain and tension, he told a visitor in his office: "My soul is cut in three parts. Part of me is French-Canadian, part is Canadian, part is policeman." In a single day all three pieces collided. First, on his way to work he was accosted by an English Canadian who asked for some street directions. Plouffe started to reply in French, when the man shot back: "Speak English." Then, at headquarters, his chief called him to say a bomb had been found lashed to Victoria Bridge, leading from the island of Montreal to the mainland. While this was federal property, and therefore the responsibility of the R.C.M.P. or the army, Plouffe was the most experienced man available—would he handle it? It was not an order; it was, rather, a citizen's duty. Plouffe grimaced as he recalled the decision. He detached the bomb at the usual considerable risk, got home, and no sooner had his shoes off, when the phone rang. An anonymous French-speaking person said that "the secret army" would take revenge by throwing acid in the eyes of Plouffe's young son. Having recounted the occurrences, Plouffe buried his face in his hands, and his visitor left silently.

If one asks Claude Bachand, the law student, whom does he consider to be Quebec's greatest figure?—the answer is immediate: René Lévesque. However, Claude Valois, the political science student, believes Lévesque is "too mercurial." His own choice as the steadfast, outstanding man in the province is the premier, Jean Lesage. But among young people generally—and many intellectuals—there is no doubt that Lévesque wins out as the most exciting and controversial personality in French Canada, and probably in all Canada. He is a member of Lesage's cabinet, as Minister of Natural Resources, but should he choose to break away and form his own party or unite with an existing group he could cause havoc in the present structure of Quebec politics. The

R.I.N. would dearly love to have him lead them, and at times Lévesque sounds like a separatist. On other occasions he comes out flatly for associate statehood as the only answer to the conflict within Canada—or, at least, the *minimum* answer.

One of Lévesque's difficulties is that he cannot control the voice that translates his quick, imaginative, and daring mind. He muses aloud—and publicly—so that even some of his closest admirers are shocked by his statements. Precisely what does he think? He once boiled it down for me to a confession of pragmatism. "I know two things for sure," he said. "First the *status quo* for Quebec must end. Second there can be no melting pot." Within these terms of reference Lévesque stretches in nervously energetic fashion—and in virtually unlimited directions—for answers. He is short —five and a half feet—and he compensates with a loping gait and staccato delivery, sentences tumbling one on the other. But he is also capable of immense and touching reflection. In one such moment, he said unexpectedly and sadly: "Perhaps it would have been better, as some of the English are saying, if French Canadians had been completely integrated as a conquered people. Then my name would be anglicized to Bishop and there would be no problem."

Lévesque was born in 1922 in the Gaspé village of New Carlisle, which, despite the name, was largely French-speaking. His father, a lawyer, pushed him into learning English when he was barely able to walk—though, he recalls, not a single one of the dozen English families who owned and operated New Carlisle ("with a Kenya mentality") possessed even the curiosity to go out and learn some French. In a way this was Lévesque's "Cookshire," except that the real reaction to it did not emerge until many years later, after his education at Laval University in Quebec City and a wartime job in New York and Europe as a French broadcaster for the Office of War Information, the United States propaganda agency. Lévesque joined the Canadian Broadcasting Corporation's French network, *Radio Canada*. Dealing with domestic and foreign issues, he soon became famous throughout French Canada as a radio and television commentator of rare bite and honesty. Lévesque in those days was an internationalist rather than a nationalist. But an event that began on December 29, 1958, and spread through the next two months, abruptly shortened his vision.

Seventy-four *Radio Canada* producers in Montreal decided to strike after management refused to allow them to organize for collective bargaining. The established unions walked out with them in sympathy—and among the ranks was Lévesque. He had nothing to gain himself; he was by now a free-lance, on a substantial contract, doing a widely followed show called *"Point de Mire"* (Focal Point). But before the strike was over Lévesque was its hero and leader. He wrote impassioned articles in the press, he toured the province with a variety show to raise funds, he went to jail as a demonstrator. Finally, on March 7, 1959, the issue was settled—with victory for the producers, but also lasting bitterness. The date was as much a key to present Quebec developments as the death of Duplessis was to prove six months later. Lévesque accused English-language newspapers of having misrepresented the producers' position; he charged that the C.B.C.'s principal negotiators were mainly English; he argued that none of the responsible federal cabinet ministers nor the prime minister, Diefenbaker (all English), did anything to intervene when the crown corporation showed shocking behavior and bad faith, at one stage agreeing to an end to the strike and then turning it into a lockout. Three thousand *Radio Canada* personnel were without work, many of them desperate financially; French listeners and viewers were deprived of a major service, and if this had happened to the English network— Lévesque added with some pertinency—Ottawa would have rushed to settle the dispute within forty-eight hours instead of sixty-eight days. "Some of us, maybe a lot of us," he wrote in *Le Devoir,* "will come out of this permanently disgusted with a certain ideal called National Unity. Never before have we felt that National Unity is something designed almost exclusively to keep negligible minorities nice and quiet. Never before have we felt that our affairs are bound to be either tragically or comically mismanaged, as long as they remain in the hands of men who have no understanding of them. . . ."

If this had been merely one man's disturbed reaction, the affair might have ended then and there. But the strike brought out latent ultranationalism in a group of highly important people with considerable influence over the public: writers, broadcasters, artists generally. It also indicated the perverseness that clouds much of the present attitude of French Canada toward English Canada, for, as *Le Devoir* pointed out in an editorial comment on Lévesque's appraisal, fundamentally this had been a strike of French Canadians against other French Canadians: the management of *Radio Canada;* even French-Canadian members of parliament did nothing to intervene. But the second point *Le Devoir* noted was gravely perceptive: "There have been some strange conversions during these last two months. Our writers and artists are generally those who used to turn up their noses at French-Canadian nationalism. And yet we've seen more nationalist slogans on the strikers' picket lines and in their meetings than at any other time or place in French Canada." What did it all mean? Lévesque's own answer, given now in retrospect, speaks for many French Canadians: "The strike convinced me that the French-English partnership in Canada was a myth. It made me realize what it means to be a minority when you don't have the strength to force the majority to pay attention to you."

The experience also revealed Lévesque's qualities as a speaker and leader. Shortly afterward he joined Jean Lesage, whose Liberals were trying to break the seemingly eternal grip the Union Nationale party had on the province even with the death of Duplessis. Lévesque stood for election in 1960 in the polygot riding of Laurier, in Montreal, and won on a platform of sweeping reform. Less than a year later his thoughts on change became apparent. As Minister of Natural Resources he was determined that Quebec's privately owned electricity companies should come under public control, a step toward diversifying *French-Canadian* industry. The growth of munitions plants during the Second World War had pushed Quebec out of a farm mentality and economy. But industrialization was still far behind that of Ontario, and what there was of it was mostly under non-French ownership or management.

Lévesque's campaign against the power companies was strenuous, but at first they did not take his talk of nationalization seriously. Who—they demanded—was capable of running the hydro complex in the event of a takeover? At one session with company representatives Lévesque pounded his desk so forcefully he shattered the glass cover. An assistant preserved a fragment, saying it symbolized a historic turning point: no longer was Quebec afraid to stand up to powerful interests. This was a misleading, if dramatic, declaration; for Lesage himself was far from convinced nationalization would work. Lévesque threatened to quit, and to take several members of the cabinet with him, unless his opinion prevailed. It was the first sample of an odd relationship and conflict, regulated by mutual need, between prime minister and minister. Eventually Lesage decided to make state ownership of power an election issue, and once again Quebecers went to the polls—this time under the slogan, *"Maîtres Chez Nous"* (Masters in our Own House). Lesage, Lévesque, and the Liberals gained a clear-cut victory, and by 1963 the takeover—at a cost of $600 millions—was complete.

In his campaign Lévesque avoided emotionalism. He relied, rather, on facts to sell his case: a refreshing departure in a province noted for political bombast and Gallic rhetoric.

His simple appeal, then as now, is that French Canadians comprise 80 per cent of the population of Quebec but control only 10 per cent of the economy. He says: Control of the economy, history shows, is essential for the survival of any culture (an argument echoed on a larger scale by Walter Gordon when referring to Canada in relation to the United States). However, Quebec, adds Lévesque, is so lagging in industry that she can catch up only with the help of considerable state planning. He cites the dollars-and-cents logic of nationalization in selected areas: cheaper power, for instance, draws in more private industry.

During the electricity controversy, Lévesque's opponents applied to him such labels as "Quebec's Castro" or "Lenin without a beard." The epithets not only missed badly the essence of Lévesque's philosophy; they ignored the fact that Ontario had nationalized its power resources back in 1903. Part of the trouble with trying to place Lévesque in a simple category—"leftist," "socialist"—is that he himself is still groping. In economics, for instance, he believes in a blend between private and public enterprise: something on the Swedish pattern. The only valid description is that he is a pragmatist—and, of course, a French-Canadian nationalist. As such he is also hypersensitive to any suggestion he considers unflattering to French-Canadian ability. One of the companies he would like to nationalize is Bell Telephone. Such a target is beyond reach in the present makeup of Canada, because the Bell Telephone Company operates in Quebec and Ontario under a federal charter. "But why the Bell Telephone?" I asked Lévesque. A case could be made for nationalizing power, I said. But why tie up millions of dollars—money that might be put to more economic use elsewhere—taking over an organization now efficiently operated? Lévesque shot back: "Don't you think *we* could do an efficient job?"

The Bell Telephone Company depicts, in Lévesque's mind, a prime example of alien, that is, "Anglo-Saxon," ownership in Quebec. In this instance emotionalism rather than logic impels him to sound almost like a fanatic. (However, and typically, a streak of practicality does intrude. The Bell Telephone Company, with its vast and modern technology, would provide an ideal jump-off point for young engineers and administrators now graduating in large numbers—for the first time—from Quebec's universities.)

One of the fascinating things about Lévesque and the very substantial though ill-defined movement he represents is that while often he expresses himself radically and creates controversy, there are friends or admirers or interpreters who step up to caution English listeners against hasty judgment. Lévesque, they explain, is hard-headed and realistic, and would not act foolishly on any serious issue—any more than would the bulk of French Canadians. In a small example, he once said in a debate with an English-speaking member of parliament that this was probably the last time in public he would use English. English Canadians immediately interpreted this as a brazen threat to break communications in the so-called "dialogue" going on between the two major races. What Lévesque meant was that there had been so much discussion—and so much misinterpretation—that perhaps he could do some good by keeping silent for a while. Claude Ryan, the erudite editor-publisher of *Le Devoir*, wrote:

> When this man speaks in public there are always several levels of perception which constantly short-circuit on the speaker's lips. There is the cold and reasonable man. There is also "the political animal" who functions at a level very near to that of vital instinct. The latter often says things which English Canada makes the mistake of taking literally, thus missing the deep meaning of what the author has wanted to communicate.

In this manner Lévesque, by his frequent references to nationalization, has kept St. James Street, Montreal's financial heart, in an anxious flutter. He has also aroused English Canadians in other parts of the country to the extent that one publication suggested his impeachment for seditiously urging students into violence. Lévesque had said in a speech before a college group that he hoped Quebec could achieve her goals without the use of terror; he left the implication that later, or under special circumstances, violence might be justified. Caught in enormous criticism from French-Canadian moderates as well as English Canadians, Lévesque then explained that he had simply meant that in certain cases—Algeria's independence struggle, for instance—force was necessary. But his original thought about Quebec still hung ambiguously in the air.

What Lévesque does say clearly—and accurately—is that he is actually a restraining influence on young people. There is no doubt that he is regarded as a semigod by many students and others. A declaration of outright separatism by Lévesque is the signal awaited by those youth—and their elders—who have hesitated to make such a decision for themselves. The results could be far-reaching, for what the extremists have lacked is strong and prestigious leadership. Since 1960 several groups of separatists have come into existence, only to fade away and leave the R.I.N. as the senior political apparatus dedicated to the splitting of Canada. And even its paid-up membership in 1965 was under ten thousand, leading Pierre Bourgault to concede that in an election it was unlikely his group could take more than two or three seats in the province's ninety-five-man Legislative Assembly. For one thing, the separatists have failed so far to make any marked inroads in the trade union movement. Organized labor has built itself up remarkably quickly since the days of Duplessis, but it is still many years behind the rest of North America in reaching desired economic levels. Trade union leaders, generally of a high intellectual capacity, are wary of separatism because they visualize a flight of capital, emigration of experienced English-speaking technicians and managers, economic blockade, trade barriers, or other measures that would cause a decline in the very standards they are now trying to raise.

The R.I.N. obviously would welcome a move by Lévesque that might offset the caution of labor. Some of the R.I.N. members regard him as Quebec's possible Kerensky, serving a temporary purpose because of stature, popularity, and relative moderation, later to be replaced by a true revolutionary. Lévesque himself says that now, in his forties, he is "too old" to take a really effective role, that some unknown young man will emerge as the future leader of a revolutionary Quebec. Meanwhile he confesses he is "pushed from below" all the time: not only by students, but by young farmers, young professionals, and intellectuals of all ages, who say: "Declare yourself." He holds them back—and himself—by insisting he wants to give Canada another year or two to prove itself.

Here is the dilemma as he explains it:

The separatists say of English Canadians, "To hell with them, they don't want to understand us. We'll never get anywhere asking for things bit by bit, or even getting things bit by bit. Let's get out now." The nationalists—and I call myself simply a nationalist—say, "Let's give this one more chance. But this time it has to work."

Now, what does he mean? Lévesque says:

English Canada objects to the use by French Canadians of the word "nation" to describe themselves. But this is precisely what we are—a nation culturally, racially, in every way. The English have to face this fact and understand that Quebec will accept no less than the recognition that it has the right of any nation to speak for itself.

Here is some of Lévesque's frank monologue:

What is the use of trying to make a go of anything when there is so much dislike on both sides? It was a phony Confederation to begin with: three English provinces (Ontario,

Nova Scotia, New Brunswick) ganging up on one French province. And the French were sold down the river by Georges Etienne Cartier (the Quebec political leader of the mid-1800's) who extolled falsely the notion of a union. It never made sense. Now what is the sense in having a bedmate when you can't stand the touch of one another? While you cannot carry the analogy of marriage too far, at least there is a lesson to be learned from an unhappy marriage—a trial separation, maybe with the understanding there could be reconciliation later. People say we might lose something by giving up a common foreign policy and common defense. What foreign policy have we had in Canada in the past score of years? We have acted "the honest broker." Is that a foreign policy? And what kind of a defense policy? Completely wasteful. We spent a half billion dollars developing the Arrow (supersonic interceptor), then junked it, and lost thousands of our best technicians to the States. All along we have made fumbles and half starts in defense; there is no reason for such huge spending when so much remains to be done at home. A separate Quebec would not have the burden of heavy defense costs—which we now share through taxation—and this money could be put to good use in education and other fields. Neutralism? In a way, but we would not disband all forces. In a Republic of Quebec we might keep one battalion, maybe two battalions, if we felt we could afford it, to be put at the disposal of the United Nations. This would be a useful service, because French Canadians are accepted everywhere in the world, and it would be a mobile force, ready to move at an instant's notice.

The foregoing is Lévesque in one of his moments of musing, as a separatist might muse. What, I asked him, did he think the effect would be on the United States if Quebec should manage to break away from the rest of Canada? Especially if there should be a vindictive campaign by English Canadians saying this was another Castro-style operation? Lévesque said he would buy radio and television time in the United States to explain what it was Quebec was aiming for, thus reassuring Americans there would be no threat to their security or investments.[4] At this stage one takes a hard and sharp look at Lévesque and his utterly naïve reply. Even R.I.N. leaders admit the one great puzzle and fear for them is precisely this point: How would the United States react? Pull out its wealth? Take physical action to prevent the St. Lawrence Seaway from falling even remotely into unknown hands? But Lévesque, who is aware that United States defense policy calls for a strong and unified Canada, is far from naïve. Therefore, much of what he says must be put down as the reflections of a man who is desperately searching for answers but is not yet satisfied with what he has found.

Lévesque has set a deadline in his own mind: 1966. That is the likely year for the next Quebec general election. It is also the year more than one million youth will reach for the first time provincial voting age, eighteen, and will make up almost one third of the total electorate. The Liberal Party is concerned with its own surveys indicating an aimless search among many of these young men and women. College and university students—about one in four—have reasonably clear thoughts of what they want in the future, generally tending toward socialism. But it is the rest who are unorganized and diffuse in their thinking. They feel cut off from their fathers' settled generation. They also show a disenchantment with politicians, even a cynicism toward them. Lévesque, in a way, might well be the beneficiary, for his background and activities remove him from any stigma.

The year 1966 has psychological importance, too, for it precedes the anniversary of Canada's centenary. If by then Quebec does not get what Lévesque thinks it should have—

[4] Direct United States investments in the Province of Quebec—in mining, pulp and paper, manufacturing—are valued at between $3.5 billion and $4 billion.

virtually autonomy—he will shout his ideas. Sentimentally he might favor separatism; realistically he doubts if it could work. He rejects out of hand "cooperative federalism," saying it is based on "perpetual improvisation." He demands, instead, a new "clear-cut contract which does not depend on mere angelic goodwill." This means a system of associated states. Privately Lévesque sometimes tells friends he visualizes a Swiss order of cantons, with Canada divided into four or five such cantons: Quebec, Ontario, the Atlantic Provinces; but he is not sure whether the regions west of Ontario would make one or two cantons. The main point is that Ottawa would have minimum powers only, perhaps in defense and foreign affairs. But in any case even such powers would be unimportant, since each canton would have a power of veto. Lévesque once admitted publicly he did not know exactly what he meant by "associate status." He said: "I am not the expert to define it." This brought exasperated reaction from the French as well as English press. Claude Ryan, who had shown patience and understanding in *Le Devoir* only a few months previously, made the remark: "René Lévesque has been an enigma for English Canada. If he keeps on chattering as he is doing, he will soon become one for us."

Lévesque and I are old colleagues. Once, in 1955, we accompanied Lester Pearson, who was Minister of External Affairs, on a visit to Moscow. East-West relations were only beginning to thaw, and Pearson was the first Western foreign minister to make the trip in many years. Lévesque, at a reception at the Canadian Embassy, showed his ingenuity and enterprise. Pearson was surrounded by five vice premiers—Malenkov, Molotov, Kaganovich, Pervukhin, Saburov—exchanging light banter about international relations. Suddenly Malenkov said, partly in jest, partly in concern: "Our conversation is being recorded." Lévesque had moved in quietly, tape recorder at his side, a microphone deftly thrust into the midst of the group. "Don't worry," Pearson assured the Russians. "We have freedom of the press in Canada. They'll print anything I tell them to." The vice premiers were not offended; at least they chuckled.

Looking back one day recently, as we walked down the steps of the legislature building in Quebec City, Lévesque confessed how he would like once again to be a "newsman" (a favorite word of his). One of the distressing changes in his life, he said, was that previously—as a "newsman"—he could afford to think he was sure of all the answers. Now he can no longer be sure. And yet he must always have a challenging situation on his hands and fight for what he considers to be social justice. Despite the bewilderment and fear he sometimes causes in English Canada, Lévesque is regarded by large numbers of French Canadians, including fellow cabinet ministers, as the leading symbol of the transformation that is taking place in Quebec—a transformation much for the better.

5.

... and the Venetian Princes

RENÉ LÉVESQUE represents the new breed of French-Canadian administrators and planners: the intellectuals and technologists who comprise a fresh and bustling Establishment, though not all its members match his radical or outspoken ways. One of the greatest phenomena of contemporary Quebec is that side by side with the struggle to find a meaning in terms of English Canada, a deep social and economic revolution has been going on within the province itself— and it is conceived by the new élite. This Establishment is made up mainly of three groups: the civil servants who have returned from Ottawa to work for the Quebec government; the social scientists sent out particularly by Laval University; the chartered accountants, economists, and business administrators graduated by Ecole des Hautes Etudes Commerciales (the commerce faculty of the University of Montreal). The constituents of this young aristocracy are labeled by one of them, Jacques Parizeau, as "The New Venetian Princes." [1]

[1] A reference to the great and noble days of the fourteenth century when a council of Venice's aristocrats ruled with efficiency and justice in place of the more usual despots. Sinister features—terrorism, secret arrests—came later, during the decline of the republic.

Parizeau, at the age of thirty-four, is a principal advisor to the Quebec Economic Advisory Council, the top planning board for the province. He first gained a national reputation as professor of economics at the Ecole des Hautes Etudes Commerciales. Now, with only the slightest trace of acrimony, he recalls that not long ago the traditional French-Canadian "in" groups consisted largely of lawyers and middle executives of English-Canadian or American companies. The bitterness is part of the prevalent feeling that the lawyers gained their prominence by acting as interpreters between English and French without particularly doing a job for their own people. As for the middle executives, the salesmen and the public relations types, Parizeau accuses them of creating, perhaps unwittingly, the false notion English Canadians had about the French Canadians being "safe." He explains:

> They drank beer and played golf with their English-speaking colleagues, giving the impression that this was the extent of any French-Canadian ambition. Thank God, we, the technologists, are out of it. French Canadians are realizing, slowly, we're not as incompetent as we thought we were, reduced to drinking beer and playing golf. We never had a chance anyway to belong to the really big Establishment, where they drink whisky. But now at least the technologists and the intellectuals have jobs with government, and we're busy. And like any other Establishment, we feel secure and just don't give a damn what others might say, so long as what we do is important.

This sense of independence and challenge has produced a rare atmosphere around Quebec City. It is doubtful if any capital in the world—including Washington in the glory of New Frontier days—ever boasted in proportion to population a greater collection of bright and talented young people. The New Venetian Princes are appropriately altruistic; their dedication, however, takes the form of patriotic devotion to Quebec itself. Jean Fournier, for instance, quit

Ottawa's Department of External Affairs in order to become chairman of the Quebec Civil Service Commission. Fournier, who had a distinguished foreign service career and headed the European division of External Affairs, turned down an ambassadorship in Latin America in order to go to Quebec. The former post would have paid, with allowances, between $35,000 and $40,000 a year; the latter pays half that amount. Many others of a similarly high caliber have switched from the federal to the provincial capital. This exodus from Ottawa offers an ironic twist, since French Canadians complained in the past that few among them could attain major positions in the federal administration.[2] Now, of course, the ratio is likely to become even smaller as the better talent is drained off by Quebec City. But on the positive side the movement indicates that Quebec has effectively cleaned house, that a provincial civil service no longer is held in disrepute, as it was during the pork-barreling days of Duplessis when corruption, inefficiency, and patronage dominated many public offices.

The Lesage government has reached deeply into university circles for scores of key people—such as Claude Morin, a thirty-five-year-old social science and economics graduate of Laval and Columbia Universities, who left an academic setting to become the premier's part-time advisor on federal-provincial matters, stayed on in a full capacity, and now is also one of the Liberal Party's principal strategists. Other professors prefer to retain their university ties, but so vital are they to the industrial and political and social resurgence that a typical Laval man who might earn $10,000 a year at the university collects another $15,000 serving on government committees and preparing reports. The opposition Union Nationale party had a difficult time finding a qualified sociologist to conduct a single study. All the trained

[2] Only thirteen of every hundred senior federal posts are held by French Canadians. A Royal Commission survey in 1962 showed that of 163 civil servants receiving $14,000 a year or more, only six were French Canadians.

people had been signed up by the government, leading Daniel Johnson, the Union Nationale leader, to observe wryly: "Lesage is calling up the class of '59." Johnson advises young people to go in for academic work, since the future demands on them will be unlimited. In the Province of Quebec the "egghead" has come into his own.

A major point made by Jacques Parizeau is that it is up to French Canadians to work out their own destiny, and here is where the young planners—the civil servants and the professors—are important.

He contends:

> We've got to offer the opportunities ourselves. There's no other way. Even if English-Canadian or American companies open their boards to more French Canadians we can't wait for them to be brought along in training or competence, not at the prevailing speed of things. We can't wait ten years. The fight we've got with separatists is a fight we've got to win ourselves. If we can offer graduates interesting jobs they'll be too busy to be separatists.

The Parizeau approach, of course, does not gain the dramatic attention usually devoted to extremists. But it reflects fairly substantially the quiet and responsible sense of purpose of the new Establishment. Broadly, Parizeau sees the future in terms of education geared to modern society (that is, producing more engineers and fewer lawyers), inducement to industry through low-cost nationalized power, and help in financing through such agencies as the province's General Investment Corporation.

The General Investment Corporation is something in the order of a holding company, but with far wider and more nationalistic terms of reference. It was conceived by provincial planners with the prime objective of saving existing French-Canadian enterprises and encouraging new ones. Part of the initial capitalization was provided by the Quebec government but the major portion was subscribed by banks and credit unions: a partnership of private and public interests rather unusual in North America, though fairly common in Europe. The Corporation's director general, Gérard Filion, in his middle fifties, is a relatively old Venetian Prince. Lesage drafted him for the job because Filion, as a newspaper editor, kept writing about the degradingly small stake Quebecers had in their own future. Now Filion has seen the Corporation off to an encouraging start, with participation in enterprises ranging from a century-old foundry to a brand-new steel complex. The foundry, typical of the province's traditional family businesses, had reached the limit of its resources and was in danger of being sold to a United States firm. The Corporation bought a controlling interest, with the intention of stepping aside after proper expansion.

Quebec can count some three hundred furniture factories —on a statistical basis probably the greatest number on the continent. But most of them are small family concerns, totally uneconomic and in constant danger of collapse. One generation later than Ontario, Filion points out, Quebec now realizes that the small or medium-sized family enterprises no longer stand a chance in North America. "A large portion of industry," he tells audiences, "is still living in the nineteenth century; it will have to get used to living in the twentieth century and prepared to live in the twenty-first century." The Corporation promotes and finances amalgamations that remain French-Canadian and forestall English-Canadian or American takeovers. But it is also after big and fresh game—not only for the material profit but also for the psychological reward of feeling that French Canadians are capable of showing technical skills. For instance the Corporation drew the French auto companies, Renault and Peugeot, into a joint scheme for car assembly in Quebec. The companies risked little, since the Corporation put up the $3.5 million for a plant; but the boost to internal morale and prestige was of importance. So it was, too, when the

Corporation organized a new company to build a steel complex, valued at $225 million, with a blend of public and private financing. Some hard-headed analysts wondered if there would yet be sufficient demand for the output. But most conceded that it was one way to attract secondary industry, and almost all agreed there was something magical or mystical about steel as a status symbol for any people striving for greater industrial strength and self-assertion.[3]

Jean-Luc Pepin, who is a federal member of parliament, can appreciate the task of Quebec planners in introducing new ideas. His own grandfather provided an example of the old French-Canadian businessman's mentality. Pepin, now forty, recalls his boyhood in the rural center of Drummondville, where his grandfather was considered an "industrialist" because he owned a small carriage factory. "He had no idea of how to work out the price for his product based on cost of materials, overhead, and so on," recalls Jean-Luc. "He simply looked at catalogues from carriage factories in Ontario, and set his price accordingly." Jean-Luc Pepin, a black-haired, handsome individual with immense charm and Gallic wit, also is aware of the pertinence of old Quebec standards that go beyond industry into education, religion, and social values generally. "The flattering way of describing anyone in my town," he remembers, "was to say, 'He is the picture of a doctor.' Or a lawyer. Or a priest. No one

[3] While government-backed development was in progress, purely private investors were moving into Quebec at an unprecedented pace. In 1965, for example, General Motors of Canada built a $75 million plant near Montreal with an annual capacity of 100,000 cars. Other recent plants included Atlas Steel ($42 million); Bathurst Power and Paper ($40 million); Canadian Electrolytic ($18 million). Because part of Quebec's revolution is industrial, one should not be misled into thinking the province lives in a primitive, agrarian economy. Quebec is primarily a manufacturing province, ranking next to Ontario in the value of its output. It leads the country in the manufacture of clothing, boots and shoes, synthetic textiles, electrical equipment, railway rolling stock, tobacco products, chemicals and drugs. It is also first in pulp and paper, and processing of nonferrous metals. Montreal, with 4,500 industrial establishments, is Canada's principal manufacturing, financial, and transportation center.

ever said, 'The picture of a scientist.' The important people —and treated accordingly with great reverence—were Docteur Garon, le médecin, Maître Marier, the advocate, and Monsieur le Curé Melançon." Pepin's own instincts were considered virtually heretical. He was enrolled in a classical college that was run by priests who emphasized, typically, preparation for the priesthood or law or medicine; but he went on to a university and became a political scientist and later a professor. Looking back, he says there can be no real resentment against the clerical teachers at his college, because "those jailors were also our saviors"—a reminder of the salient point that after the British conquest the clergy remained as the sole literate cadres for the largely illiterate masses.

Pepin's generation, with its mild sense of indignation and rebellion against the established French-Canadian order, anticipated by several years the quiet but deep social revolution currently engulfing Quebec. Possibly the most significant of the moves of the Lesage government has been in the uprooting of education from its traditional ways. Until 1964, though taxation paid for it, public education was a misnomer. Protestants and Roman Catholics each had their own school systems, with total command over textbooks, courses, and methods of teacher-training. Catholic secondary schools, and many primary ones, were controlled by religious orders whose nuns or priests served as teachers. The only avenue for French-speaking Catholics going on to universities was by way of classical colleges, which also were directed by the Church. But in 1964 a new education bill was enacted, and for the first time in history the province had a Ministry of Education. Catholic orders still retained powers and influence in religious and moral training, but now this was a part only of a much broader spectrum. The notable change was that centralized direction and curriculums were at last in the hands of a government determined to introduce some modernity into Quebec life.

The province's first Education Minister, Paul Gérin-Lajoie, a forty-five-year-old former Rhodes scholar and a brilliant lawyer, set about to disprove the widespread notion that higher education was only for the élite. In contemplated reforms, Quebec's children will engage in a six-year elementary school program and a five-year secondary school course, to be followed by study on an entirely new level of education: two years in institutes that will supplant classical colleges and prepare young men and women realistically in the sciences and other advanced subjects for universities. The scheme, which draws on the best features of education in Europe and the United States, may take a decade before it is in full stride. However, since it calls for a profound overhaul of Quebec's entire educational structure—virtually wiping the old pedagogical slate clean and starting afresh—the province, once so backward, may find itself with one of the most advanced and realistic systems in the world. In the meanwhile the wind of change is indicated by simple figures. Less than a decade ago, the majority of French-Canadian pupils left school at the end of Grade VII; fewer than 10 per cent reached Grade XI. In 1964 most managed eleven years of school attendance. Equal to the expanded enrolment was the switch in emphasis. Classical colleges, getting into line with contemporary demands, were voluntarily offering a wider choice of science subjects as alternatives to the humanities. And French-language universities reported over a three-year period a 60 per cent increase in admissions in the faculties of science and engineering.

There were—inevitably—shocked protests from the Church that Quebec's twentieth century advance in education would lead only to moral and religious degeneration. For instance, one could hear from Father Théodore Roussel, aged fifty and of the relatively isolated town of Mont Joli, that teaching should be left solely to priests ("for they are the best qualified"), and that the reason education standards did deteriorate in Quebec was because parish priests ("some of them through laziness") left matters in the hands of lay members of local school boards. Father Roussel believes that local boards should continue to be made up of the venerable triumvirate: the priest, the advocate, the doctor. His thinking, however, is in stark contrast to that of another Oblate, Father Jacques Lazure, aged thirty-five, a Montrealer and a noted sociologist. Father Lazure flatly insists that education is a secular matter. He points out that in Quebec some 1,500 priests teach in classical colleges with an enrolment of 40,000—an average of one priest for every twenty-six students. He calls this "spiritual capitalism," for in parish work there is only one priest per 1,200 parishioners. This "unreasonable imbalance" in the distribution of priests he considers dangerous. "It gives rise to anticlericalism," he says. "Almost automatically the most disturbing increase in anticlericalism in recent years has been among those students coming from classical colleges. Priests should be doing pastoral work, or missionary work in South America—but not the other kind of education in which they're involved in Quebec."

Apart from differences in their backgrounds—one with small-town orientation, the other with the sophistication that comes from a cosmopolitan city—Father Lazure sees even the brief, fifteen-year span between himself and Father Roussel as meaningful. "The conflict between generations is not confined to the lay public," he says. "We feel it acutely in the Church—the clash between the 'young' and the 'old.' " Father Lazure classifies perhaps 10 per cent of priests as "progressive," and they are generally in their twenties and thirties. Those of the average age of forty-five are fairly settled in their ways, and neither for nor against change. In their fifties, and older, they show arch-conservatism.

The story is much the same as in Latin America, or even Spain, where one meets young and progressive priests who are as yet in the minority. Obviously—as Father Lazure puts it—the complete change will be felt when the young priests now coming out of seminaries have taken over. But even today the contest essentially is not between priest and priest; it is, rather, between priest and hierarchy. Mme Solange Chaput Rolland, the writer, points out that the expression commonly heard in English Canada is that Quebec is "priest ridden," when—she continues—it really should be described as "bishop ridden." This is a fair assessment, for the fiercest critics of Quebec's new education bill were the reactionary bishops of Trois Rivières, Sherbrooke, and Rimouski. However, one of the notable exceptions happened also to be the most important churchman in the province: Paul-Emile Cardinal Léger of Montreal, to whom can be traced a new tone of liberalism in church attitudes. Cardinal Léger, aged sixty, was not always identified as a liberal, but the undoubted transformation in his thinking in recent years reflects the stirrings that went on in Quebec even before the end of Duplessism. Mme Chaput Rolland long was condemned as "anticlerical," and pressure groups tried to keep her from appearing on *Radio Canada*. Jean-Luc Pepin, too, was labeled "anticlerical." In Europe both would have been known broadly as Christian Democrats. That is, they are faithful Catholics; their fight has been merely against the Church's medieval vestiges, such as its role in education.

Among the younger generation, many students today do not even bother to call themselves "anticlerical." They simply say: "We're just not religious." A prominent campus figure at the University of Montreal went so far as to argue that he had met only one "good" priest; the rest, he said, should be lined up and shot. But not many would echo this bloodthirsty line out of the Mexican Revolution. Impiety for some is due to their Marxist orientation, but for the majority it is only one part of the general rebellion against all established institutions. An awareness of this mood has created a refreshing candor among clerics ranging from Cardinal Léger down to obscure minor personalities. One of the most colorful individualists is a former backwoods teacher, Brother Jean-Paul Desbiens, who, at the age of thirty-three, became a celebrity as author of a book, *Les Insolences du Frère Untel* (*The Impertinences of Brother Anonymous*). The book, in 1960, attacked the backwardness of the Church and its domineering grasp on education, and sensitively related the restlessness of youth that would soon translate itself into separatism.

Frère Untel sold 120,000 copies in twenty-four editions, a record in Quebec publishing history. As a symptom of the era in which he wrote, Brother Desbiens was accused of indiscretion and sent by his Marist superiors to do penance at the Mother House in Rome, and later to continue theological studies in Switzerland. But again as a sign of the times, of the changes only a few years later, he was back in Quebec in 1964 as full-time advisor to Gérin-Lajoie, the Education Minister. Speaking out in public, he continued to warn that "youth has lost confidence in the adults" and that while "a few lean toward Marxism, many re-examine their religious positions." He did not automatically deplore the trend; he suggested that any "intellectual breakaway" was in many ways preferable to the "mental apathy" that was prevalent in the past.

The changes have been wide and diversified. In 1937 a motion picture, *The Life of Emile Zola,* was banned by the Quebec Board of Censors because Zola's works were on the Church's list of proscribed books. Distributors tried once more in 1941; this time, in rejecting it, the censors added that it contained revolutionary ideas and principles. Finally in 1964, though it had long been forgotten, it was submitted again as a test case, passing without deletion or comment. There are practically no restrictions today in Quebec film censorship. In other fields it is interesting to observe that a mere fifteen years ago, Gérard Pelletier, an ardent trade unionist, was damned as a dangerous "leftist" and "Communist" by the same newspaper, *La Presse,* of which he later became editor. Married women were placed, for legal purposes, in the same category as minors and idiots. They fell under the Napoleonic Code with its emphasis on the husband as the absolute family head, to whom the wife owed complete obedience in exchange for the protection he provided.[4] A married woman, for instance, could not undergo surgery or sign a lease or take any legal action without written permission from her husband. Modern emancipation began in 1964 when the Quebec legislature passed Bill 16 making women "first-class citizens" and marriage "a partnership." The quoted words are those of Mme Claire Kirkland-Casgrain, a vivacious, attractive brunette in her thirties, who practiced law for ten years before entering politics and becoming Quebec's first female cabinet minister. She relates that the only taunts she received in her battle for women's rights were good-natured ones, when opposition members in the Legislative Assembly asked if she had her husband's permission to present Bill 16.

Jean-Luc Pepin, who went into federal rather than provincial politics, is on a difficult footing. "I see nothing inconsistent with calling myself a French Canadian and a Canadian," he says. But to many of his compatriots in Quebec he is guilty of betrayal, of having "sold out to *les Anglais*." The trend in the last few years, as we have noted, has been for bright young men and women to stay in their own province and even to renounce posts in Ottawa in order to take up work with the Quebec government. Pepin has gone against the tide by tying his future with the wider sphere of Canada. As a member of parliament, he also served as parliamentary secretary to the Minister of Trade and Commerce and in 1965 was appointed to the cabinet. Pepin, in fact, is an outstanding parliamentarian, and, simultane-

---

[4] Though the Criminal Code of Canada, based on the British code, is the same for all provinces, Quebec retains for civil law the Napoleonic Code of France, which it adopted in 1866.

ously, one of the noblest interpreters of French Canada to English Canada. Yet among Quebec's student body almost as a whole, and among a large number of intellectuals and other adults, he is virtually *persona non grata*. Equally unacceptable are other French Canadians who have been elevated to the federal cabinet.

Not all Quebecers apply this scorn, of course, but enough of the celebrated people do to make Pepin suffer inner conflict. The credo says plainly that to perform a job for Quebec you must be in one place only: Quebec itself. It is tragic, for there can be no doubting the intense love Pepin has for his home province. He speaks with enormous and ecstatic pride of recent achievements: for instance, of the billion-dollar hydroelectric project on the Manicouagan River, where six thousand men are now at work in the wilderness on the biggest construction task in North America. When it is completed in 1968 or 1969 it will feature the highest multiple-arch dam in the world and give Quebec almost three times as much hydro power as Ontario. Pepin talks with as much infectious enthusiasm, and almost as much statistical knowledge, as René Lévesque, the driving force behind the Manicouagan project. He cites the accomplishment of French-Canadian engineers who developed a radically new high-tensile cable to carry the power five hundred miles to Montreal, a process now studied by engineers in other parts of the world. "Think of what this means," he says, his brown, flashing eyes aglow. "And all the time we told ourselves we were meant to be only doctors or lawyers or priests."

This pride is obvious, too, when he addresses English-language groups. Pepin shudders with every mention of possible secession. His view, as a practical moderate, is that the French-Canadian people can survive in a country of twenty million, but not alone in a continent of two hundred million. "Therefore," he tells English Canadians, "we French Canadians have even more of a vested interest in Canada than you have." But Pepin catches abuse from both sides. English Canadians cannot understand him when he says that Quebec must have a special status, that it is not "just another province," that the British North America Act—in spirit if not in fact—makes this point clear. And then, since he preaches "cooperative federalism," he is ridiculed by such French-Canadian nationalists as René Lévesque, who refers to Pepin's "new formula for French Canada disappearing without pain."

Pepin demands changes as much as the most fiery nationalist, but he is convinced they can come—and are coming—within the present federal-provincial apparatus. He warns that a complete rewriting of the B.N.A. Act, such as Lévesque insists upon, appears "at the present time not only impossible but dangerous." This is a realistic appraisal of how far English Canada would allow itself to go, and also an implicit expression of fear that Quebec, left too much on its own, might destroy itself.

Such talk does not win him popularity among the less objective French Canadians. Nor does he endear himself when he warns against "the cult"—the "excessive concern for the particularities of race, language, culture, nation and state." He says: "We French Canadians should not switch from a stupid inferiority complex to a stupid superiority complex; we should not let our shyness of yesterday be converted into pretentious arrogance. The value of our quiet revolution stems from the fact that it is a revolt against ourselves, against our past deficiencies, and especially a will to become competent, to achieve progress for the future." He also tells English Canada to stop holding so many well-intentioned but fatuous seminars on French Canada, and to start finding its own common denominator so that the English-French dialogue will have some reality. And this is the whole story in a way: the bewilderment of contemporary Quebec, as portrayed by one of its own sons. At one instant it looks inwardly, and at the next it snaps out, indiscriminately, at the rest of Canada. And those who attempt an assessment with moderation are often deprecated, both by their own people and by the people they are trying to reach.

The new "pretentious arrogance" of which Pepin speaks should be surveyed only in the light of the passivity to which he also alludes. Professor Gilles Auclair, an industrial psychologist at the University of Montreal, has directed some fascinating studies on how the French Canadian reacts to leadership and to responsibility. His point, as he explained it to me, was this: "The French Canadian has been successful in operating small firms, but he breaks down in large operations. Why?" Auclair, after ten years of work on the subject, does not claim to have the answers, but he can produce some specific illustrations of what he means. As a consultant for one of Canada's largest industrial complexes, he conducted a course for a score of key executives, four of whom were French Canadians, to show how people can become better managers and improve over-all staff relations by working as a team. The men were staying at a motel on the outskirts of Montreal, and at noon one day Auclair gave them a five-part problem to solve, saying the answers had to be ready by 2:45 P.M. Immediately—as he relates it— one of the French-speaking executives asked: "What about lunch?" Auclair replied: "That's up to you. You have a deadline. Do what you want about lunch." The four French Canadians drove up the highway to an elaborate restaurant and did not get back until two o'clock. They had time to answer only one of the five parts of the problem. The English-speaking executives snatched a sandwich at the motel and were at work in twenty minutes, managing to answer four fifths of the problem. One of the French-speaking men then said to Auclair: "Why didn't you tell us it would take so long, or that it was so important?"

Auclair says:

> Basically the French Canadian has to learn self-discipline. Up to now he has relied on the English Canadian for discipline—maybe because of a psychological result of the British conquest. At least that is what the historian or the sociologist says. But I'm not entirely sure. It may be too simple an answer. There *is* a difference between the Anglo-Saxon and the French approach, and I'm not prepared to concede that it is entirely due to the conquest or a minority feeling. Perhaps it's because of our Latin trait—a desire to talk and discuss, rather than to do.

His belief is that self-discipline must be developed before Quebec can really function on its own; at the same time he recognizes that French Canadians have always stopped short because of the excuse that the English, over them, made the decisions.

In contrast to this submissiveness—or as a delayed reaction against it—is the "arrogance" deplored by Jean-Luc Pepin. Perhaps "chauvinism" or "parochialism" or "pride" would be equally precise. Nevertheless, there is little doubt that imperious mannerisms are showing themselves. They range from small matters to potential racism. If "Anglo-Saxons" have been guilty in the past of insolence in ignoring the French language, so there are now many bilingual French Canadians who refuse to speak a word of English. This could be put down as a relatively unimportant bit of reprisal and petulance, but it illustrates the more serious trends. Mme Solange Chaput Rolland wrote in collaboration with an English-language author, Gwethalyn Graham, a book called *Dear Enemies*. It was presented, in the fashion of the day, as a dialogue: an exchange of letters between the two discussing the differences that divide French and English Canadians. *Dear Enemies* struck some shrewd observations and came to some useful conclusions about what could be done to pare the mutual ignorance. The book sold well in the English-language edition, was widely reviewed in English-language publications, and the authors were invited to make several personal and television appearances across the country.

By contrast, the book made hardly an impression in its French edition; not a major French-language periodical bothered to review it, and there was a solitary interview on French television. Why was it ignored? The question is particularly puzzling since Gwethalyn Graham, author of the highly successful novel *Earth and High Heaven,* is a sensitive participant in both the English and French cultures of Montreal and possesses as deep an understanding and appreciation of French Canada as one could hope to find in a non-French Canadian. One explanation is that French Canada, disgusted with being shunned in the past, simply did not want to hear anything English Canada had to say. It wanted English Canada to listen, but not to speak out. Thus, a so-called dialogue in reality was a monologue.

At its extreme, this inward-looking trait of the Quebec revolution becomes glaring at an R.I.N. convention when separatists heatedly debate whether future "Republic of Quebec" citizenship should be granted only to those of French-Canadian ancestry. Its immediate application, however, is more mundane. Until recently the National Film Board, the federal agency for the production of cinema and television documentaries, ran as a unit, with French and English producers drawing finances and technical teams from a common pool. But, at the insistence of French producers, this was broken down into distinctive French and English operations. French-language producers even gravitated to their own districts in the Film Board's main building in Montreal, causing eighty-six telephones, among other fixtures, to be rearranged. Such additional expense, they felt, was minor, since the Film Board—reflecting the belated national concern with the Quebec mood—was offering English staff members courses in French language, at government outlay and on government time. French-Canadian employees posted on the bulletin board a letter saying that since they had learned English on their own time, it would only be fair of management to offer them some sort of compensatory expense-paid course. They suggested lessons in ballet. It was one of the very few examples of humor in the whole of the English-French debate.[5] It was also, of course, whimsy based on bitterness. The National Film Board has a heavy concentration of separatists.

A sinister form of introversion is sometimes found among professional groups. An association of psychologists, most of whose members were French Canadians, planned a congress at which leading men in the field were to be invited to present papers. Some of the French-Canadian psychologists demanded that the main speakers be drawn from France and Quebec because they would speak in French. Language itself was not the factor, since almost all participants had done graduate work in English-Canadian or American universities. French for the sake of French was plainly the issue. Another member of the association, a European by birth and memory, was shocked. He stood up and said: "What is this—a scientific body or an echo from Nazi Germany? Are we to invite people because of their knowledge or because of their nationality?" He found himself threatened with ostracism unless he quieted down.

The noteworthy feature about the incident is that it demonstrated not only prejudice with racial overtones but a new affinity for France. For two centuries Quebec felt no particular fondness for the mother country. This was due only in part to a sense of having been abandoned in the 1700's. It was due also to an inferiority complex of the French Canadians and a superiority complex of Frenchmen. French

[5] Another of the rare cases of good humor was seen in the English-language satirical revue, *Spring Thaw,* originating in Toronto. In one of the skits an observer commented on French Canadians: "It's time they stopped thinking of themselves as second-class citizens and remember that *all* Canadians are second-class citizens."

Canadians, when not busy saying "les maudits Anglais" ("cursed English"), were saying "les maudits Français" ("cursed Frenchmen"). There was hardly a Frenchman alive who did not consider French Canadians as colonial boors. Even French-Canadian students in Paris were usually disillusioned by the indifference shown by the local people. At best they were treated, in the French manner, merely as strangers who happened to speak French—and at that a rather ancient and distorted brand of Norman French. But the more marked irritant came when intellectuals and artists from France visited Quebec and showed impatient contempt because of the lack of incisive culture. In return, Quebecers paid little attention to France during the long period when she was considered a waning power.

In recent years, however, and particularly in the 1960's, two developments have altered the picture. First, Charles de Gaulle spoke up—and acted—to express a grandeur not only for France but for all peoples who could boast of French heritage. Second, French Canadians, drawing away from English Canadians, needed to identify with someone, if only for the sake of morale and culture, and the logical connection was with other French-speaking peoples. Quebec's revolution, whether or not it leads to an independent state, has made many French Canadians feel like members of a newly emerged nation. There was satisfaction for them when a Paris publisher's representative arrived on a world mission to compile an anthology of poetry in the French language from such disparate places as Algeria and Quebec. He spoke incongruously, but glowingly, on a television program, *Aujourd'hui,* about the "freedom fighters" of Algeria and the "freedom fighters" of Quebec. There was even greater pleasure for Quebecers when de Gaulle received Jean Lesage in Paris with the ceremony usually reserved for the president of a country rather than the premier of a province or the governor of a state. De Gaulle sent over to Quebec his Minister of Culture, André Malraux, to remind French Canadians of their cultural ancestry and by implication to suggest its superiority over "Anglo-Saxon" culture—a notion not displeasing to Quebecers. It helps French Canadians also to gain confidence and a sense of importance when they know that Raymond Aron, France's most eminent commentator and analyst—with a stature and acumen at least as great as Walter Lippmann's—is talking about them. Aron said in a front-page article in *Le Figaro* that independence for Quebec was a distinct political possibility. Moreover, argued Aron, a separate Quebec—contrary to the belief of English Canadians—could be viable economically.

But after these items are recorded, it would be a mistake to exaggerate their significance, or to think of a secessionist Quebec as fitting into a grand design by de Gaulle to shock the United States and gain a foothold in North America. While French-Canadian nationalists draw comfort from the existence of France, there is no evidence that the interest on France's part has been other than of a minor, cultural nature. Even the economic side is undramatic. French businessmen have given no indication of desire to swarm into Quebec, a lamented fact that aroused a Quebec newspaper to comment: "Don't send us Malraux. Send us industry."

Intrinsically, therefore, the upheaval in Quebec remains a Canadian affair. Characteristically, too, it goes in such cycles that rigid forecasts are meaningless. In the spring of 1964 the atmosphere was so tense that some English-speaking Montrealers were quietly selling their homes and moving to other provinces. By the autumn, however, the immediate tone of violence had subsided to the extent that some dialogue was possible. The essentials remained unchanged: the revolution would go on, and English Canada would have to be prepared to make concessions. But among French Canadians a few of the realistic questions about separatism were being discussed more openly and honestly. For example, despite the opinion of such men as Raymond Aron, could a separate Quebec survive economically? Of the one hundred professors and other members of the faculty of social sciences at the University of Montreal, at least half were debating precisely that question. The early argument was that even at the risk of a decline in living standards, Quebec should be prepared to strike out on its own. This was gradually matched by other points of view: The decline might not be merely of a slightly sacrificial nature; it might be disastrous. In theory a Republic of Quebec could continue to ship newsprint and iron ore to the United States, and manufactured goods to Canada. But what would happen in the event of a boycott?

In another department of the university, the Institute of Public Law, the brilliant Professor Pierre-Elliott Trudeau speaks out and says that separatists talk blandly of a "viable" Quebec carrying on economically, as in the past, in a customs union or common market with Canada and the United States: "It doesn't occur to them for one minute that English Canada would be so hostile it would rather go barefoot than buy shoes in Quebec—or that Washington might not be at all sympathetic to a new country on its border." Trudeau—like Gérard Pelletier, with whom he co-founded the liberal review *Cité Libre* in 1949 to combat Duplessism—is frowned upon by many young students as an old man in his forties. His voice, always strong in intellectual circles of his generation, is hardly listened to by youth, especially when he condemns separatism as "a counterrevolution." That is, the true revolution of Quebec had begun even before the death of Duplessis and was showing itself in a decline in dogmatism of State and Church; moreover, there was a marked development not only in freedom of expression but in entry into the world of science and technology.

Now, Trudeau fears, separatists merely would return to another kind of dogmatism that would strike out all the recent and considerable advances. In this apprehension he has auspicious company. Father Clément Lockquell, professor of French literature at Laval University, says: "What prevents me from being a declared separatist is a fear of isolation, of being in a cultural ghetto. We have suffered a lot from provincialism. After the First World War, and especially after the Second World War, we were opened to the world. But under separatism we might narrow rather than widen our scope." Marcel Trudel, professor of history at Laval, has two points to make: first that under separation French-Canadian culture actually would suffer, instead of preserving itself for posterity, as extreme nationalists claim. Nothing, he feels, can stop the fact that French-language newspapers print translations of American comic strips or that French-Canadian youngsters eat the same breakfast cereals, with the same advertising slogans, as their English-Canadian or American counterparts. But at least now, under Confederation, French-Canadian culture is protected by the resources of a big country. A Republic of Quebec would, of course, have its own radio and television networks. But could they begin to match the facilities and riches of the Canadian Broadcasting Corporation and its *Radio Canada?*[6] A federally owned agency, in other words, provides a safeguard for the French-Canadian character. Professor Trudel's second point is even more compelling. He sees in his fellow French Canadians a chronic leaning toward authoritarianism. He says:

> French Canadians were partisans of Mussolini. If not exactly Fascists themselves, they had respect for a firm man, a despot. They respected also a Frenchman such as Pétain, and at home Duplessis, who ruled with a strong hand. If we have a separate state there is a great danger we will fall into a dictatorship. Confederation—with guarantees for civil liberties provided by Ottawa—is a corrective against the tendencies to which we French Canadians respond.

[6] Montreal is the fourth largest television production center in the world: after New York, Los Angeles, and London. Almost all the Montreal output is in French.

What kind of a dictatorship would there be? The obvious proclivity—to judge from the history cited by Trudel—would be toward fascism. But a new ingredient to the cause of separatism has been added: Marxism. And so there is some ground now for speculation that a leftist kind of authoritarianism is possible. The Marxism is reflected in the separatist magazine *Parti Pris,* which means "position taken" or "mind made up," and which has set out to do for this generation what *Cité Libre,* in a liberal way, did for the last. Jean Ethier-Blais, a literary critic for *Le Devoir,* in reviewing a book about radical activity elsewhere, drew an obvious allusion to *Parti Pris* editors when he wrote: "They believe in hatred because they have not been taught to believe in anything else. They know only the vocabulary of hatred." In conversation later, he added his personal view: "I don't want to be run by people who write for *Parti Pris.* If extremists took over in Quebec tomorrow, one of the things that would happen would be that our so-called masters would change. I prefer English rule, which at least allows free expression."

Men such as Trudel and Ethier-Blais have expressed their doubts about separatism for several years. Among moderates, however, they represent a very small minority. Most men have been inclined toward silence, leaving to the extremists almost an exclusive field of public attention. An example of this was made forceful during a hearing in Quebec City of the Royal Commission on Bilingualism and Biculturalism. The commission, one of the most vital in Canadian history, is charged with gathering information on French-English relations, and with seeing what measures might lead to their betterment. The task will not be complete until 1967, but meanwhile grievances and suggested remedies are presented by individuals and large organizations of a variety of opinions. In Quebec City, though, one viewpoint dominated: that of separatism. R.I.N. members, strategically scattered in the audience, kept interrupting the comments of the more reasonable citizens, eventually arousing the co-chairman, André Laurendeau, to order them to be quiet. Later, Laurendeau said that what disturbed him was not the fact that the R.I.N. had tried obstructionist tactics —since these could be expected of a group agitating for a cause—but the fact that the majority of people at the hearing were not separatists, and yet no one had made a move to counteract brazen rudeness and belligerence. The implicit worry was that the moderates would forever remain mute, and the separatists would win by default.

However, only a few months later the voices of moderation began to speak up a little more sharply, largely as an unexpected result of the visit of Queen Elizabeth to Quebec City. Many French Canadians were shocked to discover how a few hundred R.I.N. demonstrators could draw world publicity, much of it detrimental to the province and its legitimate ambitions. A "backlash" element included businessmen who were fearful that upsetting news would cause a withdrawal of foreign capital. But even more important were the wise and thoughtful words of intellectuals such as Claude Ryan, the editor-publisher of *Le Devoir,* who, having earlier dismissed separatism as no answer to Quebec's problems, now rejected also the theory of associate statehood as proposed by René Lévesque. *Le Devoir,* a paper of relatively small circulation but of great prestige, especially among intellectuals, reiterated its belief in Canada as a "political reality" and in the feasibility of finding "honest agreements" between the two main elements. There were also prominent and respected Church figures, of the stature of Cardinal Léger, who denounced extremism and warned that no one in French Canada could derive any real profit from hate and violence. Perhaps most typical was the altered approach of Abbé Louis O'Neill of Laval University. Only a year or so previously, when students asked Abbé O'Neill's opinion as a clergyman, about separatism, he replied that this was a political matter for every man to decide for himself, that religion was not involved. Now, asked the same question, he still said it was a political question each person would have to ponder by himself. Then he added: "My opposition to separatism is not on religious grounds but on moral grounds. I pose the question: Do separatists show respect for other people? Have they the right to commit violence? I say the answer is that they must show respect for people and not cause them to live in fear."

The most effective note of moderation came from the premier, Jean Lesage, whose concept of "cooperative federalism" was yielding results, with Quebec receiving part of what it sought in the way of provincial power, at a cost to Ottawa of some of its federal authority. Lesage, in his early fifties, handsomely urbane and flawlessly bilingual, once had confessed to me that he felt like "a man trying to walk a tightrope." He was obviously looking for sympathy when he said:

> You have to understand the delicate position I am in. In one moment I take into account the feelings of the mass of people of Quebec—that they should have in their hands a greater control of their economic and cultural lives. In the next moment I must be very careful that anything I say, or any gesture I make, should not be considered as encouragement for the extremists.

For a while, Lesage gave the impression almost of slipping from the rope. He appeared to be floundering within his own party and cabinet, losing ground to René Lévesque, whom many felt was a greater power than the premier himself. But what was not as obvious was that a tacit working arrangement existed between the two men, a mutual respect if not affinity. Lévesque carried for the provincial Liberal Party a youthful and intellectual following; Lesage, in turn, provided Lévesque with stability and backing in many of his favorite projects. By the time the Liberals had won a few provincial by-elections, and he had gained the trust of organizers within the party, Lesage was ready to strike out with remarkable boldness and self-confidence, a leader undoubtedly in command. He called separatists "retarded adolescents" and "beardless youths" who were damaging the province's great push forward. He spoke up enthusiastically in the aftermath of Queen Elizabeth's visit and quoted a sentence of a speech she had delivered as a reminder of the importance of the crown to French Canada: "The role of the monarchy is to guarantee the execution of the popular will." To Lesage, lawyer and statesman, this was almost as significant as the candid recognition by the Queen—speaking on behalf of the federal government—that "an agreement worked out one hundred years ago does not necessarily meet all the demands of the present."

But in altering the terms of Confederation, as he was plainly determined to do, Lesage saw a process of orderly progression, not one of violence or upheaval. This distinguished him, of course, from others who were impatient or dubious that basic changes would be made. Yet in essence, what Lesage has sought for Quebec is much the same as that demanded by Lévesque. Lesage has asked for "a genuine decentralization of powers, resources, and decision-making in our federal system." The main difference between his philosophy and that of Lévesque is one of degree that has still to be pinpointed. In theory, what every French Canadian would like is to see French Canada possess the same authority as all of English Canada. This objective is automatically rejected by English Canadians, many of whom think simply in terms of majority rule; others detect finer shades to the meaning of federalism which do not permit a return to conditions of a century ago.

The question remaining, really, is this: At what point would a man like Lesage be prepared to limit the target, and at what point would English Canada insist on drawing the line? Some decentralization of power began in 1965, when Quebec took advantage of a perfectly legal process known informally as "opting out." That is, it chose to administer on its own several programs, mainly in social welfare, which, for practical reasons, had fallen under federal control during the depression of the 1930's and the Second World War and in the recovery period that followed. Though English Canadians might prefer continued centralization—because it was neat and efficient, and because it gave greater strength to English Canada—there was nothing startling about a province desiring to take over moneys and responsibilities to which it was entitled under the B.N.A. Act. The central government, in addition to relinquishing managerial dominance over such fields as hospital insurance, student aid, and unemployment assistance, was also returning to the province a larger share of the income tax dollar.

In Quebec's case, the withdrawal from joint federal-provincial schemes, to make them purely provincial schemes, was largely for prestige and political and psychological reasons. For here were French Canadians who had been allowing "Anglo-Saxons" in Ottawa unnecessary leeway in matters in which "Anglo-Saxon" minds might not understand the special French-Canadian needs. There were also some solid financial reasons. For instance, Quebec chose to promote its own contributory retirement plan rather than enter a federal project to increase the existing old age pension program. In so doing it stood to amass within a few years a fund of between \$2 billion and \$4 billion, from which the earned income would run to hundreds of millions of dollars and be put to good use in the development of the province.

But how satisfying, in the long haul, would the "opting out" be to Quebecers? The English Canadian who asks, "Doesn't this give them all the financial and political control they want?" fails to take into account the factors that press French Canadians the most. These include the intangible, yet cardinal, search for what is described in Latin countries as *dignidad,* the need for self-assertion that can be fully satisfied only when French Canadians feel they no longer are regarded as a minority but instead are accepted as partners, the development of Quebec's economy to the point where French Canadians know they are masters of it, the assurance that French-Canadian culture will be permitted to survive in French-Canadian communities outside Quebec.

"If ever Confederation fails, it will not be because Quebec —the political voice of French Canada—has separated from it. It will be because the way to keep Quebec in it has not been found." Premier Lesage, in making this statement at a convocation of the University of Western Ontario, was saying two things: first, that he was apprehensive that English Canada might have limited patience, that hostility on its part would be fatal to a moderate Quebec government trying to attain French-Canadian objectives within "cooperative federalism"; second, that the onus was on English Canada to understand the Quebec mood, and therefore to accept the difficulties of coexistence.

Just how much sympathy and goodwill could be expected from English Canada? The answer, as we have noted, varies from one part of the country to the other. It also varies within the group, for there is no monolithic character to English Canada's reaction to Quebec, any more than French Canada speaks with unanimity about the methods of pursuing its goals. In every province there are men of calm and thoughtful disposition who strive for understanding; there are also men who snap out short, impatient, intolerant rebuttals to Quebec claims. But as one generality it is safe to say that English Canadians in Quebec, as a group, are more caught up in the French-Canadian mood, and more bending to it, than, say, Albertans. Obviously geography and propinquity are factors. Partly self-interest is involved, for a spirit of compromise—as much as any sense of benevolence—is dictated by the physical stake English Quebecers have in the province. Partly, too, it is due to osmosis, the natural process by which some of the French-Canadian thinking has permeated English-Canadian defense membranes. English-speaking Quebecers—particularly Montrealers—are therefore in the logical position of acting as interpreters of French Canada to English Canada. There is nothing organized about this role, of course. Some fill it on an informal basis during business or social trips. Others—for instance professors and editors—go off on lecture tours.

But to start with, what *is* the attitude of English Quebecers to the French-speaking majority in whose midst they live? While there is no doubt that they are more atune than other English Canadians with the Quebec case, this is still only in relative terms. Substantial antagonism exists. For an extreme but revealing example: In June 1964 the festival of Jean Baptiste, in honor of the French-Canadian patron saint, was given a special emphasis. St. Helen's Island, a city park connected to Montreal by bridge, was the locale for a massive open-air public dance, with a half dozen orchestras, a fireworks display, and other attractions. More than 125,000 people showed up. To deal with the crowd, police blocked the bridge to vehicular traffic, so there was a long walk back to transportation. Shortly after eleven P.M., a sudden and torrential rainfall sent a multitude in search of limited shelter and scampering across the bridge. With buses packed, drenched pedestrians stopped every passing car and asked for a lift. Three couples—the women with dresses soaked tightly to their skins—hailed a car driven by an English-Canadian who had been listening on the radio to a report of the washed-out spectacle. "Get some of your separatist friends to drive you," he shouted, driving off and leaving behind him hatred in six hearts.

In this school are men who say the trouble is that the conquerors of two centuries ago treated the French too gently, that they should have subjugated them totally. Or, they say, even under the generous conditions left by the

British, there would be no problem with the French if Duplessis were alive to keep them in line. Economics and livelihoods affect this thinking: a sudden realization that under separatism the English position of comparative wealth hardly would be tenable. Even without separatism, the old, automatic superiority is under challenge; at the very least the English Canadian in Quebec will have to learn to speak adequate French. Coupled with this change is condescension or "Anglo-Saxon" hauteur that never recedes far from the surface. For instance: Two newspaper strikes took place simultaneously. Typesetters, members of the International Typographical Union, walked out of *La Presse* in Montreal and out of the English-language papers in Toronto. *La Presse* shut down when editorial and other workers decided not to cross the picket lines. In Toronto, the papers carried on, put together by editors and stenographers. In a Montreal English-language printing shop, a staunch member of the I.T.U. who normally would have railed furiously against the Toronto "scabs" or "finks," said instead: "Look at the Frenchmen. They can't cope, they can't put out a paper. But in Toronto, people know how to manage."

Hugh MacLennan, in a profound novel two decades ago, called *Two Solitudes*, described the dilemma of two cultures in Quebec living side by side, each mistrusting the other and fearing it might be submerged. In today's Quebec the extremists, who do not bother to pause to accept mellow points of view of others, have a relatively easy time. The moderates, the go-betweens, have the difficult task. Laurier La-Pierre, a professor of history and a stimulating television personality, is a French-Canadian federalist who feels even more acutely than English Canadians every outrage or act of violence. During the epidemic of F.L.Q. mail box bombings in Westmount, he and his wife rented a second car so they would have two cars to use in chauffeuring the children of English-speaking friends to and from school. It was a gesture shared by many French Canadians trying to ease the terror of parents who brooded over the possibility of an unsuspecting child walking by a mail box as it exploded.

In the same spirit, and in an effort to promote moderation by deepening knowledge and understanding among English Canadians, McGill University inaugurated a French Canada Studies Program. It was promptly condemned by the chairman of the department of history at the University of Montreal, Michel Brunet. He called it an insult to French Canadians, comparable to a study by foreign researchers of "Laplanders" and other "natives." The French press, almost in a bloc, chastised Professor Brunet for his attitude and touchiness. The papers recognized that even if McGill, an important center for the English-Canadian Establishment, was showing a long overdue expression of interest, at least it was finally trying to do something, so why quibble?

Part of the difficulty is precisely the point that English Quebecers are paying belated attention to their French-Canadian neighbors and hoping that crash courses in basic French will make up for all the past indifference. But also to the point is the fact that not all English Quebecers are as vicious as the inhospitable car driver or as arrogant as the unpredictable printer. At the opposite, positive end of the line are such men as Eric Kierans, an alert, appealing, English-speaking Montrealer who is full of bounce and ideas. One of his ideas was that it was essential for English Quebecers to identify themselves with the new Quebec and its aspirations. And so in 1963, at the age of forty-nine, he left behind him a career as director of the School of Commerce at McGill, and latterly as president of the Montreal Stock Exchange, and started a fresh career: in politics. He became the province's Revenue Minister, a post that places him squarely in the midst of Quebec's drive to withdraw from many of the joint federal-provincial programs and to bring home again tax and fiscal powers.

But contracting out—Kierans insists—does not mean a desire to cut ties with the rest of Canada. Rather it means that no longer will all the responsibility and authority be confined to a central government remote from regional problems. "It is this tutelage of the 1940's and the 1950's that is outdated in Quebec and against which we are rebelling," Kierans explains. His liberal economic views are directly related to Quebec's insufficiencies. Kierans argues that where you have unemployment of 10 to 12 per cent—as in Quebec —you cannot wait for Adam Smith principles to take over. "The only way to solve the economic problems of Quebec is to think in big units," he says. "For example, if you need a steel mill, get it. And if you can't get it with private capital, then get it with government money." This talk of "state enterprise" induces some of his former English-speaking colleagues on the stock exchange to call Kierans a "traitor," or a "socialist," or a "Communist." Curiously, too, Kierans is afraid that one day French-speaking people may turn on him as a Trojan Horse sent by *"les Anglais."* But so far the results have been beneficial in letting French Canadians know that some English Canadians understand them and can act as effective liaison officers with the rest of the country.

Another of the English-speaking moderates with great insight into the entire field of English-French relations is George V. Ferguson, editor-in-chief of *The Montreal Star*. Ferguson, who spent the early part of his journalistic career in Western Canada, is in the distinctive position of knowing intimately the history and attitudes of early homesteaders and their descendants in such provinces as Manitoba, and at the same time of discerning the meaningful developments in Quebec over the past score of years. One of the redeeming features of the Quebec crisis is that the major newspapers in Montreal, both English and French, have shown responsibility and restraint in dealing with key issues. Ferguson warns English Canadians against taking the stand that French Canadians must fit into Canadian society on the settled, established terms of the majority. "This is a position quite untenable," he says. "It must be changed, at least to some substantial degree, for there are basic problems of dignity involved which we disregard only at our peril." Then he tells French Canadians: "It is not right for spokesmen in Quebec to remark that Quebec is worse off than any banana republic or that it writhes in torment. Let us maintain some balance and good sense." He rejects "associate statehood" as "disguised separatism" and condemns any device that would reduce the federal power to "a shadowy thing" involving rule by two nations, each with a voice and a veto. The bridge, the hope, he offers is this: "English Canada has not by any means been the best of partners. It has played its part in creating and maintaining the solitude of the French-Canadian people. Its ignorance of realities, its stubborn belief that, if it pretends there is no Quebec problem, that problem will go away—that is already changing. If the penitents' bench is not yet crowded, it will be in due course."

An impressive degree of responsible thinking is also in evidence among English-speaking university students. Brian Mulroney was one of the few English Canadians enrolled in law at Laval University. But such is his grasp of the nature of the Quebec revolt, and so sensitive his comprehension of youthful French-Canadian minds, that he was elected president of the university's law society. Mulroney, a member of the federal Conservative Party, is highly sophisticated politically. He says that whenever he hears separatism discussed by French Canadians of his age group —middle twenties—he reacts instinctively as an English Canadian and opposes it. But then, privately, if he imagines himself in the position of a young French Canadian, he can feel its appeal. Mulroney is convinced the only answer is for English Canadians to be yielding. "If we can do this for twenty-five years—give and lean backward—we can keep the country together," he believes. "Otherwise it will break apart."

Much the same position is taken by some of the students

at McGill University who feel a unique opportunity to act as honest brokers between English and French: a challenge, they claim, that Montreal adults have failed to meet adequately. David Goldenblatt recalls how, as editor of *The McGill Daily,* he was tempted on a particular occasion to write a sharp editorial rebuking French Canadians over an irksome stand they were taking. But he restrained himself, "because otherwise we would have had two sets of angry people. I say we shouldn't give away anything we feel we have the right to, but you'll never get any compromise if everyone is burned up at the same time. The idea is to keep calm." A survey on the McGill campus showed that 83 per cent of the students felt that French Canadians were justified to at least some degree in their demands for changes; 43 per cent thought they were either mostly or fully justified—a much higher proportion than obtained among older English Quebecers.

However, the elders undoubtedly are making gestures. In Montreal only a few years ago it was almost impossible to find in an English-language newspaper office a typewriter with a French keyboard. Now the same newspapers have gone to the trouble and expense of fitting not only typewriters but linotype machines with accents so that a man such as René Lévesque will appear in print fully clothed. Large corporations with purely Anglo-Saxon titles have scrambled to conform to the bilingual trend. The Royal Trust Company became also Compagnie Trust Royal. The Canadian Pacific, in constructing a new skyscraper hotel in Montreal, is calling it simply Le Château Champlain. Not many years ago, when the Canadian National built the Queen Elizabeth Hotel, there were angry comments from English Montrealers because it was christened also Hôtel Reine Elizabeth. Even Chinese fortune cookies have gone bilingual. At Bill Wong's restaurant one is informed in the first line, "Ne croyez pas les flatteurs," and in the second line, "Do not believe flatterers."

Now, too, when la Ville de Montréal requests the suburban City of Westmount to change the name of one of its streets, from Western Avenue to Boulevard de Maisonneuve, so it will be consistent in its length through both municipalities, there is not a moment's demur. Now, too, the Château Frontenac, a Canadian Pacific hotel in Quebec City, has taken away the bronze bust of Wolfe that dominated the entrance to the main bar, thus removing an irritant to some French-Canadian residents who did not want to be reminded of the British conquest every time they sought a quiet drink. The hotel got around to this act after extremists toppled a monument to Wolfe on the edge of the Plains of Abraham. In its own way the Château Frontenac then went extremist, posting staff notices in French only and printing even match folders in French only. This, in turn, aroused a cynical response from French Canadians who wondered why violence was required in the first place to awaken their English neighbors.

The awakening is real enough in some cases. The Bell Telephone Company for many years has had an enlightened policy of hiring and training more and more French-Canadian executives. The fact that it is in a vulnerable position— the target of nationalists such as René Lévesque—may be an incentive. Nonetheless, the company is genuinely opening on a wholesale scale posts formerly held by English Canadians only, in contrast to some firms that still refuse to hire even French-Canadian salesmen. Midway between the two extremities is Domtar, boasting a modest but significant program. Domtar, with head offices in Montreal, is among the industrial giants of Canada, with sales of $350 million annually in a half dozen main divisions, including chemicals, construction materials, and paper. Its senior level of executives is virtually all English-speaking. Of twelve hundred employees in the middle level of management—junior executives and plant supervisors earning between $8,000 and $20,000 a year—only fifty in 1964 were

French Canadians. But today the company is engaged in active surveying and testing to see how quickly French Canadians can be pushed into positions of greater authority. Domtar normally hires each year between thirty and forty graduates of engineering schools. In 1960 it took in two French Canadians. Now at least half of its new engineers are French Canadians, and the proportion would be higher if more were available. Other companies are in competition for the available crop, a situation familiar in the United States where major corporations have discovered the prudence of hiring Negroes for executive training. "We haven't a crash program," said a personnel officer at Domtar, "but we are moving at such a pace, in contrast with 1960, that it seems a crash program."

The Canadian National, whose president, Donald Gordon, was hanged in effigy in 1962 for claiming no French Canadian was qualified to be a vice president, now boasts two such vice presidents (of a total of eighteen). It has also, as a state-owned railway, installed in its passenger cars printed instructions in French as well as English (such as how to snap down your berth in a roomette). Air Canada (formerly Trans-Canada Airlines), also a state service, now compels all officers and stewardesses on flights leaving Montreal to be bilingual. Language courses have become *de rigueur,* especially for junior executives, in supermarket chains and department stores, as well as in industrial corporations. Some companies buy block contracts with language schools: thousands of hours of lessons which are handed out, bunches of lessons at a time, to interested employees. Others conduct classes in their own plants, or take advantage of courses offered by the Quebec government or the University of Montreal. Some of the statistics are impressive, at least on the surface. Domtar showed as many as one hundred and twenty in its office staff studying French, but that was out of a total of 10,000 English employees. The Canadian National had five hundred enrolled in courses at the height of its program; this declined to 350 a year later.

The irony is that as much as French Canadians talk of the need for English Quebecers to speak French, and as much even as the gesture is appreciated, language is not really the index. Rather more deeply French Canadians are searching for assurance that English Canadians *want* to understand them, *want* to know why they behave as they do. That this is more than a matter of spending six or eight hours a week in a language school—or that at least part of the responsibility for understanding lies also on French-Canadian shoulders—is borne out by a submission to the Royal Commission on Bilingualism and Biculturalism. Getting down to root simplicities, the brief, prepared by the Alumnae Society of McGill University, points out how even school textbooks contribute to the perpetuation of the "two solitudes." Distortion of history, in both camps, starts at the age of nine or ten, when even the fundamental facts of the end of the French era and the beginning of the British era are at variance. The text used by the elementary grades of English-language schools in Montreal describes the situation of Wolfe in 1759, just before the Battle of the Plains of Abraham, as hopeless. Wolfe was sick, he was waiting in vain for reinforcements, and winter was coming on. But he learned from his scouts that the French had neglected to guard carefully one cove. Moreover, the English history book observes, "The French had avoided battle, believing they were safe, because they had more men than the British, and plenty of supplies."

The version as read by children in Montreal's French-language schools: "By their spies the English knew of the French movements and their pass-word at the cove.... At daybreak, five thousand English soldiers stood ranged in battle-order. Four thousand French soldiers assembled in a great hurry to meet them ... a little company, badly armed, and out of breath."

6.

Ontario: Key to English Canada

ONTARIO, THE MOST populous of Canada's ten provinces, is also the richest—and, despite an intense British tradition, superficially the most Americanized. As though this seeming contradiction is not enough, Ontario is the most content to remain purely a part of Canada. Its people show far fewer doubts about the wisdom of Confederation than the people of Quebec or even the Atlantic Provinces or British Columbia. Public opinion polls indicate that not one in four desires political union with the United States, though the majority are dependent on industries that have their origins in the United States. If there is any trouble with Ontario today it is simply that it happens to be relatively untroubled. Having attained prosperity a number of years ago, it suffers none of the uncertain novelty of affluence that has come to the Prairie Provinces only in the last few years and is just beginning in the Atlantic Provinces. Moreover, Ontario, onetime stronghold of the Loyal Orange Order and its virulent anti-Catholicism, is now relatively the least embittered of the English-speaking regions of Canada toward Quebec and its agitation. The province, in brief, is a quiet study in paradox and self-confidence.

The first remarkable feature is that Ontario was settled originally by "defeated remnants from the south" (the words of Arthur R. M. Lower) or by "leftovers" (the description of another historian, Gerald M. Craig). While the largest group of United Empire Loyalists went by sea to Nova Scotia and New Brunswick, another branch came overland through New York to establish themselves alongside the lower St. Lawrence River and Lake Ontario, as far west as the Niagara peninsula. In contrast to the more aristocratic soldiers and civil servants who chose New Brunswick, the pioneers in Ontario were generally of a hardy and humble farm stock. Craig points out that an examination of early land titles reveals that of six thousand Loyalists who signed for homesteads, four thousand made their mark with an X. Moreover, many came not out of conviction but because they had chosen the wrong side during the Revolutionary War and were afraid of reprisals. "This is an image," says Craig, "that was forgotten in the efforts of the last century to enshrine them." But the functional result was that land was cleared, new communities developed quickly, and a stable society—Protestant, puritan, and practical— emerged. If Ontario did not remain quite so homogeneously "Loyalist" as New Brunswick, it was only because the province offered too many attractions to be left to six or seven thousand settlers and their descendants. Almost from the moment Upper Canada was formed in 1791, immigrants crowded in. At first they came simply from across the border, then in later years from Britain and Europe. Of the 2,180,-000 migrants to Canada since the end of the Second World War, more than half have taken up residence in Ontario.

What is the allurement? Ontario, though geographically smaller than Quebec, is so big it could swallow Texas and still have nearly 150,000 square miles left over. The twin cities of Fort William and Port Arthur, on Lake Superior, are closer to Winnipeg, Manitoba, than they are to Toronto: an interesting indication of dimension that also brings with it one of the very few instances of conflict within the province. Inhabitants of Fort William and Port Arthur sometimes talk like true Westerners in condemning "Eastern bankers" and complaining of the concentration of industry around Toronto. Once in a while someone even revives the notion of separatism for the "head of the lakes" district into its own province. But a practical streak prevails, for facts are facts. Great mineral wealth—nickel, copper, gold, uranium—contributes to the industrial importance of the province as a whole, and "Aurora" (the name already arrived at by secessionists) might come forth as a prouder but poorer place in which to dwell. On top of this, Ontario produces half the nation's manufactured goods, and even if the Toronto area does have most of the factories within its grasp, some of the benefits of income spread to the hinterland. The Toronto Stock Exchange trades a greater volume of shares than the New York Stock Exchange (mainly because of penny shares). Within a radius of one hundred miles lies about one third of Canada's purchasing power.

Toronto itself is a big mass of suburban complexes and subdivisions, with mile after mile of bungalows and housing projects—one of the biggest such conglomerations on the continent. Its boosters like to compare the city with Chicago or Los Angeles, quoting even the claim that Toronto has the third highest car registration per capita in the world: one for every three persons. The odd thing, to the outsider, is that Toronto, with chrome and tall buildings, *is* like Los Angeles or Chicago—or Des Moines, or Cleveland, or any one of a dozen other large cities of the United States. Physically it lacks distinction, to the extent that when a television soap opera, *Moment of Truth,* was filmed in Toronto for showing on the C.B.C. and on N.B.C., a press release proudly hailed it as a "typical American town." The irony is that Toronto not long ago was stiffly proud of its number of downtown churches (some of monstrous nineteenth-century architecture), righteous code of behavior, and semblances of Old England. Built on a bedrock of puritanism, it rejected bars and embraced blue laws, leaving itself open to such crude quips as, "I spent a week one Sunday in Toronto," or, "The best place in the world in which to die is Toronto, on a Sunday, when the change between the living and the dead is so slight as to be imperceptible." The remarks usually were made by Montrealers, brought up in a highly cosmopolitan atmosphere and with a sense of immense superiority.

Little more than a decade ago people in Toronto considered it exciting to drive to Buffalo, on the other side of Lake Ontario, for the week end. Harold Town, artist, says that working in Toronto made it harder to prove himself to his fellow Canadians—a peculiarity of the country that will be elaborated on in another chapter—but there were advantages, for distractions were at a minimum. "I felt no temptation to stop at sidewalk cafés," he recalls, "because there were none. Instead, there were just squalid surroundings and ugly buildings." Changes began in the early 1950's, when Toronto took on a kind of frontier spirit and growth that extended itself to the theatre and arts generally, and erupted with bustling liveliness particularly in the last three or four years. Town acknowledges that the "phenomenon" Toronto talks about—including the introduction of civilized restaurants and decent architecture—is not unique; it has happened to many cities in North America in the postwar era, and in Montreal's case has simply added quantitatively to the charm and sophistication that were already there. "It is just that no one expected it in Toronto," says Town, "and so the transformation came as a shock, especially to Old Torontonians."

The Old Torontonians, who thought their community safe from evil forces abroad, comprise a WASP Establishment that, going back far enough, can be broken broadly into two sections: an "upper class" tending to belong to the Church of England, and a "middle class" largely of

Methodist or Presbyterian ancestry. The stamp of puritanism can be traced to the middle class, and, though bars now flourish, and cinemas do a big business on Sunday, vestiges of extreme piety hang on. The drapes in T. Eaton's huge department store are still pulled tight to hide window displays on Sunday; and tobacco is never sold inside. But these tributes to a vanishing age only tend to emphasize the changes that have taken place. A mere generation ago, when a "typical" Torontonian talked about "loyalty," there was some doubt as to whether he meant obedience first to the United Kingdom or to Canada; for many, the patriotic identities were synonymous. Strong strands of sentiment and allegiance for Britain endure, of course, but often these fall into clichés. The stuffy private clubs frequented by Bay Street autocrats, the private schools that encourage the playing of cricket rather than baseball, exist more in caricature than in actuality.

One of the best indices of the alteration in the Toronto mentality is provided by the trend in federal elections. As recently as the 1950's, the city's industrialists and businessmen, mostly Conservative, regarded Liberals as akin almost to Marxists; certainly they were too Canadian. If a single date had to be selected to signify the closing of one door and the opening of another, it probably would be 1956 and the Suez crisis. Lester Pearson, the foreign minister at the time, condemned British action; and Tories accused Liberals of being treacherous in letting down the "mother country." This theme was partly invoked in the next year's general election, and the Liberals managed to win only one of the eighteen seats in the Toronto area; the rest went to the Conservatives. But by 1963 the Liberals took sixteen of the ridings, with the other two going to the New Democratic Party.

In the interim the "typical" Old Torontonian had been pushed aside by the "typical" New Torontonian. The new breed is not even necessarily a native of the city. Of the 1,900,000 inhabitants of Metropolitan Toronto, at least one quarter have moved in from other parts of Canada since the war, and an equal number have come from abroad. Thus, half the city is made up of nonnatives. Among the "new" Torontonians are about 150,000 Italians, 75,000 Germans, and between 50,000 and 60,000 each of Poles, Ukrainians, Hungarians, and French Canadians. It is doubtful if any city of comparable size on the continent has absorbed so many strangers in such a short time.

Toronto is not a romantic city; the setting for two of Morley Callaghan's most successful novels has been Montreal rather than his home town. But it is the television and publishing center of English Canada, and other Canadians sometimes find it glamorous. Europeans are likely to consider it cold and materialistic, and filled with American-type gadgets and frivolity. This aspect of Americanization is reflected in one small example. In Toronto itself, the Canadian Broadcasting Corporation attracts less than one quarter of the potential television audience; the majority watch Buffalo channels. Though the *Ed Sullivan Show* is carried locally, the curious fact is that the Buffalo station which also carries it gets a larger and more loyal Toronto following. "It feels realler, somehow," said one Torontonian, "when I pick it up in the States." Nevertheless—or perhaps because of the American example—Toronto offers its newcomers physical comfort and an almost unlimited variety of occupations and opportunities.

The most heartening change is due to the European influx; every third Torontonian is now a Roman Catholic, and this means that the old image, Anglo-Saxon and Protestant, in part United Empire Loyalist, in part Loyal Orange Society, is in fragments. Less than fifteen years ago Orange Lodge political workers spoke of getting out the "black votes" of Catholics and Jews. Anti-Semitism used to be an open characteristic of Toronto, but of the last three mayors, two have been Jewish.

Scarcely fifty miles from Toronto is the town of Orangeville. The name is deceptive, for this is not a rabid community of Orangemen. But it is Tory in politics, conservative in habit and sentiment, and representative of much of Ontario outside the big cities. Its people are concerned more with local prosperity than with issues that do not touch them directly or immediately. Their attitude toward French Canada and the United States is revealing, and is stated fairly typically by three men of different generations: a young editor, Charles E. Wadge; a middle-aged merchant, Gordon Martin; and an elderly dentist, Dr. H. G. Campbell. Orangeville, in agricultural country, has a population of 4,930, and this is of moment—because it is a declining population. Other rural centers, of course, cite the same disturbing experience when farming becomes highly mechanized and industry does not move in to absorb the unemployed hands; thus people are pushed into jobs in the cities.

Wadge, thirty-four years old and editor of the weekly *Orangeville Banner*, says that hardly anyone ever comments on Quebec. One of the few outside events that he can recall ever arousing reaction was the assassination of President Kennedy, when men and women wept openly on the streets. Otherwise, the town is absorbed in its own economic ups and downs. When a precast-concrete plant—employing fifty men—closed down, all of Orangeville was plunged into financial or spiritual depression. Later the pall lifted, for three new industries—one to make plastic bags, another electrical appliances, the third industrial fans—set up operations promising to hire a couple of hundred men. Stories about these developments filled the *Banner* for two full years, during which period not a single editorial about Quebec appeared. "Quebec is a bit unfair demanding attention," says Wadge. "Perhaps it's entitled to a better deal, but when it starts pushing so hard, we resent it." As for the United States, he rejects any notion that Canada would be better off with closer links, and he says he is "shocked" to read letters in the Toronto press urging union between the two countries. "Everyone here," he says, "is quite happy with the set-up as it is."

Gordon Martin, fifty-one years old, a past president of the local chapter of the Canadian Legion, and secretary-treasurer of the Merchant's Supply Company, says: "I certainly wouldn't entertain any idea of becoming a United States citizen. I'm conscious of one thing—and that is, there's a difference between a Canadian and an American." What is the difference? By way of an answer, Martin tells of an experience that he thinks truly reflects the contrasts in "outlook and living habits." As one of the organizers of a school hockey tournament, he escorted a group of Orangeville youngsters—twelve and thirteen years old—to play teams in West Berlin, New Jersey. The bus ride, of close to five hundred miles, was uneventful—except that Martin remembers vividly how at two stops for meals on the United States side of the border, the group were complimented for their decorum. In one instance, it was by the waitresses who served them; in the other by the manager of a restaurant. Later, the Orangeville boys were guests for the day at a West Berlin school, and—says Martin—"they couldn't get over the lack of discipline there." The principal of the West Berlin school was so impressed by the Canadians' behavior that he said to Martin: "You must have hand-picked them." That was the whole point, Martin avers: "They were just average boys from home. On the way down in the bus, for instance, they acted up, and I had to get them to tone down. But basically they were so much better behaved than the American kids that they stood out."

If Martin sounds as though he has a sense of exaltation, it is a fairly common defense mechanism in towns of Orangeville's nature. Martin also says he is "reasonably interested" in hearing about French Canada's problems but he refuses "to be pushed around." Dr. Campbell, in contrast, did not even wish to learn about Quebec's complaints. A remarkably spry man, still practicing dentistry at the age of eighty-six when I saw him, he recalled that his first contact with French Canadians was in the early 1900's when he played lacrosse in a league that included two Montreal teams: the English-speaking Montreal Amateur Athletic Association, and the French-speaking "Canadiens." He enjoyed playing the M.A.A.A., but hated playing "the peasoupers" because French-Canadian fans were so unruly "they threw beer bottles at us." From that time on, Dr. Campbell took the policy of not giving an inch. "All that the peasoupers want to do now," he said, "is break up Canada and turn us all into Americans."

In the earlier 1870's even the most enlightened journal of the day, *The Nation*, was outspoken against "the French" and harsh in its attitude towards Roman Catholicism.... A slight softening of this extremism may be present in its successors *The Bystander* and *The Week*.... While "the French" are still reprehensible, for being everything which an Englishman is not, yet on balance, they have a right to exist. Specific points about their society earn drastic criticism, such as the casual, even antagonistic attitude towards vaccination during the great Montreal smallpox outbreak in 1885.... Race, it would seem, was even more divisive than religion. If no casual gathering of Protestants was ever happy until its members, by various indirections, had ascertained whether there were Catholics present or not, still Catholics who spoke English, while they were misguided and unfortunate, were friends and neighbors... whereas no one could understand the "gibberish" the French talked: they were mostly away off there in Quebec by themselves, and no one was able to find out what they were up to. Luckily for the country, it was only now and again, at the moments of crisis ... that their existence was brought to the attention of the average man in English Canada, though it remained true that a large fraternal organization continued to devote itself to the task of keeping the flame of hatred alive and that many men of prominence belonged to it.

—Arthur R. M. Lower [1]

The fraternal society was The Loyal Orange Society (or Order), and possibly more than any other single institution it branded Ontario with a special characteristic that has begun to fade away tangibly only in the present generation. The Order, formed in Northern Ireland in the 1790's, took its name from William of Orange and was avowedly political in aim: to secure Protestant supremacy wherever possible. Semisecret in makeup, it spread its lodges to England and the British colonies, especially to Canada. Irish Protestant soldiers, who came to fight in the War of 1812, brought their hatred for Catholics with them, plus a tendency for Orange bluster and street battle against "papists" (so violent was the record in Ireland and England in the early 1800's that parliament was compelled several times to suppress the Order).

The Orange Society never caught on in the United States, since it was dedicated not only to Protestantism but to the British Crown. The Order in Ontario, however, quickly recruited English and Scottish colonists, so that by the middle of the nineteenth century it included a wide mixture of Presbyterians and Methodists. It also became a kind of Protestant Tammany Hall, with every young politician in Ontario, who aspired to success, seeking its support. Sir John A. Macdonald was an Orangeman in 1841, though he did not indulge in sloganeering ("Service to the Protestant Church, Canada, and the Empire"). In the Upper Canada legislature of 1857 no fewer than twenty of the sixty-five members were active Orangemen. A newspaper account at the time described the police force of Toronto as "one vast

[1] *Canadians in the Making.* Longmans, Green and Company. 1958.

Orange Lodge and the gaolor a present Grand Master." Much the same applied as recently as twenty years ago; to be even a civil servant in Toronto, or Ontario generally, was almost an admission of one's membership in a Loyal Orange Lodge.

Twenty years ago, too, there were massive Orange parades, with hundreds of thousands of people lining the streets, in honor of "The Glorious Twelfth." [2] There are still eighty lodges in Toronto alone, claiming a membership of 40,000 (compared with 50,000 in 1944), and parades continue to be held every 12th of July. But no more than a few thousand of the Orangemen participate, and fewer than a hundred thousand Torontonians bother to watch. A university professor recalled for me his mixed emotions when in 1964 he asked his sixteen-year-old nephew if he was going to see the parade the next day. "What parade?" said the youth, who, it turned out, had never even heard of the Loyal Orange Society. The professor, who said that in his own youth it was required of every Protestant Torontonian to witness this display of fealty to crown and religion, confessed: "I had a conflict within myself, wondering what was happening to the teaching of history in our schools. But at the same time I was pleased beyond measure that today's youngsters are not influenced by the pernicious Order."

Not all middle-aged people feel this way. There are many who deplore the diminished stature of the Orange Society at a juncture when the French-Canadian nationalist organization, the St. Jean Baptiste Society, is engaging in Montreal in bigger and better parades every year. Some refer to themselves openly and proudly as "WASPs," and say that this is just the moment—with growing communities of Ukrainians and Poles and Italians—for "ethnic" groups to

[2] July 12 celebrated the Battle of the Boyne, a seventeenth-century victory of King William's Protestants over the Catholic followers of King James II. "The Glorious Twelfth" in Toronto was a signal, even a generation ago, for Catholic parents to keep their children indoors and out of the reach of marauding bands of Protestant youths.

declare themselves. But one senses this is said with resignation, a reluctant recognition that WASPs, even in Toronto, are close to a minority status and certainly have lost their onetime political omnipotence. It was only in 1954 when Leslie H. Saunders, Past Grand Master of British America, Loyal Orange Society, was mayor of Toronto. Today, in the printing business, he is hardly a figure of importance, though he remains active in the Order, turning out tracts and writing a column for the weekly *Protestant Action*. The current manifesto of the Order proclaims: "Unswerving and untiring allegiance to the Mother Country and the British Connection; no grants of money from the public purse for sectarian purposes; no separate schools." Saunders adds his personal touch: "The R.C.'s and the Doukhobors [3] are the only people who cause dissension in this country." Saunders also talks, as Orangemen did a century and a half ago, of "a papal plot to spread Catholicism." But he brings in a contemporary note: "There are no Protestant countries that have turned Communist."

Anybody who bothers to look at the statistics is usually surprised to learn that there are almost as many French Canadians in Ontario (648,000) as there are English Canadians in Quebec (697,000). Thus the minority positions are almost precisely transposed—but with a significant difference. While English-speaking people in Quebec hardly are in danger of assimilation by French Canadians, the latter are rapidly losing their identity in Ontario. Of the 648,000 who say they are of French origin, only 425,000, according to the last official census, can speak French. In other words, about 35 per cent have lost the use of their mother tongue; in 1951 the figure stood at 32 per cent, and in 1941 it was a comparatively low 23 per cent. Projecting into the future, sociologists at the University of Ottawa estimate that in another generation 60 per cent will be absorbed into the

[3] A sect, of Russian peasant origin, that survives in Western Canada.

Ontario melting pot. This trend may be applauded by English Canadians, since it suggests a solution to the problem of English-French relations. But it is unacceptable to those who speak of retaining a distinctive bicultural character in Canada. Curiously, the unease is expressed most sharply by Quebecers. Franco-Ontarians themselves, for the most part, seem unperturbed; there is comparatively little organized pressure from them for rights greater than the ones they now possess.

These rights go back to 1841, when what are now the two central provinces were united for a brief period. Separate schools for the religious minorities were established on a *quid pro quo* basis: Roman Catholics had their own institutions in Upper Canada (Ontario), while Protestants had theirs in Lower Canada (Quebec). These arrangements continued under later terms of Confederation. Today in Ontario the French-speaking citizens are covered at the elementary school level; public funds provide for adequate facilities, though there is constant complaint that corporation taxes are unfairly held back. Except for a few individual communities, however, there are no provisions for publicly financed French high schools. French exists as a language course in the regular high schools, but Franco-Ontarians who desire full tuition for their children in their original tongue, send them to private schools. It is a contentious issue, with the Ontario government caught in the middle. The Orange Order and some Protestant church groups demand that the line be held where it is. The government agrees that full extension of the dual school system beyond the elementary level would be financially unfeasible: an argument that causes some bitterness among Franco-Ontarians, since, it is pointed out, the Protestant minority in Quebec enjoys a complete public school system.

Extremists in Quebec continually warn of retaliation one day against the English-speaking minority there unless Ontario matches Quebec's example. But any belligerent talk is confined to French-speaking Quebecers. "The Franco-Ontarian mentality," said a sociologist at the University of Ottawa, "is quite different. At the most there are only 10 per cent who really defend the cause of a continuing culture or are willing to agitate for it." One can even note a disdainful manner among Quebec students who are enrolled at the University of Ottawa. They speak of Franco-Ontarian students as "traitors" because of their moderate attitude toward English Canada. Franco-Ontarians find themselves in a quandary over the realization that while they may be raised in French environment at home, they must enter an English world of commerce and culture. One student commented: "Some of us brood about it, but my guess is that for nine out of ten there's no real conflict. We accept the fact that we live in an English world."

The antagonism from extremists in Quebec sometimes annoys the Franco-Ontarians for much the same reason it annoys, as we shall examine subsequently, French-speaking people in New Brunswick and in the West: Quebec presumes to speak for all of "French Canada." In North Bay, which has a large French population, a lawyer said: "For a hundred years we've been getting along without Quebec. Quebec never gave a damn about us. Why should we care about what Quebec says now?" The one thought that most concerns French-speaking Ontarians—again in common with those of New Brunswick or Manitoba—is that a separate Quebec would mean the end of such French-language media as government television and radio. Charles Bruyère, for thirty years a newspaperman in Ottawa, and more recently a public-relations officer, says of himself and many of his fellow French compatriots: "A Franco-Ontarian cannot be a separatist. Where would he go? Quebecers generally say, 'We're trying to save you.' Trying to save us from what? We don't want to be saved." He mentions this while deploring—but shrugging off as a sad fact of life—the speedy decline of the French-Canadian personality in Ontario's fast-developing affluent society.

One of the most interesting aspects of English-French relations was revealed when the Canadian Broadcasting Corporation announced that one of its two Toronto radio stations would be converted to French broadcasts in the autumn of 1964. The station, CJBC, had been maintained by the C.B.C. purely for local programing while its other station, CBL, carried national shows. The network argued quite logically that Toronto still would be served in English by an additional half dozen private stations featuring local news and programs; Torontonians also could pick up several stations in Buffalo and other nearby American centers. But for the 67,000 French Canadians who lived within CJBC's 100-mile radius, there was no broadcasting in their own language. This was not, obviously, a huge number—though, as the C.B.C. mentioned, it was "the largest group of Canadians, French or English, not now receiving national service in their mother tongue." Since a prime purpose of the C.B.C. was to help blend Canada's regional and racial groups into something resembling a nation, the introduction of a French station in Toronto was not out of order.

The CJBC episode provided in capsule form some of the problems that confront efforts to consolidate Confederation. First, there were outbursts of resentment and claims from Toronto's Italian and German communities, larger numerically than the French, that they should be provided with a special station before anyone else. The point overlooked, of course, was that neither Germans nor Italians were participants a century back to an arrangement that gave their language official status. A deep principle was involved; for the first time in the rather tense issue of French Canada vis-à-vis English Canada, English Canadians were being asked to give up something tangible in the interests of biculturalism and bilingualism. Politicians, on the local, provincial, and federal levels, took up the cry of the Italians and other ethnic groups, using it as an excuse to deplore righteously that "we are having French rammed down our throats." This was the most common expression, coupled—predictably —with the undertone that Roman Catholicism was on the march.

Writers of letters to newspapers urged that militant lobby groups—the Orange Society, the Independent Order of Daughters of the Empire, Sons of England, the Canadian Legion—join forces to prevent what one typical correspondent said was "a minority group depriving a majority of what was rightfully its own." One person threatened to retaliate by listening only to Buffalo stations: "My ancestors came to Canada 129 years ago and passed by Quebec to a land where there was a promise of freedom from state and church dictatorship. Please don't make us join the U.S.A. where we wouldn't be forced to listen to propaganda in French." The C.B.C. observed that in Quebec City, where the vast majority are French-speaking, a C.B.C.-affiliated station exists solely to serve the tiny group of English-speaking residents. "Yes," acknowledged a letter writer in the *Toronto Star*, "there is an English-language station in Quebec. Wolfe won it for us." A radio columnist reported that of one hundred and fifty letters about CJBC that crossed his desk in two weeks all but four were strongly opposed to the changeover.

This reaction induced the newspaper *Montréal-Matin* to conclude bitterly that "Toronto is as intransigent as twenty years ago, and closed to any cultural contribution unless it is within the Anglo-Saxon context." The heartening aspect, however, was that not all the response was antagonistic, that, in fact, the CJBC controversy brought out some of the best of Toronto's elements. "To be able to tune a radio station and hear beautifully spoken French at any time," one woman felt, "is a wonderful opportunity, as well as great fun, and I am sure others must feel as I do." The obvious comment, too, was that the C.B.C. move was in the proper spirit. "As an unwilling ex-Quebecer of English origins," wrote a worried Canadian, "I deplore the smug attitude of Ontarians to my former kindly neighbors of French descent." A number of intellectuals and liberals stepped forward firmly. Scott Young, a distinguished columnist for *The Globe and Mail,* regretted the "strong echo of nineteenth-century hoofbeats," and said that Toronto should have a French television outlet as well as a radio station—not only to improve the prospect of future unity but to give English-speaking Canadians a chance to improve what little French they might command. Young recounted an ironic riddle: What do you call a man who speaks three or more languages? Answer: Multilingual. What do you call a man who speaks two languages? Answer: Bilingual. What do you call a man who speaks only one language? Answer: an English Canadian.

Ron Haggart, of the *Toronto Star,* looked askance at one feature of alleged liberalism. He noted first how "white liberals" in the northern United States often were the greatest allies of the Negroes in their struggle for civil rights—so long as the issue was fought in Birmingham. But they shrank back in discomfort if the battle line crept farther north than Baltimore. Then, drawing a parallel, Haggart remarked:

> There is no doubt that a sizable portion of ordinary, decent people in Toronto believe that French Canadians have a catalogue of justifiable complaints. . . . They are all in favor of the French revolution, these decent people of Toronto, so long as the revolution is confined to Quebec. They had not realized that creating the reality of a French and English partnership in Canada would require some sacrifice in Toronto.

Listeners who complained they would virtually perish without the suddenly discovered high quality of the local coverage of CJBC won from Haggart the observation:

"These people are not, of course, defending CJBC; they are defending their own illusion that revolutions can be comfortable."

Actually, Haggart may have been too harsh. There were commentators of the type of Arnold Edinborough, editor of *Saturday Night,* who suggested that Quebec was Canada's greatest obstacle in its quest for unity and therefore the province's secession might be a good idea.[4] But there were also statements from other editors and opinion makers who showed a deep understanding of the nature of Canada, some of the very best thinking in the whole of the country, and a frame of mind certainly farther advanced and more reassuring than in the Atlantic Provinces, or the Prairies, or the West Coast. "Who are the separatists among us?" asked the *Toronto Star,* which then went on to give the provocative answer that in this context the separatists were not French Canadians but English Canadians "who cannot imagine that the French Canadians have any grievances worth discussing." The *Star* continued: "Our separatists most emphatically include those who have never really accepted the idea of a French-English partnership at all, who think that specifically French-Canadian rights ended (or should have ended) with the English conquest."

"It would have been impossible to say this fifteen years ago," observed Beland H. Honderich, editor-in-chief of the newspaper, in a reference to the old, explosive Orange sentiment. The *Star* in recent years has urged broader facilities for French-speaking students in Ontario, and also the wider

[4] Edinborough was joined in this negative plea by the Glengarry Historical Society, made up of descendants of the United Empire Loyalists, who, in a brief to the Royal Commission on Bilingualism and Biculturalism, said the interests of all Canadians would be served best if Quebec quit Confederation. A nickel miner in Sudbury, Ontario, also told Quebecers through the Royal Commission: "For God's sake, separate from us. I'll help you. I'll fight for you so that the rest of the country can build a nation without religious and racial segregation. If you push us too far, there are those of us who are prepared to start a movement to join the United States."

teaching of French in English-language schools. Partly because of the newspaper's campaign—and undoubtedly as a reflection of a new attitude by parents—for the first time in the history of Toronto's public schools French is now a regular part of the curriculum; it is being pushed, as well, in other parts of the province. That this development is not a "concession," but rather should be regarded as an appropriate effort to redress legitimate grievances, is a point made by Ramsay Cook, of the University of Toronto's history department. Cook, an articulate and knowledgeable interpreter of French Canada, told the Ontario Welfare Council: "It seems to me that we English Canadians will have great difficulty in answering those French Canadians who want to balkanize our country, either through separatism or some form of associate status, as long as we in effect balkanize ourselves—if we tell the French Canadian that he can only be a French Canadian if he lives in Quebec."

At the University of Toronto itself, students show an unusually high degree of interest in learning more, and understanding more, about French Canadians. There is empathy, and it reveals itself in small ways: the letterhead of the Students' Administrative Council carries in equal size type Conseil Administratif des Etudiants. Students have organized conferences on Quebec, and on one occasion marched —in a formation of three thousand—to demand more flexibility on the part of other provinces and the federal government in relations with French Canada. The student newspaper *The Varsity* has featured series of articles on Quebec, and even editorials written in French as a gesture of fraternity. Exchanges of students between the two provinces have also been successful. One Ontario undergraduate, fresh from a trip to Quebec, wrote:

It is time that we in Ontario moved closer to our French-speaking neighbors whose warmth and intelligence are an asset to Canada. The drift towards complete Americanization of our culture can only be stopped by more exposure to the language and ideas of our sister culture. The chance to develop a distinctive Canadian way of life should be exciting to anyone who sees Ontario and Canada sinking into an American-oriented cultural rut.

Obviously, some of the newly expressed interest in French Canada, on the part of older as well as younger people, comes from an instinctive awareness that it is Quebec's presence that makes Canada distinctive and offers a safety valve against complete Americanization. Regardless of the motive, the fresh and unprecedented statements in Ontario excited in Claude Ryan, of *Le Devoir,* the acknowledgment that "ounce for ounce, an Ontario man has a better insight into the Quebec point of view than any other Canadian." Ontario, in Ryan's accurate view, remains the "key force" in shaping English-Canadian attitudes toward French Canada. "To the extent that Ontario offers constructive leadership to English Canada, many apparently insoluble problems will be solved," he predicts.

The public statements by John P. Robarts about Quebec are friendly and sympathetic, though not so heavily loaded that he might be accused of "softness." He correctly assesses much of the Quebec restlessness as "a state of mind," and says that many problems must be solved within that province itself. Meanwhile, he also says: "I don't think there's much Ontario can do except be patient and thick-skinned." This in itself is a remarkable allowance for a premier of Ontario to utter aloud. Only a few years ago, Robarts' predecessor, Premier Leslie Frost, displayed so much antipathy for Quebec's Premier Maurice Duplessis that he refused to meet him in Quebec. By contrast, Robarts gets along well with his opposite number, Premier Lesage, and is warmly received in Quebec. A mere half generation ago, the kind of strains and bitterness that crept into Confederation in 1964 might have brought from Premier George Drew the suggestion that the federal government send troops into Quebec. Robarts, instead, invited Lesage to address the Ontario legislature. Lesage and a large Quebec delegation were met at the entrance of the Queen's Park parliament building in Toronto by a choir of Ontario civil servants singing "O Canada"—in French.

Robarts, aged forty-seven, is a ruggedly handsome man. He is big—slightly under six feet and weighing two hundred and ten pounds—and conservative enough in dress (charcoal suit, white handkerchief peeping discreetly from the breast pocket) to look as though he possesses all the proper credentials for membership in the Ontario Establishment. On the face of it, he does indeed seem a sturdy representative of Old Ontario. He grew up in London, Ontario, a most proper, English-oriented city, where his father was a bank manager. He played football for the University of Western Ontario, studied business administration, was a member of the Delta Upsilon fraternity, belonged to the London Hunt and Country Club, took law at Osgoode Hall, and had a solid practice until he gave it up to devote himself full time to politics in 1959. But here the stereotype ends. Apart from the fact that his age group was beginning to emerge from the Empire Loyalist and Orange grip, Robarts was favored by what he describes as "an enlightened Anglican upbringing, in a home with a live and let live atmosphere." And then, most important, he had five years of war at sea. "It was an experience you can't overrate," he says, "for war helps you develop an affection for people." Robarts started as an ordinary seaman, and earned a commission and a mention in dispatches; four of his five years were with the British in cruisers of the Royal Navy. He tells an almost typically Canadian story of one day hearing some British shipmates speak in a disparaging way about "those Yanks" in a United States warship tied up nearby. Robarts asked: "Have you ever met any Yanks?" The British admitted they had not. That night Robarts invited three Americans back to the wardroom for a meal; everyone, of course, got along well, and later his ship-mates thanked him for the simple lesson in human relations.

He extends the message today by talking of his affinity for French Canadians, whom he has always found colorful and exciting and stimulating. But the main point is that he understands Quebec, and says: "I just feel these people are trying to achieve in eight or ten years what we did in twenty-five years." The emphasis here is on industrial expansion. But having made this observation, Robarts then confesses he is sometimes discouraged, because while he preaches moderation and understanding to fellow Ontarians, he is undermined occasionally by René Lévesque. (The day of our conversation, Lévesque gave a speech that the Toronto *Telegram* reported with a massive headline: QUEBEC ULTIMATUM). "Remarks by Lévesque," said Robarts, "are like blotting paper. They achieve nothing positive but just serve to blot out goodwill, to stiffen the attitude of people in English Canada." One of the reasons he gets along so well with Lesage is that he feels the Quebec premier is a moderate who can keep Lévesque and extremists under control.

Robarts' conception of Quebec and its needs is based more on materialism than on the intangible or social side of the revolution, though, as already mentioned, he recognizes that a vague kind of dissatisfaction exists. In general, he says of the squabbling that sometimes disturbs Canada: "To me this is like a family. At some stage, one of your brothers or sisters throws a stone at you, but this doesn't alter your relationship. It's part of growing up." Equally, however, he deplores the lack of continuity or sense of history in the Canadian makeup, and confesses that even he feels embarrassed in expressing "Canadianism," since it is not supposed to be part of the Canadian nature to be flag-waving. He thinks that perhaps Canada could have learned more than creature comforts from the United States;

it could also have learned the meaning of nationalism and patriotic indoctrination.

On the question of the United States, Robarts testifies that "anti-Americanism is a luxury we cannot afford." Here simple statistics enter the reckoning: there are more United States branch plants and subsidiaries manufacturing in Ontario than in the rest of Canada combined, with such giants as General Motors, Ford, Chrysler, General Electric, Westinghouse contributing to a direct United States investment in the province of about $7 billion. "If you're anti-American in Ontario," reasons Robarts, "it has to be in abstract, not in individual terms." Ontario borders on a half dozen states, and Ontarians are in constant personal touch with Americans. Robarts does not fear economic expansionism by the United States. "This is an enormous place," he says. "You couldn't swallow up Ontario. It's too big. Furthermore, no one wants to." Then, inevitably, the conversation reverts to Quebec and the possible effects of separatism. Robarts deplores even contemplating such a possibility, and he refuses to dwell on it for long. However, he believes that Ontario could survive in an English Canada without Quebec, since secondary industries are developing at an enormous rate; on top of this, he predicts that virtually every head office in Montreal would move to Toronto. "The hard-headed men in Quebec realize this," he says. "That's why nothing will happen."

Robarts is well aware of the key position Ontario occupies in Confederation. The province supplies the federal government with at least half its revenue. By demanding a greater share of taxes, or by pulling out of major federal-provincial schemes, it could cause great upheaval to the whole system of central government. But the Ontario of 1965 is not the Ontario of 1935, when it was undergoing trade union and industrial growing pains and Premier Mitchell Hepburn made spectacular and vituperative attacks on federal authority. Contemporary Ontario enjoys the comfortable situation of a settled, secure middle-aged individual. In contrast, the Atlantic Provinces, representative of the have-nots, demand a greater share of the national kitty; and British Columbia—as we shall note later—resentfully says it is paying too much into the pool. Robarts acknowledges readily, and gratefully, that Ontario is in the strange and enviable circumstance of not soliciting anything or feeling trodden upon. Therefore, it is impossible to identify it by label— such as "restless"—that fits the big neighbor of Quebec. Robarts has not been happy about some of the developments in federal-provincial relations that appear to favor Quebec. And while he welcomes the industrial growth of Quebec, he stands back occasionally and wonders how Quebec's state-financed programs, such as steel-making, will affect the trade of Ontario; he warns Quebec against any business practices that might discriminate against Ontario goods. But these are vague and as yet unfelt problems. Of greater concern and immediacy is the question of how far provincialism can be permitted to expand in a federal system.

Robarts is fully conscious of the fact that Ontario in the next few years will provide much of the lead to English Canada's response to Quebec. Ontario, with a population one million greater than Quebec's—and a province richer and more powerful in every other area—is regarded instinctively as the natural one to keep a sharp watch on French Canada and to stand up to it if necessary. This, in turn, narrows down to the basic conflict of English Canada seeing itself growing and flourishing within the frame of a strong central government, while Quebec believes itself to have the diametrically opposite need of increasing its own authority.

One of the representative spokesmen for centralism is Charles Lynch, chief of the Southam News Service, and a widely followed Ottawa commentator, who says of the Quebecer: "If he's going to burst into the twentieth century and find it wanting, he's not going to reduce me to his level in terms of emotion or logic. I haven't any feelings of guilt about Quebec. On the contrary, I rejoice in Quebec's situation—the boom, the way the gap between wealth and poverty is closing, the way the language has been retained." Lynch expresses renewed astonishment, on each visit to Montreal, over the enormous changes: the new skyscrapers, the construction of a subway, the preparations for the World's Fair in 1967, plus the lavish restaurants and fine new hotels—and finds it not only the most exciting city in Canada but one of the most stimulating cities in the world. He does not feel that Quebec has been sinned against by English Canada or that the "conquest" was harsh. And what he demands foremost is robust centralism to allow the expansion of the country as a whole.

What Robarts has yet to resolve is just how far he must go to meet those English Canadians who accuse him of failure to snap back at Quebec. Any reluctance to cater to extremists within English Canada is impelled partly by his belief that Lesage will restrain his own impatient ones; but also Robarts has healthy visions of statesmanship, of showing always patience and understanding so the Quebec crisis will not grow into disorder. He says he wants to impart a sense of history, and he means it. When I had a long talk with him in his office at Queen's Park, an almost ceaseless ringing of the phone was stopped only after he instructed his principal secretary to handle all calls. But one call was allowed through. It had to do with Robarts' two children—his daughter Robin, aged eleven, and son Timothy, aged seven—who were coming to the legislature the next day to hear the speech from the throne by the lieutenant-governor opening the new session. Robarts had planned for them to be seated at the rear of the chamber, so they could slip away quietly after the main event. But this was not feasible, and now they would be in the front row, forced to stay through all the proceedings. "They'll be a bit restless perhaps after an hour's speech," said Robarts, "but I want them to be able to think back on this fifteen years from now, to develop a feeling for history."

Robarts has to be applauded, for his sensitive and intelligent approach to French Canada is of cardinal importance. But his problem really revolves around a matter of Canadian identity, of national character, of historical purpose: a challenge that has confounded statesmen since Confederation. The challenge has not yet produced homogeneity in English Canada, let alone unity between French and English Canada. "Toronto must be reckoned the capital of English-speaking Canada," wrote Mordecai Richler in Britain's *New Statesman:*

> The most serious WASP cultural failure, Toronto's true tragedy, may yet be the undoing of a country. It is that after ninety-seven years it has still failed to provide Canada with a mythology, an inbred sense of nationhood, so that when the French Canadians in Quebec say, emotionally, they *are* a nation and want to get on with it alone, all Toronto can muster by way of reply is a troubled and rational but uninspired plea—yes, yes possibly, but the business of government, the gross national product, the C.P.R. and the C.B.C., works better this way. Yes, it works. But so does I.B.M. Toronto will have to come up with a better reason for the country than that.

We hear again from the impious Mr. Richler in a later chapter.

7.

Blow-Me-Down, Canadian Yankees

CANADA'S YOUNGEST PROVINCE, Newfoundland, also claims distinction as Britain's oldest possession—a conflict in terms that might suggest some split loyalties. The quandary does occur, not so much because of sentiment toward Britain but because of the historic fact that Newfoundlanders managed to keep a distinctive identity for three or four centuries only to have themselves swallowed, in 1949, in the big and busy machine known as Canada. There is much material compensation—such social security benefits as children's allowances, or, as Newfoundlanders prefer to call them, "baby bonuses," and old age pensions. There is also the broader sense of assurance that a great white father sits in Ottawa and will not let islanders starve, as virtually they did in the 1930's when one out of four was on dole of six cents a day for food allowance.

But the more wistful types philosophize by saying material gain alone is not always enough, especially if it cannot compensate for a loss of "independence" or "dignity." Old-timers still use these words in referring to the price of a Confederation that many opposed: almost half, to be precise. Therefore, it is somewhat chastening for a "mainland" Canadian to be reminded that even today many Newfoundlanders regard "Canadians" as imperialists and carpetbaggers who ignore local sensitivities in the cold rush for the almighty dollar. The technical point that Ottawa puts great sums into Newfoundland is ignored. Canada, some old-timers would have you believe, has made a captive market of Newfoundland and its 488,000 inhabitants. Younger people are more realistic and appreciative, and—generally if they are under the age of twenty—even call themselves "Canadians." But on the whole Newfoundland presents an interesting case history that is new to Canadians, though an old and sad refrain for Americans: You cannot always win affection by plowing money into an underdeveloped area; the very least risk you run is to be accused of greedy intent.

The more perceptive Newfoundlanders add a note: Those mainland Canadians who ponder whether there should be union between Canada and the United States might stop to think what it would be like to have an alien flag fly overhead. This was the strange feeling Newfoundland suffered little more than fifteen years ago when the Red Ensign, serving as Canada's flag, went up over customs sheds and federal buildings. Proof that nostalgia for the past is part of Newfoundland's trauma came more recently when Joey Smallwood, the premier, said that no newfangled maple leaf flag ever would take precedence over the Union Jack or the Red Ensign, either of which at least contains a British symbol.

The irony here is that Smallwood is one of Canada's most devoted citizens. This, however, does not stop him from being Newfoundland's greatest promoter: a whiz-bang of a man, sixty-four years old and five feet five inches tall, who practically with single hand and single purpose brought Newfoundland into wedlock with the mainland. He also ran —and continues to run—the island almost single-handedly in the tradition of a benevolent lord of the manor. Newfoundland has always been operated this way: first as a private colony of various pseudo-governors sent from England, and in more modern times as a private trading post for a half dozen wealthy families. Smallwood at least gives something in return for his power: schools, roads, and the ever-important ingredient of security. He is idolized. "Our Joey" is a common expression among people of the outports who up to a few years ago were among the most isolated and primitive of North Americans.

Smallwood is not averse to drawing a little poetic license from their trust. In 1958, after John Diefenbaker had been Conservative prime minister of Canada for less than a year, a federal election was called. Smallwood took to his usual intimate tour of the outports to gather support for the fledgling Liberal chief, Lester Pearson, and throw denunciation on Diefenbaker. In one village he said to a weatherbeaten old fisherman: "Tom, I'm counting on you to vote for us again." Tom puckered his brow and replied slowly: "Well I dunno, Joey. Look at the rise Diefenbaker gave us in them old age pensions." Unperturbed, Smallwood said: "That wasn't Diefenbaker, Tom. That was the Queen who gave the rise." And calmly he pulled from his pocket a printed copy of the Act which began in standard language: "Her Majesty, by and with the advice and consent of the Senate and House of Commons of Canada, enacts as follows...."

Smallwood is a member of a distinctive breed, fiercely possessive on behalf of Newfoundland. He is, additionally, an energetic and natural-born publicist. His first job, after he quit school at the age of fifteen, was as a printer's apprentice and then as a newspaper reporter. He moved around, working for several years on papers in Halifax, Boston, New York, and London. He also showed an inclination toward trade unionism and politics, combining them by helping to arrange street rallies in New York for the American Labor Party. Then he returned home, to reorganize a local of the International Brotherhood of Pulp, Sulphite, and Paper Mill

Workers at Grand Falls, and to start a new one at Corner Brook.

What makes this part of the record noteworthy is that years later, as premier, Smallwood was faced with entry into Newfoundland of the International Woodworkers of America, who were attempting to organize the province's lumberjacks. The need to build up a stable force of permanent loggers, in a principal industry that had stumbled along with seasonal workers, was recognized by some of the island's own economists. The union's intention was to ensure stability, but this did not suit Smallwood's needs, and so he smashed it with police acting as strikebreakers. Such tactics shocked people on the mainland. But by and large Joey had the support of his islanders; among other things they accused mainlanders of not understanding Newfoundland's distinctive problems.

Joey's love for the island has never been doubted. It was plain to every Newfoundlander more than a quarter-century ago when he took to the radio as "the Barrelman," the name given to the lookout on a sealing boat. Joey was selling soap and other products handled by a St. John's merchant. Every night, for nearly seven years, he went on the air to tell people stories from their own bountiful supply of folk lore and adventures. For many of them, living in outports with no roads, their only physical communication with one another by sea, his was the voice of comfort and pride in Newfoundland's epics and achievements. There was the story, for instance, of two brothers who were seal-hunting on a remote strip of ice. They were tied together, for their own protection, by a length of rope. The ice cracked, and one tumbled into the sea, leaving the other standing on a fragment barely large enough to support him—and certainly not strong enough for two. The brother on the ice said: "One of us got to get ashore to look after the old man." The one in the freezing water answered: "I got no knife." The one on the ice said: "I got a knife." And so saying, he slashed the rope.

The paucity of words to tell a tragic and powerful tale is typical of Newfoundlanders, who, over the centuries, have learned of hardship almost as a routine course. Joey the Barrelman did not have to look far for material. The whole of the island's past and present was filled with conflict, either against Nature or against man. John Cabot discovered Newfoundland waters in 1497, and the island was destined to remain little more than a fishing camp for the next three hundred years. England decided that Newfoundland's importance lay in its role as a base for fishing fleets, and ruled out any notion of permanent settlement. It refused to provide it with a government or treat it as a colony, arranging instead for command by "fishing admirals." The captain of the first vessel to arrive in a harbor each spring became the local lord, "the fishing admiral," for the rest of the fishing season, dispensing justice in his own rough fashion. As a further discouragement against permanent colonization, the private ownership of property ashore was forbidden. Nevertheless, a few hardy fishermen-settlers put down roots. It was not until the eighteenth century that royal governors were appointed; but these were still attached to the sea, for they were naval officers with supplementary civil authority. And not until the early 1800's could a Newfoundlander call his house his own by procuring title to prove it.

The real breakthrough finally came in 1824 when the British parliament passed laws that gave Newfoundland the privileges of an official colony. Responsible government and eventually full dominion status followed in the next century. But the economic pattern—crude and harsh—already had been laid. A small number of people, most of them totally dependent on fishing, were scattered in 1,300 communities along a coastline of 6,000 miles, their backs to the land. The impassioned patriotism of Newfoundlanders reflects itself in the nomenclature they gave their villages and coves, many of the names incongruously out of keeping with the forbidding landscape to which they are attached. Heart's Delight and Happy Adventure were so called, not because of scenic beauty, but because they were the first points of land sighted by seamen weary after long Atlantic voyages. Other names illustrated the wry recognition of life as a hardship: Seldom-Come-By, Come-By-Chance, Maggoty Cove, Deadman's Bay, Blow-Me-Down.

Just about the time Smallwood was reaching these outports by radio they were undergoing their worst depression of all time. Newsprint mills had been in operation since 1908, and mines had brought some further diversification to the economy, but it was still precarious and reliant largely on fishing. The stock market crash in New York in 1929 had its echoes along the coast, and Misery Point was never more suitably named. Between 1929 and 1932 the value of fishery exports dropped from $16 million to $6 million. The island exhausted her credit. Between one quarter and one third of the population were on relief, the government having difficulty meeting even the six-cents-daily grant for food. Finally Newfoundland, in 1934, appealed to Britain; London agreed to change it from a dominion to a dependency, and assumed financial responsibilities and debts. For the next fifteen years the island was run by a six-man commission directed from London, an arrangement that made no one happy.

After the war Newfoundland was faced with a re-examination of its status. What form of government suited it? Continuation of British control? A dominion again? Union with Canada? A national convention was set up to explore the alternatives. Looking back now, one sound and cautious appraiser, Fred Scott, a St. John's radio producer of long experience, told me that if Newfoundlanders had been given a full choice, 85 per cent would have voted to join the United States. The other 15 per cent, he said, would have been swayed by "excessive flag sentiment" to declare for dominion status or some other form of British association. The lure of the United States, as we shall see later, was in part financial, for by now United States bases in Newfoundland had made a deep impact in the island's social and economic life.

But in 1946, when the convention opened, the thought of entry into the United States was not taken seriously. While, theoretically, there would have been no legal obstacle, no one even suggested sending a delegation to sound out Washington. It was inconceivable, Newfoundlanders told themselves, that Britain would let its oldest possession drift into American hands; nor could anyone really expect the United States to place its British ally in an embarrassing situation by encouraging such an idea. This, at least, is the way Newfoundlanders reasoned it out. Hardly a person even today asks the modest question whether the United States would have been interested in Newfoundland or its awesome economic burden. Bases were being held on a long lease anyway, so such military value as existed was already covered.

In any event, union with the United States was never an issue. The big battle was over Confederation with Canada, a move Newfoundlanders had stubbornly opposed for more than three quarters of a century. Joey Smallwood was convinced that Canada offered the best future. The Canadian government itself kept out of the affair, though it had made it known since 1943 it would give "sympathetic consideration" to any application from Newfoundland to join Canada. Canada's contemporary interest was inspired by strategic as well as psychological reasons. Newfoundland's admission to the family would truly complete the concept of one nation —"from sea to sea"—above the United States border. But Newfoundland also dominated the approaches to the St. Lawrence River and therefore Canada's heartland. It was, in the words of Newfoundlanders, "the stopper in the Canadian bottle." (Even more picturesquely, Winston Churchill called it "an orange in the mouth of a suckling pig.") However, Ottawa adopted a strict policy of noninterference in the Newfoundland debate, by now resolved to the alternative of responsible self-government or union with Canada. This seeming aloofness was dictated by an awareness that islanders felt deeply hostile to a Canadian identity.

Smallwood pulled it off virtually by himself, with the aid only of a simple, concrete argument, and a lusty, energetic stamina. His selling point was Canada's substantial social security program. He managed first by radio. The familiar voice of the onetime Barrelman assailed outport ears again, though now the product was Confederation rather than soap. Then Smallwood took to the outports in person, getting there mainly by float plane. "A plane," he said, "is the most spectacular form of campaigning. You circle a village and come down on the sea. The plane coasts in as people rush to the shore." It was indeed spectacular, especially since very few of the outport residents had ever seen even an automobile. Smallwood sometimes did not bother going ashore. Landing at Little Paradise, for instance, he would speak into a microphone, his head stuck out the open door, and loudspeakers on the wings would carry his words. "Soon," he recalled, "the plane would be surrounded with people sitting there silently in their drifting skiffs, elbows on arms, chins in cupped hands, listening." But often he would go ashore, to shake hands, to learn to call voters by first name, and to tell them as individuals that under union with Canada they would never again face the cheerless, moneyless days of the past.

In a national referendum, the vote for Confederation was only 78,323, but at least higher than 71,334 for responsible government. Canada's Prime Minister Mackenzie King called the decision "clear and beyond all possibility of misunderstanding." Opponents called it, almost as accurately, "a shotgun marriage." The formal event took place on March 31, 1949, making Newfoundland Canada's tenth province. It was not long before Smallwood was engaged in another campaign, this time in Newfoundland's first election to choose a provincial government. Smallwood's Liberal Party won, as it has won handily every election since then.

Through it all, Smallwood has never forgotten the personal contact and the confidential touch. Before the referendum, there were people who feared that a great big federal power would come along and take away their village property: a hangover into history when no private property could be owned. Smallwood convinced them this would not be so. After Confederation, when mail from Ottawa did arrive, bearing the first family allowance or pension checks, some people refused to open the envelopes; they looked suspiciously like tax assessments. Smallwood again provided the voice of reassurance, so that after a while, when outport folk could not figure out precisely what was the role of a central government or the meaning of federal-provincial relations, they would simply say: "If Joey is for it, it must be all right."

One does not have to travel as far afield as Little Paradise or Joe Batts Arm or Wild Cove to sense the allegiance Smallwood enjoys. Petty Harbour is just a few miles from St. John's, the relatively urbane capital of 90,000, but in reality it exists in another time and place. George Whitton, aged sixty-nine, is doyen of the sixty families of Petty Harbour, almost half of whom live in homes clustered around the Catholic church, the rest around the Anglican church. The frame houses are perched on austere hills that slope into jetties covered with cod split and drying. Whitton showed me the scars on his feet accumulated during fifty-eight seasons of hooks and knives. How did he treat these wounds? "Turpentine and a rag or two," he said in an accent not quite of Irish origin, or English, or Scottish, or anything, except a blend distinctively Newfoundland. Whitton still put in a day's work, but he planned soon to give his son, aged forty, his boat. "In December," he said, "I'll start gettin' my old age pension. Joey with his Confederation did all that." Then he went on: "If not for Joey, how many would be fishin' here now?"

By that he meant that fishing no longer is the number one industry in Newfoundland. In dollar value it comes after pulp and paper, and mining. Partly the decline is due to outmoded fishing and marketing methods, partly because of stiffer competition for foreign markets. But since Newfoundland suffers from chronic, heavy unemployment—up to 20 per cent of the labor force—men must be kept busy, and fishing still engages the most hands. Raymond Chafe of Petty Harbour is twenty-nine, and a year or so ago he bought his first boat. It cost $600, but he received a government rebate—or "bounty," as he called it—of $220, so that his outlay was only $380. This was part of Joey's technique of encouraging younger men to stay in the industry. The other inducement, of course, was unemployment insurance which would enable a man to work from June to November, the usual season, and earn about $1,000 and enough federal stamps to collect money for the rest of the year. ("Fishin' for stamps" is a common expression.) Chafe, however, does seasonal logging and speaks of putting his son through college one day, an attitude and ambition unheard of in Petty Harbour a few years ago.

Another great advocate of Confederation is Mrs. Hubert Noftall, who has five children ranging from the age of five to thirteen. Her husband, a construction worker, was laid off his job in St. John's. Rather than remain there—and pay $60 a month rent—they decided to move to Petty Harbour, Mrs. Noftall's home village, where rent is cheaper and where a cod big enough for a family meal can be bought for twenty-five cents. Between Noftall's unemployment insurance and the children's allowances, they collect $180 a month, more cash than many Newfoundlanders used to see in a year. Production of "baby bonuses," in a sense, has become a prime industry. Newfoundland's birth rate today is the highest in the country, leading one woman to comment of the men: "Before, they used to starve us to death. Now they breed us to death."

When the inevitable question is put to Smallwood— "What has Confederation meant to Newfoundland?"—he often replies: "It was the greatest blessing from God, next to life itself, ever conferred upon the people of Newfoundland." Or, as he explained it to me:

> The thundering great significance of Confederation for Newfoundland is that it ended forever our ancient, if honorable, isolation. We paddled our own canoe for nearly five centuries, but we landed on the rocks—bankrupt. Now the first profound feeling is that we cannot go down unless Canada goes down. And if Canada goes up, Newfoundland goes up. This gives us the psychological freedom to plan for the future, just as men plan ahead for themselves and their families.

Newfoundland must still rely heavily on federal financial assistance, but, as Smallwood often points out, it has changed more truly in the brief period since its union with Canada than in the preceding two hundred years. More than 3,000 miles of roads have been built or reconstructed to connect 500 outports—over one third of the total—giving them, at last, land contact with the capital. With the opening of hundreds of new schools, the provincial expenditure on school buses alone is greater than the government's pre-1949 budget for the whole of education. There is a sharp decline in infant mortality, and there are decreases of 90 to 95 per cent in deaths from diphtheria and tuberculosis. Newfoundland has still a long way to go to make up for its grave shortage of doctors and dentists.[1] But Smallwood has introduced an offer to pay the tuition and expenses for fifty

[1] Some coastal areas, dozens of communities strung loosely together, can claim no more than one doctor for every 15,000 inhabitants. The provincial average is one for every 1,600, the lowest in North America. Even this figure is misleading, since most practitioners stay near the relative comforts of St. John's or one or two other centers.

young Newfoundlanders who are accepted in medical schools in Canada, the United States, or Britain, each year for the next several years. In return, they will be expected to spend their first four years as doctors in outports assigned to them by the provincial health department.

Smallwood obviously is imaginative and daring. In 1952 he conceived the idea of developing some of the immense hydro power that abounds untapped in Newfoundland's Labrador, and shipping it to industrial markets as far away as New York. Such a scheme would involve capital on a huge scale. Since it also involved verve, Joey flew to Britain and enlisted the moral support of another bold individual, Winston Churchill, who was especially intrigued by the notion of exporting power from the sub-Arctic. The Churchill meeting led to an introduction to the London banking house of N. M. Rothschild & Sons. The Rothschilds agreed to promote and raise finances for the British Newfoundland Corporation, more familiarly known as Brinco, and soon a half dozen of the world's largest corporations—among them Bowaters, English Electric, and Anglo-American Corporation of South Africa—were part of the consortium. By the time the Churchill River (formerly Hamilton River) project is completed, hundreds of millions of dollars will have been spent in Joey's Labrador.

In 1949, the Smallwoods, including three children, shared a cramped five-room apartment in a frame building in an unpretentious district of St. John's. Now the Smallwoods boast the Russwood Ranch, an expanse of six hundred acres, fifty miles from St. John's, on which Joey and his two sons raise chickens and cattle. The elaborate Smallwood bungalow lies between two private lakes and alongside a handsome swimming pool. An opposition member asked in the House of Assembly in 1961 how it was that Smallwood had been able to convert a twelve-year income of $180,000 as premier into "an estate valued at half a million dollars." Joey was on a vacation at the time, and the acting premier,

Attorney General L. R. Curtis, rose to decry what he called "a vicious personal attack on the premier." Curtis explained that Smallwood had built Russwood Ranch—worth at the most, he said, $100,000—with every cent he owned "to show his faith in the farming industry of Newfoundland." Moreover, the premier was heavily in debt and repaying loans out of the income from the sale of eggs: in the previous year almost a dozen eggs "for every man, woman, and child in Newfoundland." Curtis added: "It is a pity that a man cannot try to build a great farming industry without being attacked."

There was a point here, for one of Newfoundland's serious deficiencies is in agriculture; 90 per cent of the food that is marketed has to be brought in from the mainland. Partly this is because the island lacks experienced farmers, but mainly it is because the soil, with large patches of bog and rock, is nonproductive. The British, some of the more objective economists say, showed sense when they prevented pure colonization in the early days. Newfoundland is a difficult place for man to sustain himself. Its principal dollar earners, forestry and mining, become smaller and smaller employers with an increase in mechanization.[2] There has been a pickup in the construction industry—highways, federal buildings, hospitals, and schools—but Newfoundland retains the lowest standard of living in Canada and the highest rate of unemployment in North America. Fundamentally, to maintain itself at a general Canadian level, it should not attempt to support more than one third of its present population, an observation that rarely is expressed in public by economists or visitors because of the intense Newfoundland pride.

Albert Perlin, who combines the running of a large family dry goods business with the writing of scholarly editorials for *The Daily News*, the St. John's morning paper, is just as fervent a son of Newfoundland as Smallwood, though far

[2] In 1955, 17,000 men were engaged in logging; in 1965, 8,000 men, using power equipment, did the same job.

from convinced of the value of Confederation. "We haven't seen a sympathetic gleam in the mainland eye since Confederation," he says. By this he means that a combination of carpetbaggers and politicians have let Newfoundland down. "Having come into Confederation, and not knowing Canada," he comments, "we nevertheless had a concept of Canada as a nation with single purpose." Perlin attended his first federal-provincial conference in 1957 and was "shocked" to discover "the degree of balkanization" that was evident. One premier after another stood up to demand a greater share of the national wealth, while Ontario and Quebec wanted decentralization to avoid the price of carrying the poorer provinces. In this context he argues that the rest of Canada made a "captive market" of Newfoundland, which, until Confederation, was free to trade with any nation that suited it.

It is in this area, too, that the mainland visitor in return receives a shock, for if the province of Newfoundland does indeed buy about twice as much from central Canada as it did before Confederation, it receives value for money. On the other hand, the antimainlanders do not recognize the hard economics of the fact that Newfoundland gets back from the federal government at least two and a half dollars for every dollar it pays into the kitty. This pricks a delicate spot, for Newfoundlanders, like poor relations, are immensely sensitive to any inference that a rich uncle is supporting them. It is a phenomenon all too familiar to Americans who have learned the contradictions of dealing with nations not so well endowed.

The Newfoundland touchiness is even more acute than in instances of countries receiving straight nation-to-nation aid, for islanders suffer from a lingering inner conflict over having joined Canada in the first place. While the majority recognize the material advantage of Confederation, essentially what they would wish is the security plus their old distinct nationality as Newfoundlanders. Very few people over the age of twenty call themselves Canadians. Sentiment, parochialism, and patriotism die hard, especially in a people who have fought a heavy battle for centuries to survive on a barren island that became of interest to North America only when it took on some strategic value, a value that later declined with the start of the missile era.

Another generation probably will elapse before the inner conflict resolves itself, but already there are signs that youth brought up since Confederation has a broader identity. At Memorial University, in St. John's, I met Chesley Chard, sixteen years of age, who said he experienced a great thrill a while ago when he left the island for the first time, to visit Nova Scotia, and realized the potential scope of being Canadian. "Nowadays," he said, "people have to keep together. It's old-fashioned to remain apart." How, I asked him, did he think Newfoundland would have made out without Confederation? "We'd be back in the Dark Ages," he said. Chard, who is studying for a degree in education, received a provincial grant of $600 to cover part of the cost. In exchange, he promises to spend two years teaching on the island. Later he intends to move to Toronto. "After all," he says, with obvious pleasure, "I'm a Canadian. I can go anywhere in Canada."

But the young enthusiasm of such people as Chesley Chard is still uncommon. Many islanders find "mainlanders" arrogant or indifferent to Newfoundland's problems. Albert Perlin says bluntly he prefers Americans to Canadians. Perlin, speaking now as a businessman—representative of the old clique that once controlled much of the island—said that when he was free to trade with Americans, under Newfoundland's own tariff arrangements, he found them friendly and helpful no matter how minor the orders. He bought textiles in New York from a firm that did an annual business of $50 million. "We were insignificant," he recollected, "yet they treated us always with warmth and courtesy." After Confederation, nothing irritated him more than the remarks he heard in Toronto or Montreal: "We're glad to have you with us, glad to be of help." Such "condescension" he considered an insult to Newfoundland's dignity. Then his Canadian suppliers—"once they realized Newfoundland was securely behind Canada's tariff walls"—became indifferent and slow in delivery.

Perlin has vested business interests, one may argue, that prejudice his views of Canada. But in fact a great many Newfoundlanders show more kinship with the United States than with the Canadian mainland. Joey Smallwood himself points to the traditional gravitation southward that has made Boston "Newfoundland's biggest city." There are no "Yankee Go Home" signs in Newfoundland. On the contrary, when the United States announced it was closing its Fort Pepperrell base in St. John's, protest marches were held through the streets of the capital, demanding that the Americans stay on. Economics, of course, lay at the root, because it meant a substantial financial loss to have the base close down. But the affection went deep into time. "There has always been a great reservoir of good will toward the United States," said Michael Harrington, editor of *The Evening Telegram* of St. John's. His own family record provides something of an example. Harrington's father was one of fourteen children, of whom all but three emigrated to the Boston area. During the Second World War, Harrington counted eleven first cousins in the United States armed forces, but not one on his father's side in the Newfoundland forces.

The family relationship which almost every Newfoundlander can trace in the United States made way for a poignant situation in 1941, when the first United States servicemen landed on the island to set up American bases. The British had agreed to exchange bases in the Caribbean for desperately needed destroyers; Churchill threw Newfoundland in gratuitously under a ninety-nine-year lease. The Americans established four sites, and thousands of Newfoundlanders found themselves employed on a regular footing for the first time in a decade. For many who had lived on a barter economy in outports, where merchants accepted fish catches in payment for supplies and food, it was the first time they had ever seen cash in any quantity. Smallwood estimates that during the war years the United States spent a billion dollars in the island. Americans also took home with them some 30,000 Newfoundland brides. Three of the original bases remain. At Goose Bay, Labrador, an air station is operated jointly with the R.C.A.F.; in Argentia, on Avalon Peninsula, a naval air station is used mainly in the radar defense network of the continent; at Stephenville, on the West Coast of the island, Harmon field serves the United States Strategic Air Command. These three bases, Smallwood figures, still bring in about $20 million a year, making defense Newfoundland's fourth largest industry (after forestry, mining, and fishing).

At no time has Newfoundland ever opposed the presence of the bases. However, in 1949, when Newfoundland became a province, some Canadians took note of the ironic fact that Canada—after many generations of guarding jealously its soil against American incursions—finally was confronted with a *fait accompli*. But under the circumstances the objections were half-hearted. Canada accepted the responsibility of the original agreement signed by Britain, the lease for the bases having another ninety years to run. In turn, when Washington decided to close down its Pepperrell base, it assumed automatically that the valuable property should go to the federal government. But, as one of the State Department men assigned to the technicalities informed me, "We had never run into anything quite like this before. It took us two and a half years to give away $70 million worth of buildings." What happened was that Joey Smallwood simply said this was not a federal affair, but purely Newfoundland's own concern, and that every nut and bolt the United States was giving away belonged to Newfoundland. Ottawa said the base hospital could go to the province, for the benefit of civilians, but the military installations should be federal since logically they would be used by the Canadian navy, the army, and the R.C.M.P. Smallwood remained adamant. The case went to the Supreme Court, but eventually was settled out of court much along the lines of the original federal proposal.

The relations between United States servicemen and Newfoundlanders remain amicable and profitable. At Stephenville a few hundred fishermen once struggled for survival barely inside a monetary economy. Now the Harmon base is big business, employing 1,300 Newfoundlanders with an annual payroll of nearly $5,000,000. Another estimated $5,000,000 from the payrolls of the 4,700 servicemen and their families finds its way into the community. The 8,000 residents of Stephenville, with no other industry, are totally dependent on Harmon, which is a refueling stage for the big bombers. Since the manned bombers are due for retirement soon, the big question I heard among the local inhabitants was: What fate will befall the base? Will Harmon, like Pepperrell, be "phased out"? Meanwhile, the tranquil setting of Newfoundland appeals to many of the Americans. There is hunting and fishing, the people are friendly, and there is liberal application of a word Newfoundland uniquely and succinctly has given to mankind: "screech." At one time this was the name of a potent home-brewed rum, but it continues in use even now that Newfoundlanders can afford to buy the more palatable liquor from Jamaica.

Another attraction for servicemen is that Newfoundland is classed as a foreign post, with attendant living allowances and pay benefits. Yet it is easily accessible, connected to the rest of North America by commercial airlines and a car ferry. Many servicemen and their families go on home leave by driving the 108 miles to Port-aux-Basques and then taking the six-hour boat trip to North Sydney, Nova Scotia.

As one U.S.A.F. officer pointed out, "This is the only over-seas air force base in the world you can get to by car."

Before Newfoundland entered Confederation, Canada's three most easterly provinces, Nova Scotia, New Brunswick, and Prince Edward Island, were known as the Maritime Provinces. Smallwood claims credit for the fresh identification to embrace not only neighboring Newfoundland but a new spirit. "I coined the phrase 'Atlantic Provinces,'" he told me, "because I declined to be part of the Maritime Provinces with their whining history of complaint. They don't whine any more, but they did at the time we were going into Confederation. It has always been our philosophy in Newfoundland not to whine." One can quibble with Smallwood's natural predilection for Newfoundland nobility, when in fact the islanders sometimes sound irritatingly greedy to mainland Canadians. But perhaps this is only because Newfoundland has had relatively few years to get used to its new family setup and is still blunt in its language. Maritimers took almost a century to learn subtlety in complaining about "Upper Canada"[3] gouging and neglecting them.

Smallwood, in any event, is perfectly accurate in describing the altered mood of the other Atlantic Provinces. Only rarely does one hear now the lament: "We of the Maritimes rocked the cradle of Confederation, but, sad to relate, when Canada grew up it forgot those who gave it birth." Instead, there is a fresh air of assurance and expectation that the old Maritimes are at the start of an era of industrialization and prosperity, the like of which has not been seen since the opulent days of sailing vessels. What makes the mood particularly fascinating is that it comes at a time of dramatic developments in Quebec and talk

[3] Maritimers use the term imprecisely. Historically speaking, Upper Canada means Ontario, while Lower Canada is Quebec. But Maritimers prefer to combine both simply into "Upper Canada" in a symbolic sense.

of secession. Maritimers ask themselves obvious and crucial questions: Would the region be able to survive in union with the rest of Canada if an alien Quebec stood in between? Or would it turn its eyes, as it has in the past, toward the United States? The fact that the questions even arise, at a juncture when Maritimers feel they should be enjoying their revived self-confidence, has induced unprecedented hostility toward French Canadians.

In a way it is misleading to clap together the Atlantic Provinces as a homogeneous unit. Each has its own interests and problems. But they do share the same remoteness from the wealth of central Canada, and what they certainly have in common is size. They are the smallest of Canada's provinces; the original three total in area about a thousand square miles less than Maine, New Hampshire, and Vermont combined. These three also claim the staunchest of Canada's historic ties with Britain, being settled in the main by opponents of the American Revolution. Americans sometimes forget that not all people in the Thirteen Colonies objected to British rule; as many as one third supported the crown. But short of returning to England itself, what were they to do after 1783? Other nearby colonies, still under the allegiance to Britain, were for some the obvious places in which to settle.

The colony of Nova Scotia at the time stretched to the Quebec border and had a population of about twenty thousand. Many of these pioneers were New Englanders by origin, and in sympathy with the revolutionaries, but for a variety of reasons they had not risen to arms. For one thing, Nova Scotians did not have the same complaints as New Englanders about the economic regulations that Britain employed to keep her Empire together; on the contrary, the system of a protected British market worked to their advantage. Small numerically anyway, they reasoned that they could do little to help the colonists to the south, especially since Halifax held a large garrison of British troops.

And so a passive, split kind of attitude had developed, marked by some sentiment for the American cause and simultaneously by awareness that Halifax was prospering as a military depot for British forces battling the revolution. "The neutral Yankees of Nova Scotia," was the phrase that described them.

The people who fled the United States of America were, on the other hand, clearly and notably "United Empire Loyalists." The largest group, about thirty thousand, went by sea from New York to Nova Scotia. For the sake of simpler administration, the British then divided the territory and established the colony of New Brunswick, with its capital at Fredericton, far enough up the St. John River to be immune from Yankee sea attack. Thus was laid the newer foundation of the Maritime Provinces, with other Loyalists going farther afield to what is now called Prince Edward Island. Fredericton retains to this day much of the gentle flavor and tree-lined tranquility that was handed down by the original civil servants, scholars, and soldiers who settled here. Memorials to Loyalists abound, some of them merely graveyard markers indicating the final resting places for people who came to the new colony after "the recent disturbances in America." Ninety miles south of Fredericton, at the point where the river enters the Bay of Fundy, lies the commercial city of Saint John. One of its distinguishing features is the old Loyalist Burial Ground, probably the most valuable piece of real estate in town, for it dominates the shopping and financial districts that grew up around it.

In a sense the burial ground is retained as a reminder to Maritimers not only of their history of political struggle in America but of their economic struggle in Canada. Loyalists and their early descendants went through a period of great prosperity, to be followed by a period of great dismay and depression. Many of them were merchants who combined business ability with accessible lumber resources and the ship-building skills of the French-speaking Acadians whom they found in the area. By the 1860's Nova Scotia especially possessed one of the world's great merchant fleets. Her vessels were making profitable voyages to Europe and Asia, but the busiest and most natural commerce was with Yankee cousins along the Atlantic seaboard. When a move was made toward uniting the existing colonies of British North America many Nova Scotians shouted in opposition, for the prevalent trade patterns would be bound to alter. On her own, as a colony with a large measure of self-government, Nova Scotia was fine. But in a Confederation to form Canada there was uncertainty.

Such was the controversy and bitterness that a Montreal journalist, on a visit to Halifax on July 1, 1867, the day of the birth of the new dominion, noted: "The majority of the Antis are so from horror of having their country opened up, and from an innate stupidity and cupidity peculiar to a certain class of people. You cannot get sense from a blockhead, nor anything but a grunt from a certain animal. Is it any wonder that Antis should hoist flags half-mast high and put mourning on their buildings?" Those in favor of Confederation celebrated appropriately, with torchlight processions and fireworks. But the misgivings of the "Antis" soon turned out to be accurately forecast. By a stroke of ironic timing, Confederation coincided with the death of wooden ship-building and trade allied to it. Halifax had been busy not only as a port for Maritimers. Sailing vessels coming from the other side of the Atlantic were so relieved to see land that they would dock there before going on to New York or destinations farther south. With steam vessels, however, it required little more effort to head directly for New York or even St. Lawrence ports.

The argument goes on to this day about the reasons for the slump that began almost immediately on the entry of Nova Scotia and New Brunswick into union with Quebec and Ontario. Professor W. Y. Smith, head of the department of economics and political science at the University of New

Brunswick, says of his native Maritimes: "Our age of prosperity was in the 1860's when we were geared to a pattern of overseas trade. Then Confederation integrated us into continental trade." Smith, who at forty-four is one of Canada's outstanding economists, continues:

In many countries, a national system of tariff protection has been one of the factors contributing to disparities in regional incomes. Historically, this is true of the United States and Canada. Protection was one of the "spoils" the North took after its victory in the Civil War. The central provinces of Canada were the great protagonists of the national policy of tariff protection that came into being in 1879. Tariff protection has raised costs in the Maritimes because it has forced us to import many goods from Ontario and Quebec which we could have obtained from other countries at a lower price. This rise in costs has reduced the capacity of our exporting industries to compete in world markets.

A couple of hundred miles away, at St. Mary's University in Halifax, another professor of economics, Joseph Vorstermans, disputes the Smith thesis and says the trouble with the Maritime Provinces is that they failed mentally to keep abreast of progress represented by the introduction of iron ships and the end of wooden ships. Vorstermans blames the decline of regional economy on the fact that it was heavily based on lumber going into schooners. "People have wasted time wailing," he argues. "Without Confederation we would be worse off. Now we share the wealth of the nation. It was time, not Confederation, that made wooden ships obsolete."

Vorstermans, forty-eight, admits that his views are not typical of Maritimers, nor popular among them, since he speaks with subdued passion and sentiment. A Netherlander by birth, he migrated to Halifax in 1955, and he says he has enough objectivity to note a couple of points. First, "The trouble is that Maritimers compare their standard of living with the rest of Canada and find it lower. But it is still a very high standard we enjoy here. People should look to Holland for comparison. There the standard is infinitely worse than here." Second, what astonishes him is that everyone has talked of "economic problems" of the Maritimes, and yet no one got around until a few years ago to pinpoint the problems or do anything about them: "Mostly it was loose and vague talk about being done wrong by in Confederation, of land being uneconomic, of population drifting away—with no real studies to show causes or remedies."

The economic picture, as almost any native knows by heart, is simply that the Atlantic area needs secondary manufacturing industries. It cannot offer enough employment in its principal fields of pulp and paper manufacturing, mining, fisheries, and agriculture. The traditional and tragic cry, that while the Maritimes used to ship to the world lumber, fish, and other renewable products, they now export mainly brains, has diminished slightly over the last few years. But the unfavorable statistics have yet to be overturned.

The outward movement is impelled by limitations both in scope of opportunity and earnings. The average income in the Atlantic Provinces is about $500 a year less than in the rest of Canada; in terms of the United States, even the relatively unprosperous Maine has a per capita income almost 75 per cent higher than New Brunswick's. During the decade between 1952 and 1962 the investment in the Atlantic Provinces in fixed assets was scarcely two thirds of the national average. It was a vicious circle, of course. The lower investment, which resulted in fewer industries and therefore less employment, was due largely to the small population in the first instance. The perennial cry of manufacturers was that there was little justification for locating plants in Prince Edward Island, New Brunswick, or Nova Scotia, when among them they could muster only 1.5 million people, hardly a major home market in contrast with the more than 12 million concentrated in Ontario and Quebec. And so, by forced habit, Maritimers have bought most manufactured goods not from nearby factories but from the much-resented "Upper Canada," which has grown richer as a result.

Two recent developments, however, are making a change in the over-all picture. The first is the switch in movement of young Maritimers apparent in postwar years. Instead of heading for Boston or New York, a greater proportion now move to Toronto or Montreal: still away from home but at least contributing to the general economy, which, in turn, benefits the Maritimes. Partly the lower emigration is inspired by the improved opportunities in Canada, and partly by the growing sense of Canadian nationalism. In addition, there is a practical consideration: Canada has no peacetime conscription, and immigrants in the United States are just as subject to the draft as native-born Americans.

The other development is even sharper in impact. The Atlantic Provinces themselves decided to forget the old negative attitude that fate had been cruel, that they were victims of "Upper Canada" and its protected industries, that even geography conspired against them because it cut them off from the heartland: in other words, that little they could do themselves would help. One of the first moves was to take a lesson from old Yankee cousins in New England, who, over the years, too, had felt left behind while other parts of the United States were industrializing. In 1925 New England businessmen set up the New England Council, a sort of super chamber of commerce, to study regional difficulties and create new enterprises. It took Maritimers thirty years to follow the example, but finally they set up the Atlantic Provinces Economic Council.

APEC, as it is better known, is a nonpolitical, nonprofit organization composed of businessmen and economists with the broad mission of stimulating local activity and sharing in the national prosperity. Arthur C. Parks, APEC's director of research, contends, in a refreshing kind of candor, that the area up to now has preoccupied itself with attempts to adjust freight rates and cling to safe, familiar patterns almost to the exclusion of new ideas and enterprises. "In regional industrial development," he told fellow Maritimers not long ago, "freight-rate adjustment alone is likely to have little effect."

It was a most daring concept to be uttered aloud, for one of the symbols of rearguard action fought by Maritimers for many years had been the mining of coal in Cape Breton and the cost of hauling it to the rest of Canada. Cape Breton Island, at the tip of Nova Scotia and connected to it by a causeway, boasts some of the longest collieries in the world —running three and a half miles beneath the Atlantic Ocean. Maintenance charges and the long pull to the surface make the operation expensive. Even though a few collieries have shut down in recent years, coal mining in 1965 was still a leading employer. Keeping it so, by getting the coal to the industrial centers of Canada, is the major problem. Pennsylvania coal fields are close to Toronto and the big factories and power plants of Ontario; Cape Breton is 1,200 miles away. A token tariff of fifty cents a ton is placed on United States coal, while the Canadian government uses a system of subvention—a subsidy on freight charges—to make Cape Breton coal competitive in price. This subsidy costs Canadian taxpayers between $13 million and $15 million a year. Is this an economic way to run a nation?

When I put the question to several Maritimers I received virtually the identical answer from all. William "Bull" Marsh, active coal miner until 1958 and now president of the district branch of the United Mine Workers of America, said:

> The history of our country is a social and political one, rather than economic. That's what keeps us together. Look at the way the government handed out assistance to wheat farmers in the West or protected car manufacturers in Ontario with a tariff wall. It's the price we all pay for Con-

federation. What is the difference between doing those things and making coal salable? Why should we in the Maritimes be treated any differently?

Here, of course, was the classical application of the Canadian economic dilemma: a country trading 4,000 miles along an East-West strip instead of in the short, logical North-South direction. The explanations and the arguments of the historians and economists often are lost in academic wordiness. It remained for another coal miner in Cape Breton to give a no-nonsense elucidation. "The trouble with this country," he said, "is she's too goddam long and narrer, and we're at the arse end."

The formation of APEC set off a chain reaction. Provincial governments, inclined in the past to sit back and await federal assistance, took steps of their own to agitate the economy. In Nova Scotia, Premier Robert L. Stanfield organized Industrial Estates Limited, a lively crown corporation that raises money through the sale of debentures and then sets out to promote industry by building plants and leasing them to private companies at reasonable rentals. Stanfield, before entering the public field, was a quiet and cautious lawyer-businessman who inherited an old and prosperous family firm that manufactures long john woolen underwear. (A regiment commanded by an uncle during the First World War was known as "Stanfield's Unshrinkables.") Stanfield, who became premier in 1956 at the age of forty-two, showed built-in conventional traits, almost in the pat tradition of Nova Scotia, but he burst through with drive and initiative rare enough in the region in the past century.

"You can't get too much done unless you believe something can be done," he said, and then proved it. Cape Breton, for instance, reliant almost exclusively on coal and steel since 1900, is gaining an entirely new industry: a $30 million plant for the commercial production of heavy water used in the creation of nuclear power. Stanfield was able to outdraw heavy competition from Western Canada partly by putting up $12 million of the plant's cost through Industrial Estates Limited. The premier was a hero in Cape Breton even before the heavy water feat. He had worked out a pension scheme retiring miners at the age of sixty, thus enabling men with less seniority to stay in the pits despite dwindling employment. Coal miners, to show their appreciation at the last provincial election, rejected every socialist candidate, for the first time in twenty-five years, and elected instead Stanfield's Conservatives. "Stanfield," says "Bull" Marsh, "has outsocialized the socialists. A few years ago no one could possibly have dreamed of a government pension such as is available now."

More to the point, a few years ago no one would have expected a provincial government in Nova Scotia to do much about anything. R. MacGregor Dawson, a political scientist who made a voluminous postwar study of the province, said his fellow Nova Scotians were "apt to spend too much time bewailing their handicaps and too little time bestirring themselves." Stanfield in the last few years has attracted two dozen new secondary industries, ranging from the weaving of carpets to the manufacture of cement. One of his most dramatic achievements was getting Volvo, the Swedish car company, to open a plant in Dartmouth, Nova Scotia—the first assembly plant established by a foreign car maker in either the United States or Canada. Volvo was drawn by favorable terms offered by Industrial Estates Limited and by a wage structure almost 25 per cent lower than in the rest of Canada.

From a practical or financial point of view it meant little advancement for Nova Scotia, since Volvo was using as a plant a disbanded sugar refinery and employing at its peak no more than a few hundred men putting together parts and bodies already largely assembled abroad. But psychologically it was a morale booster for the whole of the

Maritimes.[4] Volvo executives said they believed in the ability of Maritime workers and in the potential growth of the Atlantic region, both as a steady market itself and as a supplier for central Canada. An eighteen-year-old youth in Saint John commented: "All my childhood I heard nothing but stories of how anyone with ambition has to clear out of here. My parents talked that way, and I'm sure *their* parents talked that way. It's nice to hear something else for a change." He still was not certain what his future would involve, but at least he was considering it in terms of New Brunswick and not automatically in terms of Ontario or Massachusetts.

New Brunswick shows fresh promise under a bouncy and energetic young Liberal premier, Louis Robichaud, who spends much of his time outside the province extolling for possible investors such virtues as natural resources, a stable labor force, and a year-round seaport. New paper mills, fertilizer and chemical plants, and a steel complex—representing more than $200 million in value—opened or were under construction in 1965. Even tiny Prince Edward Island, which up to now has lived off such agricultural products as potatoes and such tourist attractions as the small clapboard farmhouse that supposedly was the setting for *Anne of Green Gables,* has new industry. The government gambled a couple of million dollars of provincial money to lure two frozen food companies, one Canadian, the other American, with attractive leasing arrangements. It was not so much the money itself—a pittance by other standards, but fairly substantial for a population of 107,000. What was significant was the demonstration of provincial action.

One of the main questions now is the extent to which the old Maritimes with Newfoundland can work in harmony to

---

[4] It also set something of a trend. The Japanese motor industry, deciding, too, to establish a production beachhead in the North American market, expects by 1966 to assemble 200 Toyota and Isuzu cars a week at a former naval base in Cape Breton.

handle common problems, such as transportation, and move toward some sort of economic union. There is some doubt about how much coordination can be expected in a region that, despite united mistrust of "Upper Canada," has been split into internal rivalries. Halifax and Saint John compete as year-round ports. The contest between Nova Scotia and New Brunswick is such that if New Brunswick herring appears in the shops of Halifax there is a public outcry: What is wrong with Nova Scotia herring? Louis Robichaud talks of complete integration, political, social, economic, of the four provinces into one, a notion that has been discussed by Maritimers on and off for more than a century. Joey Smallwood, however, sees little likelihood even of economic collaboration, because "provinces, like people, are selfish and have to think of themselves first." Joseph Vorstermans, the economist, points out that one of the errors of "Upper Canada" is to think of the Atlantic Provinces as a bloc. "The truth," he says, "is that Nova Scotia has nothing in common with New Brunswick except underdevelopment." The only reality, he says further, is for the four premiers of the area to present a common front in Ottawa in seeking understanding and financing—which is precisely the kind of thing that led to the establishment of the Atlantic Development Board, a federal agency with $100 million in reserve and loose terms of reference to stimulate the work of existing agencies such as APEC and Industrial Estates Limited.

But no matter how deep or difficult the task of making economic sense out of the region, the impressive fact is that a hopeful spirit has come into existence. "We're still asking for Maritime rights," remarked a Nova Scotian, "but at least we've come up off our knees."

"There's another kind of separatism in Canada," observed an Ontario letter-to-the-editor writer.[5]

[5] *Maclean's,* January 25, 1964.

I found it during my ten years in the Maritimes: down there they all want to join Boston. In fact that city is already overrun with Nova Scotians who claim natural ties there—with good reason. Their natural trade routes are along North-South lines, not to the West, and the people around the coast towns like Bridgewater and Lunenburg still think they can return to the grand old days when trade flourished with United States ports. The only difference, as I see it, between Quebec's separatists and the Maritimes' is that in Quebec they have a different language.

The case is somewhat oversimplified, for Quebec's separatism involves not so much raw economics as it does the emotional claim of French Canadians that they are treated as "inferiors." A century ago, when Joseph Howe, the powerful patriotic champion of Nova Scotia, spoke of "our nation" —meaning the nation of Nova Scotians—the feeling was of superiority toward the rest of Canada. This haughtiness was based on the hard economic fact that Nova Scotia was a prosperous trading country in its own right. Howe wanted it to stay that way, independent of the dominion being formed, and free to send its schooners where it pleased, especially in sensible commerce with New England. Howe finally changed his mind and entered the federal cabinet. But there remained after him a strong Nova Scotia sentiment against the union: so much so that in 1886 the provincial government passed a series of resolutions blaming the "unsatisfactory and depressed condition of the province" on Confederation and declaring the province's right to secede.

The gestures, if not the language, became revolutionary again during the depression years of the 1930's, when at least one Nova Scotian, a man named William Rand, insisted on flying his flag at half-mast each July 1, just as other anti-Confederates had done in 1867. Rand and those who thought like him were rebuffed when a neutral commission, looking into Nova Scotia's problems, said bluntly: "From a purely economic point of view secession would be sheer folly." Of course by this time no one was taking seriously the notion of a complete breakaway as an independent nation living in isolation. Rather, any questions revolved around the hypothetical advantage of the Maritimes falling back on natural trade routes by becoming part of the United States.

Romantic ties with New England never really disintegrated even after the flight of the Loyalists. During the War of 1812 Maritimers had little heart in the fight against Americans, with the result that higher education in Halifax benefited. An expedition made up of Imperial forces—that is, from Britain, but also including a number of native Nova Scotians—sailed from Halifax to occupy the Maine port of Castine, at the mouth of the Penobscot River. But instead of engaging in warlike actions, they allowed Atlantic vessels to land cargoes destined for New England; first, however, they extracted the prevailing customs duties. The money, amounting to £10,750, was diligently turned over to the governor of Nova Scotia, Lord Dalhousie, who, not knowing what to do with it, founded the university that bears his name.

The affection and affinity have been even more pronounced in this century, with mass migrations involving all the Atlantic Provinces. Everyone does indeed look to Boston, if not with personal ambition at least with the knowledge that a blood relative probably lives there. As Joey Smallwood pointed out, there are more Newfoundlanders in Boston than in St. John's. An estimated 1.5 million residents of Massachusetts are Canadian-born or the offspring of Maritime parents. The big movement took place before the Second World War, but even today many Nova Scotians refer to New England as "the Boston states." A Prince Edward Island cabinet minister told me, as a matter of fact and pride, that most of the police in the Boston area are of Maritime descent. He went even further and boasted whimsically: "If you have Maritime license plates on your car you can park in front of any Boston fire hydrant—and you're home free."

Curiously, on a much broader and more important level, many Maritimers take the same easy privilege for granted when they discuss the question of whether or not Canada should join the United States. The point that a significantly high number of Maritimers consider this possibility seriously is borne out by the *Maclean's* survey of 1964; 39 per cent of Maritimers questioned said they favor political union with the United States. This was by far the highest proportion in the country (it contrasted with 24 per cent in Ontario), and it stood in inverse relationship to income: the lowest in the country. The question very few Maritimers, along with Canadians in general, stop to ask is whether the United States would want any part of a political union with Canada, or with segments of it, such as the Atlantic Provinces.

In Halifax I questioned a leading newspaperman, Harold Shea, about the selling features Nova Scotia could muster in attempting to convince the United States that union would be beneficial to the United States. He took some time to list three main attractions: first, Nova Scotia is the biggest fish-processing area in North America, and besides 90 per cent of the province's fish already go to the United States; second, Nova Scotia has large deposits of gypsum—more than Canada could possibly use in a century; third, Halifax offers a deep natural harbor, a base for North Atlantic defenses. On reflection, Shea confessed it was not an impressive catalogue, and from a dispassionate economic consideration Nova Scotia would be a liability to the United States, just as Newfoundland is today to the rest of Canada.

From a Canadian standpoint, Alasdair Sinclair, an economist at Dalhousie University, notes that the cliché that trade should be freely North-South has never been tested in modern times, and he is far from convinced it would be an advantage to the Atlantic Provinces. "We're the same as New England in our main products," he points out. "So maybe Maritimers are as well off as can be expected, given the geographic isolation and lack of growth industries." He also argues that even with lower incomes Maritimers have greater security—through family allowances, pensions, hospital insurance—than New Englanders. To him, therefore, union with the United States is not necessarily the answer.

For some, the answer to the economic deficiencies of the Atlantic region simply involves capital. Joey Smallwood, speaking of the benefits that have fallen to Newfoundland since Confederation, said: "Only one of my forecasts didn't come true—that large blocks of Canadian capital would flow into Newfoundland. I was a Newfoundlander, not aware then as I am now that Canada as a whole depends on the United States for capital—that Canadians look outside, just as do Newfoundlanders." Today, of course, Newfoundland counts its major mining developments in terms of American investments. Premier Stanfield of Nova Scotia put it to me in a different way: "We do not believe that our province will ever develop satisfactorily if dependent entirely on central Canadian industrial leadership and capital, because central Canadian businessmen naturally have a central Canadian bias when considering plant location. We find that Americans approach this question with a more open mind." A large portion of the heavy water project in Nova Scotia is financed by United States capital.

What is the general feeling of the six out of ten in the Maritimes who apparently prefer Canadianism to Americanism? It was summed up by Dr. Henry Hicks, President of Dalhousie University, and a former premier of Nova Scotia, who believes that "the advantages of holding Canada together as a nation make it worthwhile to pay high prices." The advantages, as he sees them, are standard: a difference in political thinking, a Canadian system of responsible parliamentary democracy capable of greater flexibility than the United States system. His conclusion is this: "Canadians are developing as a distinctive people. We amount to something in the world as Canadians. We wouldn't as an appendage of the United States."

Dr. Hicks speaks with an ancestry deep in history. His family has lived in the New World four centuries, the first hundred years in New England as planters. The pioneer members in Nova Scotia arrived before the Loyalists; to his chagrin he confesses that they helped drive out the Acadians. But then, as though making amends, he claims that a part of him—perhaps one sixty-fourth—is Acadian. This link with the past is interesting, for the whole of the stubborn affiliation between the Atlantic Provinces and the rest of Canada would fall apart in the event of a breakaway by Quebec. Even a remote possibility of Quebec secession agitates Dr. Hicks as it does many Maritimers, for Canada would then look geographically something like East and West Pakistan.

> Only along the shore of the mournful and misty Atlantic,
> Linger a few Acadian peasants, whose fathers from exile
> Wandered back to their native land to die in its bosom.

Longfellow wrote the narrative poem *Evangeline* to celebrate a tragic and brutal experiment in mass transfer of population. Acadia, now Nova Scotia, New Brunswick, and Prince Edward Island, was settled first by the French, but a century later most of the area was taken over by the British. The Acadians agreed to a modified oath of allegiance to the British crown in exchange for freedom of religion and exemption from military service. Then in 1755, with Britain and France at war, the governor of Nova Scotia demanded that the Acadians take up arms against kindred French in Quebec. They refused. The governor ordered them banished from the land they had cultivated. Their thatched cottages and tall churches were put to the torch, and about eight thousand men, women and children were herded into ships, to be dispersed among the other English colonies along the Atlantic seaboard.

The British belief, of course, was that in time the Acadians would lose their identity. Many of them did. Some drifted as far away as Louisiana. But others managed to trek back, and joined the bedraggled clusters of Acadians who had hidden in the forests or remote fishing villages. Gradually they came out of seclusion, at first treated as pariahs by English settlers who had been given the titles to their old holdings. Longfellow wrote of them, in 1847, as a pitiful, vanishing people. But he failed to take into account the effectiveness of "la revanche des berceaux" (the revenge of the cradles). In 1784, the year the province of New Brunswick was founded, Acadians numbered only 1,500. But by 1871, the year of the first federal census, their birth rate was considerably higher than that of the English; they made up almost 16 per cent of the province's population. Now they comprise 40 per cent and flourish as a distinct and different group from their distant cousins in Quebec.

They do not call themselves French Canadians or *Canadiens*. They are *Acadiens:* in their minds an enormously important distinction. *Les Canadiens,* the French inhabitants of Quebec, were handed basic rights of government, religion, education, by British law. *Les Acadiens,* despite the fact that legally they still are a deposed people with no special privileges, have managed through quiet perseverance and pride to *attain* a position of eminence. Eighteen of the fifty-two members of New Brunswick's provincial legislature in 1965 were Acadians. Even more graphically, an Acadian, Louis Robichaud, was premier, in the land from which his ancestors once were barred. Acadians speak French and have their own schools and colleges, won slowly and gently over the years. Now, however, they are once more concerned about their identity and security: this time not because of any Anglo-Saxon ruthlessness but, ironically, because of Quebec developments and the growth there of French-

Canadian nationalism. The primary fear is that if Quebec goes its own way, the whole of the Atlantic area will be isolated from the main body of Canada, eventually to be drawn into the United States, with Acadians entering a melting pot which they have so far successfully resisted. They have learned to live gracefully with the majority who are not French-speaking, and say that Quebecers should learn to do the same.

"We have learned the meaning of compromise because legally we can claim no rights," was the way Emery LeBlanc, an outstanding Acadian spokesman, expressed it. "If we have to ask twenty times for something we do not regard this as a defeat. We just put it off and ask again until we get it bit by bit. This is a method Quebec refuses to understand." LeBlanc, in his middle forties, has a broad and warm face fringed with gray hair that gives him a mildly elfish look. He was editor of *l'Evangéline,* the Acadian newspaper, for eighteen years before entering the field of public relations. "Even if we had a majority in population tomorrow our business still would be conducted in English," he said. "This is a fact of life we have come to expect and to accept." A main irritant he feels is Quebec's claim to speak for all of "French Canada," when in fact Acadia ceased to be a part of French Canada more than two centuries ago. Moreover, Acadians regard Quebecers as overly assertive and pushy, so that if Quebec ever should set up an independent state, Acadians, if given a choice, would vote against joining it.

LeBlanc, in speaking of this incompatibility, concedes that Quebecers have a point when they denigrate Acadians as a submissive, cowed people. In the Acadian sense of submission, he confesses without rancor, lies an instinctive respect for authority. One detects in LeBlanc a kind of wistfulness when he relates an illustration used by Acadians themselves: A priest, who had just finished preaching the doctrine of love for one's fellow man, turned to a little Acadian girl and said, "Do you love the English?" She nodded, and he asked:

"Why?" "Because," said the little girl, "they are above us." A practical translation of this attitude was observed in Moncton, New Brunswick, when the Canadian National Railways, the biggest single employer, circulated a questionnaire asking workers whether they preferred to speak English or French. One Acadian, who marked English as his preference, later confessed that he wanted to put down French. But mistrusting the innocence of the questionnaire, and afraid it might denote some sort of English-Canadian snooping, he said frankly: "I also wanted to keep my job."

Fundamentally this is what bothers many Acadians about the Quebec belligerence: the danger that it might cause repercussions and antagonism among English-speaking Maritimers who would show their resentment by classifying together *Acadiens* and *Canadiens*. They fear not only for their livelihoods. The whole of their culture is at stake. In a break between Quebec and the rest of the country, the French-language radio and television services of the Canadian Broadcasting Corporation, originating in Montreal, no longer would be available in the Maritimes, and so a strong linguistic and cultural influence would end.

Even now many are wary of the vexation among non-Acadians who feel that Acadians have maneuvered the education system to suit themselves. Partly involved is the question of religion; there is a tendency to identify French language with Roman Catholicism—an old and persistent characteristic among Canadians. The Reverend Maurice C. Boillat, a Swiss-born French-speaking Baptist who trained as a missionary in Toronto, is a vociferous critic of what he considers Acadian expansionism. Working out of Moncton, and preaching the message that "a person does not have to be Roman Catholic to be a good Frenchman," he says:

> The New Brunswick School Act clearly states that schools should be non-sectarian and that there should be no religious teaching in them. But there are also regulations which allow members of religious orders to serve as teachers. Many

teachers in schools attended by Acadians are nuns. They make use of catechism; crucifixes hang in their classrooms. In effect we have a system of parochial schools under the guise of a public school system. Little by little the English-speaking people have let a situation slip to a point where it has got out of hand.

Acadians admit frankly that since they do not possess the legal rights of French-speaking people in Quebec, they have had to operate surreptitiously. Any religious aspect is only incidental; the main effort is to keep the language alive by maintaining a grip on youth. In New Brunswick this technique has been effective; 95 per cent of the province's 240,000 Acadians retain a substantial use of French, in contrast with Nova Scotia's 80,000 Acadians, almost half of whom have lost all knowledge of French. In Newfoundland, which once had a sizable French colony, virtually no French is spoken today; even names have become Anglicized, Le-Blanc converting to White. American visitors are usually bewildered by the debate about retention of tongue and culture, for it does not occur to any real degree in their own lives. Not long ago a group of Louisiana students, who traced their ancestry to the Acadian expulsion, made a light-hearted pilgrimage to old Acadia. None spoke French, none had a conflict over loyalties, because, as one of them put it, "We are *Americans*."

Acadians stand part way between the crucible concept of the United States and the duality advocated by Quebec. Certainly the Acadian student is far more integrated into the mainstream of Canada than is the Quebec student. Léonel Méthot, a twenty-one-year-old commerce graduate at the University of Moncton, has an Acadian mother and a Quebec father. He says he prefers to be known as an Acadian rather than a French Canadian "because I admire Acadian history more." He even feels more at home with English-speaking students than with Quebecers. This view is not automatically shared by all Acadian students, but it came fairly close to the general mood of a small group who held a debate for my benefit. Present among them was a separatist from Quebec, an eighteen-year-old engineering student named Michel Pelletier, who insisted: "Quebec is not going to stay in Confederation just to save the rest of Canada." Lucille Fougere, aged twenty, who comes from rural New Brunswick, said: "If Quebec were to secede it would be a tragedy for us especially. We would be engulfed by English Canada or by the United States." Pelletier answered: "I don't see what you would lose here, because I don't see what you've got now." Lucille, thoughtfully and sadly, expressed distaste at the alternative of having to move to Quebec to retain French as a language, or having to unite with the United States out of economic necessity.

Hardly anyone in the Atlantic Provinces, of Acadian or non-Acadian origin, visualizes the region surviving on its own or even as part of Canada in the event of a Quebec rupture. Premier Robichaud, who believes separatism would be an economic catastrophe for Quebec, says equally it would be disastrous for the Maritimes. "We cannot get to the rest of Canada by jumping over Quebec or building a tunnel," is the gloomy way he put it to me. Premier Stanfield, a bit more reservedly but with equal concern, said: "One would have to ask very seriously whether Canada could survive as a nation." Because practical awareness exists, Maritimers are acutely sensitive to Quebec developments. They do not take lightly the attitude, heard expressed sometimes in Ontario and west of it, that if Quebec wants to quit Confederation no one will try to stop it. Sentiment for history and old tradition—and it exists strongly among descendants of United Empire Loyalists—is not even the main factor. For English-speaking Maritimers, just as for Acadians, economics dictates a firm attitude toward Quebec.

"Separatists should not talk of two nations," said Russell Harrington, President of the Nova Scotia Light and Power Company. "They should really refer to three nations: everything west of Quebec would be one, Quebec another, while we in the Maritimes would make up the third because Quebec would form a natural barrier. The Maritimes would drop off—not through any nationalistic feelings but simply the need to trade south. First would come economic union with the United States, then political union." A Halifax judge, Peter O'Hearn, disagreeing drolly, said: "If separation does take place, the Atlantic region is likely to be the only part to remain independent. No one else would want us." On a more serious plane, however, he agreed that an attitude of intense animosity toward Quebec has been created by the Maritimes' own growing sense of security and prosperity; this is a curious and new affinity Maritimers have with Westerners, as we shall see in a later chapter. Those Canadians who are sampling for the first time a sense of well-being, or feel at least optimism for their economic future, are especially resentful of the distractions caused by Quebec.

One night in the bar of the Lord Beaverbrook Hotel in Fredericton, I sat next to two men from Saint John. They were feed salesmen, and one of them, slightly drunk, said: "No one can sell more feed than me." The other, quite coherent, asked, when he heard I was from Montreal, "What's going on with all those Frenchmen?" Recently he had been to a company convention in the Laurentians, with colleagues from Quebec and Ontario, and he noticed how "sensitive" the French Canadians seemed. "Some didn't even stand up for the playing of 'God Save the Queen,' " he said, obviously with remembered annoyance. Then he paused, peered at me closely, and said: "You say you are from Montreal?" "Yes." "But you're not French?" "No," I said. Now, he said, he could talk frankly. During the war, when he served on a destroyer, he found of "four Frenchmen" aboard "there was only one good one—and he was very good." By this he implied that only one had demonstrated courage. Projecting the sample a little, he was convinced that "75 per cent of French Canadians are gutless." He concluded: "If the rest of Canada stands up to them, they'll soon forget any fancy notions." The other man at the bar, now quite drunk, commented: "Those French women sure are good . . . know how to doll up . . . put on paint . . . sure got something."

In somewhat loftier words, Dr. Henry Hicks of Dalhousie University also urges a stern policy toward Quebec. "Every pseudo-intellectual in English Canada has been climbing on the bandwagon and saying the French are badly treated," he asserted. "But has Quebec been so badly treated? On the economic side Quebec is far better off than the Maritimes. We've treated French Canadians like children and allowed them to think that everything that has happened to them is the fault of English Canada. They should be treated now as adults." Was he implying force if necessary? "Canada," he said slowly, "would have to preserve the integrity of this country regardless of the consequences. I would hope it would not have to come to the painful process that occurred in the United States a hundred years ago." But, plainly, if it would, Dr. Hicks was prepared to fight.

In Charlottetown, Prince Edward Island, another approach was taken by J. David Stewart, the provincial secretary: "There's a strong feeling here anyway that we would be better off as a part of the United States. In mileage alone, we're closer to Boston than to Montreal." Would there be any appreciable mood to resist physically if Quebec should want to secede? Stewart, who is a former commanding officer of an infantry regiment, the Argyll and Sutherland Highlanders, said: "Not at all. If Quebec seceded, that would be that."

And so here were two points of view, one suggesting bloodshed before separatism, the other saying freedom for Quebec to do what she wants. But underlying each point of view was the common factor of economics and the pull toward the United States. Those who are prepared to resist strenuously the physical division of English Canada into two parts would do so largely because they oppose union with the United States. For the others, the representative word, perhaps, was from G. Cecil Day, owner of a flourishing weekly paper in the town of Liverpool, Nova Scotia. Liverpool's main industry is the production of newsprint, which is shipped to New York, Washington, and Richmond. "As far as I'm concerned," said Day, "Quebec could go. We could survive quite comfortably without it. But we couldn't live without the United States."

8.

"Wacky" Bennett and His Empire

It may be a coincidence, or possibly the result of geographic conditions and needs, that two of Canada's most dynamic political figures are provincial premiers at each of the extreme ends of the country. J. R. Smallwood rules with a benevolent, autocratic hand in Newfoundland, cut off from the mainland by the Gulf of St. Lawrence. W. A. C. Bennett, combining techniques learned from Louisiana's late Huey Long and Quebec's late Maurice Duplessis, runs an empire in British Columbia, aloofly isolated from the rest of the nation by the Coast Range and the Rocky Mountains. Not since 1872—the year an eccentric Tory premier, William Alexander Smith, called himself Premier Amor de Cosmos (Lover of the Universe)—has British Columbia seen such a controversial and pugnacious leader. Bennett, who looks like a sixty-four-year-old, slightly heavyset version of a one-time matinée idol, may not be quite as mystical as Smith, but his financial sorcery, under the bewildering guise of Social Credit, drives many people into frustrated anguish. Several years ago, after a campaign promise to make the province debt-free, he called in about $200 million worth of long-outstanding bonds, on which as little as 3 per cent interest was being paid. Ceremoniously he had them piled onto a floating raft, and, with press photographers present, fired a flaming arrow into the bundle. Then, to finance new projects, he blandly borrowed new money at 5.5 per cent interest.

Such shenanigans, instead of ridding the province of its obligations, have given it one of the highest per capita debts in the country. And yet, brazenly, British Columbia's immense natural wealth and steady market in the United States distinguish it as possibly the most self-sufficient of all the provinces. If Canada should ever break up, British Columbia could survive economically as a separate unit, though the logical amalgamation would be with the United States because of affinity with the Pacific Northwest as a whole. Bennett makes much of this point while trading on British Columbia's built-in suspicions of Ottawa and Eastern Canada, an antipathy that has given the province its own belligerent secessionist movement from time to time.

British Columbia, which covers an area greater than the combined states of California, Oregon, and Washington, was one of the last regions of North America to be explored and settled. Captain James Cook led two ships into Nootka Sound, on the west coast of Vancouver Island, in 1778, and this was the forerunner of other expeditions by British explorers and fur-traders. But colonization as such had a slow beginning, and for many years the area was a no-man's land. In 1818 Britain and the United States established the 49th parallel as the boundary line from the Lake of the Woods to the Rockies; but since both claimed the territory beyond the mountains they agreed it should be open to traders from either side. Posts of the Hudson's Bay Company were planted in strategic parts of the coast and interior as symbols of Britain's stake. But meanwhile a battle cry, "Fifty-four forty or fight," was being sounded by United States Democrats who won the 1844 election on a campaign for Oregon's admission to the Union and right to territory on the Pacific Coast up to the latitude of 54°40'. When President James K.

Polk offered a compromise, extension of the 49th parallel to the Pacific, with a dip south around Vancouver Island, the British accepted.

The British had not believed a boundary dispute in the distant wilderness worth a war. But almost from the start there was concern with movements from the United States. Many Americans were obsessed with the philosophy of Manifest Destiny. Having acquired in rapid succession Louisiana, Florida, Texas, and California, they considered it the mission of the United States to occupy the entire continent. No one expected a fixed boundary to halt American settlers, and in London at least one man, Earl Grey, the Colonial Secretary, saw that if the remote Pacific coast of British North America should ever take in a majority of people from below the border, nothing would prevent a successful demand for union with the United States. And so, in order to discourage any influx of Americans, the British government granted Vancouver Island to the Hudson's Bay Company, whose task was to colonize it. But by 1858 only a few hundred British settlers, most of them employees or former employees of the company, had come in. Then the discovery of gold in the Fraser River region, on the mainland, brought a rush of thousands of fortune seekers, many of them by boat from San Francisco. The British, anxious now to strengthen a tenuous hold, bought back Vancouver Island from the Hudson's Bay Company, and in 1866 proclaimed the new Colony of British Columbia, embracing the mainland as well as the island.

Within a few years, British Columbia was confronted with a major debate: Whether to apply for annexation to the United States or to join as a province in the Dominion of Canada that had just been formed in the East. From a practical, material aspect, union with the United States made sense, for here was an isolated settlement of no more than ten thousand people, most of them Americans, living near a relatively easy North-South axis of the sea, while an impassable mountainous land barrier lay between them and the Canada that existed thousands of miles away. Only the former Hudson's Bay Company men and the small number of pro-British settlers from the East spoke with any enthusiasm about joining the Dominion. In 1869, when the governor of British Columbia died, Sir John A. Macdonald, Canada's prime minister, shrewdly persuaded the British government to appoint a successor who favored federation with Canada. His next step was to promise a railway, to the East, within ten years.

In 1871 British Columbia decided to become Canada's sixth province, but the marriage was an unhappy one at the start. The railroad deadline was not met; instead of completion by 1881, construction actually did not start until that year. Indignant British Columbians threatened to secede. Even when the Canadian Pacific Railway, a momentous engineering achievement, finally was pushed through the Rockies and Coast Range in 1885 it did not signal prosperity for British Columbia. On the contrary, the fledgling province was spending at a rate far beyond revenues, so that by the turn of the century the public debt totaled more than $12 million for a population of 178,000. Many of the residents insisted once again that the cost of operating a province so far away from the rest of the land always would be uneconomic, and therefore British Columbia should join the United States. Eastern Canada thought differently; the other provinces, through Ottawa, agreed that B.C. should receive federal grants to help it along.

By the time the Panama Canal opened, offering a relatively cheap way of shipping British Columbia timber, fish, and other products to the eastern seaboard and Europe, the province was moving toward its present distinction: an exciting boom or bust mentality attracting people from all parts of the country. Many, however, are merely refugees from the biting winter of the East, for Nature provides the West Coast with gentle enough temperatures for roses to bloom at Christmas, in addition to a magnificent backdrop of snow-capped peaks. Grouse Mountain is eight miles from Vancouver for winter skiing, and in the summer English Bay, ten minutes from downtown, has its beaches and easy access to fishing and sailing. In this respect the West Coast is by far the most attractive part of Canada.

Today's population of British Columbia, 1,730,000, display a curious mixture of the brashy go-go-go of Los Angeles and the conservatism of Britain. Four out of ten British Columbians live in Vancouver, which flaunts the Bayshore Inn, a gaudy motel with the doorman dressed as a Tower of London "Beefeater" and the bellhops as Chinese coolies. But across the Strait of Georgia in Victoria, the capital, the staid old Empress Hotel features immense glass greenhouses and solariums with potted ferns and aspidistras. Some of the elderly patrons, sipping tea and nibbling scones, still occupy the same places in the lounge they kept for the forty years Billy Tickle and his trio played quiet music at teatime. It is a canard to liken this atmosphere to Bournemouth, for Bournemouth was never so English. Billy Tickle was retired in 1960, and the Empress tried to appeal to a younger set by converting a wing into a motor hotel. But the fundamentals never changed, and Victoria remains the last haven on the continent for a folk striving to cling to a gracious and dead era.

Originally, the name of the province was New Caledonia. Queen Victoria renamed it herself, much to the annoyance of the Duke of Newcastle, who protested that "British Columbia" was not "very felicitous." Columbia was the title early American poets gave to the United States, hardly an appropriate allusion to anything British. However, the B.C. historian Margaret A. Ormsby wisely considers the name is suitable, since this is Canada's most American province and simultaneously its British side stands out for every tourist to behold. If the scones abound, so do the addictions to California-style divorce and suicide rates, and to strange religious sects of all nuances. Texas creeps in, too, for British Columbians love nothing better than to tell of the two ranchers sitting in a Hotel Vancouver room calmly playing poker at a hundred dollars a chip, with a private airplane thrown into the kitty. The story may be apocryphal, but there is ample evidence of fruit farmers from the Okanagan Valley deciding to take a week-end flight to Hawaii with no more luggage than the suits on their backs.

British Columbia has always had its contradictions: the great wealth a few industrialists made from the trees, and at the same time some of the worst depression riots in the country. In the hungry 1930's people drifted in from the Prairies because it was easier to subsist in a place where at least the climate was hospitable. This heritage left a radicalism in politics—an unorthodoxy that is reflected in Bennett's power today—plus the lingering question of how meaningful is a central government that, in the bitter memory of Westerners, cannot see much beyond the Great Lakes. The sense of isolation, whether it is physical or psychological, brings with it additional contradictions that make it impossible for B.C. to be described as wholly in tune with the rest of Canada, or, for that matter, in complete harmony with the United States.

On one side there is this picture:

Ninety-five years ago, when the colony's delegates traveled to Ottawa to negotiate entry into Canada, they went most of the way by a United States railway, the Union Pacific, that had just been completed across the Rockies to San Francisco. Terms of the union with Canada reached the West Coast by way of telegraph in the United States. In more recent years two lines of steel and national airlines have thrown aside the barrier of the mountains, but it was only in 1962 that the final link of the Trans-Canada Highway through the Rockies was formally opened, making it feasible to drive from one end of Canada to the other without having to swerve into the United States. Almost the first lesson British Columbians draw for visitors from the East is how much more normal it is for them to gravitate southward than eastward. The ads do not invite Vancouverites to spend a week end in Toronto, a distance of 2,500 miles. Rather, they say: "Enjoy a Sun Break in Las Vegas. Just a few hours and $84.10 via Western Airlines!" All along the Canadian-United States border, of course, people are at ease crossing into one another's cities. Buffalo is barely a two hours' drive from Toronto; Montreal is an hour's flight from New York. But a trip to any of these places has something of the tone and pace of a visit to a foreign city. On the West Coast, in contrast, adjustment is almost unnecessary. The whole of the Pacific Northwest is integrated to the extent that people in Vancouver set out on the four-hour drive to Seattle as nonchalantly as they would to one of the nearby inlets of their own coast. In turn, people in Seattle say they speak a language more akin to that of Vancouverites than to New Yorkers. The mountains and the sea do impart common nomenclature and values that stretch a thousand miles from San Francisco north through Oregon, Washington, and British Columbia. Vancouverites take it for granted that even the islands in the straits, through which the boundary runs, should be a mixture of Canadian and American, occupied by vacationers or permanent residents whose nationalities are indistinguishable.

But then a curtain comes down, at least for some Canadians:

"We're the same, until we get on the subject of politics or international affairs," said a C.B.C. producer. "I've always regarded Oregon and Washington as pretty liberal; just look at their record of voting. But there are a couple of major issues about which we simply do not talk the same language: Cuba and China. We refuse to tremble with every mention of communism. The notion that we are basically the same as Americans falls apart at this point." This, of course, is an intellectual approach, applicable to a small minority. But a difference shows itself oddly in other areas as well. While the Oregon Trail nurtured a distinctive type of individual who spilled over both sides of the border, a simple glance at Vancouver newspapers will demonstrate that despite the North-South movement much of the sentiment and communication is East-West. Very little Seattle news is featured in Vancouver. On the sports pages the main stories are devoted not to the Western Hockey League but to headlines such as "Wings Win but Howe Whiffs," describing a faraway game between Detroit and Montreal Canadiens. There are also lengthy analytical stories about the trials and potentials of Eastern Canadian football teams, one of which will meet the winner of the Western Conference for the national championship represented by the Grey Cup. The link goes deeply into history and is consciously catered to by the radio and television networks of the Canadian Broadcasting Corporation. In serious issues, such as military enrolment or commitment in wartime, there can be no doubt about B.C. loyalties; and trade unions—a force in B.C. affairs—can be loudly antagonistic to affiliated United States groups they consider meddling in Canadian matters.

And yet, in the complications of Canadian life, one comes back inevitably to the compelling facts of geography: the hard-headed logic of routes and trade North and South. In the 1964 survey by *Maclean's* 29 per cent of British Columbians, among Westerners as a whole, favored joining the United States. The figure was lower than in the Atlantic Provinces—perhaps deceptively so, for economically the West was enjoying a boom. Nor did the statistics take into account indifferent men such as Thomas J. Campbell, who told me he "wouldn't like to join the States, but if it happened I wouldn't be so heartbroken." Campbell, aged thirty-seven and a self-made millionaire, is representative of the ambitious, new, fast-moving breed who tend to overshadow the more traditional types of easygoing British Columbians. Campbell, whose father was a policeman, grew up in Vancouver's east end, which he describes as "tough, like the east side of any city, only more so." Now he is one of the biggest real-estate operators on the West Coast, with skyscraper apartments and other revenue-producing properties worth $10 million. As an alderman he opposed a measure to improve city social services, saying: "Too many do-gooders helping too many no-gooders."

He also boasts that he never watches or listens to the C.B.C. ("that tripe"), but instead tunes to United States channels. Vancouver received television programs from Bellingham, on the Washington side of the border, long before the C.B.C. opened a transmitter, and so Campbell asks: "Who needs the C.B.C.?" One of his main complaints is this: "Out here we feel that instead of being dominated by the States, we're too dependent on the East. Head offices in Toronto are milking everything from B.C." When I reminded him that he had boasted, only minutes previously, of obtaining a mortgage of $1,550,000 from an insurance company in London, Ontario—twenty-four hours after requesting it—Campbell agreed with some chagrin that this was true. "But the local office," he argued, "didn't have the authority to let me have it. They had to phone Ontario." It was then that he suggested liaison with the United States would be at least as acceptable as the present arrangement in Canada.

In the past, any drive for union with the United States has taken place in a time of depression and has been preceded by talk of breakaway from Canada. "If the truth were known," wrote Jack Scott, former columnist of *The Vancouver Sun,* "there's probably a greater, and more natural, appetite for separatism this side of the Rockies, latent though it may be, than you'll find in Quebec. Because of our geographical isolation, compounded by our parochialism, we may be more ripe for a good, rabble-rousing secessionist movement than the French Canadians." Scott goes on to point out that "the Canadian" who is inside every British Columbian, "dying to get out," would be willing to put aside his jealous provincialism if he felt there was a real Canadian identity.

Ironically, fighting Ottawa and the East has long been a profitable pastime of British Columbia politicians, and hardly can be considered a contribution to Canadian identity. Bennett, though more expedient than many, is in a sense a "typical" British Columbian. He was born outside the province (in New Brunswick), and this makes him, like most converts to British Columbia, more zealous than the natives. He carries a deep dislike for Ontario and Quebec, is almost totally ignorant of the forms the ambitions of French Canada have taken, and, as a consequence, is almost totally intolerant. In some ways he is almost a caricature of the austere puritan (he neither smokes nor drinks) whose stock was British, United Empire Loyalist, and Presbyterian. He was a young man when he moved to Alberta to take a job as a hardware salesman. Then, at the age of thirty, he moved again, to Kelowna, B.C., where he started his own hardware business. This has since grown into a chain of five stores, managed by his sons, and turned him into a millionaire.

Bennett's introduction to politics was as a Conservative. He was elected to the provincial legislature in 1941. Ten years later, shrewdly sizing up the electorate's disenchantment with the orthodox parties, he quit the Tories and turned to Social Credit—not because of doctrine, which to this day is not followed, but because it offered a fresh label and a chance at leadership. As he crossed the floor of the legislature, Bennett told a reporter: "I'll be premier in six months." His forecast fell short by a few months, but he did form British Columbia's first Social Credit government and has retained the premiership in the four elections since then. In his last campaign, in 1963, when his principal opponents were the New Democratic Party, he fought with the slogan of "Social Credit or Socialism," and won with an increased plurality. What made the slogan a pious fraud was that in 1960 Bennett had campaigned as a defender of private enterprise, and then, safely back in office, nationalized the huge B.C. Electric Company. In actuality, British Columbia, under Bennett, became a bigger practitioner of socialism than Saskatchewan under a socialist government. Apart from the takeover of power, Bennett operates transportation services —ferries between the mainland and Vancouver Island, the Pacific Great Eastern Railway—and other public enterprises valued at nearly $1.5 billion. Yet he calls himself "a Social Crediter among Social Crediters."

When I asked him to define Social Credit he recounted a visit paid to him by Viscount Montgomery. The British general, who spent four days in Victoria, repeatedly asked Bennett what Social Credit stood for, and, in common with virtually every one else, could not grasp any of the various explanations. Finally Bennett told him: "You're a military man, in charge of a campaign in North Africa, and in order to conduct an attack you take an inventory of the men, materials, and the problems. Then you attack."

"In an unorthodox way?" I asked, looking for amplification after the pause.

"No, not that. As I told Montgomery: You do the impossible in wartime, we do the impossible in peacetime."

"Unorthodox?" I again asked.

"We do the common sense. The other parties are the unorthodox. They don't do the common sense."

When all this bewildering interpretation is finished, it is Bennett himself who sums up the attraction felt by the voters: "They see in me what Social Credit stands for—it gets things done." There is hardly doubt that the party's success is due to the political acumen and popular appeal of Bennett. Despite his rigid personal habits he makes a vigorous impression. He has little in common with, and little affection for, his neighbor and fellow Social Crediter, Premier Manning of Alberta, whom he regards as too much of a Bible-thumper and too austere to muster emotional appeal. Bennett admits to having learned on a tour of Louisiana many years ago a considerable amount from Huey Long's flair for political handouts. He is also a great admirer of old Duplessis methods. He has built more roads, bridges, and tunnels than all the administrations in the previous eighty years, though they are not necessarily in the busiest places. Personally incorruptible, he retains key portfolios for himself, including finance. He runs, as Duplessis did, almost a one-man show, with scant tolerance for divergent opinions. A few people in his cabinet apply to him sometimes the Duplessis label of "Chief." Otherwise he is known as "Cece" (from William Andrew Cecil) or "Wacky" (from W.A.C.). Another title is "Commodore," given freely and with gratitude by the public in recognition of his buildup of a flotilla of ferries that offer far more extensive and speedier service than the old private companies. Basically, Bennett trades on the resentments of the obscure middle-class man who feels cut off from the high echelons and trodden on by the "Establishment." Bennett gladly takes on such federal figures as Pearson and Diefenbaker, and this makes him a hero.

Intellectuals, and many urban voters, oppose him, but it is obvious that enough voters are satisfied with pork barrel politics. Even one of Bennett's critics conceded: "You don't shoot Santa Claus." The fact that some gentle subterfuge might be involved is incidental. Most people accept it on face value when Bennett declares that the province is unique, that it pays its way as it goes. What he says is that the British Columbia government is free of "direct" debt, and so it is. In the B.C. Electric takeover, for instance, Bennett characteristically had the nationalized company itself issue bonds to pay off the former shareholders. The province guaranteed the bonds, but in Bennett vocabulary this was not a "direct" debt. By such gobbledygook British Columbia, little more than a decade after Bennett's entry as premier and finance minister, merely had "contingent" liabilities of $1.3 billion. A psychologist in Vancouver explained the Bennett charm in these words: "He's a real huckster who knows psychology, especially of the insecure little fellow." His home-owner grant is an illustration. The municipality bills you, say, $300 for taxes—less an allowance of $80 provided by the province. This makes a net to you of $220. But the municipality does not collect the $80 in direct form from the province, and as a consequence has to raise its rates. In the end the tax-payer pays for everything. But to the modest homeowner, scrimping to make ends meet, it is a good, reassuring feeling to have $80 knocked off the immediate bill. An economist-sociologist, Stuart Jamieson of the University of British Columbia, says that Bennett is getting away with his "funny money" methods because they depend on an expanding economy, and British Columbia is booming. But with the slightest recession or setback there could be real disaster, as in Alberta in the 1930's when bonds fell 50 per cent in value.

So far, however, the opposite is happening. "Despite all the lunacies of our government, business in B.C. is better than ever," said Stuart Keate, publisher of *The Vancouver Sun*. In the past decade, he pointed out, about $400 million —half of it in foreign capital—had been invested in the manufacture of wood products on Vancouver Island alone. Vancouver Island, which is the size of Switzerland, has scarcely 300,000 in population. Keate, in common with businessmen generally, is quite content with the expansion of the economy, even though he continues to condemn the politics of Bennett. Wages have risen steadily so that today British Columbians are the best paid in Canada and enjoy the highest standard of living. Forestry and related products comprise the most important industry, bringing in some $800 million a year, most of it from the United States. The annual fishing catch, largely Pacific salmon, is worth about $100 million. Cattle and sheep graze on ranges in the interior, mines provide a wealth of silver, lead, zinc, copper, and coal; and more than half the oil the province uses comes from its own fields. Electric power is symbolized by the great Kitimat project that reversed the flow of a river to give energy to a huge aluminum smelter shaped in what was once an Indian village four hundred miles up the coast from Vancouver.

Secondary industry in British Columbia is relatively small, and what there is of it is tied in with primary industry: that is, the fabrication of wire rope for logging and the building of small ships for fishing. Bennett and other politicians—in and out of election campaigns—consistently have taken advantage of the irritation B.C. feels in paying a high price for central Canada's "protected industries." Traditionally, these are exemplified by automobile assembly lines, but British Columbians complain that even machinery used in logging or mining has to come all the way from Ontario. In any free trade agreement with the United States, there is little doubt that B.C. would benefit by selling its raw products as it is now doing, and buying in return cheaper textiles or television sets. It might do very well, too, as an autonomous country, provided it possessed an ironclad guarantee of continued business from its principal market, the United States.

What would happen in the event of separation by Quebec? The Atlantic Provinces, Bennett recognizes, would be vulnerable and probably would have to look for union with the United States. But the rest of Canada, from Ontario westward, could stay together. At least this is the theory held by Bennett, who adds that the sensible outcome would be a common market with the United States. "We're for one now, anyway," he told me. "A northern country like Canada has nothing to fear from a common market with the United States. But even if the rest of Canada were to leave, and join the United States, we in British Columbia would stay in the Commonwealth." On the one side, then, he calls for close economic ties with the United States, on the other political independence that could in the ultimate mean a British Columbia nation.

How far would he be prepared to go to keep the country together? What sort of adjustments would he grant to make

Quebec happy? In effect Bennett answers that he would not take the slightest deliberate step to retain Quebec in Confederation, unless this would have a direct bearing on British Columbia or its comfortable trade with the United States. In other words, the attitude is: "What's in it for B.C.?" Speaking of French Canada, he said: "It has a choice to make, and only Quebec can make it—to fulfill its destiny within the nation or without. As far as B.C. is concerned, we will never try to bargain." Bennett, who often likes to grin, was somber when he added: "You never get anywhere by trying appeasement or by making concessions. If you do try, then the rot starts." He learned this lesson, he said, as an employer in the hardware business. Even today, "If a man comes to me and says he wants to quit, I put out my hand and say, 'Good luck to you,' and off he goes."

Since this was an allusion to Quebec separatism, I said: "Don't you ever ask why?" Bennett said that he never did, because this would be construed as weakness and it would be an invitation for unknown demands. Returning to the analogy of an employee, the premier said: "He made his own decision. If you tried to find out his reasons, then everyone would come with the same demands. You cannot allow exceptions. Even if he wanted to come back years later, I wouldn't have him."

Two others were present during the interview. One, a former personal assistant to the premier, said that surely this was not so, that Mr. Bennett would make an exception if an employee admitted he had erred and wished to be taken back. The other, a Social Credit organizer and longtime acquaintance of Bennett, said: "You don't know him as well as I do. He means it." In fact, Mr. Bennett does not always mean what he seems to say. Not long after our conversation, in which he virtually dismissed Quebec as unworthy of any dealings, he grandly lent it $100 million. He proclaimed: "Do you think B.C. would have loaned Quebec $100 million if we didn't think Quebec would stay in Confederation? I'm trying to show all Canada that British Columbia not only talks for a united Canada but acts for a united Canada." He might have added that British Columbia had just come into a windfall of $275 million, and if he had thrown it all on the market at once he would have had to be content with an interest rate lower than the 5.05 per cent he was getting from Quebec. (Quebec did all right, too, by saving the $750,000 in legal fees and brokerage charges it would have paid had it gone to regular sources for the money.)

Bennett's windfall was simply tangible evidence of his astuteness and stubbornness that are taken for granted by his fellow British Columbians and are now also painfully known in Ottawa and Washington. For three years Bennett had held up both Ottawa and Washington while he demanded what almost everyone else considered impossible terms for British Columbia's essential part in the Columbia River project for power and flood control. The original understanding between the two countries called for B.C. to build three storage dams to even the flow of the river that rises in the western slopes of the Rockies in British Columbia but does most of its wasteful—and often destructive—spilling in the United States. In return, B.C. would receive half the extra power that would be generated by United States hydro plants downstream. But Bennett, at the last minute of treaty-signing, imposed two conditions. The first was that British Columbia be allowed to sell its share of the power to the United States, a demand that required Ottawa to reverse a long-standing policy restricting the export of power. The second condition was met, equally reluctantly, by the United States when it agreed to his high price for the power. The deal was worth $275 million in an advance payment from the United States (in addition to $70 million due for flood control), more than enough to cover the province's cost of dam construction. Vancouver, by a simple side process, will garner some of the cheapest electricity on the continent, and Bennett meanwhile is financially free to get into other pet projects, including money-lending.

Bennett's gesture for "a united Canada" must be looked at with some skepticism, for essentially he demands decentralization and a strong British Columbia along with regionalism. In a sense he speaks the same words as René Lévesque in Quebec. But Lévesque at least has the virtue of attempting to postulate a sincere philosophy to back his half-formed notions of a system of Swiss cantons. Bennett is an opportunist who comes no closer to philosophy than to say: "The great stabilizing force in Canada is the existence of strong provincial governments." Generally he is content to make a frank admission that British Columbia wants to retain a bigger piece of the tax pie, and is not in the slightest bit interested in helping less endowed areas in Canada. In some of his public utterances he sounds as much a separatist as Pierre Bourgault, his cynicism impelling him to declare that British Columbia does not need Ottawa, or any other part of Canada, in order to survive in prosperity. Is there such a thing as sentiment, or the noble gesture, in striving for nationhood? For instance, I asked Bennett how he would react to any idea requiring immigration officers, stationed in Vancouver, to have some knowledge of French in order to greet French Canadians arriving by ship or plane from the Far East. First he said that anyone smart enough to travel to the Far East should be smart enough to speak English. Then he said: "We don't tell the French they've got to learn English. No one is going to tell us we've got to learn French."

I pointed out that these would be federal, rather than provincial, civil servants, and possibly Ottawa might even decide to pay a bonus to encourage a measure of bilingualism. "Then we would get out," Bennett said simply. In Bennett's mind the warning was a valid, just one, because, as he put it: "We pay three times as much tax per head as Quebec. We sell the United States two dollars' worth of goods for every dollar we spend there. We save the balance of payments from being disastrous for the whole country." Apart from marked exaggeration, forgotten was the fact that hardly sixty years ago, at a time of crisis for British Columbia, the rest of the country came to its financial assistance. But sentiment had no purpose. In a reference again to Quebec I asked Bennett if he ever forgot practical arguments and thought of Confederation in the emotional sense of marriage, where if belief in the institution is strong enough, some give and take is in order. "We married in 1871," he said, suggesting that B.C. was not responsible for any English-French commitments made in 1867.

Students at the University of British Columbia on occasion hang or burn Bennett in effigy. This is partly because of his brazen anti-intellectualism. Bennett, in public speeches, pointedly emphasizes how he never finished high school but this lapse did not prevent him from going on to success in hardware and politics. The environment for intellectuals in B.C. has been weak ever since Bennett took office. Previous governments quietly built up a high standard of education and health. Bennett followed through with new hospitals and new buildings for the University of British Columbia, but failed to provide sufficient funds to staff them adequately. From a vote point of view, he can cite the structures as tangible evidence of material advancement. But neither his supporters nor Bennett himself worry about abstractions, such as the decline in morale among the U.B.C. faculty.

Little more than a decade ago the University was able to draw some of the brightest teachers from across the country. If Vancouver's climate was an inducement, so was the attractive salary structure. But U.B.C. has slipped back badly among Canadian universities; in terms of salaries in 1964 it ranked twelfth. Its library, for a campus of close to fifteen thousand students, was listed as 50th in North America, until a private benefactor in 1965 provided $3.2 million for the purchase of books. Laboratories are inadequate for teaching or research purposes, and there has been a steady, and dangerous, movement of faculty people away from Vancouver. One professor, Avrum Stoll, felt impelled, because of the "urgency and gravity" of the situation, to publish an open letter on his resignation. He blamed the province for failure to meet its financial obligations and quoted some hard results: only 6 per cent of U.B.C.'s students were enrolled in the graduate program, compared with 60 per cent at Columbia, 50 per cent at Harvard, and 30 per cent at Berkeley. Bennett's attitude was to ask: Why put money into advanced teaching, when so many graduates drift down to California or to Eastern Canada? Faculty members found it impossible, until a year or so ago, to convince him that one way to keep trained men and women content is to provide them with finances and facilities.

U.B.C. students are possibly the most outspoken in the country; certainly they are among the most liberal. In contrast to the public at large, they decided early on to try to understand contemporary Quebec a little better, and accordingly held a "French Canada Week." The students spent $1,600 of their own money, and also received a grant from the Koerner Foundation, in order to invite from Quebec universities a few speakers whose own student societies in turn paid half the expenses. In addition, Pierre Bourgault, the R.I.N. leader, attended. An average of from five to six hundred undergraduates went to the lectures. Later, some of those with whom I spoke sounded much the same as Premier Bennett in their hostility toward Quebec. Others, probably the majority, were in a state of indifference. But a key group were those who said they had learned a great deal about Quebec's aspirations and wanted to learn still more because they recognized the seriousness of the situation.

"In a way," said Jim Ward, an agriculture student, "we're more confused than before. But at least we know that French Canadians are not satisfied." The confusion, he explained, came from the realization that there are several movements in Quebec, speaking often at cross purposes. Ward concluded: "If you cannot—as I cannot—come to terms with the out-and-out separatists, then you run the risk of being labeled 'anti-French,' when in reality you are vitally interested in them." Malcolm Scott, President of the Alma Mater Society, and one of the organizers of the French Canada Week, said that while Bourgault received considerable attention in the press because of his extremist statements, the real value of the experiment was the contact it established between U.B.C. and moderates among the French-speaking students. "The French students," observed Scott, "showed they were not crackpots. On the contrary, they were quite reasonable in many respects." It turned out to be a two-way street, with the French-Canadian under-graduates gaining a better understanding of the attitude of their contemporaries on the West Coast. Even Bourgault rewrote part of his speech after conversation with young British Columbians. "Some people in Quebec feel that adjustments can be made that will keep Quebec in Con-federation," he told them. "Others feel that Confederation is doomed and nothing can be done for it, and they become separatists. As a separatist, I can't convince you of anything and didn't come here to ask for anything. I came here to inform you." He received a standing ovation.

The main effect of the French Canada Week was to stim-ulate discussion and debate. At least the U.B.C. people were trying to enlighten themselves. In general, the bulk of Brit-ish Columbians do not share the willingness of a handful of students and intellectuals to become even slightly in-formed. On arrival in Vancouver, I took a taxi from the airport, and when the driver asked me where I was from, and I said Montreal, he said: "Oh, the home of Rocket Richard." His naming of an old-time hockey hero was not mere facetiousness; it was almost the extent of his detailed knowledge about French Canada. On the whole there is either apathy toward the political and emotional turmoil of Quebec, or outright enmity. Possibly what is most irritating, especially to French-Canadian visitors from the East, is not the discovery of anti-Quebec feeling but rather the fact that most British Columbians simply do not care one way or the other. Partly this is because of the Coast's general ignorance of, and attitude toward, the East. British Columbians, in common with people of the Prairies, simply lump Ontario and Quebec together in one and the same omnibus term: "the East," an area to be avoided if possible, and certainly to be mistrusted. If Quebec is thought of with any distinction, it is because it has a different religion from Ontario rather than a different language.

In an early public meeting in Vancouver of the Royal Commission on Bilingualism and Biculturalism, many of the speakers indicated that ignorance was breeding intolerance. The consensus of several groups was that British Columbians were unaware of the complexity of the present phase in Canadian history. One citizens' body blamed "the shortcomings of the news media." Desmond Owen-Turner, a research officer with the B.C. Telephone Company, said that most reports received in the province about Quebec were of a "sensational and violent variety, and are actually performing a disservice rather than a service." At an open forum there was the predictable outburst of a man who condemned "English" politicians for "giving in" to "the French." He shouted: "If the French language is forced farther afield, the politicians will also want Chinese—because our politicians will cater to any group." In more sober breath, a teacher of French, Daniel Dorotich, a Yugoslav immigrant who spent ten years in Quebec before moving to Vancouver, said he was "appalled by the tremendous ignorance on both sides." Mrs. Blair Neatby, French-Canadian wife of a former U.B.C. historian, said she was constantly amazed to find that British Columbians do not even know that there is a French-speaking community in their province.[1] The principal conclusions of the Commission session were that British Columbia is more closely allied to the United States than to the rest of Canada, that the Rockies are a great liability, and that insularity or regionalism exists in both East and West.

If the attitude in British Columbia toward Quebec hovers mainly around indifference, it also includes some of the harshest judgment I have found in Canada. Partly this is based on religion. In Victoria, a government official referred to "those men in black garb who want to make Canada Catholic." Some confirmation of the prevalence of this mistrust was contained in a statement by a Vancouver historian, S. Mack Eastman, who told the Biculturalism Commission that W. L. Grant's *History of Canada*—"one of the best textbooks ever written"—was pulled out of B.C. schools because it was considered "too Catholic" and "too friendly" toward French Canada.

However, there are, as we have observed, contradictions even within the soul of the empire beyond the Rockies. One November day, at the height of disturbances in Quebec, a columnist on the *Victoria Daily Times,* Arthur Mayse, summoned his fellow English-speaking Canadians to arms: "We will keep Confederation, and Quebec within Confederation. We will not permit you (in Quebec) to make good your addle-pated dream of a North American Monaco or Luxembourg thrust between Ontario and the Maritimes. These are harsh words, but if you ever attempt to make good the Principality of Quebec, the reality will be harsher." Just about a year later the mayor of Victoria received a delegation of Quebec mayors whom he had personally invited in an effort to introduce the French side of Canada to the other. It was a warm, gratifying experience. The people of Victoria who met the mayors and their wives discovered a cross section of the reasonable and sober mass of French

[1] About 67,000 B.C. residents, or 4 per cent of the population, are of French origin. But only 23,000 list French as their mother tongue.

Canadians, given neither to *habitant* quaintness nor bomb-throwing. Nevertheless, the old image was hard to shake. One B.C. civil servant, of middle age and senior position, asked in quiet seriousness: "Don't you think if the Pope had told the people of Quebec to be nice to the Queen everything would have been all right?"

9.

The Prosperous Prairies

ONE OF THE biggest American communities outside the United States is in Alberta, a Canadian province that has assumed some of the whirl and whoop of Texas. For ten days every summer at least half of the 300,000 residents of Calgary, the most booster-conscious city in Canada, reach for their ten-gallon hats, levis, leather jackets, studded belts, and high-heeled boots. It is Calgary Stampede time, and every loyal citizen is expected to convey the flavor, and to conduct business in this garb or wear it to the supermarket. The Stampede attracts about 600,000 visitors from all states in the United States, from all provinces, and about forty other countries. The Indians descend from the reservations, the Mounties put on their scarlet tunics, and the Stampede grounds shudder as the chuckwagons race around the mighty curves. It is called—at least by Calgarians—the greatest show of its kind in the world, or in an equally familiar phrase: "Bloody terrific." The use of "bloody" is a faint reminder that some old English stock—of an adventurous strain—makes up Calgary's base, even if "terrific" is a concession to modern times and the American invasion.

Some of the Americans came as long ago as the 1880's,

from Montana just to the south, and others even drifted up from Texas and Oklahoma to lay claim to magnificent ranchlands in the foothills of the Rockies. But the major penetration has taken place only since 1947, when enormous oilfields were discovered. The colony has now expanded to maybe as many as 100,000—including descendants of the originals—of whom almost half live in Calgary. It is not, however, an aloof country-club ghetto, of the style one finds in other oil centers such as Caracas. It features, instead, a curious kind of assimilation in which many Americans retain their United States citizenship but are keenly active in every community enterprise short of politics. Americans are prominent on the Stampede's board of directors; and of the past dozen presidents of the Calgary Petroleum Club, an elaborate social establishment, at least five have been from below the border. William H. Christensen, the former United States consul general, recalls saying to a prominent Albertan something about "us foreigners," and being told curtly: "Don't call yourself a foreigner in Alberta." And yet, in the closest thing to an integrated North America, Albertans are consciously Canadian. In the mid-1950's, at the height of the influx, there was some ill feeling among the old families of Calgary about the "brash Americans" taking over, a sentiment that crept into newspaper stories. But this attitude has died out now that the oil business itself has simmered down from a boom tempo into more orderly business routine. "You can be sitting next to a man at lunch," said a Calgarian executive, "and likely as not he'll be an American. But you'll not be sure, either from his accent or manner." Some native Calgarians forget their hard "a" or "er" tones to affect a Texan drawl. Or are these really Texans?

The free and easy integration is such that Bob Brinkerhoff, who arrived from Dallas in 1949 on an assignment from a firm of drilling contractors, elected later to set up his own company and stay on; he preserves his United States citizenship. On the other hand, Eddie Laborde, of Shreveport,

Louisiana, became a naturalized Canadian while in his forties and after establishing himself as an independent operator in oil exploration and development. "I felt if I wanted to earn a living here I should be a Canadian," he explained. Then, after something of a pause, he added: "After all, it wasn't like becoming a Venezuelan or an Arab." The number of Americans is significant not only because it represents a substantial percentage of the province's population. It also symbolizes a twofold phenomenon that has taken place since the Second World War: Oil production has cut sharply the traditional dependence of Alberta on agriculture; at the same time the petroleum and gas industry, infused with some $5 billion to $6 billion in United States capital, has developed into a standard illustration used by those who fear the Canadian economy is in danger of total domination by the United States.

Alberta is one of the three Prairie Provinces that stretch a thousand miles between Ontario in the East and British Columbia on the West Coast and fill 750,000 square miles. The others, Saskatchewan and Manitoba, are also in the midst of transformation from a primarily farm economy to one of diversification. Few Easterners are aware of the dramatic change in far less than a generation. For most Easterners the Prairies automatically arouse an image of endless fields of wheat and huge herds of cattle, with hardly a smokestack in between. Part of the cliché remains true. Saskatchewan is still the "bread basket" of Canada, and Alberta the chief producer of beef, while agriculture continues to be important to Manitoba. But in over-all statistics, manufacturing and mining and service industries in the Prairies today bring in greater revenue, and employ four times as many people as farming.[1] The major change, how-

---

[1] The figures also reflect the increased efficiency of agriculture. Thirty years ago a farmer produced enough food for only ten persons; now he supplies thirty-one. An example of the meaning of mechanization is reported by the University of Manitoba, where a student—a man in his 30's—commuted sixty miles every day to classes, earned a science degree in agriculture, and still managed to work his farm of 600 acres of cropland and 30 head of cattle. The only help he required was during harvest.

ever, is psychological: a sense of confidence and buoyancy that comes with economic prosperity and the feeling that the world is not going to end in a dust bowl. The combination of a record crop and wheat sales to Russia and Communist China gave Saskatchewan farmers in 1963 the highest income per family they had ever enjoyed—$6,750—in contrast to the hungry or "dirty thirties" when four out of five were on relief. But beyond this is the implicit security in the knowledge that Saskatchewan has been rescued from the tyranny of a single commodity and the whims of Nature and world markets. It has a rapidly expanding oil industry, with five hundred new wells erupting every year. Its potash deposits, the biggest on earth, attracted by 1965 almost $300 million in investments, even though the mining itself came into operation only in 1962.

The first finances for the tapping of this bonanza arrived from the United States and abroad, not from "the East." "What else could anyone expect?" said a middle-aged government official. For, what has *not* altered in Saskatchewan —or in Alberta or Manitoba—is the perennial disdain for "the East," the lingering suspicion that it cannot be trusted or counted upon. "The East" embraces Ontario, Quebec, and the federal government at Ottawa. For older Westerners there are stories their parents told of how the Manitoba government tried desperately to break the monopoly of the Canadian Pacific Railway and its high freight prices for wheat; provincial legislators enacted several laws to allow for shipments to the eastern seaboard by way of the United States, each time to be overruled by Ottawa. For other Westerners, with fresher, more personal recollections, there are stories of how manufacturers in the East have always sheltered behind tariff walls to make farmers pay high prices for equipment, and, inevitably, of eastern banks and trust companies foreclosing because of unpaid farm mortgages during the depression. "Exploitation" is synonymous with the East and devilish Bay Street in Toronto and St. James Street in Montreal, havens of the capitalists.

In a vague way even the current restlessness of Quebec is regarded as another eastern attempt to abuse the rest of the country. For, in many Prairie minds, whatever Quebec is up to she is doing because she is a slippery *eastern* province. The fact that Quebec says it feels itself a colony in the midst of Canada is hardly appreciated, despite similar cries in the past from the Prairies. As early as 1884 English-speaking Manitoba farmers talked of rebellion against the federal system because of freight rates; as recently as the 1930's there was a small but bitter secessionist movement in Saskatchewan, which considered itself a badly treated "colony." The language of separatism, therefore, is not new to the Westerner. But what is especially irksome right now is first that it comes from the East, second that it comes at a moment in history when Westerners are just beginning to harvest the long-anticipated rewards of perseverance.

The status symbols of new cars and deep freezers exist for the first time in almost every Prairie home. But beyond this fact, the West, undergoing its own industrial revolution, hardly has the patience or inclination to look with sympathy on Quebec's social and industrial upheaval. If anything, Quebec's noisy transition is dismissed as thoughtless or inconsiderate since it threatens to disturb the country when people have reason to relax and enjoy themselves. Prairie people, alluding to the 1930's and beyond, are inclined to say: "Where was Quebec when we had problems here? It was busy making money while we were starving." Quebec was starving and struggling in those days, too, but few Westerners are willing to recognize this point. Basically, everything goes back to the same old point: Quebec is the East, and so is Ontario, and both are greedy and selfish. A Manitoba farmer, speaking of separatism, mixed old acrimony with facetiousness when he said: "Quebec can do what it wants and go where it wants—so long as it takes Toronto."

People of the Prairie Provinces, peculiarly enough, are the nonconformists or the true rebels of Canada. In a sense this is because geographic remoteness placed them in a position where they had to find their own way while the heavier areas of population remained in the East. Minneapolis, five hundred miles to the south, is closer to Winnipeg than any big Canadian city. But Winnipeg is essentially a Canadian-minded city, with a "mosaic" of Manitobans of Ukrainian, German, French, and Icelandic descent; the original settlers were from Scotland. Winnipeg is also the beginning of the West or the beginning of the East, depending on the direction from which you approach it. At one time it was simply a big warehouse for goods made in the East and destined for transshipment westward. Now it turns out an increasing number of manufactured products itself—such items as plastic containers and women's sports wear—and part of the flow is eastward. It has attracted so many people from the hinterland (more than 40 per cent of the 958,000 Manitobans live in Winnipeg) that the Manitoba Telephone System prints only two directories. One lists the Winnipeg numbers, the other lists all the other numbers stretching from the border of North Dakota to Hudson Bay.

The Winnipeg phone book indicates another unusual feature, at least in comparison with the United States. It contains this listing: Communist Party of Canada, 607 Main St., 942-8985. Winnipeg elects the only avowed Communist in public office in North America. He is Joe Zuken, alderman for Ward 3, a medium- to low-income working-class district that has had a Communist representative on the city council since 1933. Zuken's predecessor was the highly respected Jake Penner, who retired in 1961 at the age of eighty. Both Penner and Zuken won support because of unstinting community service. Zuken does not spend much time at 607 Main Street, which is a rather threadbare assembly hall with a forlorn portrait of Lenin on one wall and few other decorations. He works usually from his law office in the Confederation Building, a few blocks away.

Zuken, in his early fifties, grew up in Ward 3, which he calls an "ethnic hodgepodge," and as a child understood hardly a word of English, managing better in Yiddish or Ukrainian. But today, as he told it to me, he is appalled by the Prairies' preoccupation with "multiculturalism" and its ignorance of the legitimate grievances of French Canada. "We have yet to come to grips with an understanding of the concept of a two-nation state, the fundamental of Confederation," he said. "If we have separatism in Quebec, it will accelerate our absorption by the United States. Even now we're in the process of slipping into economic and cultural subservience. Communists for a long time have been talking of what has only now moved into the center of the stage—our relations with the United States." Zuken is concerned because the legal and open position the Communist Party enjoys in the present structure of Canada obviously would alter in any union with the United States. Not long ago the Manitoba Court of Appeal, in a controversial case dealing with labor relations, sent an official letter inviting "The Communist Party of Canada (Manitoba Section)" to present a brief along with other interested groups—"a situation," Zuken notes tersely, "impossible in the United States."

Zuken will not say how many party members there are in Manitoba. Estimates go no higher than three thousand. Voters in Ward 3, which has an adult population of 50,000, almost invariably say they pick Zuken because he is an honest and conscientious alderman, interested in their welfare, and that is all they need to know. Those who might think twice about any political inference say simply, as one man expressed it, "He is a *Canadian* Communist." This is not a new attitude. The history of economic and political radicalism, in all shapes, is deep in the Prairie Provinces.

Alberta gave the world its first practical look at the unorthodox doctrine of Social Credit. Saskatchewan for twenty years was the first and only socialist state in North America, long ago facing and meeting social problems the rest of the continent is only now beginning to acknowledge. Even though there was a change of government in 1964, Saskatchewan still provides a bigger portion of its budget for education and welfare than any of the other nine provinces, and boasts the only comprehensive medicare program in North America.

Ernest Charles Manning has been premier of Alberta since 1943 and his Social Credit party has flourished in office since 1935, making the longest and possibly most successful political stories in Canada. Manning is still in his middle fifties, and only a few flecks of gray in his sandy hair detract from an almost boyish visage. There is serenity in his manner, due originally to an evangelical background and training as a Baptist preacher, and more recently to the fact that his government can count on an income of $175 million a year from oil and gas, a godsend that encourages Social Credit largesse. Twice Manning has issued "citizens' participation dividends"—checks for $20 in 1957, and $17.50 in 1958—to every Albertan over the age of twenty-one. This was in real money (a total of $20 million), and quite different from the "prosperity certificates" his predecessor, William "Bible Bill" Aberhart, put out in 1936. Aberhart, however, is given credit for the introductory demonstration of Social Credit in action, Social Credit being the economic doctrine invented by an English engineer, Major C. H. Douglas. The Douglas scheme was reduced to a famous theorem: $A + B = C$. Simply stated, A equaled wages, B the other expenses of production, and C the total cost of a product. Douglas reasoned that since C was always greater than A, the producer's purchasing power, there would never be enough money available to buy available goods. The answer was for the government to issue a "social dividend," or, more bluntly, to print scrip that would be accepted as money. This is precisely what Aberhart did. Shopkeepers and other practical economists rejected the "prosperity certificates" as "funny money," followed eventually by the Supreme Court of Canada, which ruled that the Alberta government had exceeded its legal powers in attempting to control banking and credit.

This is all ancient history now and steeped in a depression period. The Social Credit party has become thoroughly orthodox in practice and financing, even if it clings to some formal ideology. Once a year Manning delivers a traditional speech at the party convention and utters expected platitudes about how the money problems of the world would be solved if everyone adopted Social Credit principles. Delegates applaud politely, then go home to forget the speech until next year. They are, as I saw at a convention in Calgary, a rather stern-faced group, elderly for the most part and ready to nod in agreement when Manning makes one of his frequent biblical references to illustrate a point. A whole generation of Albertans have grown up under the fundamentalist preachings of Aberhart and Manning, though only the most devoted followers of Social Credit share the feeling of holiness. "If they could get away with it, they'd still be burning witches—and among the witches would be editors, pro-fluoridationists, and professors," said a newspaperman who under the circumstances preferred to remain anonymous.

The *Calgary Herald* did not mind identifying itself in an editorial:

> There are many, many non-Social Crediters in Alberta who vote Social Credit because, on the whole, it has given reasonably efficient government. The same people feel their souls shrivel when Social Credit occasionally reveals its deep-down strains of anti-intellectualism, anti-professionalism, even anti-Semitism and the kind of hill-billy funda-

mentalism which cringes and runs in the face of new thought and criticism.

The *Herald* was especially worked up at the moment because Manning was railing against newspapers and what he called their abuse of freedom. Back in 1935 Aberhart had ranted against the press and its "mental hydrophobia," and pursued it with Canada's most vicious and notorious press-gag legislation, "An Act to Ensure the Publication of Accurate News and Information." This was disallowed by the Supreme Court, along with the other dubious legislation, but now the *Herald* was taking no chances. It was warning Manning against any utterances which, it said, "smack of semi-fascism."

In the past, newspaper attacks on Social Credit were even sharper, for some members of the party used to speak of the "Turko-Mongolian conspiracy," meaning in an obtuse way that all troubles could be blamed on Jews. Although such remarks are not made openly today, there is a suspicion that anti-Semitism is a latent force in Social Credit. Actually, Manning is a quiet and cautious type of man; rarely does he make an ill-considered remark that he has to explain away. He has little use for his neighbor in geography and doctrine, Premier Bennett of British Columbia, whom he regards as an opportunist and author of brash statements. Bennett, as we have already recorded, responds with contempt for Manning's austere personality. Manning is indeed reserved in his personal relations; almost no one knows him well enough to call him by his first name, and in a sense there is the same kind of remoteness and personal mysticism that marked another highly successful political figure, the late Mackenzie King.

To many Albertans Manning is spiritual godfather as well as premier. The son of a migrant English homesteader, he took early to fundamentalism, largely as a result of listening to Sunday Bible broadcasts by Aberhart. Aberhart, he once recalled, taught him "the complete infallibility of the Scriptures." At the age of nineteen Manning enrolled at the Prophetic Bible Institute, a Baptist organization in Calgary, and three years later became the school's first graduate lay preacher. He lived with the Aberharts and took the role almost of adopted son. Aberhart was a high school mathematics teacher who turned to preaching and later to a search for practical solutions to the economic problems of the depressed, drought-stricken 1930's. It was only natural that Manning should follow him into Social Credit. On Aberhart's death, Manning became the leading radio evangelist of Alberta, an area that has more disciples of fundamentalism than any other part of Canada. He still delivers a weekly sermon that goes out over a radio network and is listened to by more than a million devoted Canadians and Americans.

In this Back-to-the-Bible Hour, every Sunday, his subject can take in—as it did not long ago—an interpretation of Egyptian hieroglyphics in biblical terms. He uses the same sonorous, precise way of speaking in handling a political foe: a courteous technique that can be devastatingly effective. American residents are particularly fascinated by Manning, so calm and dignified does he appear in contrast to more familiar and flamboyant politicians. Among Canadians even old-line businessmen, Liberals and Conservatives, speak with respect for Manning and his successful financial policy. There is some controversy over oil rights, a few people claiming the province has sold its soul to barons from the United States. But the majority of Albertans feel that the petroleum side of government has been well handled and that Manning has never allowed himself to be stampeded into improvident legislation.

The postwar oil business burst into view, and suddenly, in 1947. Until that time Alberta could think of itself mainly as a big farmland with wheat and cattle, and as a scenic wonderland with Banff and Lake Louise in the Rockies.

Then a wildcat well called Imperial Leduc No. 1, twenty-one miles south of Edmonton, blew into production with a heavy flow of crude oil. The event set off a chain reaction that reshaped and speeded the growth of Prairie economy, and with it the over-all Canadian economy. More than $4.5 billion has been invested in Alberta oil exploration and development alone, aside from further billions represented in pipelines, a dozen refineries, and sixty-seven gas-processing plants. No one knows precisely the total value, but it is at least $6.5 billion. The unique feature, in comparison with Texas or Oklahoma oil booms, is that relatively few individuals have garnered big profits. Instead, the provincial government is the direct beneficiary, meeting something like half of its public expenses through revenues from oil and gas. The apparent magic occurs because, while Texans as private citizens have made fortunes because they retained mineral rights to their farms or ranches, in Alberta the state holds mineral rights to about four fifths of the land. If the present wells were on entirely freehold property, fewer than 10,000 people would benefit financially, instead of the whole population of 1,427,000.

In effect, the provincial government holds auctions, leases out its mineral rights in parcels to the highest bidders, and then sits back to collect, in addition to rent, a royalty on all the oil produced. Carl Nickle, who is publisher of the authoritative *Daily Oil Bulletin,* says this gives Alberta a better deal than Middle East countries and Venezuela, which work on profit splits, and at the same time keeps the door open to competitors. Alberta's regulations are now a model for other oil-rich lands. Even the Saskatchewan government, socialist in principle, followed Alberta's example when it found itself Canada's second largest oil producer.

Where the controversy arises is over the amount of foreign ownership—the proportion of Alberta's natural resources that flows through non-Canadian hands. Again precise figures are difficult to arrive at, because of the interlocking relationships of the big international oil companies bearing even Canadian names. But the broad estimate is that between 75 and 90 per cent of Alberta's oil and natural gas is tapped under American auspices. "We don't know who's who," said H. H. Somerville, Alberta's Deputy Minister of Mines and Minerals. "All we require is that a company be registered here, and all we know is that the money being spent here is in Canadian dollars. We don't worry so long as it is not Cuban pesos." Somerville recalled that as far back as 1937 the Minister of Mines, N. E. Tanner, approached financial groups in Toronto and Montreal in search of capital for oil exploration. "But if anyone came here to have a look," he said, "we didn't catch sight of him." In 1938 Tanner sounded out British interests, but again, according to Somerville, the response was negative. So the Social Credit government declared as an official policy that anyone was welcome to hunt for oil, and to extract it.

Premier Manning's position is that United States capital arrived strictly on Alberta's terms. "We dictate the conditions under which our resources are developed," he told me:

> We make the laws; the laws are not made by the United States. Therefore it is within our power to determine where the line should be drawn so that the investor can be ensured a fair return for his money and the risk he takes, and at the same time our people should get a fair return for their natural resources. If there is any "exploitation" by the United States it is because we permit it. Since Canadians haven't shown themselves anxious to supply risk capital, we wouldn't be where we are without American support.

Some cynicism greets these remarks. An editor rejected as a distortion of history the argument that Alberta was turned down by financiers in the East. "Their problem," he said, "was not how to put money into Alberta but how to get it out." For, in 1935 and 1936, the Social Credit government repudiated provincial bonds worth $160 million, and its reputation was at an all-time low. A Calgary lawyer, who was once active in negotiating major contracts on behalf of oil companies, flatly accused Manning of selling out to United States interests in order to save the provincial treasury. "No sheik, nabob, dictator, or other despotic owner of oil ever disposed of it so imprudently as Manning has, or so far in advance of its use," said the lawyer:

> American companies are buying up rights as fast as they can—not that they need the oil now. But it's cheap to make a deal here, and, unlike the Middle East or Venezuela, the oil is safe in Canada. Manning has sold the rights to some ground for as little as eight cents a barrel. He did it to get quick money. We are stupid—just as the Indian was in giving up his rights. But Americans shouldn't take advantage of a stupid government, even if the white man did the Indians. It will rebound on them later.

This was, I found, a minority opinion. Alex G. Bailey spoke, more typically, for the majority. Bailey, an engineer and former provincial civil servant dealing with oil and gas conservation, made a success of his own exploration and development company when he struck out after the Leduc discovery. Later he became president of the Alberta Gas Trunkline, $150 million worth of pipeline within the province, with 87 per cent of the stock owned by Canadians. He said,

> In my view, the Americans haven't taken over anything. When they come in and build oil wells or refineries they build capital assets for us. When and if they go home they can't take those holes in the ground or plants with them. But the main thing they can't take is the know how they've taught us. I've been in the oil business twenty years, and I know that everything the Americans have done they've done in good faith. They've leaned over backward to avoid any political entanglement; they're frightened to death even of being accused of it. Besides, I'd rather do business with an American than a Canadian from the East. I can talk more frankly.

The implicit message here—and it is sensed frequently—is that many Albertans, in retaining a distaste for the East, look for economic ties with the United States. These do not presume political liaison. I met young oil engineers, men under the age of forty, who, as employees of large United States concerns, felt that they were limited in advancement, that key positions always would be given to Americans. But these men were on the outnumbered side. Most with whom I spoke expressed gratitude for the advancement they had made, the high salaries they received, and the opportunities ahead. There also appeared recognition of a fact of economics: It was only in 1962, for the first time since the Leduc strike in 1947, that the oil industry took in more revenue from production than it spent the same year on exploration, development, or administrative costs. It has still a long way to go before recovering its cumulative investment, yet Alberta continues to collect a healthy annuity.[2]

The opening of the Canadian West was not marked by the general bloodshed and Indian fighting that accompanied the opening of the West in the United States. But there occurred in the Prairies the Riel Rebellion, Canada's closest equivalent of the United States Civil War. The comparison is made not because of any scale of battle, which was minute and brief, but only because the Riel Rebellion tore apart a nation that had barely been born and accentuated latent suspicions and grievances between one faction and another. Canada's counterparts of Northerners and Southerners were

[2] At the moment, with a world surplus of oil, Alberta wells are producing only at about half capacity. All Ontario west of Ottawa uses Canadian crude, but the rest of Eastern Canada gets its oil from Venezuela because it is cheaper to bring it in by tanker than to ship it across the continent by pipeline. About 30 per cent of Alberta's average daily production of 800,000 barrels goes into areas of the United States that are close by and deficient in domestic oil. Undergoing development in the northeast of the province are the Athabaska tar sands containing a volume of recoverable crude oil equal to the entire world's presently proved reserves of conventional crude oil.

the English Protestants and the French Catholics, and their descendants suffer to this day some of the same divisions.

Louis Riel was born in St. Boniface, a settlement in Manitoba territory, in 1844. His father, French-speaking, was of mixed blood—a typical product of the marriages between French hunters, *coureurs de bois,* and Indian women who founded "la nation métisse," "the mongrel nation." The Métis developed most of the characteristics that today are accepted as normal for any nationality: mainly a determination to retain a distinctive social organization and language. But in those days there was ridicule of the Métis on the part of the pure whites. Riel's mother, the offspring of the first white woman to come to what was then known as the North West, was an intense, highly strung person who passed on to her son fervor and religious obsession. After early schooling in St. Boniface, Riel was sent to Montreal to be educated for the priesthood. He was rejected because of mental instability. To the Métis, however, he stood out as an able and natural and eloquent leader.

The Métis lived in a French-speaking colony on the Red River—the realm of the Hudson's Bay Company—and along with English settlers enjoyed virtually an autonomous life. Then, in 1869, after lengthy negotiations, the Hudson's Bay Company gave up its claim to the Canadian West in return for $1.5 million and title to 7 million acres of land. The arrangements with the Dominion government were made without consultation with the Métis. Soon English settlers, who had shown contempt for the Métis, were boasting that an army of colonists from Ontario would swamp the "halfbreeds" and their customs; when surveyors from the government of Canada moved in, the Métis felt they were being dispossessed. Riel's protests to Ottawa went unheeded, and finally he and the Métis took to arms. The insurrection was a fiasco, but in the process Riel showed his defiance of central authority by ordering the execution of Thomas Scott, a young Orangeman from Ontario ("a troublemaker," some historians have called him). This was in 1870, three brief years after English Protestants and French Catholics in the East had, in theory, settled their differences through Confederation. But now the enmity, never far from the surface, broke into the open. Quebec sympathized with Riel and the Métis in their desire to preserve language and identity; Ontario demanded Riel's life. Riel took sanctuary in Montana.

But it was far from the end of his role in history. The railway came to Manitoba, and thousands of immigrants settled around the Red River. Many Métis left their homes and moved westward on the Saskatchewan River, to establish a new colony free from the domination of people they regarded as interlopers. But by the 1880's a new wave of surveyors and settlers brought by the advancing railway created a new crisis; the Métis, who had never established legal claims to their fresh landholdings, again felt threatened. The Indians as well as the Métis were worried that the settlers would destroy the buffalo herds on which they relied for food and clothing. Canada's West never had been subjected to the horrors of an Indian War. The combination of the North West Mounted Police, to keep white men in check, and the official policy of placing wandering tribes on reservations had been fairly successful. But now a few tribes—notably the Cree—gave signs of sullen restlessness. "I never saw the Indians mean business before," a government agent reported in 1884. "The thing has got to be looked at seriously and precautions taken before it is too late." In Ottawa the warnings were largely ignored.

The Métis called out once again to Riel, who was now a schoolteacher in Montana and an American citizen. He was also fifteen years older, and since his last effort at leadership he had spent some time in an insane asylum. "The whole race is calling you," the Métis implored in a letter, and Riel, suffering from religious and political delusions, agreed to come back. The Métis promptly elected him president of a provisional government in Saskatchewan territory. The atmosphere turned out to be far uglier than in 1870, for the Métis were now in alliance with the Indians. In March 1885 a detachment of Mounted Police, sent to investigate a Métis gathering, was driven off by force. Immediately afterward, the Cree rose, and, led by Chief Big Bear, attacked a settlement at Frog Lake, where they massacred the men and carried off the women and children. Many tribes bided their time and refrained from joining the movement immediately. Nevertheless the Cree, directed by such chiefs as Poundmaker, Spotted Calf, and Almighty Voice, won a few more early victories along with the Métis. Ottawa, at last aroused, sent a strong military contingent. Within three months the rebellion and the threat of a general Indian uprising were at an end. Riel surrendered and was taken to Regina, Saskatchewan, for trial.

Once more the East was bitterly split. Ontarians called for Riel's execution as a revolutionary and the murderer of Thomas Scott. Quebecers eulogized Riel as the defender of Métis and indirectly of French-Canadian minority rights. Even the moderate Wilfrid Laurier, who was later to become the first French-Canadian prime minister, said: "Had I been born on the banks of the Saskatchewan I would myself have shouldered a musket to fight against the neglect of governments and the shameless greed of speculators." Riel, however, was found guilty and sentenced to be hanged. The jury, Quebec noted with sharp resentment, was entirely English-speaking and Protestant. It had rejected the plea of defense lawyers that Riel was insane and therefore not responsible for his actions; but Riel's English-speaking lieutenant, William Jackson, was declared innocent after a similar plea. Sir John A. Macdonald, the prime minister, was faced with pressure from two sides, for Riel stood as a powerful symbol. Quebec demanded commutation, Ontario insisted on fulfilment of sentence. A Quebec newspaper declared: "Riel executed, everyone understands, means the triumph of Orangeism over us." An Ontario newspaper warned: "We British subjects believe that we shall have to fight again for the Conquest.... (Quebec) can be sure of this, there will be no new 'Treaty of 1763.' This time the conqueror will not capitulate."

Macdonald allowed the sentence to stand, in the erroneous belief that French Canada would soon forget. One early result was that Quebec, which traditionally had supported Macdonald's Conservative party, began to swing toward the Liberals, an alignment that has survived into present times. The broader effect was equally lasting and even more significant. "Riel's execution," notes Ramsay Cook, the historian, "caused Quebec to turn in on herself and re-examine the position of a cultural minority within Confederation. Macdonald's decision to let Riel die, despite Quebec's opposition, was the first warning to French Canadians after 1867 that on issues which united English-speaking Canada the minority would have to accept defeat."

Riel's body was brought from Regina, where he was a villain, to St. Boniface, where he was a hero and martyr. The exact location of his grave, in the cemetery adjoining the St. Boniface Cathedral, is not known. There was some talk at the time of burial of keeping it a secret to prevent desecration. But Father Maurice Deniset-Bernier, rector of the cathedral, reasoned, as he showed me around, that probably nothing so mysterious happened. The grounds were altered and some plots simply were overrun when the cathedral was rebuilt in 1904. Now a stone marker in the graveyard merely says, as a general indication that the body is in the vicinity, "Here reposes Louis Riel, 1844-1885." A rehabilitation process has been going on for many years. Today Riel appears even to English writers neither as a disloyal rebel nor a ruthless murderer. At worst he is thought of as a tragic and unbalanced figure; some authors suggest his only crime was to be born in the wrong era. In a modern world Riel might have been considered a noble upholder of man's dignity and a protector of minorities. But even his nineteenth-century rebelliousness was not entirely wasted. Riel enjoyed a moment of glory in 1870 when, as a consequence of the Red River uprising, the federal government created out of the North West territories the Province of Manitoba, with guarantees for the rights of the Métis and French-Canadian settlers. Since more than half the inhabitants of the new province were French-speaking, the same provisions of Confederation applied as in Quebec: French, along with English, was to be an official language, and Roman Catholic denominational schools were to be maintained out of public taxation.

The arrangement lasted twenty years only. The Manitoba legislature revoked the federal contract for a dual system of Protestant and Catholic school boards, and said that henceforth there would be one system of public schooling, with English the language of instruction.

The legality of the Act of 1890 has long been debated, touching as it does the tender area of provincial versus federal rights. To at least one authority on the constitution, Professor Murray Donnelly of the University of Manitoba, there is no doubt that the provincial legislators committed transgressions not only against the law but against the spirit of Confederation—a development that has present significance. "Their action illustrated perfectly Anglo-Saxon arrogance," says Donnelly. Moving up to current issues in Canada as a whole, he adds: "If the French have got to give up their resentment that they're a conquered people, we've got to give up the feeling that we possess the divine right of Anglo-Saxons to rule."

The Act of 1890 was fundamentally an act of Orangemen determined to crush Catholicism. By that year, Protestants in Manitoba were in the majority, but a fresh influx of homesteaders had begun from France and Belgium as well as Quebec. Among the migrants from France were devout men and women fleeing the anticlerical mood of Paris, Toulouse, and other cities. The obvious strategy, in discouraging an invasion of Catholics as a group, was to hit at education and language. In recent years the proportion of Catholics has dwindled to about one third of Manitoba's population, but the betrayal of seventy-five years ago is still felt acutely. Most provinces maintain some sort of arrangement for turning over tax dollars to separate school boards where there are sizable French-speaking communities. Franco-Manitobans, in contrast, complain of a "double tax"—that is, they pay the usual levy for all public education, but if they want their children trained adequately in French they must open schools at their own expense.

In what has come to be known as the School Question, a certain way to infuriate English-speaking Manitobans is to suggest that French Catholics have a constitutional right to their own schools supported by tax money. From a politician's point of view it is difficult to find a more sensitive or perilous issue. Fifty years ago a premier, Sir Rodmond Roblin, wrecked a political career partly because of the School Question. As recently as 1959 Protestants in Winnipeg formed a citizens' committee to fight a Royal Commission's recommendations that the provincial government give funds to the parochial schools. Letters of abuse against the commission filled columns in newspapers. The School Question was pushed aside until the current premier, Duff Roblin, grandson of Sir Rodmond, and a forty-seven-year-old Conservative of deep integrity, offered a compromise solution. Roblin, in 1964, put forth what he called a "shared services" plan which would allow separate schools to send their pupils to tax-supported schools for such neutral subjects as mathematics and science. Roblin knew, as he expressed it to me, that intense emotionalism "is still with us, it smolders explosively beneath the surface of our political and community life." The reaction to his "shared services" plan—the only positive offering any politician had made in recent times—was instantaneous and hardly pleasing. French Catholics called it dangerous because they felt it would force them irrevocably into the kind of integrated school system they were struggling to avoid and thus would bring them one step closer to total assimilation. A member of the legislature from St. Boniface said: "We will continue to fight. We know that our rights come from God and not from Mr. Roblin." The general Protestant attitude was summed up by another member who said: "I am against any aid directly or indirectly given to parochial schools. I will defend the rights of the majority."

The irony was that in almost any other province Roblin's plan might have been considered masterful—modest enough to offend no one, yet at least a move forward in solving a vexing, passionate issue. But in Manitoba the School Question, beyond its religious overtones, runs headlong into what is called the "Manitoba mosaic," a euphemism for "melting pot" without the melting. Visitors from the United States are constantly astonished at how the various ethnic groups, particularly the Ukrainians, have retained ancient identities. While relatively few second-generation Americans speak Ukrainian or German or Italian or the language of their immigrant forefathers, in Manitoba there is a conscious effort to remember a mother tongue, to speak it at home, to dress in costume on old national days—in general to cling to the past while residing in the present. Franco-Manitobans, though a substantial force of 8 per cent of the population, are not the largest minority group. The biggest are the Manitobans of Ukrainian descent, who make up 15 per cent of the population; next are the 12 per cent of German origin.

The Ukrainians are highly organized and vociferous, arguing that the French have no special rights. Premier Roblin, on the other hand, possesses an acute appreciation of the duality of Canada. He took an early interest in the French heritage of his own province, speaks excellent French, and has a profound understanding of Quebec. His thinking about accommodation with French Canada is based on a simple belief: "I cannot visualize Canada without Quebec." Roblin's view, shared by Manitoban intellectuals generally, is that there is "a difference between cultural and constitutional levels." In other words, as he explains it, "By accident or history, or whatever you want to call it, the French-English business is part of our constitution. As real as are the contributions of the Ukrainians, the Germans, and others, these are contributions to culture and have no place in the constitution." The inference, of course, is that Ukrainians and others should fit themselves into one of the *two* melting pots in Canada. But any such open suggestion brings immediately a fiery rejoinder. "I don't see how you can have two states in one country, unless you want a repetition of the way Austria-Hungary used to be," said John Syrnick, a leader of the Ukrainian community. "What the French fail to realize is that Canada has changed tremendously since 1867. Millions of people of origins different from the French or English have come here and have contributed to the development of Canada. They do not wish to be put in the category of second-class citizens."

What does Syrnick, managing editor of the *Ukrainian Voice* and a typical spokesman, want? Broadly he wants an end to any notion that Ukrainians, among other ethnic peoples, should swim in the mainstream of either of the two principal cultures. Specifically, he wants an end to what he regards as "concessions" to Franco-Manitobans. Ukrainian is taught as an elective subject in high school, along with several other languages, but there is deep resentment that it is not given the same prominence as French: a "prominence," as we shall soon note, that hardly satisfies the Franco-Manitobans. One can almost conclude at this point that Winnipeg is a modern miracle of a metropolis, for it manages to convey the image of a *Canadian* melting pot despite the inner conflicts of interest and Syrnick's rejection even of the term "Manitoba mosaic." He prefers something called "cultural pluralism," a phrase that supposedly makes clear that different ethnic groups are integrated but manage to keep their original backgrounds more distinctly than in the United States. "A melting pot," says Syrnick, "impoverishes a nation culturally, morally, and spiritually. A person who has a sense of belonging to a certain cultural group is a more valuable citizen."

This concept reached an almost farcical height a few years ago when Manitoba's Ukrainian community erected outside the legislature building a statue to the nineteenth-century Ukrainian patriot and hero, Taras Shevchenko. There was immediate dismay among non-Ukrainian groups, especially those of British descent, when it turned out that the Shevchenko statue was slightly taller than a nearby one of Queen Victoria. The Ukrainians justified their enthusiasm for a non-Canadian hero by saying that if the Robert Burns Society could honor the Scottish poet regularly, there was no reason why they should not do the same for one of their great men. They rejected the counterargument that Burns at least reflected one of the two languages that entered into the official structure of Canada.

In the same vein, since the Ukrainians label French Canadians as an "ethnic" group, they cannot accept it when Franco-Manitobans refuse to participate in activities for "ethnic" groups. Charles E. Dojack, who is of Czech origin and publisher of periodicals in Ukrainian, Croatian, and German, tells of his experience as chairman of the Red River Exhibition, an annual fair. He rounded up for the main festivity several national groups in traditional costume—Icelandic, Polish, Indian, Ukrainian, and so on—but failed to enlist French-Canadian representation. He tried every Franco-Manitoban musical and educational society he could think of, and was turned down consistently. Finally, in a moment of supreme desperation and irony, he hired a trio of Ukrainian musicians, dressed them in *coureur* costume, and had them sing French songs. Interpreting the Franco-Manitoban boycott, Léo Rémillard, French-program director for the Canadian Broadcasting Corporation in Winnipeg, said: "I find it offensive to receive an invitation even to a cocktail party in honor of so-called ethnic groups."

Franco-Manitobans refuse to regard themselves in the same positions as Ukrainians for the simple reason that they were given rights constitutionally on a partnership basis with Anglo-Canadians—and just because those rights were taken away illegally, they say, is no reason to succumb to diminished status. Their main demand is for French as a language of instruction in the schools. One fascinating aspect of the rather depressing battle between minorities is that 95 per cent of Ukrainians, according to John Syrnick, still speak Ukrainian at home. In contrast, of the 84,000 Manitobans who call themselves French in origin, fewer than 75 per cent consider French as their mother tongue. The decline has been steady over the years, and intellectuals as well as religious leaders fear the eventual death of the language. Even among those who speak French habitually, the impurities of English infiltration are far greater than in Quebec, which itself is hardly a haven for stylists. To plug in a block heater in the subzero weather of St. Boniface, one says: "Plugger mon char." A professor recalled that during a telecast of a Grey Cup football game the French announcer, who used comparatively pure language (he was from Quebec), described a play as "un botté de dégagement." The Franco-Manitobans watching the telecast stared blankly at one another until someone in the audience translated it simply as "a punt," the English expression being understood by all.

In practice, in some rural areas of predominantly French-speaking population, French has been used in teaching, though as a bootleg operation, with the government closing its eyes. But in general Franco-Manitoban children go to public schools where subjects are taught in English; if they want to, they can take French from Grade VII, but merely as they would any foreign language. Now, however, it is becoming slightly more available than in the past, a development that arouses the Ukrainians. A few years ago French was introduced as a language course in some Grade IVs, and in 1963 Roblin put it into Grade I. The major push from Franco-Manitobans for entire tuition in their own tongue and in their own schools came with the flareup of separatism in Quebec, which stimulated discussion of French culture as a whole. But the push is relatively gentle. For one thing, the Franco-Manitoban, in an isolated minority, accepts far more than a Quebecer that he needs English—even at the price of French—in order to survive economically. For another, more than one quarter, and possibly as many as one third, of French-speaking Manitobans trace their immediate ancestry to France or Belgium, and so there is no emotional or historical pull toward Quebec itself.

Generally, Franco-Manitobans take much the same position as Acadians and are concerned with how a separate Quebec would affect their lives and effort to cling to their remaining identity. Like Acadians, they ask a crucial question: What would happen to C.B.C. radio and television, which they now receive in French, if Quebec went its own way? Léo Rémillard says: "We believe in a united Canada; otherwise we are finished." Robert Trudel, a forty-year-old lawyer in Winnipeg, accuses French-speaking compatriots in Quebec of insensitivity. "The Quebecer," he says, "is an isolationist—ignorant of the practical problems French Canadians face in other provinces. I don't think he knew us at all until talk of biculturalism arose. He knew us perhaps as a struggling minority. The French Canadian in the Province of Quebec is convinced that he is *the* French Canadian." Having said this, and while deploring the bombings and militant symptoms of extremism, Trudel adds softly: "The new attitude of Quebec has helped. It has stirred up enough interest in French-Canadian problems to shake the minds of a number of English Canadians in Manitoba. They are beginning to show an interest in French as a language and maybe do away with some of the old Orange attitude that French words and Catholicism are synonymous."

Trudel is left with the dilemma he himself outlines: How to cope, in a practical way, with the fact that Franco-Manitobans are cut off from the main source of language and cultural stimulus, and how, simultaneously, to fit into a growing English-speaking world. "Everyone has to find his own way," he says simply. Trudel's law practice is entirely in English; so is much of his social life. In addition, Trudel, an actor of some ability, has appeared in many English-language plays, and for years portrayed the part of a farm character named Rip Callahan in a C.B.C. soap opera. But to discipline himself in French, and to improve grammar and diction, he joined the Cercle Molière, an amateur theatrical group. His main concern is continuity in the future, since even less French is spoken now than when he was a youngster. If a separate Quebec should come about, bringing the total isolation of the French-speaking community in Manitoba, Trudel says he would seriously consider moving to Quebec: as much as he deplores the parochialism of Quebecers, and despite the fact he would have difficulty practicing law there. "I would want," he says, "my children to know that French literature is just as rewarding as the literature of any other language."

Trudel, by his own reckoning, is among only a handful of people. The majority of Franco-Manitobans, if faced with an absolute choice between English and French, would pick in all probability English—and stay in Manitoba. In Saskatchewan and Alberta something of the same situation prevails, with about one quarter of those of French heritage even now unable to speak the language. Louis A. Desrochers, President of the French-Canadian Association of Alberta, in noting that only about 55,000 in the province still consider French as a mother tongue, says their major problem involves education. His young son goes to an Edmonton public school where there are three classrooms for Grade I: one in English, one in French, one in Ukrainian. But from Grade III onward the program is entirely in English. French, along with Ukrainian, becomes an elective course. Even this much, Desrochers points out, is due specifically to the generosity of the Edmonton school board. In most parts of Alberta there has been no sympathy for French tuition and therefore it is nonexistent.

Like Trudel, Desrochers has a split reaction to the Quebec upheaval. He says: "We resent—maybe not so strongly as Acadia—Quebec speaking for all French Canadians, especially in provincial-federal relations. But at the same time it has drawn attention to our existence." Frequently he is asked to appear on television or radio panels to explain what French Canada wants. He tells his Alberta audience: "We are not asking you to learn French. We simply want to get rid of the idea, the stigma, that French is a foreign language." Sometimes the invitations betray awkwardness steeped in historical prejudice and in ignorance. "Would you object," Desrochers is asked, "to giving an address before an Anglo-Saxon Protestant group?" The invitations drop to almost nothing whenever there are incidents of physical violence in Quebec. In such periods many Albertans withdraw even token signs of interest in Quebec motivations; instead they show hostility toward all matters French-Canadian.

One has to travel West to be reminded of phrases that go back to the time of Riel and hardly exist outside of history books. I heard, for example, that the Quebec revolution is a "Roman plot," meaning that the Catholic Church is back of it so that it can spread its influence. The expression was used by a farmer near Regina just a few days after it was uttered by a public relations man in Edmonton. No matter how diligently I tried to explain that a substantial part of the Quebec revolution is anticlerical, the notion remained that ancient and mysterious forces were at work to dominate the whole of Canada. Somehow, too, the French language is equated with Catholicism, almost in the childlike belief that if you keep French muffled behind the borders of Quebec you keep Catholicism isolated. In a broader sense, Westerners, brought up far removed from the intimacy of the Quebec scene, fail to understand that French Canada's demand for wider recognition of French as an official language is as much psychological as it is political. A Calgary newspaper published an article about "the world's ten most important languages"—important from the point of view of the numbers of people speaking them. The list featured Chinese and Hindi; French, by this measure, was not included. The paper made no comment, but the malicious moral was clearly evident.

"What do they want?" The question is asked over and over again. An insurance agent in Edmonton said: "Just because they're French, do they want to run the country? There are still a lot of people here who remember that when Albertans were in the war, Quebecers just weren't anywhere to be seen." On a train from Edmonton to Calgary I sat next to a salesman who said: "Where the hell were they when I was up to my knees in mud in Italy?" The definition of Quebec's role in war or peace—bitterly distorted in the Western mind—was summed up brutally on the same train. A routine railway notice affixed to a washroom wall warned— in both English and French—against such offenses as gambling or spitting. Someone had scrawled over the French version: "For frogs—how true!"

The anti-Quebec feeling is particularly pronounced in the so-called "Bible Belt" of Alberta, where Premier Manning's voice has long claimed devoted listeners. Manning says: "Many of our French-Canadian citizens feel they have been short-changed. They regard Canada as a union of two founding races. I find it difficult to follow this concept." And so he is opposed to the federal attempt to study biculturalism and bilingualism because, as he puts it, "the objective is vague and indefinite, and there is little ground left for retreat." In this case, the retreat implied would be by English Canada, a possibility he refuses to consider. Manning can be quite charming when he speaks on the subject. In one public address, which I heard, he drew laughter from the assembly by saying he wished he spoke French, "because I know some jokes that don't sound funny in English but might in French." Then he was coldly serious as he warned: "You will never make bilingualism by passing statutes."

Among a few, mainly of the intelligentsia, the situation is seen in its subtle shades. But for most people there is only limited patience and a desire to avoid even discussion. Donald Simpson, a sixty-year-old farmer in Melita, in the southwest corner of Manitoba, said: "I can't fathom Quebec. I don't know what they're trying to do, and that's about the size of it. As for the language, let them keep it in Quebec. I don't want it here." George Marlin, a twenty-three-year-old student from Regina, said: "I would like to see the character of my background, Anglo-Saxon, preserved. I want multiculturalism, not biculturalism." In a distinct minority opinion, Michael Moore, twenty-one, said at the University of Manitoba: "I think Quebec has a point. The French came into Canada after they were conquered by the British and acquired certain rights. The Ukrainians and the others came to Canada under terms already in existence. They could have gone just as easily to Australia."

And in between, with possibly the most cogent observation, was an economics professor at the University of Manitoba: "If the French become more extreme they will arouse hostility—because even if the rest of Canada has not shown much awareness of Quebec, Quebec in turn is ignorant of the Prairies and our problems."

Max Seidlitz owns a farm on the Regina Plains, one of the richest grain-producing areas on the continent. His "farmhouse"—ranch-style and resembling a color page from *House Beautiful*—reflects the affluence that surrounds him and his family. The living room, thirty-five feet long, is tastefully furnished and equipped with stereophonic record player and twenty-three-inch television set. Mrs. Seidlitz works in a kitchen of walnut-paneled cupboards, and a built-in television set, too, so she can be entertained while switching on a variety of electrical appliances: wall oven, garbage disposal unit, dishwasher. It is something of a contrast to the kitchen pump and coal-oil lamps she once knew. Max Seidlitz says he would not sell his land, home, and machinery for less than $275,000. At the age of fifty-five, he also remembers other times—the nightmarish Great Depression of the 1930's, when 80 per cent of Saskatchewan's farmers were on relief. Between the eras of depression and dishwasher the province chose a socialist government—the first of its kind in Canada or the United States—and introduced medicare.

Seidlitz' story is enlightening. Though he was among the minority who did not require relief, and he has met recently with more than average success financially, in other respects his background has the main ingredients of the Prairies: the fight against greedy merchants and speculators, against the East, against perversities of Nature. Seidlitz' parents migrated from Germany in 1904. His father worked for a year, at $1 a day, on construction of the Canadian National Railways—a job that saved many a farmer because it provided winter employment. When Seidlitz senior started farming on a quarter section, a free homestead of 160 acres, his only cost was $10 for the registration of title. In those days, as Max recalls hearing it, the problem was not farming as much as it was marketing: "You would haul grain twenty miles with a team of oxen to a private elevator where the operators knew you were not going to haul it all the way back again just because you didn't get your price. So they knocked down the weight and grade, and gave you 25 per cent less than it was worth."

As a result of such malpractice, Saskatchewan farmers were early supporters of cooperatives that ran storage elevators on their behalf and did the marketing. The Saskatchewan Wheat Pool, the largest primary grain-handling organization in the world, grew out of the pioneer cooperatives. The Pool today is owned by 85,000 farmer-members who draw on facilities worth $80 million: grain elevators, terminals, a flour mill, vegetable oil extraction plant, livestock yards. The cooperative movement is one of the distinctive features of Saskatchewan. It extends itself into petroleum refining, insurance, and supermarkets. Cooperatives handle more than half the grain produced in the province and almost half the cattle. One quarter of the groceries bought in Saskatchewan are from cooperative stores. Consumer cooperatives in hardware, lumber, household appliances, and other items account for 8 per cent of all retail sales in the province.

It was not quite so tidy when Max Seidlitz went into farming on his own in 1933, with savings accumulated while he worked for his father. The first wheat he sold was thirty-three cents a bushel (today, thanks partly to the federal government's Wheat Board, an instrument of orderly marketing, Seidlitz sells his wheat for around $1.85 a bushel). He says of farming in his early days: "You either appreciated it, or left it. I appreciated it because even with the hard times I saw worse poverty in the towns. If we had a poor crop, we at least had potatoes and eggs to eat. You could exist with hardly any cash." Still, those were the "dirty thirties," filled with dismay and natural disasters: grasshopper plague and drought. Crop failure in 1937 cut the yield of grain to an average of 2.7 bushels per acre (compared with the record of 27 bushels per acre in 1963). Kansas and other wheat areas in the United States were badly hit, too, but Seidlitz feels that Saskatchewan suffered just a little more. Some farmers got no yields at all, and were forced into a vicious cycle. In order to survive, they sold their livestock, despite pitiful market prices. There were instances of farmers shipping cattle to Winnipeg and then receiving a freight bill, for the sale price did not even cover the cost of transportation.

The cities in the East suffered in the depression, too, but Seidlitz says that nothing could have been as bad as in the Prairies. "It was terrible here," he says, "because it was so humiliating. You had to ask someone for food for your table, even though you were a farmer." The shadow of the deep 1930's has receded as a new generation has grown up without even much curiosity to ask questions; but Max and his older neighbors still tremble when they compare old experiences. Seidlitz managed to avoid the degradation of public assistance, except that in one year the federal government handed out some flour and coal, which everyone collected automatically. In the 1940's he underwent the humiliation of applying for a bank loan and being turned down. It was a local credit union that finally advanced him $5,000. The result is that Max remains antagonistic toward banks, trust companies, and others dealing in money and mortgages, especially since most headquarters are in the East. The enmity is not very pronounced, for prosperity finally has come to the West. In 1961 Seidlitz' land, of which he has 2,000 acres under grain cultivation, was worth $65 an acre. Now it is worth at least $110 an acre. Prices have gone up in recent years because of bumper crops matched by huge sales to the Soviet Union, China, and other Communist countries—a move in Canada's West that pushed the United States into doing similar business with Russia, if not with China. Even city people are putting money into farmland as pure investment—a gesture of confidence uncommon a few years ago.

How does Seidlitz feel about the sale of wheat to China? Naturally he likes the financial returns (in one year alone he sold grain worth $34,000). He also says:

> I'd rather sell it to the Chinese than have them come over and take it. It makes for better relationships than if we starved them. I had cousins in Germany who starved for five years after the First World War, until they moved over here in 1923. It took them a long time to get over their bitterness toward us even after they were here. If you starve

people long enough they'll hate you forever. That's how Hitler got his start.

Seidlitz cannot understand the reasoning of Americans who refuse to have dealings of any kind with Peking. But then his conditioning—in keeping with the majority of the Prairie farmers—is of a fairly liberal direction.

The interpretation a Saskatchewan farmer commonly gives to politics is this: "If anyone asks me what party I belong to, I say, 'the wheat party.'" Depression years led many Prairie people to believe that both of the major federal parties—Liberals and Conservatives—were incapable of understanding the problems of farmers and assisting them in periods of need. Now there is some assurance that in drought or disaster a more sensitive and a wealthier central government will step in and provide loans or outright grants. Moreover, there is awareness that no Canadian government ever will permit again 30-cent wheat. But the fact remains that profound suspicion of traditional politics and methods of eastern origin, plus confidence in cooperative activity generally, led Saskatchewan to elect in 1944 a "socialist" government. It was the government of a distinctive party, the Cooperative Commonwealth Federation, and the word "socialist" has to be placed in quotation marks, for it was of a relatively mild order. When the C.C.F. party came into power it tried a few dabs of nationalization. It owned, for instance, a boot factory and a woolen mill, but not for more than a few years. The cooperative movement itself continued to flourish, but the province as such was content to run a bus service and a small airline to serve isolated communities. It also operated the hydroelectric system, but so, too, did the provinces of Ontario, British Columbia, and Quebec. Medicare, its most radical or daring innovation, was brought in only in 1962. Otherwise, Saskatchewan, under a so-called socialist government, hardly could be compared with a Conservative Britain in terms of state ownership.

Most of the men in the C.C.F. government graduated from a background of farming or teaching. The last cabinet included four working farmers, three schoolteachers, two lawyers, a railroad telegrapher, a trade unionist, a municipal clerk, and a couple of small merchants. There were no bankers or big businessmen. All were men who struggled through the "dirty thirties" or knew the decade's history. The party leader, Woodrow Lloyd, a former teacher, and unpretentious to the point of ushering a visitor into the kitchen for a cup of tea, was once a doctrinaire socialist. But as premier he soon took the pragmatic view that the best way to encourage economic growth was through a combination of private enterprise and cooperative and public ownership, with the emphasis on the private sector. The development of oil and potash mining was left completely in private hands. Oil leases were granted and royalties collected by the province much as in Alberta.[3]

Potash provides a striking example of how private capital is willing to step into a mixed economy; it also repeats the familiar pattern of how Canadian resources fall by default into non-Canadian direction. Saskatchewan's potash deposits—enough to fertilize all the earth's cultivable soil for the next four or five centuries—were known as long ago as the early 1950's. But so deeply embedded were they that mining was considered economically impractical. In any case, no risk capital showed itself in Canada. However, with a growing world demand for this essential plant food, and discovery of new techniques for extraction, foreign interest was aroused. By 1957, International Minerals and Chemical Corporation, a United States concern, was prepared to drill; and in 1962, after an investment of $40 million, it began actual mining. In its first year it extracted one million tons of potash

[3] Saskatchewan's 6,000 oil wells in 1965 were producing about 225,000 barrels a day. They accounted for more than one quarter of the total Canadian oil production. The annual income for the provincial government was $40 million.

(worth $20 to $25 a ton), and by 1967 expects production of four million tons annually. Two other United States companies, Kalium Chemicals Limited, a subsidiary of Armour and Company and Pittsburgh Plate Glass Company, and the Potash Company of America, a Denver firm, each invested $30 million. A German and French consortium invested another $50 million. Not until much later, 1965, did the first Canadian company, Consolidated Mining and Smelting, venture in with the first domestic capital: $65 million. In total, a score of companies now hold potash exploration rights. As with oil, the province leases properties and collects royalties on the amount of potash mined. After a hard history of shackled dependence on a precarious grain-and-cattle economy, Saskatchewan has found itself with an entirely new industry promising millions of dollars a year in direct revenue in addition to thousands of new jobs. In 1965 an excited government announced yet another major step in industrialization: construction of a plant, worth $46 million, for the manufacture of heavy water used by nuclear power stations.

Saskatchewan still supplies more than half the nation's wheat, but the image has changed. Nonfarmers now outnumber farmers by two to one, and the nonfarm income is reckoned no longer in millions but is well over a billion dollars. Prosperity is reflected in the new sights of handsome university buildings and splendid community social centers. What has not altered, however, is the sense of distance, geographically and emotionally, from the East. Jeannine Locke, a perceptive writer for the Toronto *Star Weekly*, wrote of her home province on a revisit after an absence of thirteen years:

> I see everywhere change but no decay of loyalty in the concept of the Last Best West. It was fired for many years by the feeling that Saskatchewan was a colony within the Canadian colony. Oppression by the imperialist East (which began at Winnipeg) kept local patriotism perfervid. Early

in the 30's it mounted to a fever of separatism. Today the province merely feels misunderstood. It has been transformed in the last ten years without the rest of Canada noticing.

The C.C.F. government was defeated in provincial elections in 1964, with fewer than one thousand votes separating it from the victorious Liberal Party. There were several explanations for the reversal. For one thing, the public, after twenty years of rule by the same group, was ready for a change of faces, especially since the Liberals were committed to continue the basic pattern of government. But another, equally plausible, interpretation was that farmers, in their affluence, desired "respectability." Having supported a socialist doctrine after the lean 1930's, and having fought for the protection the C.C.F. offered, they now thought of a move into the realm of a more orthodox-sounding party. In effect it was something of a status symbol to suggest you voted Liberal: an implication that you no longer were beset by the economic anxieties of yesteryear. Some of the older farmers may have given a vote of sentimental gratitude to the C.C.F. But younger men—the average with land and equipment worth $75,000—hardly could recall troubled times. In any event, the new premier, Ross Thatcher, a onetime C.C.F. Member of Parliament who defected in 1959, was pledged to the continuity of what had been, only two years previously, a highly controversial issue: medicare.

Saskatchewan long ago had pioneered a system of state-financed hospitalization that relieved patients of the awesome burden of paying their own hospital bills. Now it was to introduce North America's first government-operated compulsory medical care program, to cover medical, surgical, and obstetrical services by a physician. Though the benefits did not extend to the cost of drugs, and dental and optical services, it was the closest thing to the nationalized health system of Britain ever attempted in the territory of the

Canadian Medical Association and the American Medical Association. The C.C.F. government received a mandate for its plan during an election campaign. Promptly there arose a furore that attracted attention throughout Canada and the United States. Doctors everywhere saw in Saskatchewan a threat against the entire pattern of private practice so carefully erected over the centuries. For patients there was concern over the effect medicare would have on the quality of medical attention The doctors in Saskatchewan made much of this point, warning there would be regimentation, a sharp decline in standards, an exodus of practitioners, a drop in the number of new medical students, a rise in taxes, and introduction of bureaucracy that would suggest life in an authoritarian state. The provincial government said that none of these evils would come to pass, that the main effect would be simply to have bills sent directly to a government office rather than to the patient. The patient still would have the freedom to choose his own doctor.

The plan came into effect on July 1, 1962. Most Saskatchewan doctors immediately shut their offices and refused calls. Technically, they said, this was not a "strike," because limited emergency service was still provided at some hospitals. But in fact it meant a strike and a crisis that shook not only the province but the whole of Canada. Inside Saskatchewan the lines were drawn on the basis of politics and economics, with businessmen forming the hard core of opposition to the government move; the farm population was split, with those who customarily showed indifference to cooperatives of any kind joining in the opposition; the press was on the side of the doctors. Outside the province there was widespread condemnation of the walkout. Newspaper editorialists across the country likened Saskatchewan physicians to irresponsible anarchists who defied the law of the land. University professors signed open letters pointing out that if the doctors did not approve of the medicare legislation they could challenge it in the courts or in an election.

Medical men who felt strongly that the Hippocratic oath of ethics had been violated, flew into Saskatchewan from other parts of Canada, from the United States, and from Britain, to help treat the sick.

After twenty-three days, and a compromise that eased their objection to billing the government directly, the Saskatchewan doctors reopened their offices. Nearly two years later a McGill University professor who had written a widely circulated letter, saying that the democratic way of demonstrating disapproval of any government's action is to vote it out of office, received a reply. A Saskatchewan Liberal scrawled across the professor's original letter: "We did it!" A new government had indeed come into office, but not on the question of medicare. In fact it had undertaken to carry on with the C.C.F. program because medicare in practice had won general approval even from many people who initially opposed it. None of the doctors' caveats—for instance, that the health of children would suffer—proved well founded. On the contrary, standards were maintained, and in some areas improved because of the guaranteed availability of funds.

Some obstructionist tactics continued for a while, mainly in small centers served by community clinics. Several of these clinics were staffed by doctors who had come over from Britain during or immediately after the 1962 crisis. The British doctors charged that they were being denied the customary privilege of having their patients admitted into hospitals —a reprisal, they said, for their support of medicare. In general, however, Saskatchewan physicians have learned to accept the system. Even the anticipated flight of doctors has not taken place. As it was explained to me by Dr. R. W. Sutherland, former executive director of the Medical Care Insurance Commission (the government's medicare agency), Saskatchewan has always known a high turnover of M.D.s. About a hundred municipalities, long before medicare, had programs guaranteeing substantial incomes for doctors who otherwise would not have been attracted to the hinterland. Young physicians, fresh from internship, came out from other provinces and countries on a contract of from two to five years and accumulated practical experience and enough money to return home and set up permanent practice. In the two-year period before the medicare bill was enacted, the turnover of doctors was 260. In the two years during and after the crisis, it was 281. The gap was more than filled by the migration of medical people from Britain. A few specialists—principally a neurologist, two gynecologists, and an allergist—moved away at the height of the controversy. Otherwise specialized services remained unimpaired. Saskatchewan now boasts one thousand doctors—a greater number and higher proportion than ever before in the province's history: one per 940 population. Since the medicare program includes a generous schedule of scholarships and bursaries, administered by the University of Saskatchewan, there are also more applicants to medical school than ever before. The dean of medicine cites an advantage not realized previously. Now when a worthy or talented student is spotted in undergraduate years he is urged to consider medicine rather than another field; in some cases the scholarships and bursaries determine the difference between a nonmedical and a medical career.

Other fears of doctors proved erroneous. They were wary, for example, of any possible threat to their traditional right to set their own fees. The fee structure continues to be decided by doctors themselves, through the College of Physicians and Surgeons. And doctors are earning more than previously, partly because all bills are now paid while in the past an average of 15 per cent went uncollected. The year before medicare the average general practitioner in Saskatchewan earned $18,000. The year after medicare he earned $22,000, considerably more than the national averages in Canada and the United States. Specialists earned upwards of $30,000. Part of the increase, of course, is due to the greater frequency with which people turn to doctors now that they are not picking up the direct bills themselves. But while doctors are busier, they are not necessarily working harder or cutting standards. At least this is the way Dr. Neville Smith, chairman of the public relations committee of the College of Physicians and Surgeons, put it. Basically what happens, he said, is that a patient may have to wait two weeks instead of one week—as previously—for a routine appointment. In other words, doctors are merely behind schedule.

Seventy-five per cent of medicare's expense is made up through increased sales tax, corporation tax, and income tax.[4] The balance comes from premiums: a family pays $24 a year, a single person $12 (apart from a family premium of $48 for full hospital care). Ironically, the bureaucracy feared by the doctors was of their own manufacture. The initial plan of the province was for the doctors to send all bills directly to the Medical Care Insurance Commission. This was one of the more fiercely contested parts of the medicare bill, the doctors contending it would be a dangerous and degrading process that would make them hardly more independent than civil servants. The province's compromise was to allow them to submit charges in any of three ways: directly to the Commission, directly to the patient who would be reimbursed by the Commission, or through old private medical insurance companies that in effect would survive as collection agencies. In the first year, the doctors' hostility was such that 70 per cent sent their bills through agencies. From the patient's point of view it did not matter how the billing was handled, for this became a technicality once the government started to pay one way or another. But the red

[4] A main point is that while surcharges based on income may compel a wealthy family to pay more toward medical costs than it would without medicare, expenses are spread to the advantage of those less able to afford heavy bills. By government estimates, families in the $7,000 income bracket pay about $115 a year in extra taxes; those in the $4,800 range, $65; and families in the $4,000 group, $50.

tape behind the scenes was unnecessarily cumbersome. Doctors' accounts would be accumulated by the agencies and submitted every day to the Commission. The Commission would then add up the totals and send a check for a lump sum to each agency, which, in turn, would pay off the doctors. Gradually doctors began to admit the redundancy and time waste of this method, especially if there were any queries on claims, and more and more were bypassing the agencies to deal directly with the Commission.

On another level, the most interesting result of Saskatchewan's experience was the reaction among such bodies as the American Medical Association and the Canadian Medical Association. United States concern at the height of the crisis was enormous. Doctors with whom I later spoke in Saskatchewan said the A.M.A. regarded their resumption of services after the three-week walkout as a "betrayal" of the profession as a whole; letters from some medical men in the United States had urged withdrawal even of emergency services. Many physicians across Canada were equally belligerent. Later, however, the extent of damage to the medical image became apparent. In 1964, when a Royal Commission recommended medicare on a national scale, the Canadian Medical Association said that regardless of its opposition to some aspects of the proposed plan there would be no repetition of the 1962 Saskatchewan walkout.

If a hard, practical, position paper were being prepared on all possibilities for Canada's future, what would be the position of the Prairie Provinces in the event of disintegration of Confederation? The question shocks many people. Premier Manning of Alberta told me he would not even wish to speculate about an end to the union. "In my view," he said, "it is inconceivable, and such talk does a disservice to Canada." Yet the question is approached, in an academic fashion, by theoreticians who also look at bread-and-butter facts. Apart from the casual but compelling force of English-

Canadian nationalism, the cultural and political heritage of the Canadian Prairies makes them different from the states in the United States Midwest. Any affinity the farmer of Manitoba has with a Minnesotan is in the matter of general farm economics; certainly there is no intimacy over the history of the Riel Rebellion or the political philosophy of the American Progressives in 1913. The key, therefore, is economics. Professor Sol Sinclair, agricultural economist at the University of Manitoba, expresses it thus:

We in the Prairies are influenced more by the over-all Canadian scene than by the American scene. We are interested in relations with the British Commonwealth, where our trade has been for so long, or with Communist China, where our trade is just beginning. Thirty years ago in the Prairies there was a mild secessionist sentiment—not a strong movement, but we knew it was there. The cry was that the logical trade route should be with the United States, that Ontario and Quebec were milking us. Now there is almost none of this talk. If there were a break-up of Confederation tomorrow, you would find the three Prairie Provinces getting together and saying to Ontario: "We will try to work out a good arrangement with you, but if this is not feasible we will be forced to ask admission to the States." The point is that, unlike the people of the Maritimes or British Columbia, we are not inclined to look automatically southward. Here the problem is more diffuse. On the question of wheat, we would be better off in the United States getting price support and having a market for our high quality grain. On the question of cattle, we might be better off selling in the Ontario market. Forgetting, for point of argument, sentiment, it would really come down to an economic evaluation of where we would get a better deal: in Ontario or in the States.

10.

The North's Frontier: Myth and Fact

We are fulfilling the vision and the dream of Canada's first prime minister, Sir John A. Macdonald. But Macdonald saw Canada from East to West. I see a new Canada—a Canada of the North.... This is the Vision!

> —John G. Diefenbaker, Canada's
> 13th Prime Minister.

THE STEWARDESS on the plane carrying me to the Yukon said that she had panned for gold. But it was as a tourist that she had done so, at one of the special little camps maintained for dude sourdoughs on Bonanza Creek, a few miles from Dawson. "Within fifteen minutes," she recalled, "I could understand why the old-timers stayed year after year. You can actually see bits of gold—flakes and dust—and you just *know* the next pan will have a nugget."

A rewarding way to begin any exploration of the North is in the Yukon Territory, for here lingers not only some of Canada's most colorful history but a blend between North and West. The Yukon, with a flavor of the pioneer frontier, attracts both individualists and the vicissitudes of boom or bust. Its principal city, Whitehorse, was established during a gold rush, received its greatest influx of two-fisted men during a war, and now serves as an uncertain mirror to Diefenbaker's Vision. It likes to call itself the gateway to the North, since it is a transportation center. It cannot claim title as the most northerly capital in Canada. Yellowknife, in the Northwest Territories, is closer to the Arctic Circle. But Whitehorse is undoubtedly the most westerly city in Canada. This information usually comes as a shock to people in Toronto or Montreal, 3,000 air miles away, who think of Victoria, British Columbia, as the far end of the country. Only in recent years, with the appearance of the Yukon on television weather maps, have Victorians themselves been made aware that they live five hundred miles to the *east* of Whitehorse.

The thing that really counts, anyway, is the latitude. Victoria is below the 49th parallel, while Whitehorse is away up there—1,200 miles up there in the sub-Arctic, well past the 55th parallel and the line of sight of the majority of Canadians. If most Americans are in ignorance of what goes on beyond their northern border, Canadians, living in a snug belt along that border, are equally unacquainted with what happens over their shoulder. There is a vague cognizance that a couple of electronic fences, the Distant Early Warning Line and the Mid-Canada Warning Line, stretched across the frozen part of the continent because on the other side of the North Pole are the Russians. But it would be expecting too much to have everyone read the government pamphlets that talk of potatoes, cabbages, carrots, and beans thriving in places where the permafrost is just a few inches below the surface of the ground. Nor does it mean a great deal to hear that the average January temperature in Whitehorse is warmer than in Winnipeg, just seventy miles from the United States border. The main difference between "northern" and "southern" winters is in length; winter in the sub-Arctic lasts for eight or nine months. The rest of the truth is that vegetables usually grow as freak specimens; and the problem of permafrost—permanently frozen ground—affects almost every enterprise contemplated in the North. For the average Canadian, therefore, the North remains a great big unknown mass, cold and forbidding.

At the same time, for the average Yukoner the "outside" is a world to be grasped someday in retirement, but until then to be pitied for its false pace and failure to come to terms with itself. Yukoners have a point. In a nation given to regionalism, factionalism, and resentment of central authority, it is refreshing to find a quiet little oasis of contentment. The oasis, even in November, the time of my visit, is a trifle chilly. But the people who inhabit Whitehorse are almost identically of warm and good nature. They also form a lively melting pot that could be a model for any believer in multiculturalism.

A century ago a few fur traders of the Hudson's Bay Company infiltrated the Yukon. By the 1880's a handful of hardy prospectors had begun to look for gold. The occasional man of the cloth and the itinerant government official, in search of Indians, also ventured into this remote area. But that was about the sum of the notice paid to it until August 17, 1896. On that day George W. Carmack, and two Indian guides with the names of Skookum Jim and Tagish Charlie, panned the rich black sand of Bonanza Creek, a tributary of the Klondike River, and found gold. Such is the whimsy of the North that Carmack, a Californian, had been sent to the site by Robert Henderson, a Nova Scotian who had prospected the area unsuccessfully for two years. Carmack, in his excitement to register his find, failed to tip off Henderson as agreed. By the time Henderson did hear the news, other speedy claimants had moved in on Bonanza Creek ahead of him. His only eventual reward was to receive a pittance of a government pension and to become glorified as co-discoverer of the Klondike's gold. Carmack's reward was wealth.

In another example of its capriciousness, the North created at the junction of the Klondike and Yukon Rivers a lusty and thriving metropolis of buildings, tents, and wooden shacks—Dawson, the largest North American city west of San Francisco—and in less than a half dozen years abandoned it to history. Dawson City had a population of some 40,000, 80 per cent of them Americans who had thrown over their jobs, left their wives and families, sold their homes and businesses, and headed northward in the stampede for flake and nugget. The trip to Dawson took as long as a year. Some men thought they could hack their way through the raw hills and disorder of brush guarding the Yukon's southern perimeter, and they failed disastrously. Some men made it by sailing 3,000 miles to the mouth of the Yukon River, then 1,700 miles of its length to Dawson. But this was time-consuming and arduous and costly. The most practical way of all was overland from Skagway, Alaska. Ten thousand amateur sourdoughs started this trip in a single year, but only two thousand finished. Many died along the way from disease, cold, and starvation; others simply turned back.

Still, the endless lines of men, bent and struggling up the slopes of the Chilkoot or White Passes, became symbols of human determination. Then, when the major stakes had been claimed soon after the turn of the century, the adventurers of '97 and '98 vanished as abruptly as they had come. The descendants of the few who remained form the core of the Yukon's present population, constantly augmented by a new type of sourdough in search of a livelihood and tranquility rather than quick fortune.

Over the years Dawson has become almost deserted while Whitehorse has taken on some of the old pioneer glamor. Whitehorse was merely a staging post during the gold rush, and later its chief reason for existence was as terminus for the 110-mile railroad that was laid across the White Pass. It was able to count fewer than four hundred inhabitants.

Then, in 1942, another temporary invasion took place when thousands of army and construction men swarmed into the Yukon to build the Alaska Highway, the great military route that ran 1,523 miles from Dawson Creek, British Columbia, to Fairbanks, Alaska. Forty thousand of the men, highly paid and free-spending, were based at Whitehorse. Eventually the big wartime boom tapered off, and now Whitehorse is quite content with a population of about five thousand. Its residents say, almost as one, that they do not wish for any additional great spurts or overnight bonanzas. They are constantly reminded of the North's fickle character and ask only for a steady and normal growth. There may have been drama and symbolism in the battle sixty-five years ago to get over the Chilkoot Pass, but what matters now is the regular grind to succeed economically.

Whitehorse exists mainly as a federal government administrative center. Four out of five residents are dependent directly or indirectly on the Department of Northern Affairs, the Royal Canadian Mounted Police, the Army or Air Force, or the Department of Public Works. They underwrite civilization in the Yukon's 207,000 square miles, an area almost as big as Texas and populated with fewer than 15,000 people, including 2,500 Indians. Whitehorse also caters to tourists and to the relatively small number of remaining miners in the area, though in a most prosaic manner. The miners, after digging lead, silver, and zinc at Keno, find no equivalent of the ornate establishment Bombay Peggy used to operate in Dawson. Whitehorse is tidy and against commercial sin. Men who are in need of prostitutes must go a thousand miles down the line to Edmonton.

The modern route, of course, has none of the old overland hazards. Whitehorse is served daily by Canadian Pacific Airlines in four-engined luxury. From the air the formidable face of the Yukon is enough to make you marvel how any city-style prospectors, armed with enthusiasm and little knowledge of the wilderness, managed to get through. Here is terrain grooved and scarred by millions of years of erosion, with cold and awesomely black streaks of water flowing through the hills. Even the hills appear primeval, for they are generally ground to flat tops and, except for the occasional peak, of monotonously identical height. The tree line is hundreds of miles away, and so jackpine and spruce still abound around Whitehorse; but at a slightly higher level, within five miles, only shrub can be detected.

Landing at Whitehorse I was greeted by an Arctic blast of thirty degrees below zero, and promptly I was informed that this was not typical autumn weather. My informant, a transplanted Pennsylvanian named "Yukon" Bud Fisher, wore a red Mackinaw, red tuque, and a snowy-white beard, Fisher, aged sixty-three, short and slightly rotund, with clear blue eyes and a ruddy complexion, might have been posing as a Santa Claus, but in fact he was carrying out his duty as an official booster for the Yukon. Generally, Fisher is on hand to meet any plane that might be bringing in a tourist. He casually walks up and says, "Hi." It fits perfectly into the informal and friendly atmosphere of the town.

Fisher is steeped in knowledge of the Yukon and has a genuine love for this land. He adopted it back in 1929 when, after building up a small trucking business between Phoenix and Los Angeles, he sold out, loaded his wife and two children in a two-ton lorry, and drove to Vancouver. There they picked up the boat to Skagway, and then the White Pass & Yukon Railway to Whitehorse. It was as simple as that, though Fisher recalls that when he left California the temperature was ninety degrees in the shade and when he got to Whitehorse it was forty-two below. His initial reason for migrating was the recommendation of a sister who had been living in the Yukon for seventeen years and who described it as "a big, free country." Fisher has done just about everything in his thirty-five years in the Yukon. He panned for gold, and in one year amassed $14,000—far more than most of the '98ers did at the height of the boom. But in other seasons he was closer to the norm and saw hardly a fleck of gold. He built up another trucking business, eventually had a fleet of fourteen vehicles, and then was forced to quit because of a heart condition. Fisher is a rarity in the Yukon. Instead of going "outside" for his retirement, he chose to stay on and do a leisurely labor of love for the tourist bureau. The big country that first attracted him has held him, because, as he put it, "Here we find freedom and friendship. We live two thousand miles north of worry."

The same contentment affects others. The night clerk at the Taku Hotel, where I stayed, was a middle-aged Scotsman who came over from Edinburgh to visit his married daughter. The visit was supposed to last six months, but now, five years later, he was still there, fascinated by the atmosphere and the amiable life. Everyone called him "Scotty," and it is doubtful if many knew his full name. Teen-agers and adults wandered in from the lunch counter of the tiny hotel or from the main street to make personal calls from the phone on the registration desk. Invariably, at least when I was a witness, they received a cheery grin and a broadly facetious suggestion: "Ye'll nae find me objecting if ye leave a dime."

I had a quick sampling of the melting pot on my first evening, when Scotty summoned for me a taxi ("Arctic Cab Company") that turned out to be driven by a Hungarian. The taxi driver had been lured to Whitehorse, shortly after arrival in Canada in 1956, by tales of high salaries. The stories were exaggerated, but the Yukon held him. The bar to which he drove me, The '98, was operated by a Netherlander named Chris Van Oeveren, who at one time flew between Amsterdam and Montreal as a K.L.M. steward. Van Oeveren worked for a while as a maître d'hôtel in the Laurentians but never thought he could accumulate enough capital to start a business of his own in the East. As a waiter in Whitehorse, however, he managed to save a few thousand dollars and take over The '98. He converted it into a popular rendezvous complete with skins of timber wolves and black bears on the walls, an immense stone fireplace, and a brass cuspidor, which he swears was salvaged from an old Dawson saloon. The tourists like the atmosphere, but more importantly so do the residents. One of the patrons who occupied the table next to mine was an Italian carpenter still barely able to speak English despite his migration in 1955. But it was good enough for him to explain that he earned $3.70 an hour and that he thrived in the Yukon because of the hunting and fishing (he was also, he said later, escaping from a wife in Italy). We were joined by other men of German, Polish, Norwegian, English, Australian, and French origin.

Why had they come to the Yukon? The consensus was that while no one expected to strike it rich, everyone hoped to make a decent living and to save enough money for old age. Costs were from 10 to 20 per cent higher than in the "outside," but salaries were scaled accordingly and there was not the same temptation to spend on frivolities. Mrs. Van Oeveren said, "A lot of people came here ten years ago, like us, and haven't moved. I don't know why." Her husband said that periodically he goes out to have a look, then must hasten back. "I can't explain it," he said. "I don't feel at home anywhere else."

There are, obviously, a variety of reasons for the attraction of the North. One is the sheer need for escapism by men and women who cannot fit into conventional society; they know that if they do not adjust in Whitehorse there is not much farther they can run. Another is the sense of adventure that comes with the outdoors; some of the finest glacial mountain-climbing in the world is available less than 150 miles from Whitehorse. But perhaps a paramount point is that Whitehorse is a fully *Canadian* town, the most harmonious I know, despite the multitude of fresh foreign tongues. Urban centers to the south have much bigger communities of Germans, Italians, and so on. But somehow in Whitehorse the condescending term "New Canadian" is never applied. Anyone and everyone in the Yukon is a Yukoner and therefore automatically a Canadian.

The common denominator is determined by Nature, which pulls Yukoners together. No one ever talks about life being an extraordinary challenge. On the contrary, people point to the normality of supermarkets, motels, and Mounties, on patrol in sedans, issuing tickets for speeding. But the fact is that from October to April, the dark and bleak and frigid season, weather is a formidable enemy. A drive to Dawson, 330 miles away, and even a shorter expedition, must be treated with respect and caution. You load your car with bedroll, axe, and other survival gear. The inflexible rule in the event of a breakdown is to build a fire immediately; otherwise freezing sets in. Everyone is aware of the basic step of dipping rags in the gas tank to make easier the igniting of freshly hacked and chilled wood. On the Dawson road there are only three places you can stop for coffee. Thus, automatically you leave a record of your progress, and if you are reported missing there is at least a rough indication of the stretch along which you might be found.

The spirit of mutual protection is prevalent. In a small way I experienced it when the electric power in Whitehorse failed, and oil furnaces all over town went off. Since the temperature outdoors was thirty-five below, it was only a matter of minutes before the interior of my hotel was frigid. But also within minutes the phone rang. Relative strangers, people I had met only the previous evening, wanted to know if I would come over to share their wood fireplace. Phones all over town must have been ringing with the same invitation as one Yukoner was offering another a neighborly hand. Most small towns have a friendliness lacking in the big cities. But Whitehorse has the important added characteristic of a *northern* small town, where the herding instinct and subsequent sense of security are at their keenest.

"Almost everyone can be a northern type while in the North," said Flo Whyard, the wife of a Northern Affairs officer. "Even when you're posted out, you stay a northern type." The interesting thing, though, is how the northern type often elects to remain, physically, a northern type. James Whyard, a civil engineer by profession, comes from Winnipeg. Mrs. Whyard took an arts degree at the University of Western Ontario in her home town of London, Ontario. Both, then, were purely from the "outside." Whyard's first government assignment was in Yellowknife in 1945. After a few years he could have counted the North as comfortably behind him and settled into a warm niche in Ottawa. He chose, instead, Whitehorse, where the Whyards, now in their forties, have lived ever since.

Eventually the Whyards will go out, for the North is no place for older people in retirement. The summers, with long sunlit nights and cascading colors in the skies, are glorious and humbling. But the winter is too severe except for the youth or the adventurers or the individualists in full vigor. "Nothing takes root here, not even grain," said the wife of an army officer. "People don't take root either." It was a somewhat dramatic assessment, and misleading in the light of fierce loyalties people give to the North. But in fact any population over the age of sixty is supplied by the Indians; men such as "Yukon" Bud Fisher are exceptional.

The army officer's wife was a "nonnortherner." Knowing her husband shortly would be transferred, she wondered aloud why there was such a sacred feeling about Whitehorse. "I've never heard a word of criticism," she said. "I sometimes think this is a bad sign, as though everyone is on the defensive." The truth is that Whitehorse, on the surface, is rather dismal and drab, a mélange of past, present, and maybe the future. The past is represented by the frontier log cabins that still exist, including one used by Sam McGee before he was cremated in verse by Robert W. Service. A more recent hangover is Whiskey Flats, a district that became famous for its illegal stills and devastating alcohol dens during the 1942 construction invasion. In those austere wartime days, real liquor was rationed to an inadequate bottle a month, and so Whiskey Flats became an oasis for thirsty and rugged men who had spent all day hacking a road through frozen jungle. Whiskey Flats is still occupied. But now, a slum of shanties assembled from flattened gasoline cans and tarpaper, it connotes no sense of an adventurous history.

The future may be represented by the cheery school buildings and brightly painted homes of government officials. But it still adds up to the conclusion that Whitehorse, taking in its laundromats and Indian encampments, is a higgledy-piggledy sort of place. Any defensiveness is caused by a conflict between genuine affection for what it represents spiritually and a deep fear for the North's future. The fear hinges on the nagging knowledge that the North is viable only so long as it has commercial value, and this is inconstant and unpredictable. At the time of my visit there was gloom and uncertainty because the government had just announced a change in arrangements for the maintenance of the Alaska Highway, an important source of revenue for Whitehorse. Army units, based in town, were responsible for the entire Canadian length of it. Now, it was announced, the Department of Public Works would take over this operation. Merchants and others worried about how the withdrawal of military engineers would affect business, for there was no assurance that as many civilians would be employed or even that they would be selected from Whitehorse.

Another issue of the moment was the state of union itself. The Yukon may seem geographically remote from the rest of Canada, but in actuality it is more sensitively attuned to nationhood that most regions. If other parts of the country cry out against Ottawa—either for not giving enough or for taking too much—the Yukon is a happy exception. In the past some Yukoners suggested that the territory should be granted provincial status, but this is no longer a live debate. Most people are realistic and content, fully aware that the territory pays only 16 per cent of its own bills; Ottawa pays the rest. Since it is extremely unlikely that the Yukon will reach economic self-sufficiency in our time, any talk of Quebec nationalism or break-up of Confederation is distressing. Especially pained are those born and brought up in the Yukon.

During the gold rush, William Drury's father opened a trading post in partnership with another Englishman, Isaac Taylor, and this has grown into a group of stores and agencies still operated as a joint family enterprise. Drury, aged forty-four, speaks frankly of the future of the Yukon and says it depends on mining and, to a smaller degree, tourism. He cannot visualize any massive schemes for moving populations. "The North simply could not absorb them," he says. In this he has agreement from the other part of Taylor and Drury Limited—Charles Taylor, who was born in Whitehorse in 1912, thus qualifying as one of the longest residents. "It has never been proved that we have deep rich mines here," says Taylor. "They're rich maybe in base metals, but shallow, and so they peter out quickly. With the high cost of transportation, much of it is uneconomic mining anyway. Our problem is cheap transportation. Until we have transportation, how are we going to have people? And how are we going to have transportation unless there's something to draw people?" Mrs. Taylor, born in Dawson, and equally at home with the northern facts of life, makes a whimsical reference to the time when she and her husband attended an Anglican Congress in Toronto and "we discovered more people congregated in Maple Leaf Gardens than there are in the whole of the Yukon." This brought both to the heartfelt conclusion that Ottawa has done right by the Yukon. "We've been well treated, even spoiled," is the way Taylor expresses it.

And so, inevitably, Confederation—with a rich and strong central government—is the only hope for the Yukon in its present form. Drury and Taylor are convinced that if a split should come, the Yukon, impotent on its own, would be best off forming a link with British Columbia or Alberta. "If we were to join Alaska," says Mrs. Taylor, "I would leave the Yukon, even though I love it. I feel very Canadian." Curiously, the people not born in the Yukon take a different attitude. Among them the consensus is that the logical affiliation would be with the United States because of Alaska. Whitehorse is closer to Anchorage and Fairbanks than it is to any Canadian city. Alaska-Yukon sports car rallies compete on the 600-mile Alaska Highway stretch between Fairbanks and Whitehorse. High school basketball teams from Skagway and Whitehorse consider a day's trip on the White Pass railroad a normal part of northern neighborliness. The kinship, of course, is measured not only in miles but in common northern values, and these, the argument goes, would be lost in any affiliation with "southern" provinces such as British Columbia or Alberta.

The values crop up in the lusty language of the characters who continue to make the Yukon a distinctive, if unpredictable, area. *The Whitehorse Star* publishes every Monday and Thursday, but only, according to a sign, "if the staff is sober." The paper has been campaigning gallantly for years to have a hard surface laid on the Alaska Highway. An enormous banner stretches the length of the *Star* building, and even though the building is describable as little more than a shack, the message makes an impact. In one corner is a crudely sketched donkey in a cloud of dust and alongside is the battle cry: "Let's drag our ass out of the dust and pave the highway."[1]

The irreverent pace for the *Star* was set by its owner, Harry Boyle, who, during a visit of Queen Elizabeth a few years ago, wrote an advertisement: "Baths 50 cents. With soap 75 cents. Royal Fambly Free (this week only)." Boyle's philosophy about publishing is quite basic: "This is not a newspaper. It's a Yukon scrapbook." Accordingly, when the territorial government hired a man to come all the way from Ottawa to explain to Yukoners the need for physical fitness, the *Star's* headline said: "Physical Jerk from the East." Another notable Boyle line appeared with the introduction of a sports department in a local store: "Sporting House Opens on Main St."

Boyle now edits a paper in Prince George, British Columbia, but still keeps an affectionate eye on his offspring. The *Star's* entire editorial staff consists of three hands, among them Bob Erlam, who serves as publisher, advertising manager, staff artist, and staff photographer; and Mrs. Flo Whyard, who is editor, managing editor, city editor, and correspondent general. Mrs. Whyard thinks the difference between "big city values" and "Yukon values" is reflected in an incident that took place in March 1963, before she had attained the heights of editor and was still merely "correspondent general." She was alone in the editorial office of the *Star*—a musty and crowded room that must be a relic from gold rush days—when the phone rang. It was long distance. *The Vancouver Province* wanted to speak to the publisher of *The Whitehorse Star*.

Flo said: "The publisher isn't in."

There was a muffled conversation at the other end, and the operator came back with: "The editor, then."

[1] Premier Bennett of British Columbia, in an ambitious, expansionist mood, offered to pave the highway if Yukoners would abandon federal rule and join B.C. A Chinese waiter in Whitehorse said, "Bennett will have to get the money for the paving job from Ottawa anyway, so why do we need him to do it for us?" And he went on pouring coffee.

Flo, kicking aside a package of biscuits that had fallen from a cluttered desk, said: "The editor is out of town."

There were more murmurs in the distance until the operator asked for "the managing editor." Flo said, nonchalantly, that the managing editor was sick.

Vancouver shrieked: "Is there another paper in Whitehorse?"

"Yes, but it's only a weekly," said Flo, wondering what Vancouver would think if it knew the *Star* appeared only twice a week. Finally, a harassed male came on the line, spelled his name carefully, and said he was "day city editor" of the *Province,* and just whom was there for him to talk with at the *Star?* Flo said she was available.

The call turned out to be worthwhile. A report had broken in the "outside" that a Brooklyn girl, Helen Klaben, and another American, Ralph Flores, missing on a flight from Alaska to California, had been found in the Yukon near their crashed plane after surviving forty-nine days in subzero weather. Could the *Star* charter an aircraft to investigate on behalf of the *Province?* Flo took off with Bob Erlam, who got some remarkable air photos—later used in periodicals around the world—of an S.O.S. stamped in the snow near the wreck. But the frenzy shown by Vancouver puzzles Flo Whyard to this day. "Up here," she says, "we just don't think in the same way. If a story doesn't get into Monday's paper, it'll be in Thursday."

The press of half the world converged on Whitehorse, where Helen Klaben and Ralph Flores had been taken for hospital treatment. Flo with some amusement recalls the frantic jostling and maneuvering for "exclusive" stories while the pair remained in seclusion. *Life* magazine landed a task force. As Flo recalls it, a *Life* photographer was walking down Main Street when suddenly he stopped dead and stared in disbelief through the window of a barber shop. There, calmly having his seven-week-old beard removed, sat Ralph Flores. "My God," screamed the photographer, "he's just shaved himself off the cover of *Life!*"

The greatest drawing card on the *Star*, now that Boyle writes elsewhere, is Edith Josie, the paper's Old Crow correspondent. Old Crow is an Indian settlement, 600 air miles north of Whitehorse and near the Arctic Ocean. Edith Josie's charm lies in her spontaneous recording of events among Old Crow's two hundred residents: "Mr. John Joe Kay went across to see his trap on December 5, and he's lucky. He caught 4 minks and four martens. At last he's doing fine. On December 14 he went to his trap but he still gone." Edith Josie, who is forty-three, had a few years' schooling in Eagle, Alaska, and her prose remains untampered by any editor's pencil. The obituary she wrote on Chief Peter Moses had none of the hackneyed tones of metropolitan journalism. "Mr. Peter Moses," Edith Josie recounted, "has been doing lots of work when he alive on this earth. He was happy old man and friendly with anybody even with the white people. So I know everybody will miss him but hope he will have a good rest." On another occasion she reported an event involving herself: "Miss Edith Josie had baby boy." This, it turned out, was not her first child. She gave the baby—as she had the others—to a couple who needed him.

Edith Josie's column appears sporadically, only when a plane can land to bring it out of Old Crow. But it is so popular that Whitehorse readers mail copies all over the world. One of her expressions, "everything good now," has become a campus catchphrase at the University of British Columbia. Edith Josie first used it when she described how an Indian died and left his widow with the carcasses of six caribou.

In contrast, the news from Dawson is not so bright, even though the *Star's* correspondent, Iris Warner, reports: "A large herd of caribou is in the Chapman Lake district and most families in town have caribou in the pot now." The

Dawson story is perhaps the most colorful in modern Canadian history, and also the saddest. This once vibrant and passionate town, focal point of the greatest gold rush of all time, seems ordained for one setback after another. Not much more than sixty years ago its bank vaults were filled with gold, and sourdoughs were ready to squander a winter's work—a winter of frozen misery—on a week of pomp and pleasure. Paris gowns and caviar, along with champagne and paramours, were available. And men thought nothing of leaving gold nuggets in bowls at the banquet table, for guests to carry off like after-dinner mints.

However, after a few brief years, when the Klondike's creeks yielded less treasure, a massive exodus took place and the glamor and extravagance ended. Dawson steadfastly refused to consider itself a ghost town. Its people, clinging to the fabled romance of '98, were eternally optimistic. After all, more than $200 million worth of gold had been extracted, and even if individual mining no longer was economic, dredging operations were producing $2,000,000 a year. Dredges of the Yukon Consolidated Gold Corporation dug and sifted the black sand and gravel of the creek beds, turning the countryside upside down. Though unattractive snakelike rows of "tailings" remained as stern evidence of the difficulty of extracting gold, it was an industry and it employed from five hundred to seven hundred men. The employment, true enough, was seasonal, but it did provide the mainstay for the permanent residents and would do until someone discovered another Bonanza Creek; then the invasion would start all over again. Such was the sanguine philosophy of the old-timers. In the meantime, too, perhaps Dawson could pan some of its historic wealth by catering to tourists.

Several attempts were made to attract visitors. In 1953, Grant McConachie, president of Canadian Pacific Airlines, hit upon the idea of restoring the old riverboat *Klondike* into a floating palace. His motive was to build up tourist business on the airline's northern route. The *Klondike* was one of several of the original paddle-wheelers that lay rotting on the bank of the Yukon River at Whitehorse. McConachie spent $100,000 on her, so she could carry, in full splendor, passengers along the four hundred winding miles of the Yukon to Dawson. The first season was a great success, with passengers flying in from all parts of the continent and going home with enticing stories of how they indulged in a different kind of tour; they "panned" for gold, "staked" miniature claims, and danced in the Nugget Dance Hall at Dawson. But the next year the water in the river dropped to such a low level that the first four trips, all heavily booked, had to be canceled. This threw a curse on the rest of the season, and that was the end of the imaginative project.

Dawson's big effort to induce tourist trade came in 1962 with its "Gold Rush Festival." The initial plans developed at a meeting of government officials, leading Yukon citizens, and Tom Patterson, founder of the highly successful Stratford (Ontario) Shakespearean Festival. Dawson City was to be presented to the world in all its glory of '98. Half of the original buildings were still standing, and needed only infusions of money to bring them back to life. Ottawa put $200,000 into refurbishing the Palace Grand Theatre, so that a New York musical production—*Foxy,* starring Bert Lahr—could be a major attraction before its Broadway opening. The show ran seven weeks at a terrible loss, and so did virtually every other feature in town. The Shooting of Dan McGrew took place nightly, but hardly anyone witnessed it. Festival organizers had prepared for 100,000 visitors; 18,000 showed up. What was to have been an annual event, injecting vitality into the economy, collapsed in its first year. The public simply would not go as far afield as Dawson.

It is a pity, of course, for few places today offer such authentic touches of a vanishing age. You can wander past the Flora Dora Café, and find tied at the dock alongside it the old riverboat *Keno*. The Bonanza Hotel and the Arctic Brotherhood Hall remain, and so do some of the saloons that Jack London knew. Dawson now has a population of about five hundred, among them a dozen or so of the original sourdoughs. A few of the old-timers stand more erectly than the buildings, for timber is rotting and permafrost, which alters the shape of the ground when it melts even slightly, causes sloping and distortion. The couple of old hotels that remain open, hopefully, can be something of an adventure; bedroom floors run off at a fairly steep angle.

Dawson has, too, some modern motels built for the 1962 festival, but owners can do little more than bemoan their lot and speak tremulously of heavy debts and little prospect of paying them back. Of the 65,000 tourists who travel to the Yukon in an average year, driving along the Alaska Highway or flying, fewer than five thousand go up to Dawson. The number continues to dwindle. George Shaw, who owns a claim along Bonanza Creek and runs it solely for tourists, allowing them to pan for a dollar admission charge, says that what Dawson needs, "to save it," is permission to open legal gambling casinos. But even such an unlikely measure would be inadequate. The Yukon Consolidated Gold Corporation, the only existing industry, has announced its intention of closing down by 1966. The lights will go out in more ways than one. Dawson's ancient electric poles, looking skeletal with their dozens of cross arms, at least carry power as an offshoot of Yukon Consolidated's own requirements. Who will supply the town with electricity when the company goes? An old resident said, "When the dredges stop working, Dawson's heart will cease to beat."

The tragic lesson of Dawson is of more than local significance. It may contain a warning for the broad mass of the Northland. If the North was first penetrated by men in pursuit of furs or a Northwest Passage, its present attraction is largely because of its minerals. There is still gold around the Klondike, but it is too costly to extract. The economics of mining in general affects the whole of the North's future.

For at least two thousand years people have been exploring Canada's Northland. The fact that there are no dogmatic answers to some questions—precisely who, for instance, were the Eskimos' ancestors and did they cross the Bering Sea land-bridge from Asia?—only adds to its fascination and mystery. The Vikings were probably the first Europeans to visit the Canadian Arctic, about five hundred years before Columbus reached America. But the first specific date associated with the North is 1576, when Martin Frobisher sailed from England in search of the Northwest Passage. Many famous explorers were subsequently connected with this quest for a direct route between Europe and China, and among those who left their names on the map were John Davis, Henry Hudson, and William Baffin. They were heroes in every sense, for they sailed in vessels of thirty tons and they chose not the relative safety of the warm Caribbean or the mid-Atlantic but the unchartered treachery of freezing waters and a jagged coastline.

The first overland expedition dates back to 1770, when Samuel Hearne, on behalf of the Hudson's Bay Company, trekked from the mouth of the Churchill River, on Hudson Bay, to the mouth of the Coppermine River, on the Arctic Ocean; from there he swung south to Great Slave Lake, and then southeast again to return to Churchill. Hearne's 1,700-mile journey, in the company only of an Indian and across some of the bleakest territory in Canada, remains a saga; portions of the track he made still await the foot of another white man. In 1789, Alexander Mackenzie set out from Lake Athabaska and sighted the mouth of the great river that bears his name; it was not until the icy tide came in and swamped his gear that he realized he had reached the Arctic Ocean. John Franklin investigated many inland waterways, and ranged as far north as Coronation Gulf in the Central Arctic. Franklin disappeared in 1845, and for the next half century scores of search parties looked for him. It was one of these search parties, led by Robert McClure, that finally discovered the Northwest Passage.

By then the real concept of the staggering immensity of the northern part of the continent was beginning to be sensed. Expeditions that went on—for furs or minerals, or altruistically for knowledge—added details to generalities, but to this day Canada's North defies simple definitions. No one can say with certainty whether it has extensive mineral wealth. On an even more fundamental level, no one can even argue conclusively about what *is* the North. Pierre Berton, author and broadcaster, who spent his boyhood in the Yukon and whose books *The Mysterious North* and *Klondike* are among the most fascinating on the subject, says the North remains an enormous jigsaw puzzle with a myriad of missing pieces. And he adds,

> Small wonder, then, that our views of it are conditioned by a tangle of misconceptions. These run all the way from the romantic belief that the North is a frozen world of ice and snow to the naïve assumption that it may soon become a booming civilized community of cities and farms. The greatest misconception, of course, is that "the north" is all of a piece from Alaska to Ungava. You might as well lump Scotland and Serbia together because they both belong in Europe.

How big is the North? A pamphlet published by the federal Department of Northern Affairs suggests that Canadian territory above the tree line—the true Arctic—is relatively simple to delineate. The North as a whole—Arctic and sub-Arctic—is not so easily measured; it depends on where you draw the line. Defined in terms of climate, geography, and plant life, the North includes most of Labrador, a large area of Quebec, and even parts of Ontario, the

Prairie Provinces, and British Columbia; very broadly it is marked off by the 55th parallel. If taken to mean solely the realm of the federal government, as distinct from provincial, it embraces everything north of the 60th parallel, with the exception of the very tip of Quebec, and this includes the Yukon, the Northwest Territories, most of the islands in Hudson Bay, and all the islands above the mainland. Defined in this way alone, the North covers a million and a half square miles, or 40 per cent of Canada; it is large enough to swallow up more than half the United States.

This was the huge, elusive area about which John G. Diefenbaker, running for re-election as prime minister in 1958, spoke with messianic fever and oratory. "A Canada of the North. This is the Vision," he cried. "Canadians, realize your opportunities! This is the message I give you, my fellow Canadians. Not one of defeatism. Jobs. Jobs for hundreds of thousands of Canadians. A new Vision! A new hope! A new soul for Canada!" The dream, translated, was to mean enormous developments for the North: new arteries of communication, new cities, new power projects to give energy to the South. One of the men close to Diefenbaker in the Vision theme was Alvin Hamilton, Minister of Northern Affairs, who spoke of "the foundation for a nation of two hundred million people," and suggested that the Arctic Ocean might become "the Mediterranean of the modern world." Other Conservative Party campaigners threw a challenge at Canadians to emulate the Russians, who had built in their North flourishing communities and powerful industries.

Lining the walls of some of the offices in Ottawa's Langevin Building, the blackened gray stone structure that houses the Department of Northern Affairs, are maps that show the portion of the world projected from the North Pole. Viewed in this way, Canada is clearly a northern country along with Russia. Both share the Arctic Ocean, both are the same distance from the North Pole. "It is tempting to go on from this to draw comparisons between the two Norths—comparisons which indicate that the Russians, like good and trusty servants, have put their talents to work while we, recognizing the North as a hard master, have buried ours in the permafrost." The man who made this statement, several years after the collapse of the Diefenbaker Vision, was Graham W. Rowley, coordinator of the federal government's advisory committee on northern development. Rowley, jabbing a pointer at a wall map, traced areas of Siberia that are colored green, in contrast with the gloomy gray of most of northern Canada. In the simple gesture he made apparent the basic differences between the two regions.

The ice age had a far deeper effect on the Canadian North, scraping the soil from the hard granite of the Precambrian Shield, carrying it south, and leaving behind barren rock, sand, and gravel. Much less of the Russian North was covered by ice, and the great Siberian rivers have enriched their valleys with alluvial silt. But aside from more favorable soil conditions, the weather generally is milder in Siberia, allowing for long periods of summer growth—to the extent that the tree line in Siberia lies an average of five hundred miles farther north than in Canada. The Gulf Stream pours warm Atlantic water into the Polar Basin along the shores of northern Russia; this provides a year-round route and keeps Murmansk ice-free in winter even though it is farther north than Cambridge Bay, which is still covered with ice in July. In the whole of the Canadian North there are only two well-marked natural transportation routes: the Mackenzie River and Hudson Bay. Northern Russia has a series of navigable rivers flowing into the Arctic Ocean. They are spaced at regular intervals, and connect at the south with the Trans-Siberian Railway.

The net result is that while only 35,000 people inhabit Canada's North beyond the 60th parallel, there are more than 5 million in the Soviet North. Four places in Canada above the 60th parallel are designated as "towns" or "cities" with "substantial" populations: Whitehorse, with its 5,000 is the largest; Yellowknife, with 3,500, is the biggest settlement in the Northwest Territories; Inuvik, a new government-built town on the Mackenzie delta, has 1,300; Frobisher, in the far east, boasts 1,800, half of whom are Eskimos. In contrast, the Russian North has a dozen cities above the 60th parallel with populations of 50,000 or more. Murmansk numbers more than 225,000. Norilsk, with mines and metallurgical factories, and nearer the Pole than Aklavik, a fur-trading post, has 100,000. Other cities, such as Vorkuta, a coal-mining community of 55,000, possess multistory buildings of stone or cement, theaters, clubs, sports stadiums, and museums.

"On the whole, the Soviet North is of much greater economic importance for our country than the northern regions are for Canada," wrote a Russian glaciologist, Professor Pyotr Shumsky, in the magazine *Soviet Union Today*. Shumsky, the first Soviet official to tour the Canadian Arctic, also reported on a symposium he attended in Montreal organized by McGill University and the Arctic Institute of North America. He paid tribute to "the considerable amount of scientific knowledge and research developed by Canadians." It was clear from the symposium that the experts indeed knew a great deal about the Arctic, but not what to do with it. The effect was to show up the Diefenbaker Vision as based, at best, on myth and sloganeering, and not on the practical facts of northern life. The most optimistic statement came from Robert F. Shaw, President of the Foundation Company of Canada Limited and one of the principal builders of the DEW Line. "The Arctic," he said, "can become competitive, and I think we're very close." A journalist interjected to ask: "Competitive with whom in what?" Shaw said he was referring to the iron ore and asbestos in Quebec—but this, admittedly, was hardly in the region of the Arctic. There was general agreement that two factors more than others affected development of the North: transportation, and the cost of food and supplies.

Siberia, with its useful soil, helps to feed itself. The most northerly wheat-growing area in Canada is Peace River country, which lies between Alberta and British Columbia. The true North depends for its nourishment almost wholly on shipments from the "outside," a long and expensive haul usually by plane. In some of the more remote outposts, maintained for defense or exploration, it can cost as much as $100 a day to keep each man in food and fuel. The economics become unmanageable even in simple illustrations. A team for an oil exploration company worked in the Yukon on a drill site near the Arctic Circle. Bags of drilling mud, a necessary ingredient, had to be hauled by truck over the Alaska Highway from Edmonton to Dawson, and then lifted by chartered plane and helicopter to the location. The mud cost less than $2 a bag in Edmonton; delivered, it cost $42 a bag. In Texas or California or Alberta the average price for drilling is $7 a foot; in the Yukon experience it was $1,800 a foot. The exploration company folded after two years and a loss of several million dollars.

The irony is that even if oil had been found in volume, no one really would have known how to get it to market. The Arctic does not possess, as Venezuela does, a Lake Maracaibo, where tankers can come right in from the sea and line up beside pipelines. In any event, surface tankers would be uneconomic because of the brief shipping season. A popularly talked-about notion involves nuclear-powered submarine tankers that would move under the ice fields. But in hard-headed calculations the cost of such transportation today would be just as high as flying the oil out.

Oil has been extracted as far north as Norman Wells, 900 miles above Edmonton, since 1920. It supplies the few thousand people of the western Arctic with fuel and gasoline, but the point on the map is soon reached where it is cheaper to bring oil in from the South. There have been one or two oil flurries in recent years, on the theory that Canada's North contains enough to supply the entire world for at least fifteen years. The theory is based on surface seepages and geological formations, but exploration expenses alone discourage further proof or activity. The same factors apply to mining in general. Commodore O. C. S. Robertson, Deputy Director of the Arctic Institute, argues that even if the region is a storehouse of resources it has yet to be proved "that they exist in economic quantity." W. J. Bennett, vice president of the huge Iron Ore Company of Canada, and one of the most knowledgeable men on northern development, is blunter. "The first misconception people have," he says, "is that the North is loaded with minerals. This may or may not be true. First, there haven't been so many discoveries. Then when you do find an Ungava, the cost of bringing in the product makes it non-competitive." Ungava, in northern Quebec, provided an iron-ore equivalent of an oil flurry. An international group, with Cyrus Eaton and Krupp backing, considered a heavy expenditure in mining, only to push it aside when it became commercially unfeasible.

As a rough rule, the experts estimate that it costs at least four times as much to work a mine in the North as it does in the temperate zone. The expense goes beyond the obvious need for food, heating, and warm clothing. Machinery breaks down and wears out with greater frequency in the extreme temperatures, and permafrost exacts a high price. In territory where ground is frozen sometimes to a depth of a thousand or more feet, only the top few inches thaw each summer. Frozen ground by itself is difficult enough to deal with, but the melting makes it worse. What can appear to be Nature's solid foundation often turns to grimy water when a heated building is put on top of it. Permafrost is not an insuperable problem, but it is an expensive one. It also has its macabre side. In Yellowknife, the local undertaker, known as Burial Smith, operated for many years a small bus from which seats could be removed to form a hearse. The business slogan was: "Sitting down, 30 cents; lying down, $30." One of the disturbing sights around Yellowknife, just as autumn set in, was to see Burial Smith stalk the town, trying to estimate how many customers he was likely to have that winter, so he could dig in advance an appropriate number of pits before the ground became rigidly frozen.

Yellowknife is sustained by a couple of gold mines of lessening importance. The most shattering indictment of the Diefenbaker Vision and misleading optimism is that during the precise period in which he was claiming that a new prosperity would be created, figures in the Department of Northern Affairs showed a steady decline in the two areas with the longest record of mining: the Yukon and Northwest Territories. In 1954 mineral output in these regions amounted to $42.5 million. It was down to $35 million in 1958, the year Diefenbaker began extolling "the vast mineral resources." The descending line on the graph continued, so that by 1964 production stood at $33 million.

The drop was due to a number of factors. Mines were running out of ore, production and transportation were proving too costly, more accessible lodes elsewhere were going into competition. Of the seven places north of the 60th parallel where there had been activity as recently as 1960, only four were still functioning in 1965.[2] Major production in a new area, Pine Point, Northwest Territories, where large lead and zinc deposits are of high grade, is expected by 1966. A railroad has been built 432 miles southward to connect it

[2] Keno, the Yukon, was mining lead, zinc, and silver; Dawson was dredging for gold, though due to shut down; Yellowknife had its gold-mining; and Norman Wells, also in the Northwest Territories, its oil. In 1960, Port Radium, N.W.T., where uranium ore for the first atomic bomb was dug, closed down; a nickel and copper mine at Ranklin Inlet, Hudson Bay, came to an end the same year; tungsten mining in the Northwest Territories ceased in 1963.

with existing outlets, and eventually a town of 3,000 may rise. But the significance—indicated by Northern Affairs officers themselves—is that this is the only fresh development north of the 60th parallel.

The largest single investment in the Canadian North continues to be the billion dollars spent by the United States Defense Department in the 1950's in the construction of airstrips and DEW Line stations within the Arctic Circle. The Mid-Canada Line, on the 55th parallel, was built by Canada itself at a cost of $235 million. These installations, along with other military undertakings, have helped to speed up knowledge of the North and given it communications and transportation facilities it otherwise would not have had at this stage. But, as Graham Rowley points out, airfields or radar stations designed for strategic purposes are not necessarily in the best locations to assist economic development, "though they are certainly better than nothing." Their main function is to detect attacks by manned aircraft coming over Polar space. Despite the fact that in an age of missiles the likelihood of manned attacks diminishes, many strategists still feel that a future war would place the Arctic at the center, rather than the top, of the world. Thus the far North maintains a crucial importance, in a military if not a commercial sense.

The Diefenbaker Vision was not entirely unproductive. It set off a fairly extensive road-building program in the Northwest Territories. And even if its fanciful goals were not attainable, it reminded Canadians that the frontier steadily has been creeping upward. Schefferville, Quebec, on the 55th parallel, is representative of a modern northern mining community. Yet less than half a century ago Timmins, Ontario, only 500 miles north of Toronto, was considered virtually at the outer limit. Timmins also illustrates the inconstancy of northern development when it rotates around a single item, mining. In the old days a classic example of economic vulnerability was whaling, which received a mortal blow when corsets went out of fashion. Timmins built its strength on gold. One mine alone, Hollinger, was the most lucrative on the continent, producing more than $500 million worth. Gold never faded out of style, but its price, pegged by the United States at $35 an ounce since 1934, gradually made it unprofitable to mine at Timmins. The town was in a depressed state in 1964 after Hollinger, the largest employer, prepared to shut down. Then a new strike was revealed—this time an enormously rich lode of copper, zinc, and silver. The discovery resulted from six years of exploration by a United States company, Texas Gulf Sulphur, and touched off the biggest boom in trading of mining stocks in a decade. It also gave Timmins and its 29,000 inhabitants a fresh lease on life for the future and the renewed atmosphere of a giddy, pioneer settlement. Helicopters swarmed in from all directions with prospectors and would-be stakers. One helicopter operator, flying from dawn to dusk, earned $9,000 in a day.

If the Timmins story has a happy twist it is partly because the town itself is reasonably stable and mature. Located on a principal railway line, and in habitable climate, it scarcely can be included among hardship posts. Today's outer limit in the North is financial or psychological as much as geographical. There cannot be another West opening up in an extravagant rush of homesteaders, of numbers of individuals making it on their own. For one thing, enormous capital is required to operate successfully in the North. But aside from this is the recurring fact that the Canadian North is unable to sustain life in the practical sense of Siberia. "There's not a ghost of a chance for a population move," says Graham Rowley. "On the contrary, as people in the North become better educated you can expect them to move out."

This evokes the observation that few native Canadians are interested in working their own high frontier. Long ago the Hudson's Bay Company began a policy, which it still maintains, of recruiting young Scotsmen for many of its posts. They are considered "mature" and "born settlers." One of the first points a visitor notices about an isolated northern colony is the collection of men of foreign birth. The Russian professor Shumsky was struck by this at Mould Bay, a weather station. "I remember the warm friendly atmosphere in the messroom," he related, "and during the conversation someone asked suddenly, 'Who of the persons present is a Canadian?' It turned out that the station chief alone was a Canadian; the rest were a Russian, an American, a Spaniard, a Pole, an Englishman, an Irishman, and a Scotsman."

What is wanted is a "northern state of mind." This was the conclusion of *Imperial Oil Review* in a lively edition devoted to the North. Said the *Review:*

> One of the crucial (and largely forgotten) factors in the future development of the Canadian North appears to be nothing more or less than a state of mind. So far, Canadians have shown little interest in living there. Exploiting it, yes. Staying to develop it, no. Are we afraid of our North? Perhaps we are, with reason. This is a harsh land. . . . But the physical problems are not insurmountable, and sometimes not even important. Everyday living can be far harder on the mind than on the body.

W. J. Bennett, whose Iron Ore Company had the experience of opening a frontier at Schefferville, sums up a key judgment: "Even if the North has resources—and this has yet to be proved—you're never going to get people to settle it the way they did the lower St. Lawrence." Schefferville, on the boundary between northern Quebec and Labrador, is a multiple example of the new frontier: a story of exploration, of United States capital developing Canadian resources, of sensitivity to markets, of paid and sturdy pioneers who hacked a railway and townsite out of some of the worst wilderness in the world, and of the problems of keeping people there.

It was Jacques Cartier who, on a voyage of discovery in 1534, described the desolate St. Lawrence North Shore as "the land that God gave to Cain." The North Shore stretches its bony fingers upward to grasp a massive peninsula known as Labrador and about which another early traveler wrote: "God created this country last of all and threw together there the refuse of his materials as of no use to mankind." I have never seen raw, frightening country to match it. Even Saudi Arabia, from the air as pockmarked and lifeless as the moon, at least has light shining on it. Labrador feels black in a winter that extends nine months and not much brighter in a summer that offers unceasing rain. Three quarters of it is water, ladled into rivers and lakes that are separated by patches of rock. There is some earth, with jackpine and scrub, but it is the exposed rock, grooved and worn by Ice Age glaciers, that stamps the dead landscape.

On my flight, 800 miles northward from Montreal, I had the inevitable thought of how a forced landing could end only in disaster, without hope of survival or rescue. It was the grimness, the vastness, the emptiness that aroused fear. Occasionally, a low, eroded mountain range broke the monotony, but otherwise the lakes and dabs of land just meandered into a remote, bitter plateau and gave the impression of going on and on into the Polar regions. Man was never intended to lay hand here—or so he thought—for all was ugly and sterile. But when, less than a generation ago, iron ore was discovered in abundance, man began to infiltrate.

The pioneer picture is deceptive at first, for it does not take into account the streamlined townships that have been dropped into the wilderness. When we touched down at the airstrip at Wabush, the atmosphere was as much that of a Labrador outpost as one would expect to find. Passengers who waited to embark on the next leg of the trip included a Mountie, fresh-eyed and aged perhaps twenty-two, and looking almost fictional in his bulky blue breeches with broad yellow stripes, workday tunic of deep tan, and fur hat. There were also construction workers in hard-boiled hats of bright yellow or green, with big and sloppy high boots, and Mackinaws in a variety of checks and hues.

A tiny plane glided in from the gray skies above, and the pilot, in the luminous kind of parka that gleams from afar, dashed in with some mail for our flight—and rushed right out again before his engine froze. The Arctic wind was at its usual February gale strength, and the temperature was forty degrees below zero. In the small shack that functioned as waiting room, radio room, baggage room, and supply room, a poster brightened one of the bare frame walls. "Come to India," it said. "See the Taj Mahal." Later I was to discover the poster was not so incongruous, for people here do indulge in exotic voyages. But at the moment all I could think of was that this was almost wartime, in a makeshift headquarters in a strange, alien land; the transmitter-receiver in the corner, for all to see and hear, kept sounding a staccato of messages and the occasional "Roger" from someone in outer space.

Schefferville lay another forty minutes by air to the north. A radar station of the now defunct Mid-Canada Line served as reminder that we had reached the 55th parallel. The shack at Schefferville's landing strip was slightly tidier than at Wabush, and boasted washrooms, suggesting that Schefferville might be less of a frontier. This is so in fact, Schefferville being of the venerable age of ten years, while Wabush and its twin settlement of Labrador City trace their ancestry only to the 1960's.

Schefferville is purely a company town, the only kind of town that could have risen in this hinterland. Before the Iron Ore Company began construction of a 357-mile railway from Sept-Iles, on the St. Lawrence, and thus created a community of 4,000 at the northern end, Labrador and the adjacent part of Quebec were largely unmapped and uninhabited. Only a few geologists and prospectors had ventured inside the territory, among them A. E. Moss, a geologist with training at the University of Saskatchewan and

McGill. In 1942, with the war on, there was pressure for copper, lead, tungsten, and other strategic minerals; it was for these that Moss set out in search. The Mesabi Range of Minnesota was supplying enough iron ore for steel. But a lot of ore was taken out of the Mesabi Range, and at the end of the war—with a frustrating shortage of consumer items such as automobiles—the demand for steel, instead of dropping, went up. It was then that mining companies began to take a serious look at the iron that was known to exist in Labrador-Quebec.

Moss, a short, stocky man in his early 50's, who became chief geologist for the Iron Ore Company, recalls that he and his teams had more than 20,000 square miles to survey—the equivalent of trekking around the world at the equator through a strip a mile wide. Labrador's water surface helped; without float planes, Moss figures, the area never could have been opened up. Still, the nearest base was Sept-Iles, a hop of 320 miles to Knob Lake, the eventual site of Schefferville. And since a plane's maximum range was only about 700 miles, back and forth trips were not made lightly. Prospectors, surveyors, and drillers camped in the bush six months continuously, fighting off not only the misery of winter cold but the agony of summer black flies so fierce that many men were forced to quit in defeat. Canned meats and dehydrated foods provided the main nourishment. Fishing was—and still is—spectacular, with six-pound speckled trout in abundance. But there is little game, and nothing edible grows in the soil. "You'd starve to death if you had to live off the land," says Moss.

Most of the major deposits of iron ore, around what are now Schefferville and Labrador City, were discovered in 1946 and 1947. Moss, a taciturn, quiet type, recalls that "some ore bodies stuck out of the ground as large as a room." Fifty such bodies were located around Knob Lake alone, several up to 50 million tons in content. Around Carol Lake (Labrador City), where one ore body was seven miles long, known reserves were over a billion tons—enough for a hundred years at the anticipated rate of extraction. The problem was not how to dig it out; the deposits were covered with only a few feet of earth or overburden, and simply had to be scooped up by mechanical shovels. The problem was how to haul it through the wilderness to the outside world, and this would require both major financing and the formidable construction of a railroad.

In 1949 Hollinger and M. A. Hanna mining interests joined with steel producers—Republic, National, Armco, Youngstown, Wheeling (and later, Bethlehem)—to form the Iron Ore Company of Canada. Besides the financing provided by the partners, nineteen United States and Canadian insurance companies agreed to lend $145 million. About four fifths of the total capital was American. In 1950 a small steamer in the coastal trade slipped into the Bay of Sept-Iles with the first heavy construction equipment. Four years later the Quebec North Shore and Labrador Railway was in existence, and so was the foundation of Schefferville.

In the interval, the largest civilian airlift in history had been maintained in the wilderness. The company employed seventy-five pilots, and, at the height of operations, its planes were taking off at a rate of one every five minutes—a feat of logistics exceeded only by the Berlin airlift—to supply base camps and way stations housing and feeding close to 7,000 construction workers. Fifteen million yards of earth were shifted, much of it from ravines and escarpments. If part of the route was blighted by muskeg and stunted spruce, a portion of it also was confronted by a granite barrier that rose three thousand feet and tried to isolate the iron ore from access to the sea. Two tunnels, one a half mile long, had to be bored through the rock, and seventeen bridges had to go over the canyons and rivers. The men who put down a million and a half ties did so above a thousand treacherous waterfalls, and in the maddening haze of black flies or Arctic winds that lashed in at fifty miles an hour and sent temperatures to sixty below zero.

Forty years of mining would be required to justify the cost —$300 million—but spiritually it was a priceless accomplishment, a tribute to organized and scientific pioneering on one of the last frontiers of the world. When construction ended, Sept-Iles, which for three centuries had languished as an obscure outpost, was transformed into a booming and modern seaport capable of loading into freighters ten million tons of ore a year. Feeding the ore, from its northern distance, was Schefferville, a town with the comforting appearance and all the facilities of a brand new subdivision a thousand miles to the south. There are now close to eight hundred families in Schefferville, living in dwellings of a dozen different styles, from single bungalows to four-family apartment blocks. All the homes are colorfully finished with stained or painted asbestos shingle sidings and wood trim in attractive green or yellow or brown. Uniformity is avoided. Streets are laid out in gentle curves, radiating into the town center with its churches and modern school buildings. The commercial area includes a hotel, a bank, restaurants, supermarkets, department stores, cinema, and smaller enterprises such as beauty parlor and dry cleaning establishment. A forty-two-bed hospital is staffed by three doctors and a dozen nurses. Physically, therefore, Schefferville lacks nothing, and its inhabitants are paid high wages and salaries. There are no "miners" as such in open-pit work, no uncomfortable or dangerous underground assignments. An electric-shovel operator, scooping ore from a quarry, earns $10,000 a year. Truck drivers, hauling the ore away, earn from $150 to $200 a week. The lowest paying job, as a janitor, yields $110 weekly. Average income at Schefferville is $8,000 a year, and the value is enhanced since rent for a company-owned dwelling ranges from $32 to $38 a month for three bedrooms, from $60 to $65 for four. The most expensive houses for executives, equivalent to $30,000 homes in any moderately sized city to the south, rent for $110.

The company is generous and thoughtful on virtually every level: sickness benefits, paid vacations, extra leave, free correspondence courses, lavish recreation facilities. When the roof of the Olympic-size swimming pool proved faulty after three years, the company did not hesitate to order a new one at $30,000. "No other town of this size could afford such an extraordinary expense out of a normal budget," observed the recreation director, Bill McNeill, aged twenty-five. McNeill, as a single man, pays high income tax. But he also lives in a low-rental apartment sponsored by the company. On savings of $300 a month, it was easy for him to spend his last vacation skiing in Squaw Valley, California, and to plan his next one in Japan. "In Kirkland Lake, Ontario, where I come from," he said, "talk of Florida was for wealthy people. Here everybody can afford to travel."

What, then, are the drawbacks? Why does Schefferville suffer from the serious and chronic ailment of losing its people despite the lucrative attractions? When it first opened, and while decent housing was in short supply, the turnover in personnel was 75 per cent a year. But even now, after a decade of digging in, it is still 20 per cent. Bill McNeill provided, in one word, part of the reason for the fickleness: "Ambition." As a young man, he says, he looks upon Schefferville as an adventure and a chance to make far more money than he could elsewhere. But he recognizes its limitations and feels no sense of attachment. The average man—company records show him to be twenty-nine years old—lacks even the zest for adventure. He knows that, even with the expense of a family of two or three children, he can leave after a few years with savings of $10,000, enough to start his own business in more hospitable climate. Not all make it, of course. The quick earnings sometimes go equally hastily in expensive vacations in Europe or Hawaii. Still, one former Schefferville hand sends his old mates letters about the coffee plantation he now owns in Central America. Two young engineers, after a couple of years' experience in open-pit mining, are in Peru as partners in a profitable firm of consultants. One man, with $15,000 accumulated from truck-driving, bought a garage in Montreal, soon lost everything and went into bankruptcy. He is back again, saving a second hoard. But more representative are three others—a chef and two mechanics—who combined forces and earnings and opened a successful bowling alley-snack bar in Shawinigan Falls, Quebec.

Schefferville, obviously, cannot hold the ambitious types. Another element in the turnover is the hideously depressing sense of isolation, which prevails in spite of the railway link with Sept-Iles and a flight a day to the outside world. Whitehorse in the Yukon at least has its Alaska Highway; people can get into their cars and drive to another kind of community, thinking nothing of the hundreds of miles involved. People in Schefferville, in contrast, feel hemmed in. The town boasts eight hundred cars—in terms of population, one of the highest ratios on the continent—but only thirty miles of road, to and from the quarries. Otherwise the desolation of scrub and rock and moss and water envelops everything. Whitehorse enjoys summers of outdoor swimming. Ice lingers in the lakes around Schefferville until late June, and at no time, even in July, does the water's temperature rise above forty-five degrees. Labrador is much farther south than the Yukon, but its weather is Arctic. The peninsula is caught between two of Nature's refrigerators. The Labrador current, a stream of cold sea water and ice, pushes down from the Arctic to chill the eastern coast. At the same time Polar air of gale force, with a velocity as high as seventy-five miles an hour, sweeps in from the direction of Hudson Bay. And so it is the climate, possibly more than any other factor, that drives people away.

Even the few who have remained from the earliest days usually have the motive of accumulating enough savings to finance retirement in their 50's. Jack Jenkins, aged forty-seven, is one of the originals. He and his wife and teen-age daughter still live in the house they occupied in 1954. They are the only family left of the first fourteen in residence. In the last ten years they have had six next-door neighbors. Why the frequent changeover? Mrs. Jenkins, a hardy, self-sufficient soul, says that almost invariably it is the wives who insist on pulling out; the men can take it. "When the rain isn't falling in the summer," she says, "and the ground is dry, the red dust from the pits blows everywhere, and you can't even keep it out of the house. It drives some women crazy. And in the winter you can't go out because of the wind and the cold. When you're cooped in day after day with young babies, again it drives you crazy."

These hardships might be manageable, said the wife of a young engineer. What is really terrifying is the sensation of isolation combined with the weather. She recalled her reaction when a local doctor decided her ailing baby would have to be rushed to the Children's Hospital in Montreal: "I trembled, thinking the day's plane wouldn't be able to come in. This sometimes happens four days in a row because of the weather." The experience worked out happily, but at the end of it she told her husband: "No more children until we get out of here." And so here was the whole story again, the main question: How do you get people to live in an Arctic environment? A. E. Moss, the geologist, offered the opinion: "Maybe you could do it if you regarded the Arctic as the British used to regard the tropics. Offer enormous salaries and three months of home leave a year. But in the case of iron ore here, in competition with prevailing world prices, this would be impossible."

The average stay in Schefferville is now five years. In Labrador City the turnover of the 3,000 inhabitants is 60 per cent a year, partly because the town is in the weeding-out stage Schefferville underwent during its first several years; the hard core has still to declare itself. But Labrador City suffers even greater isolation than Schefferville. From Labrador City, which also is run by the Iron Ore Company, one can drive only four miles: to Wabush, operated by Wabush Mines, a consortium of United States, Canadian, and European steel companies. Wabush, still under construction in 1964, with only a couple of hundred housing units completed and paving yet to go in, was hardly an exciting change of pace for residents of Labrador City.

But, typical of the comforts of the new frontier, the Wabush hotel at which I stayed—the Sir Wilfred Grenfell, named after the British medical missionary—would do credit to a highly sophisticated center. Built in the style of a Swiss chalet, it makes a delightfully surprising anomaly. The picture windows in the dining room may not look over exotic scenery—exotic is hardly the word for any of the Labrador landscapes—but the food is of a finely civilized character. One can dine on escargots, imported English Dover sole sauté meunière, red brand filet mignon, or shashlik en brochette, with suitable wine, and pay an average of seven dollars a person. The prices are not out of line with local earnings, which, the same as at Schefferville, bring a high standard of living. Labrador, in which Wabush and Labrador City are located, belongs to the Province of Newfoundland. Salaries in the company towns are at least twice as high as those in St. John's, the capital; 60 per cent of the labor force at Labrador City and Wabush are from the island of Newfoundland; 20 per cent are from Quebec, the rest from other parts of Canada.

In Schefferville, on the Quebec side of the Labrador border, three quarters are French Canadians; yet separatism is almost an unknown word. There was a case, while I was there, of a man refusing to allow his son to join the Boy Scouts because this would have meant an oath of allegiance to the Queen. But this was a rare case. In fact, politics, usually a vital part of the Quebec scene, hardly enters conversation—partly because the kind of people who come here are motivated by the very simple desire to garner enough capital to get out and start a fresh life; they do not want turbulence of any kind. Partly, too, it is because of the calm and unhurried air that is breathed into an isolated place. Schefferville possesses a radio station, operated in English and French by the company as a public service. Though news is read from time to time, it is not linked with any network and so emits none of the hysterical immediacy that sometimes engulfs the individual listening to a live broadcast. Newspapers from Quebec City and Montreal come in with the train on its twice-weekly schedule. Lively events that can cause tempers to flare in Montreal have cooled off by the time of arrival, and cast hardly a spell on Schefferville.

For the most part, people's concern is about economics. There is awareness, for instance, of the uncertainty of mining as a livelihood. Schefferville was built at enormous expense to fill an unsated demand for iron ore. However, almost from the moment it came into existence, a new process for concentrating ore was being developed by metallurgists. Known as pelletizing, this cut the high cost of shipping crude ore and made such areas as the Mesabi Range, with only low-content ore remaining, economic to operate. Labrador City works on the new process, but the relatively high-yield ore of Schefferville (53 per cent iron content) no longer is as attractive as it was a mere decade ago. Schefferville, in the words of one executive, "is being pushed pretty hard." The only guarantee it has of a market is the fact that it is owned by steel companies that strive to keep alive their investment. But among employees the nagging worry is layoff. During the 1950's Schefferville shipped ten million tons of ore a year; by 1963 this had dropped to 6.5 million tons. In 1963, 1,200 men were on the Schefferville payroll; in 1964, 1,000. The Iron Ore Company of Canada, taking together Schefferville, the railway, Labrador City, and Sept-Iles, has about $500 million invested in Quebec-Labrador.

The area provides almost two thirds of Canada's iron ore, and the over-all investment—including that of operators additional to the Iron Ore Company—is close to $1 billion; 90 per cent of this money comes from the United States. If any sentiment exists on the spot against American extraction of Canada's natural resources, I did not hear it expressed. The dominant attitude was summed up by a French Canadian who said: "It's very nice to say that these are our resources. But who else is willing to take them out and give us jobs, heh?"

Although the Quebec side of the border is calm, Premier Joey Smallwood of Newfoundland has a small separatist movement on his hands. "Movement" is perhaps too strong a word, but certainly during my visit there was a mood for establishing Labrador as a separate province. Why anyone should dream of autonomy for the bleak land that God gave to Cain is difficult at first to comprehend. But the fact is that even if Jacques Cartier once wrote that Labrador could not yield even "a cartload of earth," he has been proved wrong. The iron ore of Labrador brings Newfoundland more than $10 million a year in royalties, enough to cover a tenth of the province's budget. Provincial expenses in Labrador City and Wabush are negligible, since the companies built even the schools, pay most of the teachers' salaries, and maintain other major services. Residents resent the high price for gasoline, which includes sixteen cents a gallon in provincial tax, when they receive in return no road system. Even the four miles of road between Wabush and Labrador City were laid by the companies. And so the complaint as expressed by a native of St. John's is: "The government does nothing. We'd be better off on our own, and use the revenue from the iron ore to build a library, a television station, and put in some roads, maybe to the coast, so we could have contact with the outside world." The separatist current lacks direction at the moment, but it has a serious aspect. The mood was reflected in provincial elections of 1963, when Newfoundlanders living in Labrador sent to St. John's the only independent member of the House of Assembly. This was, people pointed out, a protest vote and a warning to Smallwood not to take Labrador for granted.

In a practical sense Smallwood hardly can regard the territory lightly. Labrador is rich not only in minerals but in timber and water power. This potential was sufficiently recognized years ago, in a vague sort of way, to cause dispute between Quebec and what was then the Dominion of Newfoundland. Quebec, dating its claim back to the Peace of Paris in 1763, said it held sovereignty to all of Labrador except a strip about a mile wide along the coast. Newfoundland argued that its old title carried with it the rights to the watershed of the rivers emptying onto the coast. In 1927, the Privy Council, highest tribunal of the British Commonwealth, agreed with Newfoundland and awarded it 120,000 square miles, which turned out to contain the dormant treasures.

The provinces of Newfoundland and Quebec were still arguing in 1965—not so much about boundaries but about arrangements to transmit Labrador power over Quebec land lines. But the point was that the power was there. Topography, despite an ugly hand, endowed Labrador with the turbulent Churchill River that plunges 245 feet over an escarpment, making a waterfall seventy-eight feet deeper than Niagara. This is only a part of the heritage; a series of cataracts and a comparatively easy way to converge the river into a vertical drop of 1,040 feet would give it a power potential of six million horsepower, twice that of the largest existing power site, Grand Coulee, in the northwestern United States. The intention is to carry the power into the industrial centers of eastern Canada and the United States. New York will receive its share through Consolidated Edison. The project, a construction challenge on a scale comparable to the St. Lawrence Seaway, is expected to cost more than $1.2 billion. By the time it is completed, possibly in 1972, Broadway marquees and New York subways will be running on hydroelectric power generated more than a thousand miles away in the Canadian North.

11.

Culture on Guard

What would happen in Canada if full sovereignty were invoked and the southern border were sealed tight against American mass culture—if the airwaves were jammed, if all our comic books were embargoed, if only the purest and most uplifting of American cultural commodities were allowed entry? Native industries would take over, obviously. Cut off from American junk, Canada would have to produce her own.

—Richard H. Rovere [1]

THE DROLLERY OF THE above quotation is noteworthy for several reasons: first, because it was written by an American about a subject that is grimly serious to many Canadians, and then because it avoids the usual hackneyed question: How would Americans feel if the positions were reversed, if Canada were ten times more populous and powerful than the United States, and as a consequence inundated and frustrated it with a peculiarly Canadian brand of lore? But perhaps the quotation is interesting because it serves as an embarkation point for Mordecai Richler, one of Canada's

[1] *Maclean's,* November 5, 1960.

most gifted and belligerent authors. Richler has turned out a satirical novel about an Eskimo named Atuk, fresh from Baffin Bay, who discovers how culture can work in Canada. Among other things, Atuk keeps a group of relatives locked up in a basement in Toronto while they mass manufacture carvings for him to sell at enormous profit. Occasionally, he rewards them with a peek at television, which, they are persuaded, is his own private magic. Richler uses Atuk freely to strike at smug commercialism in the arts, in television, in journalism—and mainly at what he calls "Canadian self-inflation." He ridicules Canadian nationalism in passages such as the one uttered by a newspaper character: "Wring your hands, scratch your noggins, but the trouble with us lard-bottomed, spoon-fed Canadians is we live in a mealy-mouthed atmosphere of mumble-mumble in national purpose. When do we ever get angry?" [2]

Canadians do get angry, of course. Some of them get angry at Richler who is contemptuous of such an abiding concern for a "Canadian culture" that it creates literary figures "world famous in Canada and deservedly unknown just about everywhere else." The people who accuse Richler of being an undisciplined smart-aleck who sells his own country short (Richler, aged thirty-three, now lives in England) do so sometimes for strongly patriotic motives. They resent his suggestion that since Canada is a North American country it is therefore logical for New York to serve as Canada's cultural capital. But chauvinism is not the only stimulus. Among some Canadians there is an equally deep feeling that Canada's cultural life has fared well, that it has produced a reasonable crop of writers and artists, and the country should be proud of them.

Between the Richlers and the nationalists are the vast mass who do not really care one way or the other. They take it for granted that in the field of literature the same lettering

[2] In Canada, *The Incomparable Atuk* (McClelland & Stewart); in the United States, *Stick Your Neck Out* (Simon & Schuster), 1963.

appears in the comic strips in Canada as in the United States, that the same jingles are heard on the radio, that the same television programs are watched—along with the same motion pictures, and the same photographs in the same magazines. It is a relative handful who debate the perennial question: first, whether there is a *Canadian* culture; second, whether the United States is guilty of throttling it, just as the United States is indicted for dominating the country economically. The two charges go hand in hand, and they reflect the most serious aspects of Canada's attempt to mold a personality of its own. What is so fascinating about the whole business is that no one has yet satisfied the majority of Canadians that there is an indigenous Canadian culture that spreads much beyond the sculptures and prints turned out by Eskimos, who are almost, but not quite, in the mass production stage suggested by Atuk. And if there is no distinctive art or literature form, what is the reason? Is it because talent has not been given a chance for expression because of the presence of that big, overpowering neighbor to the south? Or simply because Canadians have not had —up until now—a great deal worth saying of interest to others? Moreover, they haven't even been encouraged by other Canadians to say it. Richler may be culpable for brashness and irreverence, but he has been more honest than most contemporary social critics in facing facts and discussing them.

There is nothing particularly new about the search for identity and the torment over its hypothetical existence, or even the indifference of the general public. The only thing altered is that the villain, aside from the Canadian himself, used to be the Briton rather than the American. A hundred years ago the scholarly journals lamented the dearth of Canadian literature; even more pungently they deplored the scant attention paid by Canadians to Canadian writers. "The intellectual classes of Canada," commented *Saturday Reader*, a Montreal periodical, "are like the Italian who preferred to go to the galleys rather than read an Italian book." Arthur R. M. Lower, the social historian, notes that from the earliest days Canadians were able to produce their own athletic games—hockey, lacrosse—and even to fashion education to suit local conditions, despite the English and Scottish influence. But in purely cultural fields—painting, literature, music, theater—the picture was bleaker and showed hardly a speck of originality. While Canada was attempting to emerge as a political unit in the nineteenth century its British overseers—"guardians of a superior culture"—kept intellectuals and semi-intellectuals under their tutelage and were openly scornful of colonial efforts at the arts.

This contempt, Lower contends, was almost as destructive a factor in discouraging the appearance of a native literature as was the importation from England of magazines and books at the expense of local publications. If sensitive Canadians once deplored this cultural colonialism of Britain, their descendants now have the same complaints about the United States—but with an ironic difference. The overseers are Canadians themselves who go through phases—ups and downs—of considering that Canadian talent is best when it is displayed at home, or conversely, that talent cannot be very great if it does not first achieve recognition abroad. This manic-depressive trait permeates much of the so-called cultural debate and is discouraging to artists and authors who would prefer to stay home but cannot endure parochialism.

Little has changed since those days of a bygone century when Canadians imported their reading matter. They continue to buy foreign publications in quantity—if not, as previously, British, now American. This gives rise to the observation that Canada is the only country of any size in the world whose people read more outside periodicals than they do their own. Magazines in Britain suffer no competition from France or Germany for a simple language reason. The United States allows the entry of periodicals from Mexico, but since these are in Spanish they can hardly rate as a challenge. The border between Canada and the United States, in contrast, does not shield it from a common language, and something like four out of five magazines picked off a newsstand in Canada come from the United States. The score of general Canadian magazines attempting to compete have not questioned so much the circulation of hundreds of millions of American copies each year; rather they object to the fact that many of them carried advertisements specifically directed at Canadian readers. This was managed through what is known as the "split run": insertion of the special advertising only in those copies distributed in Canada. The complaint was that the United States magazines, with no editorial expenses in Canada, and no interest in encouraging Canadian writers by publishing their stories or articles, were engaged in unfair economic war with genuine Canadian publications. The main expenses of the American magazines were absorbed in a home market with ten times as many consumers, leaving them free to "dump" their product in Canada and reap the advertising dollars.

This, at any rate, was the conclusion arrived at by a Royal Commission headed by Senator Grattan O'Leary, a former newspaper editor. The commission condemned the existing situation, suggested a ban on "split run" editions, and urged tax measures which, without curtailing freedom of distribution, would have cut some of the advantages held by other American magazines in competition with Canadians. Two successive governments—one Conservative, the other Liberal—talked of enacting legislation, but both steered away from the tax recommendations made by O'Leary. There were warnings from Douglas Dillon, United States Secretary of the Treasury, and by others in Washington, that any action, particularly against *Time* and *Reader's Digest,* which print editions in Canada and therefore claim a technical avoidance of "split runs," would bring about American reprisals against Canadian interests. In 1965, when the government again said it would introduce measures to protect Canadian publications, *Time* and *Reader's Digest* were declared exempt from any restrictions. And so the cultural debate became involved in two conflicts: the broad question of United States enterprise in Canada and how it affects Canadian sovereignty; and the still more diffuse question of how to develop the Canadian arts and consequently an identity. Some of the popular publications directly in danger of closing down, because of loss of advertising revenue, have made a substantial effort to interpret and portray a distinctive flavor of Canada. Notable among them is *Maclean's,* which has managed to be entertaining and informative, and to set a high standard in magazine journalism. But *Maclean's,* published in Toronto by a company with profitable trade magazines to carry the load, has suffered a heavy deficit every year since 1960 in spite of a rising circulation of 550,000 (in terms of population, equivalent to 5.5 million in the United States). Any shutting down of *Maclean's* because of economics would be a severe blow to Canadian authors who sell to it regularly. But mainly it would deprive the public of an intelligent mirror to the nation they form.

Not everyone has gone along with the O'Leary report. Some Canadians have invoked the principle of a North American culture extending beyond political boundaries. Robert Weaver is one of Canada's leading literary figures, who, as a C.B.C. public affairs specialist, has been responsible for some outstanding radio programs of high intellectual level, and, as editor of *The Tamarack Review,* a quarterly, has introduced many poets and authors of the younger generation. Weaver, in his early forties, dismisses the O'Leary recommendations as "negative and defensive." He points out that even the Royal Commission rejected any notion that "the culture of the American people is in some way an alien culture, a monolithic, inferior way of life from which Canadians need shelter." On the contrary, he uses some of the commission's own words to argue that the people of Canada, like the people of the United States, are basically North Americans: "Inheritors of the thoughts and traditions of Europe, but also the children of geography, products of the environments, the emotions, the driving forces, the faith, the dreams, and the forms of expression of the North American continent. . . . But somehow we now exist in defiance of geography, and we have to find ways to communicate from East to West when the pull is to the south." His answer is to maintain a cultural identity through subsidy.

"One magazine like *Encounter*," says Weaver, "would do more to further that cross-continent communication than any damage we may do to *Time* and *Reader's Digest*." The precedent for subsidized magazines already exists, he reminds us. *Encounter*, the English monthly, is sponsored by the Congress for Cultural Freedom. In the United States the monthly *Commentary* is sponsored by the American Jewish Committee. And in Canada itself, points out Weaver, subsidized culture was long ago established with the publicly financed C.B.C. and the National Film Board, "which have a decent tradition of biting the hand that feeds them."

If Weaver sounds heretical when talking about periodicals, he is equally outspoken in discussing the state of Canadian authorship and literary sophistication. What he demands, in place of the complaint that Canada is inhibited by the United States, is simple acceptance of the fact that the country has produced very few creative people of international stature. "We are a provincial country," he says in suggesting that Canadians assume humility and reality without looking southward to lay the blame. It always distresses him, he adds, when he meets in Jamaica or Paris, or anywhere else, someone who says: "What other important writers have you had besides Mazo de la Roche?" The author of the long *Jalna* series about the Whiteoak family and a romanticized Canada did attain international recognition. So too did the humorist Stephen Leacock and, in an earlier era, Thomas Chandler Haliburton, creator of Sam Slick, the ingenious Yankee clock peddler. But the list is not long. In contemporary terms, the novels of Morley Callaghan and Hugh MacLennan attract attention in the United States as well as in Canada; but most other Canadian authors remain hardly known even within the confines of Canada.

Some prominent Canadian *littérateurs*—among them Robertson Davies—argue that Canada has a far more impressive catalogue of literature than either Canadians or non-Canadians are prepared to acknowledge. In an explanation for American readers, Davies has agreed that if Canadian books are mingled with books from England and the United States, they are likely to be lost, for their tone is not aggressive or eccentric. But placed together as a Canadian library, and considered as the production of a land and a people, they assume a more impressive stature:

> They tell of a country which is a political rather than a geographical or racial fact. They tell of a people self-effacing and self-doubting who are being pitchforked by history into a new self-appraisal. They tell of a people who have pretended they had no ghosts, but who now find themselves troubled by all the importunate ghosts of a bicultural civilization.... But that does not satisfy us; we compare ourselves with England, with France, with the United States, and make ourselves miserable.[3]

Another critic, with possibly a less subjective view, J. Donald Adams, wrote in a column in *The New York Times* that Americans have held Canada back, culturally, by assuming the role of big brother. But that, he appended, was not the whole story: "Canada should have by now a much more vital literature of her own than she has thus far produced." One explanation offered by Adams is that "Can-

[3] *Holiday,* April 1964.

ada has been passing through a phase that we (Americans) went through in the 1870's and 1880's—great material expansion and a greatly increased sense of national identity— conditions which make for a high degree of self-consciousness, and thereby a not too hospitable climate for self-expression." His conclusion is that Canada has not yet "found herself," and this is one reason why so few books by Canadians are published in the United States.

A recurring theme, noted by many of the analysts, is how Canada's beginning was different from that of the United States, where people seized their future from the grasp of an Empire, and had to make the best of it or expire in disrepute. "That," says Robertson Davies, "was bracing; it made for a tonic intellectual climate, and fostered the seeds of myth. But that same Empire was our mother, and the navel cord was never cut; it withered as we grew." Two or three results were apparent: first, there was no spirit or fire of revolt to infuse Canadian literature as it expanded; second, the art of compromise—of learning to live with inherent British tradition alongside a dynamic nation with a tradition of nonconformity—was beaten into every Canadian, including future authors, from childhood. The miracle, if one can look at it as such, is that anything distinctive has emerged at all.

Edmund Wilson introduces another point: the overwhelming loneliness caused by such an immense stretch of land as Canada. "How can one get hold on such a country?" he asks. "Can one think of such spaces in terms of any human meaning?" This topic occupies the attention also of Canada's leading literary critic, Northrop Frye, who says the question of identity—"Who am I?"—is only part of a greater riddle such as, "Where is here?" He writes:

> One wonders if any other national consciousness has had so large an amount of the unknown, the unrealized, the humanly undigested, so built into it. Rupert Brooke... speaks of the "unseizable virginity" of the Canadian land-

scape. What is important here, for our purpose, is the position of the frontier in the Canadian imagination. In the United States one could choose to move out to the frontier or to retreat from it back to the seaboard. The tensions built up by such migrations have fascinated many American novelists and historians. In the Canadas, even in the Maritimes, the frontier was all around us, a part and a condition of one's whole imaginative being. The frontier was primarily what separated the Canadian, physically or mentally, from Great Britain, from the United States, and, even more important, from other Canadian communities. Such a frontier was the immediate datum of his imagination, the thing that had to be dealt with first.[4]

The writers in the past decade at least, as Frye points out, have begun to explore a world which is post-Canadian, as it is post-American, post-British, and post everything except the world itself. There are no frontiers or provinces in the age of television or aircraft. But Robert Fulford, a stimulating young Toronto critic, speaks of the curious fact that there are few really good expatriate Canadian authors: men and women who have fled what they consider rather drab and inhospitable climate to take refuge in New York or London or Paris, There are, of course, some who have attained stature and acceptance away from their old environment. Mavis Gallant, for instance, is a Montreal writer who migrated to Europe to write stories that have won her a faithful following in *The New Yorker*. But in general even the expatriates rarely come up with the passion of anger or rebellion or dissension. Fulford's logical explanation is the lack in Canadian history itself of wrath or other deep emotion to act as a stimulus. William Faulkner implicitly carries in his writings the troubles of Mississippi, and in a sense shows guilt feelings. But, according to the Fulford reasoning,

[4] An essay in *Literary History of Canada,* University of Toronto Press, 1965.

if Faulkner had been born in southern Ontario, instead of the southern United States, he probably would have been a mediocre writer since he would have had no racial or other major conflict to agitate him.

Shortly after hearing this expression from Fulford, I went around to see Morley Callaghan in his Toronto home. Callaghan has often made the point that Canada is a part of the North American cultural pattern, and while people in the North should have a different literature from that offered by southern writers—"we have our own idiosyncrasies up here"—in the final analysis no matter how distinctive it might seem, it still would be North American culture. He said,

> I don't think you can do anything about it. It's like the Latin tribes living outside Rome, broken into so many tribal customs. Those with strong enough tribal culture could preserve themselves from the Romans. But aside from the French Canadians, who are we in Canada? We have the same tastes as people in the United States, and you can't by an Act of Parliament decree a culture. As far as the Americans are concerned, not only are they not plotting against us—culturally, or any other way—but they'd love to see something unique emerge from us.

Callaghan's own case history adds another dimension to the trial of notable Canadian names in international literature. It is an old but recurring theme about Canadian talent being unappreciated at home and therefore drowned in discouragement. This phenomenon goes through oscillations. At the moment there is a modishness, of a sort, about Canadian talent; certainly there is a cultural boom. But it is largely a boom in the performing arts. Toronto, Montreal, Vancouver, and other cities, have new concert halls and theater centers, each of which, in Callaghan's view, is "a shrine to performers." He says: "You can fill a country with performers, but you may not produce a thing worth performing." [5] And so, carrying the thought to an obvious conclusion, men and women may believe it fashionable to go to a concert, but they will not read a book. "To sit down, and meditate, to do something by yourself, is rare," Callaghan observes. The point is that even if a Maureen Forrester achieves acclaim on the concert stage in the United States, and is received equally enthusiastically at home, the same process must take place in exaggerated form when it applies to a writer instead of a singer. "I'm convinced there is a bush-league mentality here," says Callaghan:

> By this I mean that if you have big-league talent or class and a scout picks it out, invariably people will tell the scout he picked the wrong guy. There's a kind of discomfort about *anyone* being elevated from the minors. Canadians can't recognize a talent that doesn't stay in the bush league. If a book written by someone in Indiana becomes a best seller in New York, it will be a best seller here. But it can't happen the other way round, that a book should be accepted first here.

Callaghan exaggerates, but only moderately. He himself is an example of a Canadian author succeeding almost in defiance of Canada. But the fact is that he was hardly recognized in his own country for many years, despite skillfully fashioned books of the quality of *The Loved and the Lost* and *The Many-Colored Coat,* in addition to more than fifty *New Yorker* stories. Callaghan was born in 1903, making him a contemporary of F. Scott Fitzgerald and Ernest Heming-

[5] There has never been a shortage of famous Canadian actors, singers, directors, or others in the performing arts. From the earliest times of mass entertainment, Canadians have been identified with Hollywood films: such men and women as Mary Pickford, Norma Shearer, Raymond Massey, Walter Pidgeon, Marie Dressler, Glenn Ford. The stage, opera house, and concert hall have claimed such varied personalities as Kate Reid, Glenn Gould, Oscar Peterson, Paul Anka, Teresa Stratas, George London. Until a very few years ago Canadians interested in serious drama automatically had to think of migration to London or New York. Some change came with the introduction of the Shakespearean Festival in Stratford, Ontario, in 1953. But it took a decade for the Canadian venture to feel sufficient confidence to drop the policy of hiring a foreign star and instead to rely chiefly on Canadian acting talent.

way. To many of today's younger authors, his is the first truly Canadian voice in literature simply because his stories are not parochial; whether they are set in Toronto or Montreal, or Paris or New York, the drama of human experience is authentically universal. To Edmund Wilson, he is "the most unjustly neglected novelist in the English-speaking world." Wilson, writing in *The New Yorker,* wondered "whether the primary reason for the current underestimation of Morley Callaghan may not be simply a general incapacity—apparently shared by his compatriots—for believing that a writer whose work may be mentioned without absurdity in association with Chekhov's and Turgenev's can possibly exist in our day in Toronto."

Wilson made this comment in 1960, and had occasion four years later to recall the hostile reaction it provoked among Canadian reviewers. As Wilson himself discovered, many Canadians accepted the opinion that Callaghan could write short stories, but they considered him incapable of writing novels. "They resented my praising these latter," Wilson deduced. "I was thus, from their point of view, trying to dispose of Canadian property in the same way that other Americans had done when they bought up Canadian industries or had attempted to dictate to the Canadian government the policies that our government would prefer to see it follow."

Callaghan, who has lived in New York and Paris, chose to live and work in Toronto because he was born there, and so was his wife, and he says a writer has to feel he can draw from people and situations he has known for a long time. When I remarked that this seemed only a part answer, Callaghan agreed. "I've a strange feeling," he then said, "that I need opposition. I need to say 'to hell with you' to the people in Canada who try to pull everyone down to a conformist style. There are a lot of men and women with talent here, but you have to have a curious stubbornness, a sublime egotism to overcome the weight that will try to make you smaller or drag you down." He sums up his ambiguous feelings about Canada, and its attitude toward writers, in telling of the reception of one of his more recent books, *That Summer in Paris*, a sensitive and beautifully written account of his early relationship with Hemingway and Fitzgerald. While some reviewers saw in it the rare quality of one writer talking of other writers truthfully and yet without malice, a newspaper in Winnipeg said of Callaghan: "Who does he think he is?" A Montreal critic accused him of being "a hanger on."

Sadly, Callaghan concludes:

> Canada is one of the most bourgeois countries in the world. People will not accept "art" unless it makes money, and so there's no distinction in producing a work of quality unless it pays off. Perhaps the same mentality, the same materialism, exists in the United States, but the States is so big and has so much energy that you can be poor and still have boosters. New York is forever looking for something that isn't familiar, something that is different. It may be wrong 90 per cent of the time, but at least it is looking.

Oddly, there are ups and downs in the public response to people in creative fields—corresponding, one is tempted to suspect, to the general confidence, or lack of confidence, in the country as a whole. Before the Second World War—certainly up to 1939—the automatic urge of many young men and women heading for the professions was to migrate to the United States. Even in the field of journalism the pull was strong. Friends of a student graduating from university said, as though paying him the highest compliment possible, "You should try to work on a paper in New York." The inference was that he was too ambitious or competent to be satisfied with opportunities in Canada. The war changed much of this attitude. A feeling of self-importance asserted itself across Canada, and not only because of a notable military record. The war created such institutions as the National Film Board, at first designed as a propaganda agency but soon developing into a producer of internationally recognized documentaries. Canadian talent was finding an outlet for itself also on radio, with the C.B.C. winning acclaim for its drama and current affairs programs.

The generation that graduated in the late 1940's and early 1950's did not hear so frequently the advice: "Move to New York." Apart from the boom atmosphere and feeling of fresh confidence inside Canada, there was enough disdain for McCarthyism among people in the intellectual or cultural fields to discourage them from any desire to live in the United States. Canada, moreover, was being taken seriously in international politics, and this inspired not only improved journalism but a lively outburst of commentaries that in turn gave a more provocative and original tone to literature and the arts generally. By the early 1960's, however, a slump in morale, reminiscent of the 1930's, showed itself: unconsciously, perhaps, with the realization that Canada possessed only modest international stature; consciously because Canadians felt that nationhood itself was precarious, that a basic cleavage set apart French from English, and this in its own way split wide the efforts to reach cultural distinction and maturity.

These transitions, of course, were subtle and difficult to attribute to definable forces. Nevertheless, an interesting Gallup Poll indicates a change in the general public mood in the brief period of a decade. In 1963 almost six Canadians in ten expressed the belief that Canadian artists, writers, and musicians did not have a chance to develop their talents in their own country—a substantial increase over 1953, when about four in ten held the same view. In what is obviously a vicious circle, the mere fact that people consider the outlook is negative tends to cut into morale or support for creative arts.

The net effect is to rob Canada not only of her present

intellectual confidence, but to deflate the prospects for building a stimulating future. Critic Robert Fulford makes a shrewd point when he says that the migration of a television director or a literary figure to the United States involves the loss of genes even more than the loss of the individual. When a John Kenneth Galbraith leaves Canada, the country is denied not merely the immediate call on his skills as an economist, educator, and author; it is denied also the talent and brains of all the future Galbraiths. There is an argument that the exodus of brains is offset by the infusion of aptitudes migrating into Canada from abroad. In some fields—especially medicine and science—this holds true. But it is not always true in the literary fields. The case of Brian Moore is, from a Canadian point of view, revealing and sad. Moore, one of the finest novelists in the English language, hardly can be claimed as one of Canada's own, since he was born in Belfast and migrated to Montreal only at the age of twenty-seven. But he started his writing career in Montreal, was happy to take out Canadian citizenship, and had full intentions of remaining in Canada. Now, however, for the world of readers at large such superb books as *An Answer from Limbo, The Feast of Lupercal*, and *The Luck of Ginger Coffey* will be identified as products of an author living in the United States.

Moore, who is in his middle forties, quit Montreal in 1959 after twelve years of residence. He now lives in New York. Why did he leave? When I put the question to him, Moore replied with a kind of perplexity and anguish that never would have existed if Canada had been another sort of country:

> Have I left it? It reminds me of the story of James Joyce when he was asked why he had left the Church. "That's for them to say," he said. I feel the same way. First of all, Canada treated me very well both as an immigrant and a writer, and my reasons for leaving were the same as my reasons for leaving my native Belfast. New York seemed

a more interesting and promising place to live in than was Montreal—which leads me to one of the vague dissatisfactions one feels about Canada. There is no real metropolis, no Paris of which the whole country seems proud. In the same way there is no Canada—no one country, but merely a series of squabbling regions bound up in regional prejudices and myths. No metropolis, no unity of regions, none of the pride of being North American which one feels at once in the United States. If Canadians are not proud of being Canadians, they are also curiously unwilling to admit the immigrant to full status as a Canadian. This was the one thing which irritated me constantly in my years there. Even old friends who had known me for a decade would suddenly turn on me in the middle of a discussion and say, "Of course, you don't really know; you're not really Canadian." There are no New Americans in the United States. But once a New Canadian, always a New Canadian—in other words, a foreigner.

Moore offers to illustrate "these vague feelings of affection, irritation, and dissatisfaction in my love affair with my adopted country" with one incident. Still thinking of himself as a Canadian—"even though Canadians are reluctant to allow me this supposition"—he retains his Canadian citizenship. Recently, he called the Canadian consulate in New York to inquire about renewal of his passport. A woman at the other end of the line said: "But if you're living in the States, why do you want to go on being a Canadian?" Moore's sad comment is: "Alas, this seems to sum up Canadian self-denigration, indifference, and inferiority feeling vis-à-vis the United States. In other words, if a country doesn't think much of itself, it can't expect other countries, or nationals of other countries, to think much of it. It's too bad, for, believe me, I am very fond of Canada. I *chose* it, after all."

If some authors leave, or do not find a place in Canada, others from abroad occasionally reverse the procedure and make a home in Canada. Nicholas Monsarrat, whose early fame was based on *The Cruel Sea,* is an example—though not, it turns out, for inspirational or ennobling reasons. He selected Canada because of "part inertia." Monsarrat, now aged fifty-four, spent his first twenty-five years in Britain, but then kept on the move: two years in Paris, one in Germany, six at sea with the Royal Navy, several in South Africa, and from 1953 to 1956 he was with the United Kingdom Information Office in Ottawa. Later he decided to make Ottawa a base for—ironically—the very quality Canadian writers deplore: the disdain with which people treat authors unless they are financially successful.

Monsarrat says that he too deplores this materialistic attitude, but it suits his purpose. "I'm absolutely anonymous here," he says. "I'm nothing—a writer. If you make a lot of money, you're classed as wealthy, which is a different thing. Otherwise a writer's position is not much above that of a street cleaner. People feel that because I live in Canada there must be something wrong with me. And so they leave me alone and make no demands on my time." This, in turn, enables Monsarrat to produce books at a steady clip, far more than if he lived in New York or London. And, in an appropriate twist, he has become wealthy in the process. He has twenty titles, among them *The Tribe That Lost Its Head* and *A Fair Day's Work,* making money for him in fifteen languages. In the last thirteen years Monsarrat has earned $1,300,000: an average of $100,000 a year. His rate for serialization is a dollar a word.

Monsarrat throws out the statistics with scornful regard for an "underdeveloped" country's values. Over a long lunch he said,

> Canada isn't exactly underdeveloped, but living here is like living in a civilized Congo: there's just as much search for identity. This makes it interesting. But in searching for identity you've got to sit back and let it happen. The kind of man who worries about his personality usually winds up a nonentity. It takes a long time to make a nation. You can't

force it. In any case, you're beginning to realize you have problems in Canada. Up to now you were concerned only with how to make a dollar.

The materialist and conformist character of Canada, emphasized by Callaghan and Monsarrat as repressing to the creative processes, is discerned also by Edmund Wilson. He blames the "Scottish *bourgeoisie*" of the cities who "believe that the chief aim in life is to work very hard and make money, and that an artist is a weakling and a trifler." But in addition Wilson says that it was not until a trip to Canada in 1964 that he was made so aware of the importance of nationalism as a stimulating force to literature:

> It was true of most of our own best writers till after the Civil War that they were occupied in one way or another with the attempt to give America an identity—by investing a legendary past, by idealizing an imperfect present, or by prophesying a transcended future. All these writers had a national mission. But in English-speaking Canada no such mission was felt, because no such independence and no such unity had been achieved. The English writing of Canada is scattered all across the continent; it has no center, no organic development.[6]

Strangely, French Canadians, with a long and acute striving for identity, have also failed as yet to emerge with a literature of more than regional importance. The best known "French-Canadian" work internationally is *Maria Chapdelaine.* But Louis Hémon wrote his novel of Quebec farm life a long time ago—nearly half a century ago—and he was a Frenchman from France. In more recent times, Gabrielle Roy won acclaim in 1946 for *The Tin Flute,* a novel of impoverishment in Montreal. But Gabrielle Roy comes from St. Boniface, Manitoba, and as a Franco-Manitoban is not accepted by all Quebecers, in their strident nationalist assertions, as one of them. Since Quebec today possesses a key

[6] *The New Yorker,* November 21, 1964.

ingredient for dynamic writing—conflict within itself and hostility within the broader context of Canadian nationalism—an obvious question occurs: Why has French Canada not produced literature of meaning to the world at large? Part of the answer is that a strain of inhibition—brought on by a Church that, at least in the past, feared literature as a subversive force—has still to run itself out. It is significant that there has not been a really good romantic novel to emanate from French Canada, leading to an admission from Brother Clément Lockquell, professor of literature at Laval University, that the inhibition includes what he terms "modesty."

Jean Ethier-Blais, who teaches French-Canadian literature at McGill University as well as serving as reviewer for *Le Devoir*, holds that possibly the two outstanding "French-Canadian" authors are Will Durant and Jack Kerouac, whose French-Canadian parents or grandparents were in the great trek to Massachusetts in the latter part of the nineteenth century. "They have been able to produce in America without the frustrations of Quebec," says Ethier-Blais. He adds that the French-Canadian experience is too negative, founded on hatred and rancor, to build a literature:

> We're feeding on ulcers, and this doesn't make for great works of art. William Faulkner had a hatred for the North, but he also dominated the Negroes. What French Canadians lack is a whipping-boy, the equivalent of the Negro. Jews as whipping-boys? No, they are just other "Englishmen." One day the present conflict in the soul of French Canada may result in great novels—but that day is not yet in sight.

Ethier-Blais' thesis is that there have been three dominant themes in French-Canadian writing: God and faith, the earth, and the city. The first two were linked, for the original messianic idea was that French Canadians had been sent to the New World to propagate a Catholic rural society. *Maria Chapdelaine,* according to this theory, was probably the greatest of the "earth" novels because it represented a reaction against the change that was beginning to be felt just before the First World War: a drift from the good soil of the farm to the untold corruption of the city. Ethier-Blais considers *The Tin Flute* the first great "city" novel, for Montreal—glowing as a Paris, a big and rich metropolis—delineated French-Canadian poverty without hopes of improvement. The central feature in *The Tin Flute* was a hill, Westmount, the core of the "Anglo-Saxon" part of town; a French-Canadian did not even aspire to conquer it. During the same period another novelist, Roger Lemelin, wrote also of life of the urban lower classes in *Au Pied de la Pente Douce*. Lemelin's setting was Quebec City, where the people on the hill at least were other French Canadians, and one could hope to climb it.

Both these products were by gifted writers, but essentially, as with almost all French-Canadian literature, they were inward-looking or parochial in scope. A newer crop of writers may be striving to integrate themselves more into the flow of world literature, abandoning the traditional social-political subjects and going through a psychological phase. Noteworthy is Marie-Claire Blais, who, only in her mid-twenties, has produced four books, among them *Mad Shadows* and *Tête Blanche*, translated and published in the United States. They speak of the inevitability of pain in such unremitting terms that Edmund Wilson calls Mlle Blais a "true phenomenon," and says "she may possibly be a genius." But not all her Quebec compatriots think this glowingly of her, and she is hardly known in English Canada. Here, of course, one encounters a peculiarity of Canada: the almost complete wall between writers in English and French, and between readers of both publics. For most English Canadians, translations of French-Canadian books, when they are available, usually denote a jolly, fictional French-Canadian family, the Plouffes, developed by Roger Lemelin in recent years but which even he is abandoning as tiresome. In turn, French Canadians are disinclined to read English-Canadian books merely because they are by English Canadians. "Since I do not think the two Canadas as a whole are interested in one another, I do not see how French Canadians can benefit from an Anglo-Canadian culture any more than we can from an American or English culture," comments Brother Lockquell. "Those of us who read literature are more interested in English literature than in Anglo-Canadian literature. I would like to know how many English-Canadian books are read by French Canadians, even by intellectuals."

The point is well, if sadly, taken. A revealing example is Hugh MacLennan's *Two Solitudes,* published in 1945 and still read as a thoughtful and carefully written account of strains in French-English relations. But it appeared in French translation only in 1964, and even then it bore the imprint of a publisher in Paris rather than in Montreal. "The most evident reason for the delay," says Ethier-Blais, "is the sort of intellectual provincialism, with regard to things English-Canadian, which is so typical of French Canada. I can only ascribe this provincialism to an intuitive feeling: the necessity to protect oneself against enlightened interpretation." A key question in the book is whether it is possible to be a French Canadian and a Canadian simultaneously. The answer is one of doubt, unless French Canadians are prepared to accept the abandonment of cultural nationalism—and this, of course, arouses the age-old fear of assimilation.

Essentially, however, *Two Solitudes* is a story of human relations, with MacLennan suggesting the universal tragedy that befalls intelligent people unable to overcome misunderstanding and prejudice. MacLennan, who is fifty-seven, and who has gone on to write other novels such as *The Precipice* and *The Watch That Ends the Night,* says that twenty years ago the relationship between French and English was relatively easy to portray. But in the emotional and complex climate of the 1960's he could not have written *Two Solitudes*. Here an interesting sidelight occurs, related to a sensitive English-language author in the milieu of contemporary Montreal. In 1963 MacLennan was so upset by the mood of French Canada, and the ugliness creeping into day-to-day affairs, that he headed overseas—to Grenoble, France —to spend a year in reflection and work on a new novel. Just before leaving Montreal, he confessed that he felt bewildered and he could not see clearly what it was that French Canada desired. He thought of the analogy of children, striving for self-assertion or emancipation, who want their parents around in order to feel secure; but they also want to be able to push them into oblivion. It was a terribly distressed and pessimistic MacLennan who sailed away. A bare two months later he was able to write from Grenoble: "A long expatriation is bad for a writer, but sometimes a short one is necessary." By the time of his return to Montreal he was more calmly engaged in the book he was writing—and hopeful for the future of Canada. One can believe that the passionate upheaval for this writer—one of the few distinguished authors produced by Canada—is of the sort that adds to greatness.

Edmund Wilson considers the poetry of Canada, both in French and in English, less interesting than its fiction. He accuses Canadian poets of being "fearfully imitative," especially of William Carlos Williams and Ezra Pound. But Wilson finds few supporters of this opinion within Canada itself. If there is some doubt about the over-all caliber of Canadian novelists—and their share in world literature— the poets on the whole have emerged with sturdier reputations. Names such as Douglas LePan, E. J. Pratt, F. R. Scott, A. J. M. Smith, A. M. Klein, Earle Birney are familiar to many readers, while a younger vintage is represented by Leonard Cohen. Some of them have shown, in the interpretation of Robertson Davies, "the sternness of the Canadian character at its best." The poets have managed to infuse irony and bite and direct attack in their commentaries on life in general, and Canadian institutions in particular. Robert Weaver explains this occurrence in statistical terms: a poet does not expect a large audience, and does not mind it if only a few hundred people pay attention to what he has to say; while a novelist cannot be content with a small audience and therefore is a greater conformist. Edmund Wilson concedes that two poets at least—Louis Dudek, the son of Polish parents, and Irving Layton, born in Romania—have performed a useful function "by getting rid of Presbyterian inhibitions." Robertson Davies calls Layton "our strongest voice of poetic protest."

One of the livelier clashes in the literary arena is between Poet Layton and Novelist Richler. Mostly it is about each other's appraisal of the Canadian scene and the world at large. Sometimes it degenerates to juvenile levels with Richler saying that Layton pushes so hard that "an unsigned copy of any of his books is now a collector's item," and with Layton replying, "I don't know what's bugging him. I swear I've bought a remaindered copy of every one of his novels." On balance, Layton, who is twenty years older than Richler, shows more maturity and discipline in his analysis of some of Canada's pressing problems. He quarrels quietly with Richler's proposition that the Canadian-United States border is nonsense, that the whole thing should be done away with because Canadians are Americans anyway. He says,

> What makes us different from Americans is that we are Europeans whose sensibility has been modified by living on this continent. While Americans erased the different qualities the immigrants brought with them, we have carried over some of the European traits, giving us a kind of serenity. We have defied geography to produce this strange country of ours, and now we have to be realistic and stop beating ourselves. We have to realize that despite a small number of

people scattered across a big country, despite the fact that many do not read English, despite the presence of the United States, we have produced many good writers. Maybe they're second-string writers, but how many Goethes or Schillers have other countries produced?

Layton's main point is that Canada should avoid looking at itself always in terms of the United States, but rather should simply make good use of American literature, as it would the literature of any country.

Harold Town, the artist, puts the same thought another way. "Hunting for a 'Canadian identity' is boring to me," he says. "In an age of quick communications, there has to be involvement with world movements. It still leaves room for Canadian individuality even if the language is that of the world." He says of Canada: "I love it, but I'm ashamed of its diffidence and lack of color." Part of this defect, he feels, is due to insecurity, and this in turn is caused by the same tremendous space that others speak of, "the over-shadowing of the individual under the huge sky." However, Town, a forty-year-old painter whose canvases fetch up to $3,000, is living proof that at least some Canadian art is appreciated at home and abroad. So also is Jean-Paul Riopelle, possibly the most widely recognized of Canada's painters. Riopelle's early association was with a Montreal art group known as *Les Automatistes,* who explored new idioms and introduced a vibrant quality to nonrepresentational painting that broke with a deeply conservative past and made an impact across the country.

Riopelle now lives in Paris and is considered by that city as a Parisian. But he remains a symbol of French-Canadian pride in artistic development that shines far brighter than its literary achievement. Closely associated are names of other French Canadians: Paul-Emile Borduas, who died in 1960, and Alfred Pellan, who lives near Montreal. Among English-Canadian artists of distinction are Goodridge Roberts of Montreal, Jack Shadbolt of Vancouver, and Alex

Colville of Sackville, Nova Scotia. A quarter century ago, when an exhibition of Canadian paintings was held in London's Tate Gallery, a critic noted how the preoccupation was with posterlike renderings of pine forests and wild coastlines, "passionate statements by artists who seemed to have a lumberjack's axe in one hand and a paintbox in the other, paying homage to untamed Nature." In 1964, when another exhibition by Canadians was held at the Tate Gallery, a critic in the *Manchester Guardian* observed that Nature had been subdued, that the artists had forgotten early struggles with a hostile landscape, and had absorbed many of the international mannerisms that pervade the art of today. Eleven painters were represented, and each had a point of view to express. "Out of this interesting medley," said the *Guardian,* "it is impossible to come to any precise conclusion as to the meaning of 'Canadian' but it would be only for that reason to deny that the word has a meaning. It has as many meanings as Canada has landscapes or cultures. And all of them are subtly un-English though some of them are recognizably French."

In brief, though Canada has not developed a distinctive art style—or literary style—it is trying harder than at any time in the past. Hardly justified, perhaps, was the celebrated if inebriated remark by Brendan Behan on a visit to Toronto. Behan, to show his displeasure both with the police, of whom he ran afoul, and with the state of Canada's cultural achievement, said: "Ireland will put a shillelagh into orbit, Israel will put a matzoh ball into orbit, and Liechtenstein will put a postage stamp into orbit before you Canadians ever put up a mouse."

Sitting in my room at the Hotel Vancouver, having breakfast on a foggy and rainy Pacific morning, it suddenly occurred to me that one of the greatest unifying forces in Canada is a man named Max Ferguson. Here, at 8:35 A.M., Ferguson's deep voice was coming over Station CBU, the local C.B.C. radio outlet, with characteristically irreverent and biting commentaries on Canadian and global mores, politics, and peculiarities. Not many weeks previously, on another foggy and rainy day on another coast, I had heard the same voice while I was in the Nova Scotian Hotel, Halifax. It was 8:35 A.M. there, too, despite the fact that Vancouver and Halifax are separated by a few thousand miles and five time zones. The synchronization was made possible, of course, by tape recording and rebroadcasting. But the significance of it is not apparent until the traveler meets it personally in various parts of the country.

As though the Halifax-Vancouver example was not sharp enough, I flew later to Whitehorse, the Yukon, and there—in yet another time zone making the spread six hours—I heard Mr. Max Ferguson at precisely 8:35 A.M. poking shrewd fun at some of the irksome issues of the day. The local announcer declared: "This is the C.B.C. Yukon network—CFWH, Whitehorse," an impressive enough notation (and enough to take my mind momentarily off the knowledge that fog had been replaced by a temperature of thirty-three degrees below zero) when one thinks that this service exists for fewer than 15,000 people living in the Yukon. The Canadian Broadcasting Corporation extended its facilities to the Yukon only in 1958. Until then a Whitehorse station manned by volunteers put on sporadic programs of recordings and local news; the Yukon, for all practical purposes of information, was isolated from the rest of Canada. "The day they put on the national news and Ferguson was the day we joined Canada," said a Whitehorse resident. "The C.B.C. is the best value you get for your tax money in the country."

Such a testimonial is worth registering, for it tells much about the unique nature of Canada and how some of its needs, unlike those of the United States, can be satisfied only through state measures. In Ferguson's case, more is involved, obviously, than the mere technicality of sending out the same program at the same time sheer across the second largest country in the world. This is a relatively simple engineering exercise. The importance of the Ferguson symbol is that it denotes, first, that he works for an agency that is financed through public funds yet remains virtually free from any government interference; second, along with physical links provided by the railroads and the airlines, the Canadian Broadcasting Corporation has contributed in major fashion to whatever cohesion Canada possesses; third, its standards and caliber are so high as to attract world attention and a steady audience in the United States even though its prime concern is Canada. "Canadian culture," in other words, can be developed, with the resources of government, to be distinctive and independent and influential.

Ferguson, a rather quiet, shy person of forty-one—whose exuberance and abandon are kept for the air—attracts a cult of followers dedicated to his highbrow and impish humor that shows no prejudices: it satirizes all levels of society. Imitating the voices himself, he hits at Lester Pearson's lusterless style and John Diefenbaker's pomposity—but rarely receives complaints. "A good many parliamentarians might like to complain," he says, "but they probably think it would not be politically expedient." One of the rare formal objections was lodged after he enacted a skit of Pearson and President Kennedy discussing the acceptance by Canada—following long and bitter debate—of nuclear warheads. In the skit the United States President suggested it would be interesting to see how sensitive the Russians were, and the North American "partners" could test this by lobbing just one rocket at the Soviet Union. The President thought that maybe Canada should do the actual lobbing, since it had wide open spaces and small population centers, and therefore would not suffer as much as the United States in the event of retaliation. Pearson uttered some characteristic platitudes in agreement. The protest over the show came from Robert Thompson, leader of the

Social Credit Party, who considered this an undignified way to treat Canada's sovereignty.

Ferguson, of course, stayed on the air, just as the C.B.C. itself has remained on, uncensored, after every uproar created by politicians. More than half of Ferguson's mail comes from the United States and contains such comments as: "Thank you for providing an oasis in our jungle of jingles." This refreshing twist—the reverse of the cultural trend—is manifested in many of the C.B.C.'s quality programs, both on radio and television, and especially in drama and public affairs. Americans who live close to the border and who can pick up Canada's telecasts are among the most hearty supporters. A commentator in *The Detroit Free Press* observed that while the 400th anniversary of Shakespeare's birth was being celebrated by the English-speaking world, "thus far it is a milestone that will go almost unmarked on American TV." The comment was inspired by the variety of Shakespearean plays and related programs offered on C.B.C. television. One has to remember, however, that the border deflects signals in two directions, and the overpowering impact is from United States television. About 60 per cent of all Canadians live within direct range of American channels, while the rest get their steady United States indoctrination through programs carried by the C.B.C. itself or by the privately owned CTV network. Canadians in 1965 were not deprived of *The Munsters* or *Peyton Place*.

Nevertheless, and despite the seeming contradiction, the C.B.C. provides an example of a country acting to protect its so-called "undefended border." It had its origin in the 1930's when private radio was unable financially and spiritually to offer a full national service to counterbalance the United States broadcasts that were dominating Canadian receivers. It was designed to be similar to the British Broadcasting Corporation in approach and autonomy. Today, while its main source of revenue continues to be from taxation, it differs from the B.B.C. in accepting advertising and commercial programs. In addition, Canadians always have had a choice between their publicly owned service and privately owned radio and television systems.

There is little doubt that the C.B.C. has helped to build a national consciousness, though some people charge that it has failed in a prime purpose: to act in effect as a propaganda agency and interpret the French and English populations to one another. Over the years polarization has set in, with *Radio Canada,* the C.B.C.'s French-language offshoot, growing into a major operation of its own. Toronto is synonymous with C.B.C. in English; Montreal means the C.B.C. in French. English producers occasionally venture out from Toronto to take fleeting looks at Montreal, and have little comprehension of the real mood of this center of French Canada. A rash of shows about Quebec in 1964 probably did more harm than good, since most were shallow in concept or deceptive about the degree of French Canada's grievances. The guilt was not entirely in the Toronto area. It was shared also by *Radio Canada,* which, in a spiritual kind of separatism, made only inconsequential efforts to relate what English Canada was saying or thinking, or even to describe the essential problems of other parts of the country.

This having been said, however, the C.B.C. still stands out as the most important single cultural medium in Canada. The longest television network in the world involves the Newfoundland fisherman and the British Columbia logger in the same spectacle as the Prairie businessman. If it is less than perfect in melding the two basic racial elements, it is still much farther ahead than private television both in this field and in providing a defense against the cultural invasion from the United States. Government regulations require that Canadian television stations fill 55 per cent of their time with programs of Canadian origin. Private stations barely meet the conditions; a program such as *Romper Room* rates technically as "Canadian" if it is produced locally, though the conception, the format, and even the script may originate in the United States. Standard United States attractions—for instance, *Bonanza* and *Perry Mason*—are carried by the C.B.C., but the network at least lays claim to a Canadian content above the minimum required; about two thirds of its programing is purely Canadian. Moreover, it is an important outlet for Canadian authors and playwrights, many of them engaged in experimental writing.

The tradition of high-quality visual productions in Canada began long before there was a television network. It had its origin with the National Film Board, which took form in 1939 under the guidance of one of the world's great pioneers in documentaries, John Grierson. Like the C.B.C., the Film Board is a state agency, though its aims are somewhat broader: not only to tell Canadians about their own country but also to portray the nation for countries abroad. It has created a unique place for itself, its documentaries and cartoon animations winning scores of international awards, so that Canadians, for once, do not need to make automatic comparisons with similar products of the United States. The lesson here, of course, is the same as with the C.B.C.: in a country of relatively small population, stacked alongside a mammoth, only public financing can hope to provide mass culture on a distinguished level. In Europe it is no novelty to find the state serving as a patron of the arts. In North America the leaning has been more toward private endowment and benefaction—a custom that may work in the United States with its affluence and predilection for individual enterprise. But it has proved less than adequate in Canada, where thrift and materialism have helped to keep intact some of the biggest family fortunes.

In 1951, a Royal Commission, headed by Vincent Massey —who had been Canada's first diplomatic representative to the United States and was to become Canada's first native-born governor-general—expressed its concern over the cultural assault by Americans. It proposed as the best means of resistance the establishment of a government agency to distribute public funds for "the encouragement of the arts, letters, humanities, and social sciences." A small and scattered population—at that, divided into two populations—hardly presented itself as a sustaining market for a writer desirous of making a living from his craft. Even today almost all Canadian writers have to hold jobs in television or teaching or allied fields in order to call themselves writers. But now, through the combined efforts of a tiny group of energetic and enterprising publishers and the Canada Council, a writer's lot is much more feasible than it was a few years ago. The Canada Council resulted from the Massey report, but its formation, delayed until 1957, was made possible only by a windfall: inheritance taxes on the estates of two of the country's richest industrialists, Sir James Dunn and I. W. Killam.

The total was $100 million, a substantial and ironically practical symbol of a marriage between the private enterprise that had yielded this wealth in the first place, and the traditional and benevolent attitude of a government concerned, as it had been since the days of the country's origin, with Canadian autonomy. Half of the $100 million went into a university expansion program, matched by the institutions themselves. The other $50 million, in an endowment fund, provides $3,000,000 a year for scholarships and fellowships to artists, novelists, poets, actors, sculptors, teachers; in addition, grants go to symphony orchestras, ballet and theater groups.

The Council functions independently of the government and shows flexibility and imagination in deciding who should share its money. Artists have wandered off to Athens or Rome just to soak up atmosphere; some have gone northward to live with Eskimos. Others—writers and composers —have sought merely the solace and privacy and peace of mind that a few thousand dollars can provide. For the "young"—that is, comparatively inexperienced people—the average is $2,000 plus travel expenses. For the "mature"—that is, established people—the average is $4,000 plus expenses. In the first seven years of the Council's work, 3,971 individual Canadians benefited. The list is impressive and includes notables such as Hugh MacLennan. Has the Council been able to turn back the United States invasion or stop the exodus of talent? "The time to ask this question," says Peter Dwyer, Arts Supervisor of the Council, "is a generation from now. But even today there are actual books you can pick up, and music you can listen to, that can be traced directly to the Council's existence. The main thing is the feeling that talent can be encouraged not only verbally but in a tangible manner. A government has assumed a measure of responsibility in a fairly deft fashion."

The Council has spread itself beyond government and state in an effort to arouse a wider interest in the arts among wealthy Canadians, and so build up the endowment. However, an appeal for private bequests or donations yielded only three meaningful returns. One was the gift of Stanley House, a large summer home standing on sixty-eight acres of the south shore of the Gaspé Peninsula. Deeded to the Council by an American with a sentimental attachment for Canada, Miss Olivia B. Terrell of Cambridge, Massachusetts, Stanley House is used as a retreat by scholars, musicians, and painters. Another contribution of $600,000 came from the Molson Foundation, named for an old Montreal brewery family, to provide two $15,000 prizes a year for cultural attainment. The third and most generous gift—$4,250,000—betrayed a sad Canadian sense of materialism. It was given by an anonymous donor, who, shunning the spirit of the arts and the purpose of the Council, designated it for use in medicine, engineering, or science. Council directors were slightly upset by this bourgeois approach to life, but not so upset as to show offense or raise a fuss. "If anyone turns down four and a quarter million dollars, he needs his head examined," was the way one of them put it. To retain its own integrity, and at the same time respect the scientific purpose of the gift, the Council considered for a while a study in the chemistry of painting, so that there would be at least some value to artists. Eventually it settled on a separate fellowship scheme for research in "interdisciplinary fields," a liberally vague phrase.

12.

Days of Affluence and Strain

CANADA AT THE moment is like a middle-aged man who finds material prosperity after years of ups and downs but cannot derive full pleasure from it because he is distracted by a marriage that is in danger of breaking up. Or, if he is nonchalant about such a possibility, he nevertheless suffers a vague but nagging guilt feeling that perhaps he should not be quite so relaxed. For, apart from marital troubles, he knows—or at least has been warned—that a huge corporation, namely the United States, is expanding so quickly that inevitably it will overshadow and engulf his own business. As though this is not enough, he sometimes wonders, as many men do in their middle years, if he has really accomplished much with his life. This doubt is not terribly deep, because a sense of pomposity also swirls within him. What he really craves, amidst the contradictions, is the confidence that someone wiser and stronger than himself will be available to provide reassurance and direction.

Rarely has any country undergone such a period of affluence with so little spiritual enjoyment. In the race between Canada and Sweden to see who can be next to the United States in standard of living Canada was ahead in 1965. The signs of boom and expansion were manifest in every province: in housing projects, in plant enlargements, in graphs that rose sharply and optimistically. Canada's gross national product—the total value of goods and services produced in the country—increased by nearly 9 per cent in 1964, exceeding the forecasts of government economists who had dared to hope for a rise of 6 per cent. The sale of new and used cars established fresh records, and so did the sale of furniture and other household items. The labor force was the biggest of all time, and unemployment in 1965 fell below 4 per cent. A White Paper spoke in conservative tones when it said that the expansion was well balanced, with the economy "showing no signs of excesses or distortions." Even though the rate of growth might now be slightly lower, the basic trend went on. Canadians were promised in 1965 a robust 7 per cent increase in the gross national product, a continuing advance in capital investment, further boosts in personal expenditures, and a favorable export position. To top it off, they were treated to a 10 per cent cut in personal income tax, bringing their charges on the whole below those in the United States.

The irony is that much of this happened when no one appeared to be looking. The country, if it did not want to bother keeping its eyes on Quebec, was busy squinting at Ottawa with discomfort and often irritation. Parliament was in a low state of decorum and morale. Government business was transacted only after exasperating obstructionist tactics by the Opposition or by petty procedural wrangles that often were little better than the level of high school debates. Partly this was because the familiar two-party political system—or at least the principle of solid rule by one of the two major parties—had fallen into disarray. When the Liberals, with Lester Pearson as leader, took over in 1963, they could form a minority government only, holding 129 of the 265 seats in the House of Commons. The Conservatives, though defeated after a seven-year administration, still retained ninety-five seats; the New Democratic Party won seventeen seats on a platform of mild socialism; the Social Credit Party, talking of monetary reform, took the remaining twenty-four seats but promptly split itself into two factions, so that in effect there were five parties in parliament. The three smaller parties aligned themselves on some issues with the government, but the fragmentation was enough to slow any legislative body and to handicap even the best-designed legislation. Beyond this, however, was the personality of the Prime Minister himself. Pearson, the highly successful global statesman, showed little firmness or astuteness in the tangle of domestic politics. Moreover, his choice of lieutenants in some instances proved disastrous, with a series of charges of corruption or ineptitude in high places contributing to the national uneasiness. Nonetheless, entering his third year in office, Pearson could look to two impressive achievements: he showed a deep understanding of the Quebec mood; and he put back on an amicable basis the Canadian-American relations that had fallen to a low estate under Diefenbaker.

The two men, Pearson and Diefenbaker, stood in unusual contrast even in 1965. Though both were in the same age bracket—Pearson sixty-eight, Diefenbaker a couple of years older—they represented totally different backgrounds and attitudes. Diefenbaker, the lawyer from Prince Albert, Saskatchewan, never quite lost his suspicion of the eastern "Establishment" or failed to pose as champion of the people; he spent a quarter of a century in parliament, learning the rough and ready tactics of politics, and when he was re-elected Prime Minister in 1958 he commanded the largest majority in Canada's history. First and always he was a political animal, with respect for parliamentary process, but constantly prepared for sharp infighting. Pearson, on the other hand, was an Easterner, and if not exactly an early member of the "Establishment," he belonged to the high echelon of the permanent civil service in the Department of External Affairs. Political infighting was never a part of his nature or training. Rather, he spoke softly to make his points in the diplomatic world and avoided confrontations. By the time he became a political party leader he was sixty-one, too old to identify with any grass-roots domestic movement or yearnings of "the people." Diefenbaker, after he mismanaged affairs as Prime Minister largely because of his suspicion of those around him, and his mistrust in delegating authority, lost whatever respect intellectuals might have had for him; but he could count on considerable grass-roots loyalty. Pearson, at home more at the conference table than at the hustings, never really caught on with the masses. But at the same time, even when he was criticized for a rather bumbling manner in delegating too much authority to lieutenants who could not be trusted, he retained personal stature particularly among intellectuals. Diefenbaker's rancor at being turned from office was compounded by a realization that Pearson, no matter how badly things went for him at home, would keep his prestige abroad. Diefenbaker, if he was recognized at all, was identified as the apostle of anti-Americanism.

"Anti-Americanism," as related at the outset of this book, is too simple a label to apply, for Diefenbaker never would allow himself the vulnerability of such an open emotion even if he felt it strongly. His technique, indirect yet dangerous, was demonstrated in the 1963 election campaign when he clung to his argument that Bomarc missiles could be used without nuclear warheads. An Ottawa correspondent, W. A. Wilson, put in a phone call to NORAD headquarters at Colorado Springs and reached a senior officer who said he could not become involved in a political issue but agreed he might answer a straight, factual question. Wilson asked him if Bomarcs could be equipped with non-nuclear warheads, and the officer replied that $30 million had been spent in such an effort—and it was given up as useless. Such information had been available to Diefenbaker as Prime Minister. NORAD, as a matter of routine, must have reported the telephone inquiry to Ottawa, for the next day when Wilson joined Diefenbaker on his plane, embarking on a campaign tour, the Prime Minister approached him and said abruptly: "What did NORAD say to you?" Wilson told him, repeating the statement that NORAD could not associate itself with a Canadian political issue. Diefenbaker, his eyes flashing, rubbed his hands together and said, "Oh I hope they get into this, I hope they get into this."

In 1964 and 1965 his technique vis-à-vis French Canada was much the same. Just as he would never sound openly anti-American, so he never uttered quotable remarks that could be called anti-French Canadian. Yet the innuendo was apparent. During the debate on the Canadian flag, Diefenbaker stood for the old and condemned the new, leaving himself open to the accusation that he was out of step with the contemporary needs of Canada. It was only one of several points that bothered party members; they were perhaps more concerned with a general image of infirmity he was creating. Both in 1964 and 1965 revolts were attempted by Conservative members of parliament to force Diefenbaker's removal or resignation as leader. One insurgent group was led by the Conservative chief in Quebec, Léon Balcer, a forty-seven-year-old former naval officer who was convinced that Diefenbaker was bringing disaster on an old and distinguished party by attempting to whip up an English-Canadian backlash against French Canada in preparation for the next election campaign.

Balcer always had been a strong federalist, making frequent attacks on Quebec separatists. He had served his party loyally and successfully for sixteen years, seeing it defeat Quebec's usual favorites, the Liberals, and reach heights unknown in the province since the days of Sir John A. Macdonald. But he considered it had lost its national character and had disintegrated into a partisan machine representing English Canada exclusively. When Diefenbaker outmaneuvered the mutiny in 1965, Balcer himself quit the Conservatives. He said the conflict had gone beyond the person of Diefenbaker. "It is the party's policy that has to be remade," he declared. "The majority of Conservative members supporting Mr. Diefenbaker have nothing but contempt for French Canada and all that it represents. I can no longer suffer to be at one and the same time a French Canadian and a member of that party." Many Conservatives seemed almost glad to be rid of their Quebec mainstay. When Balcer crossed the floor of the House of Commons to sit as an independent member, Diefenbaker was seen to grin in ostensible satisfaction, and several Tories thumped their desks in approval. It was a dramatic moment, but also one of great significance. It set the Conservatives on a road divorced from French Canada—doubly serious in a country where unity, though represented theoretically by parliament, is provided more by political parties whose platforms take into account regional needs and peculiarities and indirectly strike a national balance.

But not all was well with the Pearson government despite —or even because of—an effort to keep national cohesion. The Liberal Party itself was strained by internal problems related to scandal and politicians who all happened to be French Canadians. It was a Conservative member from the Yukon, Erik Nielsen, who first made public in the House of Commons the allegation of attempted bribery and subversion. The story, broadly, was this: the United States was trying to obtain the extradition of a man named Lucien Rivard, claiming he was wanted as a major figure in a Mafia narcotics smuggling ring. Rivard was already in custody in Montreal. A Montreal lawyer, representing the United States Justice Department in the extradition effort, said he was offered a bribe of $20,000 if he would not oppose bail for Rivard. There were other attempts to gain favor for Rivard, the lot allegedly made by three highly placed Liberal ministerial assistants, including a former aide to the Canadian Justice Minister, Guy Favreau. Favreau's own integrity was never under question. Rather, he was accused of "honest stupidity," "honest bungling," and "honest incompetence" for not taking action when he received a report by the R.C.M.P. about the Rivard incidents. Pearson, after vacillating and earning other epithets for his administration ("blundering," "naïve," "inept"), finally appointed a one-man court of inquiry to look into the charges and Favreau's handling of the affair. Almost at the same time he had, in a separate case, to dismiss a cabinet minister who was indicted in Quebec on charges of having accepted money illegally to promote a race track in his constituency. There were further disclosures about two other cabinet ministers who had ordered expensive shipments of furniture for their homes, without immediate payment, from a manufacturer doing business with government agencies before entering bankruptcy.

In the minds of the majority of English Canadians, the events, coming one upon the other, were equated with the old and notorious days of corrupt machine politics in Quebec. Therefore, by inference, all French-Canadian politicians were condemned, even if they were of the new and young breed. After an adverse judicial report, Pearson switched Favreau in cabinet posts, but was assailed for not conducting a wholesome cleanup of administrative personnel. His sympathizers made kind yet perceptive observations about him, one prominent Ottawa figure recalling that Sir Robert L. Borden, an earlier Prime Minister, once said that the most important quality for a Prime Minister was patience. "Pearson has that quality," said the Ottawan, "but I'm beginning to wonder if his decency—such as his loyalty to friends—may not be a handicap. A good Prime Minister also has to have a vein of iron, a degree of ruthlessness." Pearson's technique, explained an aide, is simply an extension of the method with which he ran the Department of External Affairs: "He uses the velvet approach. His attitude is to yield and if necessary let people have their own way on everything—except the big thing. He doesn't make hasty decisions. But he's ready to make up his mind when the time comes." It is here, of course, that an area of considerable doubt lies, with many saying that vagueness and ambiguity may be fine for diplomacy but are not the attributes that help in management of a nation's day-to-day affairs. And yet Pearson paraded decisiveness when he demanded action on a new flag. Essentially he proved himself a man of the present while Diefenbaker was an apparition from the past.

Pearson, basically, is a pragmatist who tailors his approach to relatively modest goals one at a time. He flaunts no grand philosophy or ideology, but rather likes to deal with facts and situations as they exist. A strong streak of right versus wrong motivates him. Pearson was born in rural Ontario, the son of a poorly paid Methodist minister. In later years a friend of long standing, a shrewd observer, noted that even a sketchy understanding of Ontario Methodism at the turn of the century helps to explain some of the qualities that have made Pearson perform with astonishing consistency. The issues with which he coped most successfully as foreign minister were those involving good and evil. All had some moral content, "and these he interpreted in terms of the thinking of the Ontario parsonages in which he had been brought up." A simple illustration occurred not long ago when, at a conference of Commonwealth prime ministers, Pearson repeated the stand he had taken in 1961 against South Africa and apartheid, and demanded a declaration of racial equality for all Commonwealth countries. His words now were aimed plainly at the white supremacist government of Southern Rhodesia. When he returned to Ottawa, even a political foe, T. C. Douglas, leader of the New Democratic Party, was happy to proclaim: "We are all proud of you."

Diefenbaker is the delight of the political cartoonists, who often depict him with fierce, bulging eyes and kinkly hair that stands high as though aggravated by a series of angry electrical shocks. Pearson usually comes out with a shy, almost insipid grin—a college boyishness added to by the bow tie he favors over a straight tie. He looks as though he would rather chew peanuts at a ball game than sit tranquilly through a symphony concert. It is a fair representation, for Pearson's intellectual curiosity is aimed mainly at government or foreign affairs. He shines best when he relaxes in a small group—a half dozen or so—and discusses the world and problems generally. It is an informal technique he used very effectively as foreign minister when he met with journalists, privately and quietly, for a background chat about a situation that interested him. In this way he put over Canada's position without committing himself officially. In return, the newspapermen, foreign as well as Canadian, showed great respect and fidelity, protecting their source. Rarely was Pearson betrayed.

If Pearson holds to any semblance of a formal philosophy it is perhaps best summed up in a speech he gave in 1961. "Today, more than at other times," he said, "greatness requires the quality of steadiness and balance; a refusal to be stampeded or bullied into the uncritical acceptance of the most strident appeal, the biggest headline, the loudest noise." He seldom turns a quick or emotionally exciting phrase—and indeed seems reluctant to do so. A literary critic, in reading a collection of Pearson speeches, noticed that even if he starts a sentence with a grand-sounding phrase, "he draws back abruptly from the brink of rhetoric." His thoughts, however, are almost invariably solid and sound. "As a people," he has said, "we are suffering from a kind of national schizophrenia—are we too British or too American; Westerners or Easterners; bicultural, multicultural, or no-cultural? I am concerned that Canada should be greater than its parts and that its national government should be strong enough to serve the whole country."

Almost from the moment he took office, Pearson was immersed in the awesome problem of saving Canada from herself. Apart from the fact that much of the tension became acute only in 1963, Diefenbaker had never shown marked sensitivity toward French-English relations. Pearson, however, talked forcefully of the special character of Canada emanating from its two founding peoples. His conception and appointment of a Royal Commission, to explore ways of improving kinship and making Confederation meaningful, relieved a part of the pressure that was building up in Quebec. Added to this was his acceptance of a new tax-distribution formula that gave Quebec greater capital with which to build its future and come closer in education and accomplishment to the rest of the modern world. But whether such measures would prove sufficient was another —and doubtful—point. What worried Pearson was the mood of the country, not the technicality of how taxes should be divided or how federal-provincial machinery could be changed. Quebec, he feels, is going through a healthy revolution—if it can be contained. But the elements that once might have kept it within bounds, including the clergy and politicians, are themselves drawn into the revolution. And so, uncertainty over the future begins with Quebec itself. It extends automatically into English Canada, where irritated people demand to know: What are those French Canadians up to, when will they be content to stop?

Quietly, though not usually in public, Pearson says that perhaps his international training permits him to look at Quebec in the reflection of what is happening in the world at large, the mood generated universally. Belgium, he points out, has had a bilingual and bicultural problem for a hundred years, too, but only in the last few years has it become dangerous. "Young people are no longer manning the barricades," is the way he put it to me. "They're attacking them. Look at what we've done to them. We've sent them to slaughter in two world wars. Now they're confronted with problems of a nuclear world and outer space. We're moving too fast, and psychologically and sociologically we can't keep up with the changes. In the 1920's we (in Canada) thought we lived in a fireproof house. Now we know we are caught up in the insecurity of the age."

Then, wistfully, he observed, "at the risk of a cliché," that "Canada is a difficult country to govern—when you add to the federal divisions the differences between the two main language groups." And because of this, "compromise has to be a cornerstone. Canada was founded as a compromise, grew as a compromise, and can only be maintained as a compromise and with concessions."

Pearson, who helped to draw up the United Nations Charter, and several years later presented the first draft suggestion of what was to become the North Atlantic Treaty Organization, is an internationalist at heart. Early on, he was suggested for the post of the United Nations secretary general, but was vetoed by the Russians who wanted a European, Trygve Lie. Subsequently, he was invited by NATO to become its secretary general, and would have accepted, except that the Canadian Prime Minister, Louis St. Laurent, persuaded him to enter active politics as foreign minister, with the understanding that he would be in line for party leadership and therefore the prime ministership. But the Liberals fell out of public favor, and the prime ministership did not come to Pearson for several more years, by which time the glory was beginning to fade from such feats as peace-making, 1956-style, when he proposed an emergency United Nations force that allowed the British and French to withdraw from Suez with some sort of honor.

Was there now a longing for a return to those days of international diplomacy—and glory and distinction—without the aggravation and hardship of domestic office? Pearson, always remarkably candid and informal in answering such a question, said that sometimes he did wonder if it was worthwhile being a Prime Minister rather than an international civil servant. But then—he added—in such moments of doubt he would go home, have a drink or two before dinner, relax, and consider that maybe it was worthwhile.

As for the old days, the mid-1950's, was it Pearson's personal skill, the timing, or what, that gave Canada such unusual prestige? And should Canada now cut its cloth a little more humbly? He replied:

> I don't know whether we developed an exalted view of ourselves. We simply took advantage of a situation that existed. We had done well in the war. We asked for nothing. We were highly regarded in a world that was groping. Everything was made to order for us. If I were coming on the scene now as Minister of External Affairs, I think I could do a few things. But I certainly can't see the same kind of opportunities I had in those days. When I look back now, there wasn't a single political incentive for what we did. We were just technicians. It's pretty hard to do anything today without getting involved in politics.

Pearson did attempt to get back into the international swing in 1965, but with disheartening results, and involvement in politics—or at least accusation of such by the United States Administration. His first mission as Prime Minister had been to make good on Diefenbaker's reneged commitments to accept nuclear weapons. Governmental connections between Ottawa and Washington had become cool to the extreme, but now, in a series of Pearson meetings with President Kennedy and then President Johnson, the old rapport was re-established. Pearson's attitude toward the United States has always been healthily Canadian. He does not believe that Washington "browbeats" Ottawa, but he does say that "everything counts when you live in the shadow" of such a mighty neighbor. He often has stressed his awareness of how the United States carries an awesome burden on behalf of the West. Marquis Childs, the syndicated columnist, refers to him as "one of the best friends the United States has anywhere." But none of this alters the prime fact that Canada's proximity to the United States makes it almost inevitable that United States actions around the world will affect Canada. If the United States is drawn into a major war, so, almost in certainty, will Canada be drawn into it. Pearson's credo is that while Canadians must never ignore the heavy global responsibilities of the United States, "we feel bound to speak with our own voice on any problems which are of concern to us." Recently he wrote: "I remember John Foster Dulles once saying to me, a little impatiently, that he would not want to have me along if he was playing golf because I would undoubtedly ask to be consulted every time he was about to putt. He accepted with good grace my reply when I said I would only interrupt him if he was using a 'nine' iron instead of his putter."

Pearson in 1965 felt that President Johnson was using the wrong club. He watched with growing concern the widening war in Viet Nam. And, in Philadelphia, to accept Temple University's World Peace Award, he said that "a settlement is hard to envisage in the heat of battle, but it is now imperative to seek one." He then suggested that the United States suspend its air attacks on North Viet Nam, which had gone on for two months without the desired effect of subduing the Viet Cong or North Vietnamese. In no sense did he advocate abandonment of South Viet Nam. What he did argue was that Hanoi might be willing to negotiate but was hesitating because it could not risk "the public humiliation of backing down under duress." Much the same was said by Prime Minister Shastri of India and by such prominent Americans as Senator Fulbright. But, in the words of reporters with access to the White House, President Johnson considered Pearson's speech "unsolicited provocative advice." Afterward, when Pearson was asked to comment on the current state of Canadian-American relations, on whether they had been damaged by such issues as Viet Nam, Cuba, and China, he said: "They are close and friendly, and I am sure they will continue that way. But they are never easy. They are too important—especially for Canada—to be easy. They should never be taken for granted." The essence of the relationship, however, was that "we can disagree and remain good neighbors, close friends and loyal allies."

The Philadelphia foray was exceptional. Mostly, Pearson as Prime Minister had to be content with memories of international diplomacy; matters at home were too critical and urgent to permit much diversion elsewhere. In any case, there was a generally modest approach in recent years to foreign affairs. First there was a recognition that the Canadian image had been tarnished during the Diefenbaker era, and had to be repolished. But this was only part of the reality. Since the mid-1950's Canada had lost the priceless virtue it possessed when newly emerged nations looked on her as unsullied by imperialism. Now these former colonies were themselves pushing for positions of prominence as middle powers, ready to snap even at Canada. Ten years ago Canada was a vigorous, chaste youth on the international scene. Now Lester Pearson and his conscientious and capable appointee as foreign minister, Paul Martin, were up against the problem of diplomatic middle age of a middle power. Martin would prefer to express it another way: "Canada has dropped the idea of a 'middle power.' The label is meaningless and confusing. Any nation with a dedicated and able public service, and a dedicated responsible government, can make an important contribution. Psychologically, it is bad to use the term 'middle power.' A nation's effectiveness depends on what it does. That was Dag Hammarskjold's way of thinking, and it is ours."

But the phrase "middle power" persists in daily usage, and Canada's effectiveness occasionally shows flashes of the old times. In 1964, when Cyprus was threatened with civil war and Turkish troops were poised to invade, Martin flew to New York to confer with U Thant at the United Nations. Formation of a United Nations peace-keeping force seemed hopelessly bogged down because of a series of interlocking conditions set up by potential participants. With time running out, Canada sent an advance party to Cyprus on a "survey mission"; technically, it was not part of a peace force. But this was the breakthrough, and soon an official United Nations contingent, including Finland, Ireland, and Sweden, was in operation. Turkey halted its preparations for invasion. "Again it was Canada that stepped into the breach with no haggling over who should pay the costs or what Canada's final involvement might be," commented *The Milwaukee Journal.* Similar tributes in the foreign press sounded reminiscent of a decade back. But it was Viet Nam, rather than Cyprus, that illustrated the dilemma of a middle power punctiliously trying to do right in life. Canada was named a member of the tripartite Control Commission, established by the Geneva Conference of 1954 to supervise the truces in Viet Nam, Cambodia, and Laos, because it was considered the most acceptable Western nation to balance the Poles, with the Indians in between. But when the Canadian team wrote a minority report in 1965, justifying the initial retaliation by the United States against North Viet Nam because of the latter's infiltration of South Viet Nam and supplying of the Viet Cong, Ottawa was labeled a "satellite" of Washington. Ironically, this was at a time when some Americans were condemning Canada for pursuing a vigorously independent foreign policy.

It is here that Americans are called on to remember some salient points. For instance, on the question of trading with Cuba and recognizing the Castro régime, it is not Canada that is out of step. It is the United States that is out of step with the fourteen other members of NATO, most of whom maintain diplomatic or commercial relations with Cuba. In the case of selling wheat to Communist China, two thirds of Canadians, according to the Gallup Poll, consider this quite proper and good conduct—and not for reasons of profit alone. They believe it is improper to deny food to others because of differences in ideology or complexion. In this sense, Canadians come closer than Americans to agreement with Arnold Toynbee's thesis that communism will no more succeed in converting the whole of mankind than did Christianity or Islam; and that, moreover, the real issue of the day is not communism but the determination of the non-Western majority of mankind to free itself from Western domination. In a curious fashion, the United States benefits from Canada's stubborn pride and autonomous way of thinking. Canada stands as thriving proof to countries around the world that the United States, which could easily strangle its difficult neighbor economically or militarily, is far more ethical and trustworthy than Soviet Russia, which had no hesitation about moving into Poland and other bordering lands.

Once Americans accept the principle that Canadians are *not* Americans, that Canada is preoccupied with remaining Canada, then Americans will be in a position to understand the problems besetting their neighbor. They will understand the interrelationship between the two key issues: French Canada in reference to English Canada, and Canada as a whole in terms of the United States. One of the best informed of Canadians, H. Carl Goldenberg, an economist-lawyer who has served on every major federal-provincial conference since 1945, sets forth the belief that the French-English problem will be resolved because English Canada and French Canada are dependent economically on one another. Goldenberg, who has the rare distinction of being an English-speaking Montrealer serving on two important provincial bodies, the Quebec Economic Advisory Council and a commission dealing with tax revision, adds a qualification: "If we were to have another depression as in the 1930's, with mass discontent, I'd not be surprised to see Quebec break away and form a separate state. But if we reduce unemployment and engage in development, as we are now doing, such a possibility becomes remote." Then he concludes: "Speaking as an economist, I'd say the American problem is the more important. When you realize the control Americans have over Canadian industry and resources, you know the strength of the wires they can pull. Even if Quebec ever decided to become a separate state, American capital could destroy it."

One can question whether Goldenberg is too optimistic about the future of Quebec in Confederation, but the importance of the American influence and impact on every feature of Canadian life is undisputed. The "unguarded" border is more accurately described as an "unequal" border. For, apart from the statistics of American domination in manufacturing and extraction of natural assets, there are emotional and psychological strains created simply by the fact that one is an ally of the United States. James Reston, of *The New York Times,* often refers to this phenomenon. "Washington," he points out, "complains, not unnaturally, that the allies are leaving everything to Uncle Sam, and the allies complain that Uncle Sam is not only protecting them but overwhelming them." Reston argues that the United States has failed to keep its friends informed on crucial issues, that the lines of communication are cut by Washington.

Indeed, a case can be made over Pearson's Philadelphia speech. The reason President Johnson supposedly was so nettled over the suggestion for a halt to the bombing of North Viet Nam was that he was preparing his own broadcast offering negotiations, and was afraid the Pearson statement might undermine this approach. Apart from the validity of the Pearson suggestion that remained even after the Johnson broadcast, there is no doubt that if the White House had forewarned the Canadian Prime Minister, among other allies, of the departure from its previous policy, there would have been greater restraint at Philadelphia. The point, of course, is that the United States is at a stage when it depends less and less on an alliance. It no longer consults —or even informs—allies because it does not require their support as much as in the past. Canadians take the position that they have every right to prod the United States into keeping a proper perspective.

Canadians themselves have some explaining to do. John Hay Whitney, publisher of the *New York Herald Tribune,* told a group of Toronto businessmen a couple of years ago that while Americans frequently are ignorant of Canadian problems they are also increasingly disturbed by what they feel is "the oversensitivity" of Canadians and the introduction into Canadian mentality of the kind of nationalism that expresses itself in "unreason." A continuation of this complaint might be that no one in the United States is trying to usurp Canadian sovereignty, and that in any case no nation in the world today enjoys an absolute degree of sovereignty. Canadians recognize the economic benefits of American capital, but since they can measure only present statistics, they project, psychologically, into the future and come away needlessly frightened.

Canadians, in hearing these charges, throw counterchallenges. They say: With changes taking place in trade patterns in the world, with the possibility of tariffs dropping between Canada and the United States, how will American companies with branch plants in Canada respond to competition from their offspring? Will these parent companies adjust to new situations that may arise—situations that were never contemplated when they came to Canada in the first place because they looked on it as a "colonial" market? Will they reorganize their total production so that instead of running duplicate lines they might develop Canadian products that would supply the United States as well as the Canadian market? Canadians who question the practicality of legislation to push for such developments say the answers to these questions will provide clues to the answers to the even bigger questions of how deeply cognizant Americans are of Canada, and how sincerely anxious they are to identify with Canadian needs and predicaments.

Part of the difficulty in striking complete harmony in Canadian-United States relations is that Canadians believe the onus for balance is on the Americans, for the unequal border is drawn lopsidedly in favor of the United States. The sheer weight or magnitude of the United States makes Canada a relatively puny neighbor. It is a bit like a mouse lying down to sleep next to an elephant. If the mouse rolls into the elephant, it does not cause a dent. But if the elephant is not careful how it turns over, it can terminate the existence of the mouse. In other words, the United States has the responsibility to be constantly awake to the vulnerability of Canada. This requires first an awareness of the existence of the country and its problems, and a realization that some of those problems might readily become the United States' own problems. For instance, if Quebec separatism does grow into a force to be reckoned with, and Canada is split up, what then? What of the present position of complacency and security enjoyed by the United States in the shadow of a dour and united country to the north? What if the Atlantic Provinces clamor for admission to the United States, as they would almost be bound to do? Would the United States say it already has enough stars on its flag, or would defense considerations alone enter its judgment? Thus, more broadly and cogently, what will be the response of the United States if the neat and comforting picture of a friendly and safe power turns out to have been a delusion? With no assurance that a republic of Quebec—gateway to the St. Lawrence Seaway and to the Great Lakes and to the heartland of the United States—will not fall under the administration of unknown or ill-defined extremists, how will the United States react? One unfriendly neighbor, on the tiny island of Cuba, caused consternation. Merely the outbreak of a revolution in the Dominican Republic incited the landing of United States Marines when there was no clear evidence of the strength of so-called leftists. The United States found itself in 1965 almost in a trigger-happy temper, shooting first and questioning afterward.

There is little Washington can do directly to affect the outcome of developments in Canada, but there is much it can do to understand the situation and at least support, even indirectly, a responsible central government by considering its stature. When a Prime Minister of the caliber of Pearson, who is already condemned by many English Canadians for being "soft" on French Canada, has his face slapped by the President of the United States, he is simply weakened in a second direction. After the 1965 Philadelphia speech, stories were leaked to the United States press that it would be "a long time" before a resentful Johnson would invite Pearson again to lunch at Camp David. Diefenbaker, apart from his knack for undermining American-Canadian relations, would, in another government, almost inevitably destroy French-English relations in Canada. The personal prestige of Pearson is important, his international stature of significance as a source of national pride and dignity.

A trace of irony exists. The Canadian fear of United States domination could have supplied Pearson with his greatest thread of unity at home. In the past, whenever a Canadian Prime Minister has confronted grave internal problems he has either sought or been handed a device providing concord. Macdonald used the need for construction of a railway, and got British Columbia to join Confederation. Mackenzie King's cry in the 1920's was for autonomy, the need to establish that Britain would not take Canada for granted, would not commit it to any act it would not welcome. King figured, accurately, that autonomy was the one issue everyone in Canada could agree on. The one area all Canadians agree on today, whether they are French or English-speaking, is the implicit threat of United States domination or Canadian involvement in a hazardous situation of American rather than Canadian making. Pearson has not exploited this apprehension, because of his superb sense of fairness and genuine respect for what the United States represents. But it is a weapon that always hangs in the background, ready to be introduced by a less scrupulous Prime Minister.

"What we have here is deeply ingrained vanity and arrogance—vanity and arrogance fed by isolation; by school histories which teach that we are indeed a peculiar people; by filiopietistic societies which insist that we are somehow superior to all other nations, morally and politically; by a thousand editorials, a hundred thousand radio and television programs, which play up . . . our own morality and nobility." These words were written about the United States, after the assassination of President Kennedy, by the eminent historian, Henry Steele Commager. They might as aptly have been written about Canada, but one wonders if they would have been received as generously as in the United States. Canadians have been going through a brooding period of self-analysis, but they have yet to learn to accept findings if they are unflattering. This is a touchy people, taking quick offense at criticism by insiders as well as by outsiders. When the first report of the Royal Commission on Bilingualism and Biculturalism was released in 1965 it aroused resentment in a large portion of the Canadian press because it was considered overly sympathetic to French Canadians. The commission, set up by Prime Minister Pearson in 1963 to study and analyze what steps could be taken to develop the Canadian Confederation on the basis of partnership between the two founding races, will not make specific recommendations until 1967. Meanwhile, on the strength of a year and a half of soundings—public meetings across the country—it came to some preliminary conclusions. "All that we have seen and heard," the commission stated, "has led us to the conviction that Canada is in the most critical period of its history since Confederation.... We must reiterate that we have found overwhelming evidence of serious danger to the continued existence of Canada."

It was, without doubt, a depressing document. But it was also a fair and unbiased one, arrived at after much thought by the distinguished co-chairmen, André Laurendeau and A. Davidson Dunton, and their ten colleagues who represented a cross section of intellectual Canada. While French Canadians were warned that they would have to do their share, the clearer inference was that English Canada's attitude would have to change if the country was to remain coupled. English Canada responded by and large by saying that the commission was alarmist, that it had conducted much of its investigation during the bomb incidents and the controversial visit of Queen Elizabeth—all in 1963 and 1964 —and that conditions had quieted since then. This was precisely the danger. Conditions had indeed become less dramatic, but in no sense less serious. Events and circumstances were merely more elusive and less tangible than a year or two earlier. But one could assume that English Canada had found what it was looking for: a convenient, technical escape hatch for avoiding unpleasant facts of life. It was likely, however, that English Canadians were deceiving themselves. "There are those," said the commission in its final words, "who feel that the problems will lessen and go away with time. This is possible, but, in our view, it is much more probable that unless there are major changes the situation will worsen with time, and that it could worsen much more quickly than many think."

And what of French Canada? Was it giving comfort to English Canada by holding back on what it considered rightful demands? Or was it continuing to probe, to test—not in a calculated way, but intuitively—to see at what stage

English Canada would rear back and say that beyond this line there would be no yielding? The answer was that the exploration, the pushing, continued, as inevitably it must, and as assuredly as it would also in the future. If an extremist government were in power, it would be easy to assume that a cunningly designed, premeditated plot was afoot, perhaps borrowing the Marxist technique of two steps forward, one step backward, but always with the objective of a net gain. Such, of course, was not the case. The Lesage government, made up of moderates, was acting purely with the instinct natural to all French Canadians: the striving for self-preservation and continuity.

Premier Lesage and his education minister, Gérin-Lajoie, asserted in 1965, for instance, that Quebec had the right to enter into agreements with foreign countries in such areas of provincial jurisdiction as education. The confrontation with Ottawa came about because Quebec was exchanging a group of teachers with France. Partly, semantics were involved. Gérin-Lajoie, a constitutional authority, carefully used such words as "entente" or "accord" in describing Quebec's arrangement, and did not refer to it as a "treaty." Nevertheless, English Canada saw in this, accurately, a basic testing of federal authority and sovereignty. No one disputed the privilege of Quebec—or any other province— to look abroad for teachers or technicians; the legality of how they were to be brought in was the issue. Even Lester Pearson felt impelled to utter a loud and unequivocal "no" to Quebec. The federal government alone, he declared clearly, had the right to sign treaties with foreign powers. Gérin-Lajoie had made the appropriate observation that a federal government, oriented to an "Anglo-Saxon" way of thinking, never would be able truly to represent Quebec's interests in education or culture generally. This was valid enough, but it was not the central point of the controversy. What Quebec really was doing was sparring: feeling out ever so gently its claim to a special status.

One of France's outstanding writers on political science, André Siegfried, a quarter of a century ago described the French-English relationship in Canada as "the modus vivendi without cordiality." Frank H. Underhill, a current chronicler of the Canadian scene, says that he will settle just for good neighborliness. "The most alarming feature of our present situation," he comments, "is that so many of the French leaders no longer seem to be led by ambition or by a wider patriotism to play their part in federal politics. If they are not attracted to our federal capital, what hope is there of the ultimate loyalty of the masses of French Canadians being attached to the larger Canadian experiment?"

Perhaps the key to the whole of the Canadian crisis or malaise is this: if the country's future seems uncertain it is because Canada began to grow toward nationhood at a moment in history when nationalism itself was becoming outmoded. The swing of French Canadians toward separatism, or euphemistically "associate statehood," was in a sense a throwback to Jeffersonian political doctrine. The central government, Jefferson believed, must be limited internally, leaving most decisions to the states and communities; its main function is to present a united front in foreign affairs. "The article nearest to my heart is the division of the country into wards," he wrote in contending that history had shown that rights and liberties flourished in inverse proportion to the degree of centralization. Jefferson wrote this in 1816, and one can reason that the requirements of modern society call for resources that only a central organization can provide. In more recent and Canadian terms, however, the historian W. L. Morton averred in 1946 that "the Canadian state cannot be devoted to absolute nationalism, the focus of a homogeneous national will. The two nationalities and the (various) sections of Canada prevent it." This, essentially, is what French Canadians are saying today when they demand a status that recognizes reality. What few French Canadians understand, however, is that while English Canada may be prepared to accept that Canada is two nations culturally, it will not accept it as two nations politically. Morton himself adds a contemporary footnote by suggesting that English Canadians can be as bloodthirsty as any other peoples, and will use force if necessary to prevent political disintegration.

A new constitution for Canada is in the making, and a new form of partnership may be evolving. Until now, the capsule definition of democracy has been "rule by the majority," as though this in itself automatically eliminates danger of abuse and protects the minority. But since more and more French Canadians think of *themselves* as a majority —at least within Quebec—the heart of the question is whether a democracy can be made up of two majorities. Many thoughtful French Canadians think it can—and must. This concept, of course, requires sophisticated rethinking on the part of English Canadians, for it runs headlong into conflict with English Canada's fundamental ideas about federalism.

It may well be that French Canadians are pointing the true direction for Canada. The perplexity of attaining a Canadian identity has been inspired largely by a desire to be different from the United States. Canada tried to find this difference in a monarchy, which failed to provide simple answers. It tried it in a parliamentary system, which has had difficulties since it is based on pure majority rule. But in the English-French amalgam there is a vague realization that Quebec does make Canada different. The problem is how to translate this acknowledgment in practical terms. Contrary to the doctrine of classical textbooks on political science, it might be said that a return to the Jeffersonian theory of decentralization would not be so bad, provided some system of economic equalization could be guaranteed to bring the poorer sections of the country close to standards of the wealthier ones. Intrinsically, what is interesting and unique about Canada is its very diversity and the challenge of arriving at a form of government that could be a model for much of the world. The melting-pot approach, even if it worked once in the United States, is impractical elsewhere. In a Europe starting with economic federalism, the ultimate goal is political union—but a union of many nations retaining their different cultural and ethnical backgrounds. The same aspiration dominates Latin America and most of the world's developing areas. Perhaps the French Canadians who think of "associate statehood," in a moderate sense working toward a loose federal structure, have stumbled on the formula of the future.

Is Canada going to know tranquility or strife? The answer will be determined more by English Canada than by French Canada. As Quebec advances in education and technology, its feelings of inferiority and insecurity, dominant now, may well disappear, and with them may decline the compulsion to assert nationalism. But in the long period required to reach this level, unsettling fluctuations of wrangle and response and recrimination will go on, with the future dependent on English Canada's ability to develop understanding. The real issue comes down to this: At what stage will English Canada say that Quebec's expressed needs go beyond any possible compromise, beyond the widest possible bounds of Confederation? The attitude of the average English Canadian so far has not been encouraging, and such harmony as does exist between the two main races is due more to government leadership than to any spontaneous goodwill. Thus, while one cannot be certain about the future, there is a broad and indispensable signpost to watch: the character of the national leadership. Quality of government is, of course, important to any country at any time in its history, but in Canada's case the next decade or so will be crucial for its union. A Pearson type of government, with a sensitivity and a liberality toward Quebec, has a better chance to keep Canada intact than a Diefenbaker type of government that would tend to be immoderate and tell French Canadians, early on, "You've got all from us you're ever going to get." Such a challenge from English Canada would provoke greater intensity of nationalism in Quebec and strengthen the separatist rallying cry.

The major question then would revolve around what would happen if Quebec decided to secede. Would it be occupied by English-Canadian forces? This would be a militarily feasible exercise that could keep Canada together physically but would destroy it spiritually. The other possibility is that English Canada would shrug its shoulders in disgust and let Quebec go its own way. Would a Republic of Quebec then collapse economically, as many English Canadians believe? In theory it would have virtually no chance to survive, but the same was said of Cuba and other modern states that have broken away from existing economic patterns and struggled on, much to the astonishment of the skeptics. The essential feature that must be remembered about Quebec is that it can be driven by emotion as much as by logic. If Quebec considers itself excessively abused by English Canada it will not stop to ponder the material side of life. It will plunge toward autonomy, not with a suicidal thought but with the righteous belief in destiny of any emancipation movement.

Index

Aberhart, William "Bible Bill," 280-281, 282-283

Acadians, French-speaking, 227-228, 241-246, 298, 300

Acadiens, 15n

Adams, J. Donald, 366-367

Africa, 109, 124

Afrikaners, 125

agriculture, 275, 275n

Air Canada, 56n, 179

Air Force, Army, 320

Alaska boundary, 59

Alaska Highway, 8, 320, 326, 328, 334, 340

Albany, 16

Alberta, 7, 35, 260, 262, 273-276, 280-287, 299, 300, 301, 340

Alberta Gas Trunkline, 286

Algeria, 116, 118, 124, 138, 162

Almighty Voice, 290

American Jewish Committee, 365

American Medical Association, 310, 314

An Answer from Limbo, 374

Anchorage, Alaska, 328

Anglo-American Corporation, 218

Anglophone, 15n

Anka, Paul, 370n

Anne of Green Gables, 235

Anse au Foulon, 16

anti-Americanism, 4-5, 7-8, 396

anticlericalism, 21, 152, 292-293

anti-Semitism, 186-187, 282

apartheid, Pearson on, 400

Arctic, 44

Arctic Brotherhood Hall, 334

Arctic Cab Company, 322

Arctic Institute of North America, 339, 341

Argentia, 223

Argyle and Sutherland Highlanders, 248

Armco, 349

Armée de Libération, 2

Armour and Company, 308

Armstrong, Donald, 95n

Aron, Raymond, 163

Asia, 109, 124

associate state plan, Quebec, 121

Astor Hotel, 84

Athabaska tar sands, 287

Atlantic Development Board, 236

Atlantic Monthly, 36

Atlantic Provinces, 43-44, 122, 181, 207-249, 257, 263, 411

Atlantic Provinces Economic Council (APEC), 231, 232, 236

Atlas Steel Company, 149

Atuk, 360, 361

Auclair, Gilles, 158-159

Aujourd'hui, 162

Au Pied de la Pente Douce, 379

"Aurora," 183

Australia, 54

authoritarianism, tendency toward, 165

Avalon Peninsula, 223

Bachand, Claude, 115-121, 131

Back-to-the-Bible Hour, 283

Baffin, William, 335

Baffin Bay, 360

Bailey, Alex G., 286

Baldwin, John, 81

Baleer, Léon, 397-398

Ball, George W., 70, 71

Banff, 283

Bank of Canada, 72

ban-the-bombers, 81-82

Barber, Clarence, 101, 102

Barkway, Michael, 93

Barrelman, the, 210

Bathhurst Power and Paper Company, 149n

Bayshore Inn, 254
Behan, Brendan, 384
Belgium, 105, 113
Bell Telephone Co., 136-137, 178
Ben Bella, 118
Bennett, W. A. C., 250, 255, 259-267, 282, 329n
Bennett, W. J., 341, 345
Berton, Pierre, 336
Bethlehem Steel Co., 349
Bible Belt, Alberta, 301
Big Bear, 290
bigotry, religious, 6-7
Bilingualism and Biculturalism, Royal Commission on, 166, 180, 198n, 270-271, 402-403, 413
Billy Tickle, 254
Birmingham, 38
Birney, Earle, 381
birth rate, Newfoundland, 216-217
Bizier, Richard, 117
Bladen, V. W., 70
Blais, Marie-Claire, 379
Blow-Me-Down, 212
Boer War, 58-59
Boillat, Maurice C., 244-245
Bomarcs, 76, 79, 396
bombings, 23, 116, 130-132, 414
Bonanza Creek, 316, 318, 332, 334
Bonanza Hotel, 334
bonds, repudiation of, Alberta, 285-286
Borduas, Paul-Emile, 383
Boston, 237, 238-239, 248
Bourassa, Henri, 103
Bourassa, Yves, 128-130
Bourgault, Pierre, 110-113, 266, 268-269
bourgeoisie, 20
Bowaters, 218
Boy Scouts, 354
Boyle, Harry, 329
brains, exodus of, 374
Brazil, 5, 7
Brecher, Irving, 94-95
Brewin, Andrew, 82
Bridgewater, 237
Brinkerhoff, Bob, 274
Britain, early relations with, 3, 12, 16-18, 20, 27, 36-41, 48, 51-52, 56, 58, 60-62, 65
British Broadcasting Corporation, 387
British Columbia, 7, 25, 31, 42, 46, 49, 50, 61, 181, 250-272, 337-340
British Columbia Electric Company, 260, 261
British Columbia Telephone Company, 270

British Newfoundland Company (Brinco), 218
British North America Act, 20, 39, 48, 52, 52n, 115, 157, 170
Broadfoot, Dave, 47
Bruyère, Charles, 194
Brunet, Michel, 174
Buffalo, 186, 256
Bystander, The, 189

Cabot, John, 211
Calgary, 273, 301
Calgary Herald, 39, 280-281
Calgary Petroleum Club, 274
Callaghan, Morley, 186, 366, 369-372, 377
Cambodia, 407
Campbell, Clarence, 123
Campbell, H. G., 187, 189
Campbell, Thomas J., 257-258
Canada Council, 390-392
Canada, French, 2, 15, 15n, 18-25, 33-35, 37-39, 40-42, 153-154, 110-180, 204, 241-246, 268-269, 270, 271n, 279, 292-302, 354, 398, 408, 414-415
Canadian-American Committee, 30, 94, 101, 107, 108
Canadian Broadcasting Company, 3-4, 46, 56n, 82, 132-133, 165, 183, 186, 196, 197, 198, 206, 244, 256, 257, 258, 296, 298, 299, 364, 365, 373, 384-389
Canadian Development Corporation, 105
Canadian Electrolytic Company, 149n
Canadian Labour Congress, 96
Canadian Legion, 33, 188, 196
Canadian Medical Association, 310, 314
Canadian National Railways, 56n, 112, 244, 303
Canadian Pacific Airlines, 320, 332
Canadian Pacific Railway, 55, 177, 178, 206, 253, 276
Canadian Pulp and Paper Association, 108
Canadian Quandary, The, 100
Canadian Students' Union, 120
"Canadian Unity," 111
Canadians in the Making, 53, 189-190
Canadiens, 15n, 17, 19, 122, 189
Canal Zone, 64
cantons, Lévesque plan for, 142
Cape Breton, 232-234
Carleton, Guy, 18
Carleton University, 127
Carmack, George W., 318
Carol Lake, 348

Cartier, Georges Etienne, 140
Cartier, Jacques, 345-346, 356
cars per capita, Toronto, 183
Castine, Me., 238
Castro, 106, 407
Cataraqui Cemetery, 14
Catholicism, Roman, 6-7, 15, 17-18
Cercle Molière, 299
CF-105 Arrow, 76, 140
Champlain, Samuel de, 15
Chapais, Thomas, 17
Chard, Chesley, 221
Charlottetown, 14, 36, 248
Chartrand, Reggie, 118
Chez Vito, 118
Chateau Champlain, 177
Chateau Frontenac, 178
Chilkoot Pass, 319, 320
China, 10, 67-69, 92-93, 256, 406, 408
Christensen, William H., 274
Chrysler Company, 203
Church, changes in, Quebec, 150-155
Churchill, Winston, 27, 213, 218, 222
Churchill River 218, 335, 357
Cité Libre, 113, 164
Clark, Champ, 52
citizens' participation dividends, 280
citizenship, U.S., retained in Canada, 273-275
climate, British Columbia, 253-254
coal mining, Nova Scotia, 232-233
Cochon Borgne, 117, 118
Cohen, Leonard, 381
College of Physicians and Surgeons, Saskatchewan, 312, 313
Colonies, Thirteen, 17, 18
Colorado Springs, 80
Columbia River Project, 265-266
Columbia River Treaty, 50
Columbus, 335
Colville, Alex, 383-384
Commager, Henry Steele, 413
Commentary, 365
Come-By-Chance, 212
Communist Party, 113, 278
Communist Party of Canada, 278
concert halls, 369-370
Confederation, 20, 36, 42, 43, 47, 48, 75, 87, 114, 129, 139, 169, 171, 181, 200, 203, 206, 213, 214, 215, 216, 217, 220, 221, 225, 228, 229-230, 246, 264, 267, 271, 289, 314, 409, 413
Congress for Cultural Freedom, 365
Conservative Party, 14, 34-35, 185, 259, 291, 293, 306, 363, 394-395, 397, 398
Consolidated Edison Co., 357

Consolidated Mining and Smelting Co., 308
consulates, 40
Control Commission, tripartite, 407
Cook, James, Capt., 251
Cook, Ramsay, 59-60, 199, 291
Cookshire, 110, 111, 132
Cooperative Commonwealth Federation, 306-307
cooperatives, 304, 306
Coppermine River, 335
Corner Brook, 210
Corry, J. A., 25-26
Cosmos, Amor de, 250
Côte des Neiges, 118
Craig, Gerald M., 59, 182
Créditistes, 35n
Creighton, Donald, 58-59
Cruel Sea, The, 376
Crysler's Farm, 58
Cuba, 10, 64, 66, 67, 80, 256, 406, 407, 412
culture, problems of, 52-53, 359-392
Curtis, L. R., 219
Cyprus, 407

Daily News, 219
Daily Oil Bulletin, 284
Dalhousie, Lord, 238
Dalhousie University, 239, 240, 248
Dartmouth, N. S., 234
Das Kapital, 118
dates, significant, 57-62
Davidson, George, 47
Davies, Robertson, 366, 367, 381-382
Davis, John, 335
Dawson, R. MacGregor, 234
Dawson, 316, 319, 323, 324, 327, 331-335, 340, 342n
Dawson Creek, 320
Day, G. Cecil, 249
Deadman's Bay, 212
Dear Enemies, 159-160
debt, British Columbia, 253, 261
de Gaulle, Charles, 41, 162
Delta Upsilon, 201
Deneset-Bernier, Maurice, Father, 291
Department of Citizenship and Immigration, 40
Department of External Affairs, 62, 68-69, 76-77, 120, 146, 395-396, 399-400
Department of Northern Affairs, 320, 325, 336, 337
Department of Public Works, 320, 326
dependency, Newfoundland, 212

Desbiens, Jean-Paul, 154
Desrochers, Louis A., 299
Detroit Free Press, The, 387
Deutsch, John J., 94
Devoir, Le, 15*n*, 134, 137, 142, 166, 167, 200, 378
dignidad, 170-171
Diefenbaker, John G., 5, 10, 29-30, 34, 35, 73, 75-79, 80, 133, 209, 316, 317, 337, 339, 341, 343, 386, 395, 396-398, 401, 402, 404, 406, 412
Dillon, Douglas, 72, 363
Disney, Walt, 3, 4
Distant Early Warning Line (DEW Line), 75, 81, 317, 339, 343
Dojack, Charles E., 296
Dominican Republic, 65, 412
Dominion of Canada, 20, 52, 52*n*
Domtar, 178-179
Donnelly, Murray, 292
Dorotich, Daniel, 270
Douglas, C. H., Major, 280
Douglas, T. C., 400
Doukhobars, 192
draft, French attitudes toward, 123
Dressler, Marie, 370*n*
Drew, George, 200
Drummondville, 149
Drury, William, 327, 328
Dudek, Louis, 382
Dulles, John Foster, 28, 405
Dunn, Sir James, 390
Dunton, A. Davidson, 414
Duplessis, Maurice, 21-23, 37, 113, 115, 133, 135, 146, 165, 173, 200, 250, 261
Duplessism, 113, 164
Durant, Will, 378
Durham, Lord, 57, 122
Dwyer, Peter, 391

Earth and High Heaven, 160
East Angus, 110
Eastern Townships, 110, 112
Eastman, S. Mark, 271
Eaton, Cyrus, 341
Eaton, T., 185
Eayrs, James, 51
Ecole des Hautes Etudes Commerciales, 144, 145
Economic Council of Canada, 94
economics, concern with, 52-53
Eddy, Nelson, 8
Edinborough, Arnold, 198
Edith Josie, 331
Edmonton, 284, 300, 301, 340
education, 193, 292, 302
education, changes, Quebec, 150-152

Eisenhower, Dwight D., 12
Elizabeth, Queen, 33, 36-39, 167, 169, 209, 272, 329, 414
emancipation of women, 155
Empress Hotel, 254
Encounter, 365
England, 15*n*, 18
English Bay, 254
English Electric Co., 218
Erlam, Bob, 330
Eskimos, 335, 360, 361, 390
Ethier-Blais, Jean, 166, 378-380
Evangeline (l'Evangéline), 241, 243
Evening Telegram, 222
exploitation, 87
exploration, Far North, 335
exports, 67

Fair Day's Work, A, 376
Fairbanks, Alaska, 328
Faulkner, William, 369, 378
Favreau, Guy, 399
Feast of Lupercal, The, 374
federalist, cooperative, 114*n*
federalists, 1-3, 173
Ferguson, George V., 175, 176
Ferguson, Max, 384-387
Festival, Shakespearean, 370*n*
fifty-four forty or fight, 251
Figaro, 163
Filion, Gérard, 148
Financial Post, 92*n*
Financial Times, 93
Finland, 407
Fisher, "Yukon" Bud, 321, 325
fishing, 211, 215, 216, 262, 348
Fitzgerald, F. Scott, 372
flag, Canadian, 33-36
Fleischer, Nat, 118
Flora Dora Café, 334
Flores, Ralph, 330
Ford, Glenn, 370*n*
Ford Motor Company, 90, 203
forestry, 262
Forsey, Eugene, 96
Fort Duquesne, 17
Fort Pepperrell, 222, 223
Fort William, 182, 183
fortune cookies, bilingual, 177
forty-ninth parallel, 251
Fougere, Lucille, 246
Foundation Company of Canada Ltd., 339
Fournier, Jean, 145-146
Fowler, Robert M., 108
Fox, Paul W., 49-50
Foxy, 333
France, 105, 161-163

Franklin, John, 335-336
Fraser River, 252
Fredericton, 227, 247
Freedman, Sam, 47
free trade, 101-105
freight rates, 276-277
French Canada Studies Program, 174
French-Canadian Association of Alberta, 29
Frobisher, Martin, 335
Frobisher, 339
Front de Libération Québecois (F. L. Q.), 36, 116, 117, 119, 124, 130-131, 173
Frost, Leslie, 200
Frye, Northrop, 367-368
Fulbright, J. W., 405
Fulford, Robert, 368-369, 374

Galbraith, Gordon, 104
Galbraith, John Kenneth, 374
Gallant, Mavis, 368
games, 362
Garigue, Philippe, 128
General Electric Company, 203
General Investment Corporation, Quebec, 147-149
General Motors, 89, 90, 149*n*, 203
George III, 14
Gérin-Lajoie, Paul, 151, 154, 415
Glengarry Historical Society, 198*n*
Globe and Mail, The, 197
Glorious Twelfth, 191, 191*n*
Gold Rush Festival, 333
Goldenberg, H. Carl, 408-409
Goldenblatt, David, 177
Goldwater, Barry, 45
Goose Bay, 223
Gordon, Donald, 112
Gordon, Walter, 3, 72, 73, 84-86, 90-96, 102, 105, 106, 136
Gould, Glenn, 370*n*
Grace, David, 104
graft, 21
Graham, Gwethalyn, 159, 160
Grand Coulee, 357
Grand Falls, 210
Grant, W. L., 271
grants, cultural, 390-391
Great Slave Lake, 335
Green, Howard, 29, 63, 76-77
Grenfell, Sir Wilfred, 354
Grey, Earl, 252
Grey Cup, 257, 297
Grierson, John, 389
gross national product, 394
Grouse Mountain, 254
Gulf Stream, 338

habitants, 18, 19
Haggart, Ron, 197, 198
Haliburton, Thomas Chandler, 366
Halifax, 6, 44, 209, 226-227, 228, 229, 236, 238, 239, 247, 385
Hamilton, Alvin, 337
Hammarskjold, Dag, 406
Hanna, M. A., 349
Happy Adventure, 212
Harkness, Douglas, 78
Harmon Field, 81, 223, 224
Harrington, Michael, 222
Harrington, Russell, 246
health and medical care, Newfoundland, 217-218
Hearne, Samuel, 335
Heart's Delight, 212
heavy water, 233-234, 240, 308
Hellyer, Paul, 83
Hemingway, Ernest, 372
Hémon, Louis, 377
Henderson, Robert, 318
Hendrick, Max M., 79-80, 83
Hepburn, Mitchell, 203
Hicks, Henry, 240-241, 248
history
    1605-1760, 15-18
    1760-1867, 18-20
    since 1867, 20-50
History of Canada, 271
Hitler Youth, 117
Holiday, 366*n*
Hollinger mine, 344, 349
Holmes, John W., 28, 68
Honderich, Beland H., 198
Hotel Vancouver, 384
House of Assembly, Newfoundland, 218
House of Commons, 1, 34, 35, 62, 77, 78, 209
Howe, Joseph, 237
Hudson, Henry, 335
Hudson Bay, 337, 338
Hudson's Bay Company, 55, 251, 252, 253, 288, 318, 335, 344
Hull, Cordell, 65
Hutchison, Bruce, 25, 30, 45
hydroelectric development, 156, 218, 262-263, 357

IBM, 206
Imperial Leduc No. 1, 284, 286, 287
Imperial Oil Review, 345
income, wealth, per capita, per family, 119, 230, 276, 309
Incomparable Atuk, The, 360*n*
Independent Order, Daughters of the Empire, 196

Indians, 15, 16, 17, 55, 273, 287, 289-290, 318, 320, 325, 331
Industrial Estates Ltd., 233-234, 236
industry, 87-109, 147-149, 233, 234, 235
Insolences du Frère Untel, 154
Institute for Economic Affairs, Canadian, 28, 68
International Bank for Reconstruction and Development, 72
International Brotherhood of Pulp, Sulphite, and Paper Mill Workers, 209-210
International Falls, Minn., 11
International Minerals and Chemical Corporation, 307-308
International Monetary Fund, 72
International Typographical Union (ITU), strike, 173
International Woodworkers of America, 210
interpreters of the U.S., Canadians friendly, 5
Inuvik, 339
investments, United Kingdom, 88-89, 101
investments, U.S., 88, 90-96, 105, 203, 275, 285, 286, 307-308, 343, 344, 345, 349, 356
Ireland, 15*n*, 407
Ireland, Northern, 190
Iron Ore Company of Canada, 341, 345, 348, 349, 354, 355

Jackson, William, 290
Jalna, 365
Jamieson, Stuart, 262
Jean Baptiste, festival, 172
Jenkins, Jack, 353
Jesuits, 15
Jewett, Pauline, 97-98
Jews, 128, 186
Joe Batts Arm, 215
John Labatt Ltd., 91-92
Johnson, Daniel, 23, 147
Johnson, Harry G., 7, 99-100, 101
Johnson, Lyndon B., 51, 102, 404, 405, 409, 412

Kalium Chemicals Ltd., 308
Kapital, Das, 118
Keate, Stuart, 262
Keirstead, Burton, 84-86
Kennedy, John F., 62-63, 65, 71, 72, 77, 187, 386, 404, 413
Keno, 334
Keno, 342*n*

Kerouac, Jack, 378
Kierans, Eric, 89, 174-175
Killam, I. W., 390
Kilowna, B. C., 259
King, Mackenzie, 27, 49, 60-62, 214, 282
Kingston, 14, 26, 53
Kirkland-Casgrain, Claire, Mme, 155
Kirkland Lake, 351
Kitimat hydro project, 262-263
Klaben, Helen, 330
Klein, A. M., 381
Klondike, 336
Klondike, S.S., 332-333
Klondike River, 318, 319, 332, 335
Knob Lake, 348
Koerner Foundation, 268
Krupp, 341

labor, organized, Quebec, 138-139
Laborde, Eddie, 274-275
Labrador, 336, 345-358
Labrador City, 347, 348, 353-354, 355, 356
Labrador current, 352
Lahr, Bert, 333
Lake Athabaska, 335
Lake Louise, 283
Lake of the Woods, 251
La Macaza, 76, 81
language, French, 24
language problems, 125-143, 178-180, 191-200, 244, 266, 292-302
Laos, 407
LaPierre, Laurier, 173
La Presse, 111, 154-155, 173
Latin America, 64-65
Laurendeau, André, 167, 414
Laurier, Wilfrid, 290
Laval University, 22, 120, 127, 132, 144, 146, 165, 176, 378
Layton, Irving, 382-383
Lazure, Jacques, Father, 152
Leacock, Stephen, 366
Le Blanc, Emery, 243-244
Léger, Paul-Emile Cardinal, 153-154, 167
Lemelin, Roger, 379
LePan, Douglas, 381
Lerner, Max, 83
Lesage, Jean, 23, 131, 134, 135, 146, 147, 162, 168-169, 200, 201, 415
Les Automatistes, 383
Les Fusiliers Mont-Royal, 129
Lévesque, René, 131-143, 144, 156, 157, 167, 168, 169, 177, 202, 266
Lewis, Burton, 7

Liberal Party, 23, 34, 35, 78, 134, 135, 146, 168, 185, 209, 215, 283, 291, 306, 309, 363, 394-395, 398-399, 403

Libération, 36

Lie, Trygve, 403

Life, 330-331

Life of Emile Zola, 154

Lincoln, Abraham, 13

Lindemann, John, 95n

Lippmann, Walter, 78, 163

Little Paradise, 214

live stock, 275, 304

Liverpool, N. S., 55, 249

Lloyd, Woodrow, 307

Locke, Jeannine, 308-309

Lockquell, Clement, Father, 164-165, 378, 380

London, George, 370n

London, Jack, 334

London, Ont., 201, 258, 325

Long, Huey, 250, 261

Lord Beaverbrook Hotel, 247

Los Angeles, 254

Louis XIV, 16

Louis XVIII, 105

Louisiana, 57; Acadians in, 242

Loved and the Lost, The, 370

Lower, Arthur R. M., 34, 53-54, 125, 182, 189-190, 362

Lower Canada, 19; *see also* Quebec Province

Lower Canada College, 128

Loyal Orange Society, 6, 181, 186, 190, 191, 192, 193, 196, 201, 288, 290, 292, 298

Loyalist Burial Ground, 227

Luck of Ginger Coffey, The, 374

Lunenburg, 237

Lynch, Charles, 204-205

MacDonald, Jeannette, 8

MacDonald, John A., 13-14, 47-49, 87, 88, 190, 253, 291, 316

Mackenzie, Alexander, 335

Mackenzie River, 338

MacKinnon, Frank, 14

Maclean's, 46, 103, 236-237, 239, 257, 359n, 364

MacLennan, Hugh, 173, 366, 380-381, 391

Macmillan, Harold, 77

Mad Shadows, 379

magazines, U.S., in Canada, 363

Maggoty Cove, 212

"Maîtres Chez Nous," 135

Malraux, André, 162-163

Manchester Guardian, 384

Manicouagan River, 156

Manifest Destiny, 6, 52

Manitoba, 49, 126, 175, 194, 275, 287-302, 377

Manitoba Telephone System, directories, 278

Manning, Ernest Charles, 260, 280-283, 285, 286, 301-302, 314

Many-Colored Coat, The, 370

Maria Chapdelaine, 377, 378

Marlin, George, 302

Maritime Provinces, 48, 225, 227, 271; *see also* Atlantic Provinces

Marsh, William "Bull," 232-233, 234

Martin, Gordon, 187, 188

Martin, Paul, 406, 407

Marx, Marxism, Marxists, 117, 118, 153, 166, 185, 415

Massey, Raymond, 370n

Massey, Vincent, 389, 390

Matthews, Roy A., 30, 101

Mau Mau, 118

Mayse, Arthur, 271

McCarthyism, response to, 6, 373

McClure, Robert, 336

McConachie, Grant, 332

McCormick, Bertie, 52

McGee, Sam, 326

McGill University, 41, 94, 101, 128, 174, 177, 180, 378

McGill Daily, 177

McGraw-Hill Publications, 109

McLaughlin, R. S., 89

McLaughlin Car Company, 89

McNeill, Bill, 351

mechanization and unemployment, Newfoundland, 219n

Medical Care Insurance Commission, 311, 313-314

Medicare, 280, 309-314

Melita, 302

Memorial University, 221

Memphis Commercial Appeal, 36

Merchants' Supply Company, 188

Mesabi Range, 348

Méthot, Léonel, 245-246

Métis, 288-292

Mexico, 6, 106

Mid-Canada Warning Line, 317, 343, 347

Milwaukee Journal, 407

mineral rights, 284

Minifie, James M., 82

mining, 216, 232-233, 262, 275, 276, 341-342, 342n, 343-344, 346-354

mining, Far North, 341-342

Ministry of Education, Quebec, 150-151

Minneapolis, 278
Minneapolis Tribune, 11
Misery Point, 212
Molson Foundation, 391
Moment of Truth, 183
Moncton, 244
Monroe Doctrine, 65
Monsarrat, Nicholas, 375-377
Montana, 288, 289
Montcalm, Marquis de, 16
Montgomery, Viscount, 260
Montreal, 1, 12, 15n, 16, 44, 81, 86n, 112, 116, 117, 118, 121, 122, 123, 127, 128, 135, 149n, 160, 163, 165, 172, 173, 174, 175, 177, 178, 179, 184, 185, 186, 189, 203, 231, 247, 248, 256, 257, 269, 285, 288, 317, 339, 346, 352, 355, 369-370, 371, 374, 379, 391, 398, 408
Montreal Amateur Athletic Association, 189
Montreal Canadiens, 257
Montréal-Matin, 196
Montreal Star, The, 9-10, 35, 175
Moore, Brian, 374-375
Moore, Michael, 382
Morin, Claude, 146
Morton, W. L., 40, 42, 54, 55, 416
mosaic, Canadian, 45
Moses, Peter, 331
Moss, A. E., 347-348, 353
Mould Bay, 345
Mounties: *see* R.C.M.P.
Mulroney, Brian, 176
Murmansk, 338, 339
Mysterious North, The, 336

Napoleonic Code, Quebec, 155
Nation, The, 189
National Broadcasting Company, 183
National Film Board, 160-161, 365, 373, 389
National Geographic, 36
National Hockey League, 123
National Steel, 349
nationalization of power, Quebec, 135. Ontario, 136
NATO, 75, 77, 78, 79, 81-83, 403, 407
naturalization, attitude toward, U.S. and Canadian, 9
navy, Canadian, 74-75
Neatby, H. Blair, 61-62
Neatby, Blair, Mrs., 270-271
Negroes, 119, 124-125, 179
neutralism, 82-83
New Brunswick, 20, 43, 84, 140, 182, 194, 225, 227, 228, 230, 235, 236, 241, 242, 244, 259

New Caledonia, 254
New Carlisle, 132
Newcastle, Duke of, 254
New Deal, 98
New Democratic party, 35n, 82, 185, 259, 400
Newfoundland, 50, 61, 75, 96, 119, 207-249, 250, 354, 356
New France, 15-19
Newman, Peter C., 97
New Statesman, 206
New York, 9, 256, 357, 360, 372
New York Herald Tribune, 410
New York Times, The, 9, 36, 78, 409
New Yorker, The, 368, 371, 377n
New Zealand, 54
Niagara River, 58
Nickle, Carl, 284
Nielsen, Eric, 398
Nobel Peace Prize, 28
Noftall, Hubert, Mrs., 216-217
Nootka Sound, 251
Norilsk, 339
Norman Wells, 340, 342n
Norstad, Lauris, 77
North, The, 30, 43, 336-358
north and south, trade and traffic, 233, 237-241, 248-249, 256, 257, 263, 278, 279, 285-287, 315, 365
North and South, U.S., 1850's, 41-42
North American Air Defense Command (NORAD), 75, 77, 80, 81-83, 396-397
North Bay, 76
North Sydney, 224
North Viet Nam, 405
Northwest Territories, 317, 337, 339, 342-343
North West Mounted Police, 289
Northwest Passage, 336
notaires, avocats, 20
Nova Scotia, 19, 20, 43, 46, 50, 140, 182, 221, 225, 226, 227, 228, 230-234, 236, 237, 238, 241, 249, 318
Nova Scotia Light and Power Co., 246
Nova Scotian Hotel, Halifax, 385
Nugget Dance Hall, 333

O'Hearn, Peter, 247
O'Hearn, Walter, 9
Oil, Alberta, 274, 283-286; Saskatchewan, 276
oil exploration, Far North, 340-341
Okanagan Valley, 255
Old Crow, 331
O'Leary, Grattan, 363, 364
O'Neill, Louis, Abbé, 127, 167-168

Ontario, 6-7, 19, 20, 21, 26, 31, 37, 42, 43, 44, 47, 50, 57, 58, 76, 86n, 89, 99, 119, 126, 139, 148, 181-206, 220, 222, 228, 235, 247, 263, 271, 276, 277, 288, 289, 290, 315, 333, 336, 351, 369, 400
Ontario, Lake, 182
Ontario Welfare Council, 199
Orangeville, 187, 188
Orangeville Banner, 187
Oregon Trail, 257
Organization of American States (O.A.S.), 63-66
Ormsby, Margaret A., 254
Osgoode Hall, 201
Oshawa, 89
Ottawa, 1, 10, 24, 31, 35, 40, 43, 48, 49, 65, 115, 127, 144, 146, 165, 168, 170, 194, 204, 207, 215, 223, 251, 253, 255, 259, 265, 266, 276, 288, 289, 327, 329, 333, 337, 376, 394, 404, 407
Owen-Turner, Desmond, 270

Pacific Great Eastern Railway, 260
Padlock Law, Duplessis, 21-22
Palace Grand Theatre, 333
Panama, 10, 64
Panama Canal, 59; effect on British Columbia, 253-254
Pan American Union, 65
Paris, 36, 38
Parizeau, Jacques, 98-99, 104-105, 144-145, 147
Parks, Arthur C., 231
Parti Pris, 166
Patterson, Tom, 333
pay scales, Schefferville, 350
payments and taxes, medicare, 313-314
Peace River, 340
Peacemaker or Powder Monkey, 82
Pearson, Lester B., 27, 30, 33, 78, 102, 142-143, 185, 209, 386, 395, 396, 399-400, 401-404, 405-412
Pellan, Alfred, 383
Pelletier, Gérard, 111-115, 125, 154-155, 164
Pelletier, Michel, 246
Penner, Jake, 278
pensions, 234
Pentagon, 76, 79
Pepin, Jean-Luc, 149-150, 153, 155-158, 159
Perlin, Albert, 219, 221, 222
permafrost, 317-318, 338, 341-342
Peterson, Oscar, 370n
Petty Harbour, 215

Phelps, Arthur L., 54
Pickford, Mary, 370n
Pidgeon, Walter, 370n
Pine Point, 342
Pitt, William, 16
Pittsburgh, 17
Pittsburgh Plate Glass Co., 308
Plains of Abraham, 16, 178, 180
Plouffe, Leo, 130-131
Point de Mire, 133
Policies and Practices of United States Subsidiaries in Canada, 95n
policy, foreign, 64-83
policy, nuclear, 73-74, 76-79, 396
Polk, James K., 251-252
population, ethnic background, 45; Acadian, 245; Toronto, 186; Winnipeg, 279; Yukon, 322-323
Port Arthur, 182, 183
Port-aux-Basques, 224
Port Radium, 342n
Porter, John, 127-128
Potash Company of America, 308
potash mining, 307-308
Pound, Ezra, 381
Poundmaker, 290
Prairies, Canadian, 43, 49, 55, 181, 255, 273-315, 337
Pratt E. J., 381
Precipice, The, 380
Prince Albert, 395
Prince Edward Island, 7, 14, 225, 227, 230, 234, 238, 241, 248
Prince George, 329
Privy Council, London, 48
prizes, cultural, medical, scientific, 391-392
Progressive Conservative Association, 35
Prophetic Bible Institute, 283
Protestant Action, 192
Province of Canada, 20
pulp and paper, Newfoundland, 216
puritanism, Toronto, 185

Quebec City, 16, 22, 36, 37, 85, 86n, 145, 166, 167, 196, 355, 379
Quebec North Shore and Labrador Railway, 349-350
Quebec, province, viii, 2, 7, 18-24, 31, 41-50, 54, 57, 76, 86n, 89, 99, 105, 110-143, 181, 187-188, 189, 192, 194, 196, 197, 199, 201, 202, 204, 205, 206, 220, 228, 241, 246, 249, 250, 263, 264, 265, 266, 268-272, 276, 277, 289, 290, 315, 336, 337, 341, 343, 345, 347-354, 357, 379,

Quebec, province (cont'd)
394, 397, 399, 408, 409, 411, 414-
419
Queen Elizabeth Hotel—Hôtel Reine
Elizabeth, 177
Queenston Heights, 58
Queen's University, 26

Raddall, Thomas H., 55, 57
radicalism, 254-255, 279-280
Radio Canada, 133, 134, 153, 165, 195,
388
railroad to British Columbia, 253
Rand, William, 237
Rankin Inlet, 342n
Rasminsky, Louis, 72, 73
Reader's Digest, 363, 364, 365
recession and rethinking, 28-31
recognition, foreign, needed for Ca-
nadian talent, 362
Récollets, 15
Red River, 288, 289, 292
Regina, 290, 291, 300, 302
Regina Plains, 302
Reid, Kate, 370n
Rélations, 127n
religion, 61-62, 85-86, 150-155, 184-
185, 190-192, 193-200, 259, 270
Rémillard, Léo, 296, 298
Republic of Quebec, 164
Republic Steel Company, 349
Reston, James, 409
revolution, Canadian, 57
Richard, Maurice "Rocket," 122-123,
269
Richler, Mordecai, 206, 359, 360, 361,
382-383
Richmond, 112
Riel, Louis, 288, 292
Riel Rebellion, 288-292, 300, 315
Rimouski, 153
R. I. N. (*Rassemblement pour l'Indé-
pendance Nationale*), 38, 41, 111,
113, 115, 117, 118, 119, 124, 132,
138, 139, 141, 160, 166-167, 268
Ring Record Book, 118
Riopelle, Jean-Paul, 383
riots, 123
Rivard, Lucien, 398
Robarts, John P., 200-206
Roberts, Goodridge, 383
Robertson, O. C. S., 341
Robichaud, Louis, 235-236, 242, 246
Roblin, Duff, 293-295
Roblin, Rodmond, 293
Roche, Mazo de la, 365-366
Rolland, Solange Chaput, Mme, 125-
126, 153, 159-160

Roman Catholic church, Quebec, 116-
117, 150-155, 186
Roosevelt, F. D., 27, 63, 65, 74, 98
Roosevelt, Theodore, 59
Rothschild, N. M., & Sons, 218
Rotstein, Abraham, 100-101
Roussel, Théodore, Father, 151-152
Rovere, Richard H., 359
Rowan, Carl T., 11
Rowley, Graham W., 338, 343, 345
Roy, Gabrielle, 377
Royal Air Force (R.A.F), 75, 80
Royal Canadian Air Force (R.C.A.F.),
75, 77, 80, 81, 117, 223
Royal Canadian Mounted Police
(Mounties), 6, 8, 9, 55, 131, 223,
273, 320, 346
Royal Commission, 363, 364, 389-390
Royal Navy, 201, 376
Royal Trust Company—Compagnie
Trust Royal, 177
Russwood Ranch, 218-219
Ryan, Claude, 137, 142, 200

Sackville, N. S., 384
Safarian, A. E., 95-96
St. Boniface, 288, 291, 294, 297, 377
St. Helen's Island, 172
St. Jean Baptiste Society, 129, 130,
191
St. Jerome, 125
St. John, 227, 236
St. John River, 227
St. John's, 210, 212, 215, 216, 217, 219,
221, 222
St. Lawrence North Shore, 345
St. Lawrence River, 16, 44, 182, 213,
347
St. Lawrence Seaway, viii, 43, 58,
141, 358, 411
St. Laurent, Louis, 27, 403
St. Mary's University, 229
Sanburn, Richard, 39, 41
sanctions, economic, 64
Sandwell, B. K., 8
Saskatchewan, 49, 126, 260, 275, 276,
303, 395
Saskatchewan River, 289, 290
Saskatchewan Wheat Pool, 303-304
Saturday Night, 198
Saturday Reader, 361-362
Saudi Arabia, 346
Saunders, Leslie H., 192
Schefferville, 343, 345, 348, 349-357
Schlitz Brewing Company, 91
scholarships and fellowships, 390-391
School Question, 293-302
Scotland, 15n, 18, 278

Scotsmen, 344

Scott, Fred, 212

Scott, F. R., 41, 381

Scott, Jack, 258-259

Scott, Malcolm, 269

Scott, Thomas, 288, 290

Seattle, 256, 257

Secretary of State for External Affairs, 27

security, social, 56, 56n

Seidlitz, Max, 302-303

seigneurs, 17, 20

Seldom-Come-By, 212

self-discipline, need of, 158-159

separation, separatists, *séparatisme*, 24, 46, 111, 113, 114, 115, 117, 118, 120, 132, 138, 140, 161, 163, 164-176, 183, 194, 236, 246, 257, 258, 263, 266, 277, 309, 354, 356, 388

Sept-Iles, 347, 348, 349, 350, 352, 355

Seven Years' War, 17

Shadbolt, Jack, 383

Shakespeare anniversary, 387

Sharp, Mitchell, 71

Shastri of India, 405

Shaw, George, 334

Shaw, Robert F., 339-340

Shea, Harold, 239

Shearer, Norma, 370n

Sherbrooke, 120, 153

Sherbrooke University, 120

Shevchenko, Taras, 296

Shooting of Dan McGrew, 333

Shumsky, Pyotr, 339, 345

Siegfried, André, 416

Simpson, Donald, 302

Sinclair, Alasdair, 239-240

Sinclair, Sol, 315

Skagway, Alaska, 319, 321, 328

Skookum Jim, 318

Slick, Sam, 366

Smallwood, Joey, 96-97, 208-211, 214-219, 222-225, 356, 357

Smith, A. J. M., 381

Smith, Burial, 341-342

Smith, Neville, 313

Smith, W. A., 250

Smith, W. Y., 101, 102, 228-229

Social Credit, Social Credit Party, 35n, 250-251, 259, 260, 264, 280-282, 285, 387, 395

socialism, 56, 56n, 116, 280

Somerville, H. H., 285

Sons of England, 196

South Africa, 125

Southam News Service, 204

Soviet Union, 80, 83

Soviet Union Today, 339

Spotted Calf, 290

Spring Thaw, 161n

Stampede, Calgary, 273-274

standard of living, 393-394

Stanfield, Robert L., 233, 234, 240

Stanfield's Unshrinkables, 233

Stanley Cup, 122-123

Stanley House, 391

Star Weekly, 308-309

Starnes, Richard, 4

State Department, U.S., 77-78

Stephenville, 81, 223, 224

Stewart, J. David, 248

Stick Your Neck Out, 360n

Stoll, Avrum, 268

Strait of Georgia, 254

Stratas, Teresa, 370n

Strategic Air Command, U.S., 80

Stratford, 370n

strike, Saskatchewan doctors', 310-313

Students' Administrative Council—Conseil Administratif des Etudiants, 199

students, interests of, 120

subsidies, 232

Sudbury, 198n

Suez crisis, 28

Sullivan show, 186

Superior, Lake, 182

Sutherland, R. W., 311

Sweden, 105, 407

Syrnick, John, 295-296, 297

Tagish Charlie, 318

Taku Hotel, 322

Tamarack Review, The, 364

Tanner, N. E., 285

Tardif, Marcel, 2

tariffs, 87-88, 93-101, 229, 232

Tate Gallery, London, 384

tax, interest-equalization, 71-73

tax laws, Canada, 91

tax laws, U.S., 90n

Taylor, Isaac, 327, 328

Taylor, Mrs., 327-328

Taylor and Drury Ltd., 327

television production center, Montreal, 165, 186

Terrell, Olivia B., 391

Tête Blanche, 379

Texas Gulf Sulphur Co., 344

That Summer in Paris, 372

Thatcher, Ross, 309

theaters, 369-370

The '98, 322

Thompson, Robert, 96, 386-387
threat to U.S., republic of Quebec, 411-412
Time, 363, 364, 365
Times, The, of London, 103
Timmins, 343-344
Tin Flute, the, 377, 379
Tories, 187, 259, 398
Toronto, 8, 13, 44, 57, 103, 104, 108, 127, 128, 173, 182-184, 190-192, 221, 222, 231, 256, 258, 277, 278, 285, 317, 327, 360, 364, 368, 369, 371
Toronto Star, 196, 197, 198
Toronto Telegram, 202
Town, Harold, 184, 383
Toynbee, Arnold, 408
Trans-Canada Highway, 255-256
Trans-Siberian Railway, 338
Treasury Board, 47
treaty, first international, 60n
Tribe That Lost Its Head, 376
Trois Rivières, 16, 153
Trottier, Emile, 2
Troubled Canada, 92
Trudeau, Pierre-Elliott, 164
Trudel, Marcel, 165-166
Trudel, Robert, 298, 299
Turkey, 407
Two Solitudes, 173, 380-381

Ukrainian Voice, 295
Ukrainians, 294-302
Underhill, Frank H., 53, 56-57, 416
Ungava, 341
Union Générale des Etudiants du Québec, 120
Union Nationale party, 22-23, 134-135, 146-147
Union Pacific, 255
United Kingdom Information Office, 376
United Empire Loyalists, 4, 19, 53, 84, 182, 186, 198n, 201, 227, 238, 246, 259
United Mine Workers of America, 232-233
United Nations, 27, 63, 83, 407
U.S. Air Force, 81, 81n
U.S. Information Agency, 11
University of British Columbia, 262, 267-269
University of Manitoba, 47, 54, 275n, 292, 302, 315
University of Moncton, 245
University of Montreal, 22, 112, 115, 120, 144, 153, 158, 164, 174

University of New Brunswick, 101, 228-229
University of Ottawa, 192, 194
University of Saskatchewan, 95, 312, 347
University of Toronto, 45, 49, 59, 70, 84, 100, 199
University of Western Ontario, 201, 325
Unknown Country, The, 26
Upper Canada, 19; *see also* Ontario
Upper Canada (Ontario and Quebec), 225n, 230-231, 236
Upper Canada Village, 58
U Thant, 407

vacations, Schefferville, 351-352
Valois, Claude, 121, 131
Vancouver, 44, 69, 104, 126, 254, 257, 258, 261, 263, 265, 267, 268, 269, 270, 321, 369-370, 383
Vancouver Island, 251, 252, 260, 262
Vancouver Province, 329-330
Vancouver Sun, 258-259, 262
Van Oeveren, Chris, 322
Varsity, The, 199
Venetian Princes, New, 144, 180
Venezuela, 5, 7, 107, 340
Vera Cruz, 63
Vermont, 110, 112
Victoria, Queen, 254, 296
Victoria, 254, 260, 271, 317
Victoria Daily Times, 271
Victoriaville, 112
Viet Cong, 405, 407
Viet Nam, 10, 405, 406, 407
Vikings, 335
Viner, Jacob, 11
Vorkuta, 339
Voltaire, 16
Volvo, 234-235
Vorstermans, Joseph, 229-230, 236
vulnerability of Canada, 411

Wabush, 346, 354, 356
Wabush Mines, 354
Wadge, Charles E., 187-188
Wales, 15n
Ward, Jim, 268-269
Warner, Iris, 331-332
Washington, George, 13
Washington, Columbia River Project, 265
Washington Post, 78
Wasp, 124-125, 128, 183, 191, 192, 206
Watch That Ends the Night, The, 380
Weaver, Robert, 364, 365, 382
Week, The, 189

West Berlin, N. J., 188
West Coast, 43-44
Western Hockey League, 257
Westinghouse, 203
Westminster, Statute of, 62
Westmount, 23, 125, 173, 178, 379
wheat, sale to Communist China, 69, 276, 305, 308, 408
Wheeling, 349
Whiskey Flats, 326
Whitehorse, 316, 317, 320, 321-324, 325-326, 339, 352, 385
Whitehorse Star, 328-332
White Pass, 319
White Pass & Yukon Railway, 321, 328
Whitney, John Hay, 410
Whitten, George, 215
Whyard, Flo, 325, 329-331
Whyard, James, 325
Wild Cove, 215
William of Orange, 190
Williams, William Carlos, 381
Wilson, Edmund, 367, 371, 377, 379, 381-382
Wilson, W. A., 396

Wilson, Woodrow, 63
Winnipeg, 47, 54, 182, 278, 293, 296, 298, 304, 308, 317, 372
winter, length and severity of, 317, 324-325, 346-347
Wolfe, James, 16, 20, 57, 178, 180, 196
World Peace Award, Temple University, 405
World's Fair (1967), 205
World War I, 59, 89, 379
World War II, 66, 73, 75, 90, 113, 123, 135, 170, 182, 222, 239, 275

Yanks, 201-202
Yellowknife, 317, 325, 339, 341-342, 342n
Young, Scott, 197
Youngstown, 349
Yukon, 316-335, 337, 340, 342, 352, 385
Yukon Consolidated Gold Corporation, 332, 334
Yukon River, 319, 333

Zuken, Joe, 278-280